AF601783

Exposition of Ruth and Esther

Exposition of Ruth and Esther

George Lawson
and
Alexander Carson

Sovereign Grace Publishers, Inc.
P.O. Box 4998
Lafayette, IN 47903
2001

Exposition of Ruth and Esther

Copyright © 2001
By Jay P. Green, Sr.
All Rights Reserved

ISBN 1-58960-059-2

Printed In the United States of America
By Lightning Source, Inc.

INTRODUCTION

The design of this book, say some, is to give us the genealogy of David. This certainly could not be the chief design either of Samuel, who is generally supposed to be the writer of it, or of the Spirit of God, in giving us this history. The genealogy of David from Judah is contained in very few verses, and we find it in several other parts of Scripture. Every part of the book affords rich entertainment and useful instruction.

What would we give for a piece of family history, equally ancient and authentic, of any of our own nation, or rather that nation, whatever it was, from whence we have derived our origin? The holy Bible was not written to gratify curiosity, and yet what book was ever written that can equally gratify laudable curiosity about the occurrences and manners of former ages?

This book is one of those which were written by inspiration of God, and must therefore be exceedingly profitable to us, if we read it with a due attention to those instructions which it is designed to impress on our minds. It is not one of those books in which we are to look for new instructions. The religion recommended in it is that which had been already taught by Moses; but it impresses deeply upon the mind of the attentive reader many truths highly conducive to holiness, and to the happiness even of the present life.

We find in this book, that private families are as much the objects of divine regard as the houses of princes. The sacred writers that give us the history of Saul and David, give us likewise the history of Naomi and Ruth. What are the rich and great more than the mean and indigent, before God? The greater part of the kings and princes that reigned three thousand years ago are now utterly forgotten; but the names of Boaz and Ruth will live whilst the world lasts. It is to be hoped that many other precious saints lived in these ancient times, whose names are now not heard of in this world. But the same God who caused the names of some to be recorded in that Book of Life which he has given us for our instruction, has recorded the names of all of them in another Book of Life, to be opened and read, at the consummation of all things, in the ears of all mankind.

That in this life we must expect changes, is another of the truths of which this book reminds us. 'Changes and war are against me,' said one of the best men of ancient times. Naomi, one of the best of women, met with such vicissitudes, that she wished to have her name changed to Marah. We all know that we are constantly exposed to changes, and yet we all need to be put in mind of it. One great part of our unhappiness is, that we forget the mutability of our present condition; and therefore, when trouble comes upon us, we behave as if some strange thing happened to us.

But a lesson more useful and more pleasant is impressed upon our minds by this book—that God does not forsake those who trust in Him at the time when they are visited with the bitterest afflictions. *'I will be with him in trouble, to deliver him.'* The history before us is a comment on this promise. Many were the afflictions of Ruth and Naomi; but the Lord delivered them out of them all, and, *'according to the days wherein he had afflicted them, he made them glad.'*

But what distinguishes this book from other sacred books is, the charming picture it gives us of domestic felicity in the lowest rank of life, and in persons deprived of those friends to whom men or women use to look for felicity. Naomi was bereaved, by the king of terrors, of her husband and of all her children. Ruth was bereaved of the husband of her youth, and was left childless. They both felt their griefs like women of tender sensibility; yet they were neither discontented nor unhappy. There were three things which contributed to preserve them from sinking into despondency, and that rendered them happier under their afflictions than many other persons find themselves in the most prosperous circumstances.

First, Their piety. They trusted in God. Naomi doubtless had taught Ruth the knowledge of the God of Israel before she brought her into the land of Israel; for *'she came,'* as Boaz says, *'to trust under his wings,'* (Ruth 2:12). In the low circumstances of both these women, they hoped in God, they submitted to his providence; and they could not be miserable in any situation in which his providence placed them.

Secondly, They loved one another with a fond affection; and where there is true love there will be pleasure, where there is mutual love there will be happiness.

Thirdly, Their behaviour towards one another was a continual expression of their mutual love. There were none of those brawlings, unkind reflections, and fits of sullenness between them that often embitter domestic life. Naomi never complained of too little respect from Ruth, never exercised her authority with bitterness, never distressed her daughter-in-law with peevish complaints of the afflictions of her former life, or of neglect from her kinsmen, or of her other friends. *'The law of kindness was in her mouth,'* and it was evident, from every part of her conduct, that she set as high a value on Ruth's happiness as on her own. Ruth, on her side, considered the desires of her mother-in-law as commands which she was happy to obey, and did everything in her power to compensate to her the loss of her husband and her sons. So wise and affectionate was her behavior, that the townsmen thought her better to Naomi than seven sons.

Our natural tempers will have much influence to make our lives happy or miserable. If they are happy, they will dispose us to be cheerful, and to promote cheerfulness in others. If they are unhappy, the bad effect of them will be felt by our neighbors, especially by those who are under the same roof with us. But we are rational creatures, capable of instruction and of reflection. We are all desirous of happiness; and, if we find any thing in ourselves that makes it impossible to attain happiness, is it not our wisdom to put it far from us? Why should a disease be suffered to embitter our days and endanger our lives, if a remedy can be found?

And does not the Scripture furnish us with remedies for every distemper of our hearts? The words of God are healing words. The entrance of them gives light to the understanding, peace and purity to the heart. The naturally bad tempers of men must be changed where they produce their proper effect. The wolf and the lamb, the lion and the cow, are made to feed together where the gospel is received by faith. It must be confessed, that vestiges of our corrupt dispositions will still continue to blemish our conduct till the body of sin is destroyed; but, beholding as in a glass the glory of the Lord, we are changed into the same image from glory to glory. Nor are the virtues of the ancient saints without their effect upon the attentive reader of the Bible. Although Paul never ceases to call upon us to *'look to Jesus as the author and finisher of our faith,'* yet he frequently puts us in mind likewise of the advantage we may derive from a due attention to the virtues and graces which appeared in those that have gone before us in heaven. As we all ought to walk in the steps of the faith of our father Abraham, all women, as the apostle Peter tells us, are bound to imitate Sarah in obedience to their husbands, and in meekness and goodness of spirit. Naomi and Ruth were two of those holy women, who, he says, *'adorned themselves,'* as all women ought to do, *'with that ornament of a meek and quiet spirit, which is, in the sight of God, of great price.'*

You are charmed with the lovely beauties of domestic harmony and affection which adorned these good women. You praise them. You would be glad to see mothers and daughters by blood or affinity, husbands and wives, mistresses and maid-servants, living together in amity, and contributing, as they did, to one another's felicity. Why then do you not imitate them? Are your tempers so incurable, that there is no possibility of persuading you to prefer the glory of God and your own happiness, to the gratification of humours and passions which appear to yourselves detestable?

Read this history, not to gratify your curiosity, but to improve your hearts. Remember that you are bound, by the authority of God, to imitate the meekness and gentleness of

Christ and of his saints. The grace revealed in the gospel teaches us to deny every lust of the flesh and of the mind, and to practise every lovely virtue. The power of the Holy Spirit can subdue our rough tempers, and beautify us with those graces of holiness by which the gospel of Christ is adorned; and his own Word is the great mean which he uses for fulfilling in us the good pleasure of the divine goodness. Not only faith, but every fruit of the Spirit, love, joy, peace, long-suffering, gentleness, goodness, meekness, temperance, are produced through the word of truth; and the short history of Ruth is as really a part of the word of truth, as those books which give us the history of our Lord's life and death.

The female sex may likewise learn from this book a lesson of great use to them-how they may preserve their beauty, and make themselves amiable in old age. It is the glory of those *'trees of righteousness which are planted in the house of the Lord, to bring forth fruit in old age.'* It is the privilege of those women who are adorned with the beauties of holiness, that old age does not wither, but improves their beauties. Sarah's face was so lovely at ninety years of age, that her chastity was brought into danger at the court of Gerar. The daughters of Sarah, in the most advanced period of their lives, possess beauties more charming, and less dangerous. Naomi was not less lovely than Ruth, and, had Elimelech been alive, she would have been as dear to him when she was approaching to the grave, as in the day when he first received her into his arms.

The male sex, as well as the female, may derive useful instruction from this book. Consider Boaz as a master, as a friend, as a neighbour, as a man of consequence and wealth, as an honest man. In all these respects, you will find him worthy of esteem and imitation.

If young and old, rich and poor, masters and servants, do not find useful instruction in this book, the fault is their own. It is easily understood, and scarcely needs a comment for explication. But it may be useful to have some of those practical instructions which it contains set before us, that we may be assisted in meditating upon this part of the Word of God. It was, doubtless, one of those books of Scripture in which David found such delightful and nourishing food to his soul. O that the holy Spirit, who wrought so powerfully in the heart of that blessed man, would work in us the same temper! Then we would find a feast for our souls in every portion of Scripture. Our days would be a continual festival, because we could always find food ready at hand, more delightful to our taste than honey from the comb.

THE
HISTORY OF RUTH.

LECTURE I.

ELIMELECH AND HIS FAMILY GO TO LIVE IN THE LAND OF MOAB.

CHAPTER I. 1–5.

The intention of this history, according to some, is, to trace the genealogy of David from Salmon, the son of Nahshon, prince of the children of Judah at the death of Moses. But this part of the genealogy of David and of Christ, could have been given us without writing a whole book. It is given us in not more than two verses by the writer of the book of Chronicles, 1 Chron. 2:11,12,15, and in little more than one by Matthew, chap. 1:5,6.

The reading of the book is sufficient to convince us, that it was written to furnish us with the most useful instructions in righteousness. It gives us a beautiful picture of female virtue, first shining in the midst of poverty, and then crowned with felicity. Let all women read this book, and learn those virtues which will adorn them with honor and beauty. Let poor and afflicted women read this book, and learn to bear their troubles with a becoming sense of the divine agency in their trials, with patience, with meekness, with all those gracious tempers which will endear them to their friends, and furnish them with agreeable reflections at the end of their distresses.

But why should we speak at present of all these precious advantages which may be gained from this book? Every part of it is rich in instruction, and the instruction is conveyed to us in a story, which never failed to interest any reader who was not utterly destitute of human sensibilities.

Verse 1. – *Now it came to pass, in the days when the judges ruled, that there was a famine in the land: and a certain man of Bethlehem-Judah went to live in the country of Moab, he, and his wife, and his two sons.*

We are not told the precise time of the story recorded in this book. And why should we be solicitous to know what God has not put it in our power to know? One thing appears certain, that Ruth became the wife of a son of Rahab the harlot, who was famous for her faith and her works in the time of Joshua. But we have reasons likewise to believe that Boaz, the son of Rahab, was a very old man when he married Ruth, for he was the grandfather of Jesse, the father of David. Between the entrance of Joshua into Canaan, and the birth of David, there intervened three hundred and sixty-six years, which are to be divided amongst four progenitors of that illustrious prince.

Now it came to pass in the days of the judges who ruled Israel, that is, in the time when Israel was not under regal government, but after the days of Joshua. The expression does not necessarily imply that a judge ruled at the time when Elimelech went into the country of Moab. It was a famine that drove him from his own country; and famines, with other public calamities, were most frequent in the intervals of the government of the judges.

There was a famine in the land. The land of Israel was a land of milk and honey, the pleasant land which God had chosen for his people Israel; and yet we often read of famines in this land. Think not that the fertility of a land is able to secure its inhabitants against famine, or that any earthly advantage is sufficient to secure us against any calamity whatsoever. All things are in the hand of God, and his creatures change their qualities or effects at his pleasure. Without him, we should die of hunger amidst plenty, we should be miserable amidst all possible means of happiness. But, through the kindness of his providence, many have been well satisfied in the days of famine, or in a waste howling wilderness.

But why does God send a famine on the land which he had chosen for his own people; upon the seed of Abraham, whom God had called out of the land of the Chaldees, to give this fertile land to his seed? There is no reason to doubt that this famine was well deserved by the sins of the people; for the Lord had promised, that as long as they walked in his law, they should enjoy his blessing on their land, on their basket, and on their store. But he had threatened famine, and many other calamities, as the just reward of their deeds if they should apostatize from him.

We have never felt famine, although we have well deserved it. We have indeed felt scarcity, and stood in fear of famine. But the Lord has hitherto dealt wondrously with us, in supplying us with the necessaries, and many of us with the comforts of life. Let us bless God who has hitherto preserved us from this terrible judgment. Let us be deeply sensible that, whatever we may want of the good things of this life, we have much more than we deserve. In days of scarcity, let us call to mind those famines in which the sufferers would have thought themselves happy as kings, if they could have been supplied but once in two or three days with that bread which we eat every day of our life.

And a certain man of Bethlehem-Judah went to live in the country of Moab. The Jews often gave names to persons, or places, expressive of something that was true concerning them. Bethlehem, which signifies the *'house of bread,'* seems to have been a place famous, even in the pleasant land, for its fertility. Yet even in this fruitful district of a fruitful country, famine prevailed to such a degree, that one of its proprietors was compelled, by the want of bread, to leave it, and seek food in a foreign country. We may reasonably conjecture, from the behaviour of Naomi, that her husband was a fearer of God. And yet he is forced to seek bread in the land of Moab, where his God was unknown. Men are commonly attached to their native soil; but none among us is so much attached to his native country, as the ancient Israelites were to theirs; those of them especially who were lovers of the religion of the God of their fathers. There is a great difference between a Scotsman going to America, and an Israelite going to dwell in the land of Moab. In many places in America, our God and our Saviour is as well known as amongst ourselves. Should you want bread at home, you would not account it a very great hardship to go to a strange land, where you might find bread to your bodies, and at the same time find provision for your souls. But you would almost perish with hunger rather than go to live among the Turks; and yet the Turks are not so great enemies to the name of Christ, as the Moabites were to the name of the God of Israel.

Some blame this Ephrathite for going to live in the land of Moab. Why (say they) did he not rather bear all the hardships of famine, as well as his neighbors, rather than go to dwell amongst heathens, – amongst such heathens as the Moabites, of whom the Lord had said, *'Even to their tenth generation, they shall not enter into the congregation of the Lord for ever: thou shalt not seek their peace nor their prosperity all your days for ever?'*

It is not necessary to enquire, nor is it perhaps possible to determine with certainty, whether this Bethlehemite did right or wrong in going to live in the land of Moab. Yet no man ought to be condemned, whether dead or alive, without proofs of guilt; and no certain proofs of guilt appear in the present case. Undoubtedly, the people of God were commanded not to mingle themselves with the heathens, lest they should learn their ways; but they were not absolutely prohibited to live in a strange land. When imperious necessity forced David to dwell in the tents of Kedar, or in the city of Gath, or Ziklag, he was to be pitied rather than blamed.

The children of Israel were forbidden to do any servile work on the Sabbath day; and yet when the disciples were accused for rubbing the ears of corn to prepare them for food on that day, our Lord justified their conduct on the ground of necessity, and silenced his enemies by producing the example of David; whom these hypocrites themselves did not blame for eating, when hunger compelled him, that show-bread which it was lawful for the priests only, in ordinary cases, to eat. And have we not read what David did in another case, how he sent his father and mother to the king of Moab, to dwell with him, till he knew what God would do for him?

It is not certain that none but this Bethlehemite went at this time to live in Moab. We read of Israelites that dwelt in Moab, and attained high stations in it, although we cannot tell at what period, (1 Chron. 4:22,23). Nor can we tell what connections might be formed against individuals of Israel and of Moab, when both nations were under one lord, (Judges 3:14). If Naomi's family were like herself, they could not but conciliate the regard and love of all that knew them, whether Moabites or Israelites. A sweet temper disarms the fierceness of savages.

It seems probable that this family lived under, or near the time of Ehud's administration, although we cannot certainly tell why they chose rather to go the land of Moab than to any other country. One thing is evident, that there was plenty of bread, and to spare, in the land of Moab, when little was to be had in the land of Israel. What shall we say to this? Were the Israelites greater sinners than the Moabites? or were they less favored by that God who causes the corn to grow up out of the earth? Neither of these conclusions would be just. The Moabites were great sinners, for they were apostates from the religion of their father Lot, and worshippers of Chemosh. But God then suffered all nations to walk in their own way, except his chosen people. *'Them only he knew of all the families of the earth, therefore he punished them for their iniquities.'* Because God was gracious to them, he would not suffer them to walk in their own ways, that he might turn them again to himself.

Many times was Israel afflicted by various calamities, but *'Moab was at ease from his youth.'* Was Moab, then, happier than Israel? No, in no wise. He was miserable. *'He was at ease from his youth, and he settled on his lees, neither did he go into captivity, therefore his taste remained in him, and his scent was not changed. Therefore, behold the days came at last, that the Lord sent wanderers that caused him to wander, and emptied his vessels, and brake his bottles.'* Elimelech went to live in the country of Moab; not to dwell there longer than necessity compelled him. He chose rather to dwell in the Lord's land than any where else; but who can endure the rage of hunger? We cannot always dwell where we wish, but if at any time we are forced to live at a distance from the place where God's name is known and preached, our hearts ought to be left in the sanctuary. David was sometimes compelled to live in the tents of Kedar, but he ever loved the habitation of God's house, and his heart was poured out within him when he thought of the pleasures of the sanctuary.

He, and his wife, and his two sons. It is possible that if he had wanted a family, he might have been able to live at home. In times of extreme scarcity, a family may be as a heavy burden upon the minds of the poor, who know not how to satisfy the appetites of their little ones, and cannot open their understandings to make them sensible of the necessity of wanting what cannot be had. Our Lord speaks of times when it is miserable to be with child or to give suck; and Paul tells married persons, that they ought, in times of distress, to look for troubles in the flesh. Beware, however, of dissatisfaction with the providence of God, which has given you families. Amidst all the anxiety that you feel about the means of their subsistence, would you be willing to lose any of them? Would you not rather rise early and sit up late, and eat the bread of sorrow, in laboring for their subsistence?

The man's wife, with his two sons, went with him. We are not told whether Naomi was willing to go to a strange land, but we have reason to believe that she was willingly obedient to her husband. She was one of those wives whose law is their husband's will in all things wherein the laws of God leave them at liberty. These are the women who are qualified to give and to receive happiness in the married state. But those men are brutes, rather than husbands, who put the temper of such wives to a severe trial, when irresistible necessity does not compel them. It was necessity that compelled the Bethlehemite to remove his family to the land of Moab. His wife saw the necessity of the case, and therefore she did not think of returning, when she was become her own mistress, till the necessity was removed.

Verse 2. – *And the name of the man was Elimelech, and the name of his wife Naomi, and the names of his two sons Mahlon and Chilion, Ephrathites of Bethlehem-Judah. And they came into the country of Moab, and stayed there.*

The mention of the names of the father, mother, and sons, gives an air of truth to the narration, and tends to interest us in their fortunes. When we know the names of persons, we seem to ourselves to be in some degree acquainted with them, and therefore when we hear of any remarkable event befalling any person, we wish to know his name, although we can have no opportunity of ever seeing him.

We are not told of what lineage this family was, but we learn afterwards that they were nearly related to the noblest of the families of Judah. Chilion and Mahlon were almost the nearest of the kinsmen of Boaz, who was the son of Salmon, the son of Nahshon, prince of the tribe of Judah in the days of Moses. Greatness will secure no families from poverty and want. Many who once rode in their own chariots, have been compelled to subsist on the bounty of others.

The family were Ephrathites of Bethlehem-Judah. *'Bethlehem was not the least among the cities of Judah.'* It was the city of Boaz, the city of David, the city *'of which came forth to God that Ruler of Israel, whose goings forth were of old from everlasting.'* What city ever deserved so well to be renowned, except Jerusalem, where God long dwelt; where Jesus himself preached; and from whence his word of grace went forth to the nations?

And they came into the country of Moab, and continued there. In the former verse, we are told that they *went to live in the country of Moab.* They set out from their own country with a design to live in the land of Moab. Here we learn that they actually accomplished their purpose of going into the country of Moab, and there they continued longer perhaps than they wished or intended. They hoped that in a year or two they might find it convenient to return to the land of Israel. When we go from home, it depends entirely on the will of God whether we shall arrive at the place of our destination. When we are in it, it depends no less on the divine pleasure whether we shall ever again see the place from which we went out. *'A man's heart devises his way, but the Lord directs his steps.'* Beware of bringing upon yourselves the punishment that came upon the proud king of Babylon, because he did not glorify that God in whose hand his breath was, and whose were all his ways. Do you say, that to-morrow you will go into such a city, and buy, and sell, and get gain? Say, rather, If the Lord will, we shall live, and go into that city. In Him you live, in Him you move, in Him you have your being.

Verse 3. – *And Elimelech, Naomi's husband died, and she was left, and her two sons.*

'What is our life? It is a vapour which appears only for a little while, and then vanishes away.' Elimelech went only to live in the country of Moab; but the same reasons which compelled him to go to that land, compelled him to stay in it, till a stronger necessity compelled him to go the way whence he was never to return. Amidst all your trials, remember that the greatest of all trials is approaching, and perhaps nearer than you imagine. Do you fear that you shall want bread in times of scarcity? Perhaps before they are at an end your lives may end. Are you obliged to leave your native fields? The time is fast approaching when you must leave the world. Why should dying creatures be perplexed about things that they may never need, and at most cannot enjoy long? Death will soon level the distinction between the most affluent and the most indigent of the sons of men; and, therefore, let the rich enjoy their portion in this world without abusing it, or placing their confidence in what must be theirs but a very short time. And let not the poor be greatly dejected by the want of what they cannot long need. If we can procure but *'food and raiment, let us therewith be content; for we brought nothing into the world with us, and it is certain that we can carry nothing hence.'*

And she was left, and her two sons. It was, no doubt, a grief to Elimelech, if he felt the approaches of death, to leave his wife, and his two young sons, in a strange land, in a land of heathens, poor, and, for aught we know, almost friendless. When you choose your place of abode, if you have families, or may have families, let this be one principal consideration, where you will leave them if God should call you out of the world. What cheerless prospects must present themselves to the view of a good man leaving a young family in the midst of neighbors that have never heard of the grace of God, or never paid any regard to what they have heard!

She was left of her husband with two sons. How much was this good woman to be pitied! She was left in a state of indigence. Her sons, very probably, were come to that time of life in which they might be of some use to her; but she had lost that friend in whom her hope rested for the support and government of her family in its distressed and dangerous condition. I call its condition dangerous, not because they were in a country of enemies to their nation, although the Moabites were seldom the friends of Israel, but because they dwelt in a land devoted to the worship of Chemosh. Without the comforts of religion, Naomi's heart must have died within her; yet in a short time afterwards, the Lord added new affliction to her former griefs.

Verse 4. – *And they took wives for themselves from the women of Moab. The name of the one was Orpah, and the name of the other Ruth. And they lived there about ten years.*

Many blame these young men for marrying wives of the daughters of Moab, and certainly they were much to be blamed for marrying them, if they had not a credible evidence that these young women were convinced of the folly of worshiping Chemosh, and cordially disposed to join with their husbands in the worship of the God of Israel. When Ezra was informed that the holy seed had mingled themselves with the Moabites, and with other idolatrous nations, by marrying their daughters, he was filled with almost inconsolable grief. Nothing but the expulsion of the strange wives could dispel his anxious apprehensions of the wrath of God, merited by the conjunction of the men of Israel with the people of these abominations.

If Mahlon and Chilion had good reason to think that their intended wives were sincere proselytes to their religion, they deserve no blame, but rather praise. But whether they were justifiable or excusable, or neither the one nor the other, it is perhaps impossible for any man to determine, because we have not sufficient knowledge of the circumstances of the case. Certain it is, that Salmon did well in marrying Rahab, who belonged to a worse race of people than the Moabites, for she renounced the idols and abominations of her country, and showed her faith in the God of Israel by her works. Perhaps the example of Salmon, to whom this family was related, induced them to venture upon this alliance with strangers. But why should we pronounce a sentence against any man, when we are neither called to be his judges, nor furnished with means for judging?

This we know with certainty, that whether Elimelech did right or wrong in going with his family into the land of Moab, which led the way to their marriages, and whether the sons of Elimelech did right or wrong in contracting these marriages, the providence of God, by what it did, was accomplishing its own gracious purposes. Ruth was one of God's elect. She was to be brought to the knowledge and love of the truth by her connection with the family of Elimelech. The happiness which she gained, was a good compensation for all the distresses which this family had endured–for all that the land of Israel had suffered by a ten years' famine. Little did the pious remnant in Israel know, when they were deploring the miseries of the poor, that the famine was to be subservient to the salvation of a precious soul in the land of Moab.

They dwelt about ten years in the land of Moab. It seems that Naomi could not return sooner on account of the famine. What a dreadful scourge was this famine of ten years! We need not think it strange that Elisha sent away his friend the Shunamite to live in a strange land, when there were to be seven years of famine. Every year in the course of this famine must have been a very great accession to the miseries of the poor, or rather of the whole people. We find that a second year of dearth is likely to be worse than the first, although the price of provisions is not so high, because money is more scarce. What would seven or ten years of scarcity be, although they should not amount to a famine? Blessed be God, who has not year after year turned the rain of our land into powder and dust!

Verse 5. – *And Mahlon and Chilion also died, both of them. And the woman was left without her two sons and her husband.*

Poor woman! what will she now do, bereaved of both her sons, after her husband? Might not one of them at least have been spared for her comfort? Let us not speak in this manner, lest we should seem to charge God with folly. God's thoughts are not as our thoughts. If God loved this woman, we think that he would have left her one or another, at least, of her family, if not all of them. Yet all of them die, and leave her desolate in the land of Moab, far from all their relations that were yet left in Bethlehem! The love or hatred of God is not to be estimated by our feelings, or by our reasonings, unsupported by the Bible.

Naomi might probably think that she was one of the most unhappy women in the land, when necessity compelled her to leave the land of Israel. When she afterwards lost her husband, she might think that then only she began to be miserable, and that she greatly erred when she thought herself unhappy before this calamity befell her. But when she afterwards lost first one and then another of her sons, new thoughts would come into her mind. Then she might suppose that she had complained too heavily of the loss of her husband, and was not duly thankful to God for sparing her sons. Now at last, and not before, she might think that the Lord dealt bitterly with her, and had made desolate all her company. When heavy calamities befall you, beware of speaking unadvisedly with your lips. Beware of gloomy and impatient thoughts. Say not that God has bereaved you of all earthly comforts, when he has reduced you to poverty, if your friends are preserved alive. If some of your nearest friends are cut off by a stroke, still you must not say that nothing is left to sweeten life, when others are left whom you love. It is presumptuous in mortals, in sinful mortals, to think or talk as if the Lord had forgotten to be merciful.

Naomi's thoughts of God's dealings with her upon earth are now very different from what they were when these two things came upon her, the loss of children and widowhood. All these things appeared then to be against her. But now she knows and sees that all these things were fruits of the love of God. Amidst your perplexing thoughts about the occurrences of life, it will be profitable to consider what you will think an hundred years hence of these adversities which now spread such a dismal gloom upon your spirits. Blessed are the men who firmly believe that God is wiser than themselves, and who act according to that belief by a patient resignation to God under every trial. They will see at last, and they believe at present, that *'all the paths of the Lord are mercy and truth to such as keep his covenant and his testimonies.'* At last it will be found, that we could not, without great loss, have wanted any of those trials of faith which once were ready to overwhelm our spirits.

LECTURE II.

NAOMI'S RETURN TO HER OWN COUNTRY.

CHAPTER 1:6-10.

Verse 6. – *Then she arose with her daughters-in-law, that she might return from the country of Moab. For she had heard in the country of Moab how the Lord had visited his people in giving them bread.*

Naomi would, no doubt, often say within herself, Woe is me that I dwell so long in the country of Moab; that I live year after year among the worshipers of Chemosh! Yet she found herself under the unhappy necessity of continuing among them till she could entertain the prospect of being able to live in her own country. It was David's most earnest desire, that he might dwell in the days of his life in the house of the Lord; yet, more than once, he found it absolutely necessary to dwell among heathens. But as soon as God opened to him the way to return to the Lord's land, he gladly and thankfully improved the opportunity.

Naomi justly thought that the Lord called her back to Bethlehem, when she heard that he had visited his people in giving them bread. She might now entertain rational hopes of finding the needful supports of life in her own land. She could not hope to make the figure at Bethlehem which she did in the days when the candle of the Lord shined upon her head, when her husband was yet with her, when her children were about her, when the family estate supplied it with the means of keeping a plentiful table; but she might hope, by the labor of her hands, and the kindness of her friends, to live in a manner suited to the circumstances in which divine providence had now placed her. It is not pleasant to flesh and blood to be reduced to a dependent condition. But humbling dispensations of providence ought always to be attended with a correspondent humility of spirit, unless we desire misery as our portion, and, what is still worse, to be found fighting against the Almighty. His will must be done; and, if our will stand in opposition to his, it must bend or break.

She had heard in the country of Moab, that the Lord had visited his people. In the land of strangers, she was always anxious to hear what was passing in the land of Israel. She still took an interest in that country for her own sake, for her friend's and brethren's sakes, for the Lord's sake. Although she was dwelling in a land well supplied with bread and wine, (Isa. 16:9,10) yet she felt deeply for the poor Israelites in their own land who were punished with hunger. She mourned for the long continuance of the famine, and was filled with joy in the midst of her sorrows, when she heard that the Lord had visited her people in mercy. Thus Nehemiah, at the court of Shushan, was ever careful to be informed of what was passing in the land of Judah. He was rich and great, and enjoyed the favor of the greatest prince in the world; but his happiness could not be complete unless he heard that his people were happy.

The Lord visited his people in giving them bread. 'Thou visitest the earth, and water it,' says David, *'you greatly enrich it with the river of God which is full of water, you prepare them corn, when you have so provided for it.'* The Psalmist teaches us to consider every fertilizing shower from heaven, as a kind of visitation from that God who keeps the clouds in his hand, and *'turns them about by his counsels, to do whatsoever he commands them upon the face of the world, in the earth.'* When Naomi heard that plenty was restored in the land of Israel, she saw that the Lord had visited his people, and brought with him a rich present of suitable supplies for their necessity. She had seen, that even the land flowing with milk and honey could not supply its inhabitants with the necessaries of life, unless God were pleased to *'hear the heavens, that the heavens might hear the earth, and the earth hear the corn and the wine and the oil, that they might hear his people.'*

If God after nine years of scarcity, should return to us in mercy, and give us abundance of bread to eat, would we not confess that we could never be sufficiently thankful to God for his undeserved bounty? But have we not still greater reason to be thankful, when scarcity is hardly felt in one year out of ten? Why should we need cleanness of teeth to make us sensible of that bounty by which we are fed every day of our lives? If you were in a dependent condition, and one of your friends should supply you once in a week with provisions for your table, would you not reckon yourselves highly indebted to his goodness? But would it not be esteemed by you an higher act of kindness to make a settled provision for your subsistence, that you might never want what is needful? If rare mercies from God are acknowledged with thankfulness, (and who can be unthankful for them?) what praises are due to him for mercies showered down upon us every day in our lives!

Then she arose with her daughters-in-law, that she might return from the country of Moab.

Verse 7. – *Therefore, she went forth out of the place where she was, and her two daughters-in-law with her, and they went on the way to return to the land of Judah.*

One of these young widows, we have reason to think, was still a heathen. And yet (let many Christians blush!) she, as well as her religious sister-in-law, behaves in a dutiful and respectful manner to her husband's mother. May we not say, that the daughter who behaves undutifully to her mother, and even the daughter-in-law who is an adversary to her mother-in-law, has denied the faith, and is worse than an infidel? If your parents, by nature or marriage, were rich, you would treat them with respect, because you would hope to share in their prosperity; but Naomi was poor, and a stranger in the land of Moab, and yet her daughters-in-law treated her with kindness while she lived near them, and would not allow her to leave the country without accompanying her in the way, and doing her all the service they could. Their husbands were dead. Their relation to Naomi might seem to some to be utterly dissolved; but their love was strengthened rather than abated. And why should it not? Are we to withdraw our affections from our friends because the Lord has afflicted them? The death of husbands or wives will not put an end to the friendship of those who are allied by marriage, unless there has been bad behaviour on the one side, or an ungenerous spirit on the other. That which loudly calls for sympathy, can never be a good reason for coldness.

Verse 8. – *And Naomi said to her two daughers-in-law, Go return each one to her mother's house. May the Lord deal kindly with you, as you have dealt with the dead, and with me.*

Orpah and Ruth were greatly attached to their mother-in-law, although their own mothers were still alive. They did not stand in need of Naomi's friendship, but she needed theirs. Her afflictions and desolate condition endeared her so much to them, that they seemed to pay more attention to her than to their own mothers; and, on some accounts, she was better entitled to their sympathy. She seems to have travailed in birth with them, that the promised Christ might be formed in them, and probably she was in truth the spiritual mother of Ruth.

Go, return each to her mother's house. Whether their fathers were still alive, or whether their mother's house is mentioned because their intercourse in the house of their parents would chiefly be with their mothers, we cannot tell.

May the Lord deal kindly with you! She blesses them when she sends them away, not in the name of Chemosh, but in the name of Jehovah the God of Israel; and thereby insinuates, at a time which they could never forget, and in words which were likely to be often present to their minds, that not the gods of Moab, but the God of Israel, was the eternal fountain of blessings, from whom every good and perfect gift was to be expected. Our speech ought to be always seasoned with salt, but there are particular seasons when our words ought to be ordered in consummate wisdom. The words of parting friends, who are likely never again to meet, make an impression never to be erased. Who knows what good may be done by such words, when they breathe at once the fervour of piety and of charity? They are like dying words, for our friends are then dead to us when we see them no more.

May the Lord deal kindly with you, as you have dealt with the dead, and with me. It seems these two women had been good wives to their husbands, although their husbands were poor men and strangers. If they had assumed more power over their husbands than they ought, they would probably have been supported by their relations and countrymen. But they always dealt kindly with them, and endeavored to render their condition in a land of strangers comfortable and pleasant. Nature itself, you see, teaches wives to deal kindly with their husbands, for Moabitesses were taught by it to deal kindly with those that married them. Beware, you who call yourselves Christians, of behaving worse than women that never heard the duties of wives enforced by such powerful motives. *'Submit yourselves unto your husbands as unto the Lord; for the husband is the head of the wife, even as Christ is the head of the church, and he is the Saviour of the body. Therefore, as the church is subject to Christ, so let the wives be to their own husbands in everything.'*

You know not, husbands and wives, how long you may dwell together. Death may soon come, and will doubtless, sooner or later, come and tear away the one of you from the other. When that event shall take place, how will you wish to have behaved? Behave at present as you would then wish to have behaved, for then you will not be able to bring back the present time. Many great miracles have been wrought by the power of God, but it never did, nor ever will, recall the time that is past. How comfortable was it to Orpah and Ruth to hear Naomi say, You have dealt kindly with the dead! And how comfortable was the reflection to them through life, that she had reason to give them this commendation!

As you have dealt with the dead, and with me. These amiable women extended their kindness from their husbands to their mother-in-law, the only friend of their husbands to whom they could show kindness. It is commonly supposed, that a widow may hope to live among us more comfortably with a son-in-law, than with one of her own married sons. This observation often holds good but not to our honor. Why should not daughter-in-laws behave like daughters? If husband and wife are one flesh, your husband's father is your father, your husband's mother is your mother. Why should Moabitesses behave better than many Christian wives, and merit commendations which cannot, without flattery, be given to those who have such superior advantages for knowing and for practising their duty? I say not this to shame you. I know that there are some to whom no reproof of this kind is due. But are there not others who behave less affectionately to their own mothers than did Orpah and Ruth to the mother of their husbands?

And with me. When I speak of the unkind behavior of some wives to the mothers of their husbands, let me give to every one her portion of reproof. The blame of unkindness does not always lie on one side. If there were more Naomis, there might be more Orpahs and Ruths. Naomi was disposed to take in good part the conduct of her daughters-in-law, and to express a grateful sense of the attentions that were paid to her. Some old women look upon every instance of kindness from their daughters, or their daughters-in-law, as a debt for which they owe them no thanks. Others are so sullen, so suspicious, so fretful, that there is no possibility of pleasing them. They turn the duty of their children into a hard task, which they find it impossible to perform with satisfaction to themselves, because it gives so little satisfaction to those whom they wish to serve. True, your children are bound to honor you, but they are not bound to comply with all your humors. They are bound to be the comforters of your old age; but how can they comfort you, if you refuse to take comfort in all they can do to please you? They do no more than their duty when they endeavor to gild the evening of your days by their dutiful behaviour; but are you not bound to show a grateful sense of their care to perform their duty? You see that Naomi thanked and blessed her daughters-in-law for the kindness which they had showed to herself, as well as for their endeavors to contribute to the happiness of her sons.

Verse 9. – *May the Lord grant you that you may find rest, each in the house of her husband. Then she kissed them, and they lifted up their voice and wept.*

Naomi did not wish her daughters-in-law to continue through the remaining part of their lives unmarried. She was far from thinking that their entrance a second time into the bond of marriage, would be in any degree inconsistent with all due respect for the memory of their first husbands. If ever they should again enter into this state of life, as she hoped they would do, she wished them all that happiness which they might have expected to enjoy if the Lord had been pleased to spare the lives of her sons.

There are seasons, in which unmarried persons and widows will act wisely if they continue as they are; but there are other times, in which it is in general better for the younger widows, as well as unmarried women, to marry. We cannot, indeed, fix a rule which will include all without exception, because that may be good for one which is not good for another, whose dispositions or circumstances require a different conduct. There are some who err by marrying when they ought not, or whom they ought not to marry; and there are others who sin when they do not marry, as we learn from the different advices given on this subject by the apostle Paul, (1 Cor. 7; 1 Tim. 5).

But whenever men or women marry, if they are wise for themselves, they will take proper measures to find satisfaction in that new state of life; and one of the chief means to be used for this purpose is prayer to God. '*May the Lord grant you that you may find rest in the house of her husband!*' '*A prudent wife is from the Lord,*' and a kind husband is from the Lord also; and, if in any thing, surely in this most important step of life, we are to ask counsel from the mouth of the Lord, and to implore his blessing. Let it be, however, remembered, that if you are sincere in seeking the blessing of God upon this relation, you will follow the directions of his word in making your choice. Have you not a husband or wife at present? judge for yourselves whether you ought, or ought not to marry. *Marry whom you will, only in the Lord.'* Do you seek rest in the house of a husband, or comfort with a wife? remember what God says concerning the virtuous woman, (Prov. 31) and what he says in many places of his word concerning the character of the man whose conduct he approves, and to whom he will give his blessing, (Prov. 3).

If it is to be wished that wives may find rest in the houses of their husbands, it must be the duty of husbands to do what they can to procure them rest, not only by endeavoring to provide for them what is necessary for their subsistence and comfortable accommodation, but by such a kind behavior as will promote their satisfaction and comfort. Men and women may have affluence without rest, and rest without affluence. But let women also contribute to procure rest for themselves by frugality, by industry, by such behaviour to their husbands as will merit constant returns of kindness.

Then she kissed them, and they lifted up their voice and wept. They wept because they were to part, never again to meet, all of them, together in this world. They had been happy in one another, and one of the sorest afflictions incident to this life, is the everlasting separation of those who are mutually dead. But why do we say everlasting separation? There is no everlasting separation of Christian friends. Little was known of what we know concerning the future state, by these friends of whom we are speaking, and there was little ground of hope that they would all meet in that state, if they had known it; for it does not appear that Orpah was willing to take up her cross, and deny herself, to serve the God of Israel. We that are Christians have the happiness to know with certainty, that our separation from our friends in Christ will not be eternal, though it may be long. Because it may be long, we mourn; because it is not to be eternal, we do not mourn as they that have no hope.

They lifted up their voice and wept, not only at the thought of their long separation, but at the recollection which rushed into their minds at this time, of many endearing, of many sorrowful, of many joyful circumstances of their past lives. For such is the precarious and changeable nature of worldly felicity, that even the sweetest joys of life often make way for the most piercing griefs. Our remembrance of pleasures enjoyed, and to be enjoyed no more, spreads a dismal gloom over those pleasures that we might yet enjoy. We cannot be made happy by a rich abundance of those things which give happiness (such as the world can give) to others, because we are bereaved of those things in which we place too much of our happiness.

This world is a place of mourning to all, but to some more than others, by the afflictive changes which darken many of their days. Let us all seek to be found in Him whose office it is to *'comfort all that mourn.'* Sorrow is turned into joy by him who is *'the Consolation of Israel.'*

Verse 10. – *And they said to her, Surely we will return with you to your people.*

We have no reason to doubt the sincerity of both these women in this extraordinary profession of attachment to Naomi, although one of them was easily diverted from her purpose. There is a great difference between the same mind at different times. Orpah's intention of going with Naomi, included an intention of serving Naomi's God, and of relinquishing the gods of Moab; for it is not likely that she thought she would be permitted to practise the worship of Chemosh in the land of Israel. We may therefore observe from this place, that you ought not to mistake every purpose of being truly religious, as a sign of true grace. If you turn to God from sin, with full purpose of, and endeavour after, new obedience, you are true penitents; but this full purpose is attended with habitual performance. *'Bring forth fruits meet for repentance,'* if you desire to be esteemed true children of Abraham. If, like Orpah, you promise and intend to perform, but return to your former course of life, your *'goodness is like the morning cloud, and like the early dew, that goes away.'*

Surely we will return with you to your people. They knew but very few of Naomi's people; but from her own behavior, and the behavior of her family, they judged that they were people with whom it would be happy to live. Let us all endeavor so to live, as to give strangers to religion favorable ideas of those who profess it. The lewd conduct of nominal Christians has done unknown mischief in the world. If all Christians were attentive to the cause of Christ in their conversation, stumbling blocks would be removed out of the way of the inconsiderate, and the mouths of malicious enemies stopped. *'Many, seeing our good works, would glorify our Father who is in heaven.' 'Whatsoever things are true, and honest, and just, and pure, and lovely, and praiseworthy, think on these things,'* if you desire to enjoy peace in your own minds, or to be useful to others around you.

May we see more and more of the accomplishment of the prayer of our Lord Jesus, that all his followers *'may be one in the Father, and in the Son; that the world may know that he is sent by the Father!'*

LECTURE III.

THE SAME SUBJECT CONTINUED.

CHAPTER 1:11-15.

Verse 11. – *And Naomi said, Turn again, my daughters. Why will you go with me? Are there still any more sons in my womb, that they may be your husbands?*

Turn again, my daughters. Naomi does not call them her daughters-in-law, but her daughters. They deserved to be addressed by her in this affectionate language. They were as dutiful and affectionate to Naomi as if she had borne them.

Turn again, why will you go with me? We ought not, without good reason, to leave the land of our nativity. We are not bound to live all our days in one place or in one country, but we ought not to change our condition or country without being able to give a good reason for it. There is no part of the world which the curse of God has not reached; and if we hope, by leaving our native land, to leave the miseries of life behind us, we will be miserably disappointed. Naomi had formerly too good reason for coming into the land of Moab, and she had now a very sufficient reason for leaving it; but it was highly proper that her daughters-in-law should consider, before they accompanied her to Bethlehem, whether their reasons were as good as her's. *'As a bird that wanders from its nest, so is a man that wanders from his place.'*

Are there any sons in my womb, that they should be your husbands? Before the law was given by Moses, it appears to have been customary in some parts of the East, that the wife of a man who died childless should become the wife of his brother; and therefore Judah doomed his daughter-in-law to the fire as an adulteress, when he heard that she had committed whoredom in the house of her father, where she was ordered to continue till Shelah, the son of Judah, was marriageable. But Orpah and Ruth could have no prospect of second marriages in the family of Naomi. She was now childless, and could have no prospect of other children to supply the place of those she had lost.

Verse 12. – *Turn again, my daughters, go. For I am too old to have a husband. If I should say, I have hope, if I should have a husband also tonight, and should also bear sons;*

Turn again my daughters; go your way, for I am too old to have an husband; or, if I should have an husband, I cannot expect to have any more sons; or, if I should have both an husband and sons, they would be too long in growing up to maturity for becoming your husbands. Naomi would have preferred these two young widows to all other women as wives for her sons, if any sons had been left to her. But all her sons were gone to the land of forgetfulness, and she was not foolish enough to think either of a husband or sons at her time of life. She did not indulge romantic hopes, as too many do. of what would never happen. There are some who, in a bad sense, hope against hope; but their hopes, built upon a foundation of sand, deceive them, and end in deserved misery. Naomi did not allow herself to form such visionary expectations as would end only in disappointment. The hand of the Lord had gone out against her, and robbed her of her best friends, and she would not, like the foolish Edomites, say, *'The bricks are fallen down, but we will build with hewn stones; the sycamores are cut down, but we will build with cedar.'* It would add greatly to our happiness, if we could believe and improve that fundamental principle of our religion, *'If God make peace, who can make trouble? but if he hides his face, who can behold him; whether it is done against a nation, or against a man only?'*

I am too old to have an husband. She would not so much as think of another husband in her advanced period of life. The apostle Paul seems to take it for granted, that a woman would scarcely be found at sixty years of age, or upwards, who would think of marriage; and therefore, in giving directions about those female servants of the church who could not conveniently perform the duties required of them if they were married, he says, *'Let no widow be taken into the number under sixty years of age.'* Why? Because the younger widows, if they were taken into the number, might marry.

I am too old to have an husband; but if I should have an husband, can I hope to have children? Sarah bore a child when she was ninety years of age. But it would be presumptuous to expect miracles in the ordinary course of providence.

Some people cannot think without envy, of happiness enjoyed by others which themselves cannot hope to enjoy, as if the pleasures of others were their punishment. But Naomi wished to each of her daughters-in-law rest in the house of an husband, although she herself was to continue a desolate and poor widow. And she hoped it would not be a long time till she heard that both of them were happy in another change of life. I fear few of us are possessed of the generous charity of the apostle Paul, who could say, *'We are glad when we are weak, and you are strong.'*

If I should say that I hope; if I should have an husband also tonight, and should also bear sons,

Verse 13. – *Would you wait for them until they are grown? Would you wait for them from having husbands? No my daughters, for it makes me very sad for your sakes that the hand of the Lord has gone out against me.*

Extremes in every thing are to be avoided. Some, too precipitately, rush into the married state. They do not duly deliberate about this important step of life. They do not consult with those friends who have a right to give their mind, and they do not take time to consult with God, *'from whom every good gift comes.'* But others are too dilatory about entering into the married state. The bad effects of undue delay of marriage have often appeared in the licentious conduct of the young. It was the desire of Naomi, not only that her daughters-in-law might find rest, each of them in the house of an husband, but they might find it while the years of their youth yet continued with them. Suppose the possibility that she might yet have children, *would you wait for them till they were grown? Would you wait for them from having husbands?*

No, my daughters, for it makes me very sad for your sakes that the hand of the Lord has gone out against me. She was grieved for her own sake that the hand of the Lord was gone out against her, and yet she would have borne it more easily if she herself had been the only sufferer. That she was a widow, and childless, appeared hard to her; but it distressed her no less to think that her amiable daughters-in-law were become widows in the days of their youth, especially when she thought, as she was disposed to do, that their affliction was the effect of a quarrel that God had with herself.

This is a great aggravation of the afflictions of many parents, that their children are involved with themselves. They could bear poverty, they could bear reproach, they could bear death itself, had they none who depended on them for bread and for respectability in the world. But it appears hard to them, that their innocent babes, or their affectionate children in a more advanced period of life, should suffer along with them. Under this covert, we are too apt to hide from ourselves our impatience under the dispensations of divine providence. God has the same right to rule over the fruit of our bodies as over ourselves, and to allot to them their share of the good or the bad things of this world.

It is bitterest of all, when we have reason to think that our sins have provoked God to punish us in the persons of our friends, or to inflict those strokes which our friends must feel as heavily as ourselves. Let us beware of ever exposing ourselves to such heart-piercing reflections by conduct that may bring down God's displeasure upon our families. Let us humble ourselves under the mighty hand of God, and commit to his disposal our families as well as ourselves. David procured the death of his little child, and threatenings of heavy judgments upon others of his family, by his sin. But let us remember what method David took to recover his peace of mind, and, if we are in like circumstances, follow his example; (2 Sam. 12; Psalm 51).

God's people may sometimes, without good reason, think that the hand of the Lord is gone forth against them, in the calamities which befal their families or friends. David had good grounds for humbling himself under the hand of God gone forth against himself in the disasters that befel his family; but Job had no reason to think that his children were taken away by God either for their own or their father's transgression. Satan '*moved the Lord against that good man to destroy him without cause.*' Our afflictions are hard enough to be borne by us, without the addition of groundless reflections against ourselves. At the same time, the error is much more common of insensibility to the divine displeasure, when it has been really kindled by our sins, than of vexing ourselves with unjust suspicions of God's anger. But it will be our wisdom to guard against mistakes fatal to our peace of mind, as well as those which indicate an unhumbled spirit. Nothing is more unlike a saint than stupidity under divine corrections, whether they come upon us in our own persons, or in the persons of our friends; but few things are more unfavorable to the progress of holiness than groundless jealousies entertained and cherished concerning the dealings of divine providence in the management of our concerns.

There is one thing that still remains to be considered concerning this parting speech of Naomi to her daughers-in-law. Why did she dissuade them from going with her to the land of Judah, where the true God was well known; and persuade them to return to a country of abominable idolaters, where they would be carried down the stream of general practice into the abyss of perdition? '*Because of such things*' as are commonly practised by the heathen, '*the wrath of God comes on the children of disobedience.*' Ought not Naomi, then, to have rather endeavoured to pluck her beloved daughters as brands out of the burning, by alluring them into a land where the method of salvation was known, and where the means of grace were enjoyed?

We are not bound to justify all that Naomi spake or did; and we ought not rashly to condemn her, because we know only a few of the things that she spake to her daughters-in-law. But, in charity to that good woman, we ought to believe, that, for years past, she had been endeavoring, by her practice and her converse, to recommend to her young friends the worship of the God of Israel. If they were truly turned from the error of their ways, nothing that is here said was likely to drive them back to their own country. But if they were not, why should they go forward with her into her country, where she could not support them, and where it was possible that, from the behaviour of Naomi's countrymen to such destitute strangers, they would rather contract prejudices unfavorable to their religion, then cordially join in their worship? They might have been disgusted even with Naomi's own conduct, if she had not fairly told them what inconveniences they were to encounter in going to her land, and to her people. We ought, by all prudent methods, to gain proselytes to a religion which we know to be divine; but we are to catch none by guile. When Paul says, '*Being crafty, I caught you with guile,*' he spake not in his own person, but in the person of an objector to the account he was giving of his own conduct. Far from allowing that he caught them with guile, he proves the very reverse to have been the case; for he '*renounced the hidden things of dishonesty, not walking in craftiness, nor handling the word of God deceitfully.*'

Our Lord very plainly told his followers what they were to expect in his service. To a man who expressed his intention of following him, he said, *'The foxes have holes, and the birds of the air have nests, but the Son of man has no where to lay his head.'* We may however observe, that Christ usually administered proper antidotes against the fears which the doctrine of the cross might excite in the minds of his hearers. When he told them that they must *'deny themselves, and take up their cross and follow him,'* he told them likewise, that *'those who lost their lives for his sake should find them.'* It may be doubted whether Naomi, in the dejection of her spirits, did not overlook the powerful consolations which might have encouraged her young friends to follow her into the land of Israel, and would have more than compensated all the inconveniences to which they would have been exposed in a strange land. She honestly told them that they could not reasonably expect outward prosperity if they should accompany her. But might she not have reminded them of those spiritual advantages, which made the condition of the poorest Israelites unspeakably more advantageous than the happiest state of those heathens who knew not God? Doubtless she had often spoken of those privileges to them in former time; but as yet they had not learned their nature, and perhaps Naomi now despaired of ever being able to give them a perfect idea of it.

Verse 14. – *And they lifted up their voice and wept again. And Orpah kissed her mother-in-law; but Ruth clung to her.*

Again they lift up their voices and weep when Naomi had represented her own destitute condition, and the little encouragement she could give them to go with her to her native land. They were also pierced with a deep concern for the afflictions which she had suffered, without any prospect of seeing them redressed in the manner they could have wished. But there is always a mixture of pleasure with the tears which flow from compassion and charity. Those men are not to be envied, but pitied, who feel not for the woes of their friends.

Naomi had already kissed both her daughters-in-law. Orpah now kisses Naomi and leaves her. We can scarcely avoid thinking, when we read this history, of the young man whom our Lord loved, although he would not follow him. The young man was amiable for his natural dispositions, and for his discreet behaviour; but, alas! he could not think of parting with all that he had for Christ. Orpah, in like manner, would have gladly accompanied Naomi to her people, could she have enjoyed with her those accommodations that appeared to her necessary for her earthly felicity. She kissed Naomi because she dearly loved her, but she did not love the God of Naomi so as to *'forget her father's house, and her own people,'* to serve Him. Think not that an amiable natural temper, or an affectionate behaviour to your parents and friends, are either sufficient indications of true religion, or compensate for the want of it. The young man whom Jesus loved went away sorrowful from Jesus; but his sorrow at leaving him did by no means atone for the deaf ear which he turned to his religious instructions. Nature, in its highest endowments and improvements, is infinitely below grace. There are some believers in Christ, whose natural tempers are never refined to such a degree as we might expect from their religious principles; yet they shall dwell for ever in the region of love. There are other men, whose natural tempers are affectionate and humane. Perhaps they are improved by all the advantages of a polite and learned education. Thus they acquire an uncommon degree of respectability in the world, and yet continue destitute of faith in Christ and love to God. With all their attainments, they are still in a miserable condition. The love and esteem of men will not secure them from the wrath of that God whose service they neglect; and whose, Son, the only Saviour, they despise.

Orpah kissed her mother-in-law, but Ruth clung to her. And Ruth's attachment to her was worth ten thousand of Orpah's kisses. The young nobleman in the gospel treated our Lord with high respect; but all this availed him nothing, for he would not sell his possessions at Christ's command, and become a follower of Jesus. Happy were the apostles who continued with him in all his temptations. They left all and followed him. What they left was little, but that love which disposed them to leave all was highly valued by him, and they received an hundred fold of recompense even in this world.

Verse 15. – *And she said, Behold, Your sister-in-law has gone back to her people and to her gods. Return after your sister-in-law.*

It was doubtless Naomi's grief, that a young woman whom she loved, and who loved her so dearly, went back, not only to her people, but to her gods. Naomi, it is probable, knew her too well to be mistaken in the suspicion she had formed of her conduct. If her husband, when he married her, had no better reason than Naomi now had to judge favorably of her religious sentiments, he was greatly to be blamed for taking her into his bosom. But love may easily deceive a man who is clear-sighted in ordinary matters. Jacob, in all probability, did not find it so easy a matter as he expected, to reclaim Rachel from the worship of her father's images.

She has gone back to her people and to her gods. Naomi doubted not that she was returning to her gods, although she said nothing of them when she left her mother-in-law. Perhaps she was not even thinking of her gods; but her return to her people was, in effect, a return to her gods. If she had intended to have nothing more to do with her idols, she would have fled from the temptations to idolatry which surrounded her on every side in the land of her nativity, and amongst her kindred.

There are too many, even of the professors of the true religion, who have no other reason for professing it, but the public confession of it among the people to whom they belong. Were they inhabitants of Greece, they would profess either the Turkish or the Greek religion, for the same reason that induces them to be Protestants in Great Britain. Beware of thinking that the best religion in the world will save you, if you do not receive the truth in the love of it, and in the love of it not chiefly for your fathers' and brethren's sake, but for its own sake, and for the sake of its glorious Author.

Return after your sister-in-law. Example has a mighty influence, the example especially of dear friends with whom we have long lived in habits of intimacy. If Orpah had gone with Naomi, Ruth and Orpah would have kept one another in countenance. As matters stood, Ruth was likely to be esteemed by all her former friends the greatest fool in the world. Did not Orpah leave her mother-in-law, although she loved her with as warm affections as any mother-in-law could expect? But she was not so unwise as to leave all her other friends for a single friend connected with her by a relation which was now extinguished. Ruth loved her mother-in-law with an unreasonable and romantic fondness. When Orpah, in her sight, had the good sense to leave her, and to return to much nearer friends, Ruth still kept her foolish resolution to go to a country which she knew not, with an old woman, who, instead of being able to support her, must depend on the labor of this poor young woman. Such might be the reflections of those who knew not the springs of Ruth's conduct But Ruth had sense enough to know, that neither the example nor the opinion of other people, ought to be the rule of her own conduct. *'It is a small thing for us to be judged of man; but he who judges us is the Lord.'*

Here again it may be asked, Did not Naomi cast stumbling blocks, as well as Orpah, in the way of Ruth? Was it not a sufficient temptation for this young woman to see Orpah returning to her gods? Why does Naomi enforce the temptation, by exciting her to follow the example? Does not Solomon give a much better advice, when with great earnestness he exhorts us to *'keep out of the path of evil doers,'* (Prov. 4:14,15)?

Naomi did not, certainly, wish that Ruth should return to her gods; and if she did not wish that she should return to her gods, she could not wish that she should lay herself open to temptations, such as those to which Orpah was now exposing herself. Ruth, therefore, who knew Naomi's zeal for the Lord God of Israel, would not understand her words as an advice to follow Orpah's example, but rather as a trial of her sincerity, and a modest reference of the important point to her own choice, whether she would go with Orpah to her friends and her gods, or come with Naomi to the land of Israel, and worship the God of Abraham and of Lot. We ought to be zealous for the Lord God of Israel, and to do what we can to turn sinners from the error of their ways; but we cannot compel the inclination or the judgment of our friends. Christ himself did not seek any followers that would not willingly comply with his injunctions. *'If any man is willing to come after me, let him deny himself.'* He, who works in men to will and to do, will accept of no man's doings where the will is not engaged (Matt. 16:24).

When Jesus said to a man who would have followed him, *'The foxes have holes, and the birds of the air have nests, but the Son of man has no where to lay his head,'* he did not intend to dissuade any man from following him, but to let men know that they ought, before they profess themselves his followers, to consider what they may expect in his service, and whether they are prepared to bear the cross without repining, when God calls them to endure it. When he said to Judas, *'What you do, do quickly,'* he by no means authorised Judas to execute his wicked design of betraying his Master, but rather to awaken his conscience to a sense of the danger and baseness of his intentions, by placing the intended crime before his view, and fixing his mind upon it as a crime presently to be committed; for those evils which are considered as present may strike horror, although they were far from appearing dreadful at a distance. So Naomi, in the words before us, rather warns Ruth of the danger of returning, than exhorts her to return; *Return to your people, and to your gods.* After what Ruth had learned of the God of Israel, she could not bear the thought of returning to the gods of Moab; and therefore, she would rather expose herself to every possible inconveniency and hardship in the land of Israel, than return to her own people. Let blinded idolaters *'walk in the name of their gods; we will walk in the name of our God for ever and ever!'* Never will we be so mad, if we have any true knowledge of the glory of God, as to leave the Fountain of living waters, to make to ourselves cisterns, which will prove but broken cisterns that can hold no water. The folly of apostasy will not damp, but invigorate our zeal, for why should we follow the example of those who *'begin in the spirit and end in the flesh?'*

LECTURE IV.

RUTH'S STEADFASTNESS TO HER RELIGIOUS PROFESSION.

CHAPTER 1:16-18.

Verse 16. – *And Ruth said, Do not beg me to leave you or to return from following after you. For where you go, I will go. Where you stay, I will stay. Your people shall be my people, and your God my God.*

Ruth clung to Naomi, when Orpah kissed and left her. How firmly she clung to Naomi, we learn from her own words:–

Do not beg me (or do not press me) *to leave you, or to turn aside from following you.* Dearly as Ruth loved her mother-in-law, and pleasant as her words had usually been in her ears, she was greatly distressed with what Naomi had now said. She could not really intend to persuade her beloved daughter-in-law to return to the service of Chemosh; but Ruth could not bear the slightest appearance of temptation, especially from the lips of one who was so dear to her; nor could she easily bear the appearance of any suspicion concerning her steadfastness in the faith and worship of the God of Israel.

Ruth assures Naomi, that it would serve no purpose to remind her of the inconveniences which she might expect to encounter. She had already formed her resolution, and it was so firm, that no considerations would induce her to alter it. Why, then, should any more be said on the subject? It might make her very uneasy, but her purpose could not be altered.

Where you go, I will go. Where you stay, I will stay. Should Naomi go to the end of the world, she would go with her. How much more when Naomi was going to the land of Israel, where the God whom she had chosen for her God was known and served. The land of Israel was likely to afford but poor accommodation for Naomi, and but poor prospects for a Moabitish stranger who attended her: but it was the country of her beloved friend; it was the Lord's land; it was a land where she would be freed from those mighty temptations to idolatry which were so formidable to her in her own land; and where she would enjoy religious privileges, no where else to be enjoyed in the world.

Where you stay I will stay. The company of Naomi in a cottage would be more pleasant to her than that of any of the Moabitish ladies in a palace. *'Better is a dinner of herbs where love is, than a stalled ox and hatred therewith.'* Better is the company of a poor saint in a prison, than the society of the rich and great in their splendid dwellings, if they take no delight in God, and in the remembrance of his name.

Your people shall be my people. At this time Naomi's people must have been a very poor people after so many years of famine; but they were Naomi's people, and they were the people of the Lord of hosts. If we desire to serve God, his people must be our people. If we love Christ, we must cultivate fellowship with those whom he acknowledges as his faithful followers. If his name is dear to us, we will entertain a high value for those on whom this worthy name is called. If we acknowledge him as our Lord and Saviour, we must associate ourselves with his loyal subjects, the objects of his love and care, the partakers with us of his salvation.

And your God my God. We are not to infer from these words, that Ruth chose the god of Israel for her God, merely or chiefly because he was Naomi's God. She had not so learned the God of Israel from her pious instructress. If she had chosen her God merely from respect to her earthly friends, why did she leave the God of her father and mother? Boaz was better informed concerning the moving springs of Ruth's conduct than we can pretend to be, and he attributed her voluntary exile from her own country to a principle of true piety. *'A full recompense,'* he says, *'be given you of the Lord of Israel, under whose wings you are come to trust!'*

'Your God shall be,' or *'your God is my God.'* She knew that there was no God in all the earth like the God of Israel, the only living and true God. She was instructed by Naomi, and she had probably been instructed likewise by her husband Chilion, that their God did not exclude the poor Gentiles from his covenant. They were indeed well qualified to teach her this necessary and important truth, because Rahab, the Canaanitess, that illustrious proselyte to their religion, was married into their own family. If Rahab was received by God into the number of his people, why may not Ruth also, the Moabitess, claim and expect a share in the blessings of his covenant? She appears not to have called in question her right to trust in him as her God; and she devotes herself to him as one of his people, and thereby sets us a good example of faith and obedience. The Lord requires us, in the first commandment of his holy law, to know and acknowledge him as the only true God, and our God. If Ruth, a Moabitess, one of that nation who were to be excluded for ten generations from the congregation of the Lord, is not afraid to subscribe with her hand unto the Lord, and to call him her God, why should we, from a pretended humility, call in question our right to say unto the Lord, *'You are our God?'* Or, why should we prefer any other portion, or any other Lord to him? Ought we not to say, as Jeremiah teaches us, *'Truly in vain is salvation hoped for from the hills, and from the multitude of mountains. Truly in the Lord our God is the salvation of Israel. Behold, we come unto you, for you are the Lord our God!'* Or, as we are taught by Israel, *'O Lord our God, other lords besides You have had the dominion over us; but henceforth by You only will we make mention of your name!'* (Isaiah 26:13).

Verse 17. – *Where you die, I will die, and there I will be buried. May the Lord do so to me, and more also, if anything but death parts you and me.*

Ruth was still but a young woman, and yet she thought of the day of her death; and the thoughts of that day perhaps contributed to fix her resolution of cleaving to Naomi. It is best to live with those whose death we wish to die.

Ruth supposed it likely that Naomi would die before her. This consideration was unpleasant to one who was forsaking all other friends to go with her. If she had lost one or several friends in the land of Moab, other friends would have been left; but if she went with Naomi to the land of Israel, she knew of no other friends. The death of Naomi, who was as mortal as her husband and her sons, might soon leave Ruth a friendless stranger.

She is willing, however, to take the risk. If Naomi should die, she had no intention of returning to the country from which she set out. When Naomi's friends died in the land of Moab, she returned to the land of Israel; but when Naomi died, Ruth will not return to the land of Moab. The land of Israel is henceforth to be her country. She will not return to those friends that will exert all their influence to bring her back to her ancient gods. She will continue till she dies in the land of Israel, however friendless and unprotected, and will have her grave in the same place with Naomi, with whom she hopes to live in a better world.

May the Lord do so to me, and more also, if anything but death parts you and me. What might happen before death she could not say. Her prospects were but dark, and yet she is fully determined to abide with Naomi. Neither poverty, nor the contempt usually thrown upon strangers, nor any of the wrongs to which an unprotected woman in a strange land might be exposed, would induce her to separate from such a beloved friend, or to leave the country where the only true God was served.

God do so to me, and more also. 'God inflict upon me punishments too awful to be named, and punishments still more dreadful than any that you can suppose, if anything but death parts you and me.' Ruth solemnly swears that she will still cleave to Naomi, and to the God whom Naomi served. Thus David bound his soul by an oath to keep all God's righteous judgments. Thus we all ought to lay ourselves under the most sacred engagements to cleave to the Lord as our God, and to walk in his ways. Can we be too firmly engaged to the service of Him, whom to serve is liberty and happiness?

When we consider how firmly Ruth had resolved to cleave to Naomi, and to the God of Israel, ought we not to consider whether we, who enjoy so vastly superior advantages to Ruth, are determined with equal firmness to continue in the faith, in the profession and in the practice, of our religion? Ruth was instructed only by one, or a very few Israelites, in the knowledge of religion. She never had enjoyed an opportunity of attending upon any of the public ministrations of the priests or Levites. If she had ever seen the Bible, and learned to read it, that Bible consisted only of seven at most of the many books of Scripture which are put into our hands; yet she sacrifices all the pleasures – all the friendships – of her youth, all the hopes of better days in her own country, to that holy religion which she professed. What may be expected of us who have so long enjoyed the benefit of the church-administrations which Christ has appointed for the conversion of sinners, and the establishment of saints; and who, from children, have been accustomed to read the Scriptures? We are under no necessity of leaving our native country and our friends, to enjoy the institutions of the gospel, or the fullest liberty of worshiping God in a manner agreeable to his own direction. If we are unsettled in our religious principles and practice, we cannot make the excuses that many might have made, who nevertheless were far from taking advantage of them to excuse a conduct that would admit of no excuse; for what excuse can be made for postponing the care of our souls to any thing in this world? If ten thousand deaths, or if circumstances of misery worse than any kind of death, were to be suffered by us for our religion, would it consist with true wisdom to purchase an exemption from such temporary sufferings at the price of everlasting destruction from the presence of the Lord? Yet still more inexcusable are we, if, without the temptations of any extraordinary inconveniences in this world, we prove unfaithful to our religious profession.

That we may cling with purpose of heart to the Lord, it is necessary that our hearts be renewed by the grace of God; for never will we be true followers of them who left all and followed Christ, unless we are delivered from the remaining power of that attachment to the things of the present world, which renders so many professors of religion unstable in all their ways. If God put his fear into our hearts, we will not depart from him, (Jeremiah 32:40). If we are left to the natural impulse of our own hearts, however amiable our natural dispositions may be, we will follow the example, not of Ruth, but of Orpah, who kissed and left Naomi, (Heb. 13:9).

Perhaps some may allege that Ruth, with all her firmness to her religious principles, forgot a part of that duty which the light of nature taught her. Why did she not show some attachment to her own mother, as well as to her mother-in-law? Why did she leave her parents with an intention never to return, that she might go to a land which she knew not? The answer is easy. She saw that she could not return to her mother without exposing herself to very dangerous temptations. She could not, perhaps, have lived in her mother's house, without seeing daily homage paid to false gods, and meeting with daily solicitations, and more than solicitations, to join in the practice of abominable idolatries. She might soon have been given in marriage to a worshiper of Chemosh; and it may easily be judged how little such a convert as Ruth was prepared to encounter the temptations to which she might have been exposed in the house either of a mother or a husband. She therefore *'forgot her mother's house and her own people.'* With a disinterested spirit, she embraced and held fast that religion which she had been taught, not only by her mother-in-law, but by the Spirit of God. Unless she had been drawn by that divine power, which alone can change the hearts of men, she would not have come to the Lord's land, and to God himself as her exceeding joy. We are not called, in the literal sense of the words, to *'forsake our father's house and our own people;'* yet in the spiritual sense it is absolutely necessary. We must be ready to part with every thing for Christ, if we desire to be Christ's disciples; for if any man come to him, and *'hate not father, and mother, and brothers, and sisters, yea, and his own life also, he cannot be one of his disciples.'*

While we consider the steadfastness of Ruth's religious principles, we cannot refrain from admiring likewise her fervent love to Naomi, and contemplating the happiness which both of them enjoyed in their mutual friendship. If earthly felicity seems a proper subject of envy, who would not envy this happy pair of friends, rather than Haman in all his grandeur, or Solomon in all his glory? And yet who were ever poorer than Naomi and Ruth?

Live in love and peace with all men if you can, especially with all Christians, and with none more than with those of your own house. But if you desire to enjoy the sweets of such domestic friendship, imitate the piety, the modesty, the gentleness, the patience, the meekness of these good women. Be careful especially of your tempers in the time of affliction. There are some who seem at times to overflow with good-will and kindness to their friends, but at other times, especially times of affliction, they are such sons or daughters of Belial, that it is almost impossible to live in friendship with them. Such was not Naomi. She was always disposed to take the heaviest share of her family afflictions, and to make them as light to her friends as possible. When her heart was wrung by sorrowful reflections, she spake kindly to them, and showed a warm regard to their interest. The law of kindness was ever on her tongue; and the complaints that were extorted from her were not of that sullen kind which provoke indignation, but expressive of that resignation, and that tenderness of heart, which excite compassion mingled with esteem.

Verse 18. – *When she saw that she was determined to go with her, then she quit speaking to her.*

The words of Ruth evidently proceeded from her heart, and produced full conviction in the mind of Naomi, that her beloved daughter-in-law would trouble her with no sullen reflections of her change of condition, whatever new hardships might befal her in the land of Israel. Naomi, therefore, was fully satisfied, and added not a word more on the subject. She saw that it would give pain, and do no good; and why should any man speak a word that gives pain to his neighbor, unless that pain has some advantage attending it, or likely to attend it? Words should be like food or medicine. Words of reproof or alarm may sometimes be no less useful than those drugs which are unpalatable but salutary. But should a wise man use any kind of language, especially disagreeable language, that can do no good?

When Ruth had given Naomi as good proof as she could give her of her settled determination to cling to the God of Israel, Naomi is fully satisfied, and gives her no further trouble. Thus ought we to rest satisfied with those credible professions of faith in

Christ, and steadfast adherence to his truths and ways, which are required from those who are admitted to the communion of the church. Such professions are necessary to establish that confidence which church-members ought to have in one another; and when they are made, we are deficient in that charity *'which believes all things,'* if we give place to groundless surmises concerning their sincerity. They may in the end prove insincere, for aught we can tell; but to form suspicions of them till good ground is given for them, discovers, not a godly jealousy over our brethren, but a proud censorious spirit which the laws of Christ condemn.

By her noble profession of stedfast adherence to the religion of Naomi, Ruth gained this advantage, that nothing more was said to her about returning to the gods of Moab. If we desire peace and quietness in the ways of God, let us openly avow our purpose of heart to cling to the Lord, and make it evident in the course of our profession and practice that we are sincere, and resolved to be stedfast. When the friends of Christ see evident signs of our attachment to the good cause in which we are engaged, they will treat us with confidence, and be ready to strengthen our hands by the various offices of Christian communion. When his enemies see our Father's name written on our foreheads, they will desist from those solicitations to turn from our profession which they see to be fruitless. *'If it is possible, as much as lies in us, let us live peaceably with all men;'* but let us not seek peace with the ungodly, by dissembling our attachment to those truths which they disbelieve, or those duties which they despise. If they will not live peaceably with us unless we become their servants, and forfeit the character of faithful servants to Christ, their enmity will be better than a friendship bought at an expense so unwarrantable. But for the most part, wicked men themselves despise an unstable Christian, and cannot divest themselves of an inward reverence for the man whose professions and practice are uniform and self-consistent.

LECTURE V.

RUTH'S ARRIVAL WITH NAOMI AT BETHLEHEM.

CHAPTER 1:19-22.

Verse 19. – *So they two went, until they came to Bethlehem. And when they had come to Bethlehem, all the city was moved about them, and they said, Is this Naomi?*

There is a great difference between the making, and the accomplishing of a good resolution. There are some who resolve well, but they defer the accomplishment of what they have resolved till a more convenient season, which never comes; or they begin well, but they stop short in their course. Ruth not only resolved to go to the land of Israel with Naomi, and there to continue for life, but goes along with her till she comes to Bethlehem, and there dwells without ever wishing to return. She did not so much as ask leave from Naomi, before they left the country of Moab, to go back to bid farewell to her father and mother. Doubtless a woman so pious and affectionate as Ruth, must have loved and honored her parents, and have thought with regret of leaving them for ever; but had she returned to take leave of them, they might have persuaded or forced her to continue at home; and to continue at home appeared to her too hazardous to her soul. She therefore went along with Naomi, travelling no doubt on foot, and meeting with but indifferent accommodation on the road. At last, however, they come to the ancient habitation of Naomi in safety; for the Lord, by his good providence, guarded them amidst the dangers of their journey, and brought them to their city of habitation.

The appearance of Naomi with Ruth the Moabitess, excited much surprise at Bethlehem. It is probable the inhabitants of that city never expected to see her more. She had been ten years absent, and they knew not that she was still alive. She was now to her former acquaintances almost like one who had returned to them from the land of forgetfulness.

The great alteration in her condition would likewise excite their surprise. She went out with her husband and two sons, and returned only with a stranger, whom none would expect to see, a young woman of the land of Moab. Many alterations take place in families within the space of a few years, but these alterations are the less observed that they are made by slow degrees. First one dies, and then, when he is forgotten, a second, and a third. This is the common course of things; but if two or three should die out of a family at the same time, all the neighborhood would be struck with astonishment; all the friends of the survivors would be filled with compassion. Such did the case of Naomi appear to her acquaintances, who now, for the first time, seem to have been informed of the change in her condition.

If you consider what changes have befallen many of your neighbors within the last ten years, you will be struck with a sense of the mutability of all human things. Many have within the compass of that time lost their father, their mother, some of their children, their friends whom they most loved of any thing upon earth. If you have lost such friends, God has been loudly calling you to *'set your affections on things above, not on things on the earth.'* If you have not, remember that your earthly comforts are as uncertain as those of your neighbors. The next ten years may leave you as desolate as the last ten years have left any of your friends. Your husbands, your wives, your children, are as liable to the stroke of death as theirs. While you pity them, learn to provide consolation for yourselves for the time when you will need it as much as they. Naomi now appeared in a very different condition from that in which her neighbors had formerly known her. But those who knew her piety would not think her miserable. She had lost her husband, but not her God. She might have still said, *'Although my husband is dead, and my children are dead, I know that my Redeemer lives. The Lord lives, blessed is my rock! and the God of my salvation be magnified!'* Naomi, however, at meeting with her old acquaintances, had her soul harrowed afresh by the recollection of her former enjoyments, which were now lost to her for ever.

Verse 20. – *And she said to them, Do not call me Naomi, call me Mara; for the Almighty has dealt very bitterly with me.*

Naomi now saw many of the former acquaintances of her husband and her sons. These acquaintances would expect to hear of all that had befallen them in the land of Moab, and would speak of many things that tended to revive the remembrance in Naomi's mind of the pleasant days she had passed in their society. Her heart bled at the recollection. No wonder that her words, on this occasion, express a bitterness of heart that attracts our pity; but it is the bitterness of grief, not of impatience. She is very deeply humbled under the mighty hand of God, but does not fret at the dispensations of his providence.

Do not call me Naomi, call me Mara. Naomi signifies *pleasant,* Mara signifies *bitter.* Naomi's name, when it was mentioned by her friends, added to her grief, because it brought to her mind all the pleasant things which she had enjoyed in the time of her prosperity. It is very probable that, in former days, either she herself, or some of her friends might observe how well her circumstances suited her name. As she was a woman of a pleasant disposition, she gained the love of her husband, her sons, her neighbors; and life is pleasant to those who enjoy the friendship of all around them, especially as they are disposed to make themselves happy, when happiness is in their power. But the recollection of the delightful days she had spent in the bosom of her family and in the visits of her friends, was more grievous to her. Her earthly happiness was fled and gone. She could not now be happy in a town which was emptied of those things that made it formerly delightful. She could not communicate that pleasure to her acquaintance which she once did. She could not now wear that cheerful air which once beautified her countenance. She could not mingle in cheerful converse. She had it not in her power to endear herself by acts or by words of kindness, as in former days. She might very probably think, in this burst of grief which broke forth at the sight of her old acquaintances, that her very name would be a source of perpetual affliction, and that she would not be able to hear it pronounced without a constant reminder of what she now felt. *'The heart knows its own bitterness;'* and there are little circumstances unknown and unfelt by others, that exasperate the sorrows of the afflicted in a very great degree.

Do not call me Naomi, call me Mara. We excuse these words from the time when they were spoken. They were dictated by passion rather than by judgment; not indeed by the passions of anger and discontentment, but by the passion of grief, and of grief excited by the best and loveliest affections. She thought it impossible that her days should ever again be pleasant, because Elimelech, and Mahlon, and Chilion, were no more to be her companions. But we ought not so to lament the comforts we have lost, as to think that all our future days must be spent in bitterness. Has God taken away from us every thing that can render life comfortable? Has he written such bitter things against us, that our eye can never more see good? Let us mourn for our departed friends. *'By the sorrow of the countenance, the heart is made better.'* Yet, when they are taken away from us, let us not say, *'Our gods are taken away, what have we more?'* God can give us joy for mourning. He can even turn our mourning, and the cause of our mourning, into causes of the most heart-felt joy. *'Mine eye shall no more see good,'* said Job in the days of his griefs; but he was happily disappointed, for he saw more good after his afflictions, than he had ever seen before them.

Whatever evils befal us in life, let us not forget from where they come, *'Out of the mouth of the Most High proceeds not evil and good.'* It is He that *'kills and makes alive, that brings down to the grave and brings up.'* Of this Naomi was sensible. *'Call me Mara, for the Almighty has dealt very bitterly with me.'* Had her husband and her children died by the hand of violence in a strange land, she would have seen the agency of divine Providence in the injuries of wicked men. But, as matters stood, she had none to blame for the calamities that came upon her, unless she thought, as she was likely to do, that she had brought her calamities upon herself by sin. There was no hand of man laid upon her beloved friends. Their death was caused by the visitation of the Almighty, who can do no injury to any of his creatures.

The Almighty has dealt very bitterly with me. If all our afflictions come from the Almighty, it is in vain, as well as impious, to contend with him that smites us. Shall the potsherds of the earth strive with their Maker, who has all power to do with them as he pleases? He cannot be effectually opposed, and He can do nothing that is wrong. Weak mortals may injure their fellow-creatures for their own advantage; but what profit can it be to the Almighty, that he should oppress the work of his own hands? *'Yea, surely, God will not do wickedly; neither will the Almighty pervert judgment. Who has given him a charge over the earth, or who has disposed the whole world? If he sets his heart upon man; if he gathers unto himself his spirit and his breath, all flesh shall perish together, and shall turn into dust.'* And what can we say if the Almighty should thus display his sovereign power? *'Is it fit to say to a king, You are wicked; and to princes, You are ungodly? how much less to Him that does not accept the persons of princes, and does not regard the rich more than the poor; for they all are the work of his hands?'*

This name, which we render Almighty, is by many understood to signify the all-sufficiency of God. He is able to do what he pleases, and there is an abundant and overflowing fulness with him to supply all our wants, and to satisfy all our desires; and therefore, when, by the strokes of his hand, we are deprived of the sweetest of our created enjoyments, it will be our wisdom, instead of fretting at our losses, to seek a compensation for them in the enjoyment of himself. Out of his riches in glory, by Christ Jesus, he can supply all our wants. In the enjoyment of his favor, which is better than life, we may find abundant satisfaction when all things look black and dark around us. Have we lost father, mother, children, friends? He is a thousand times better than they all, to those who choose him for their portion; (Hab. 3:17,18).

The Alimighty has dealt very bitterly with me. It is natural for mourners to aggravate their own afflictions, and to call on all their neighbors to *'behold and see if there is any sorrow like unto their sorrow which is done unto them, wherewith the Lord has afflicted them in the day of his fierce anger.'* Naomi had better reason than most persons, to think that the Almighty had dealt very bitterly with her, when she had not a single child spared to her in the fall of her family; yet Job was afflicted with heavier strokes, and after all could praise the Lord, saying, *'The Lord has given, and the Lord has taken away; blessed be the name of the Lord! Shall we receive good at the hand of the Lord, and shall we not receive evil also?'*

It is undoubtedly our duty to consider the divine dispensations towards us with attention, and to feel the scourge with which God is pleased to wound us. He will not lay upon man more than is meet; and therefore it is unsafe to be regardless of any of those heavy circumstances, by which he is pleased to embitter our earthly condition. If they are all designed for the accomplishment of some purpose concerning us, we must endeavor to answer God's designs, that we may not bring upon ourselves heavier calamities than we have yet felt. We may, however, err, by thinking our calamities heavier, when they are compared with other men's calamities, then they really are. Into this mistake, persons of a sorrowful spirit are ready to fall, to the no little damage of their souls. They may be full of complaint, when they have reason to be thankful that their situation is not worse. They may deny themselves that comfort which God is pleased to allow them, and disable themselves from giving glory to God in the fires, by that cheerful patience which is at all times our duty.

Do you ask how you may keep clear of both extremes? That you may be preserved from the unhappy effects which may result from too slight thoughts of divine correction, consider how loudly God calls you, by various circumstances of affliction, to consider your ways. How inexcusable must you be, after all God's dealings with you, if you are found indulging any of those corrupt affections which you are called to mortify, or neglecting any of those duties to which your chastisements ought to rouse you! Jeremiah, in the book of the Lamentations, teaches the church deeply to deplore her miseries; but what end? Not to inspire her with despondency, for he teaches her to say, *'The Lord will not cast off for ever; but though he cause grief, yet will he have compassion according to the multitude of his mercies.'* The true reason why the prophet wished his people to feel their calamities was that they might be thoroughly awakened to comply with his exhortations: *'Let us search and try our ways, and let us turn again to the Lord. Let us lift up our hearts with our hands to God in the heavens.'*

To prevent the bad effects that might result from too deep sensibility to our distresses, as if they exceeded the bounds which God is ordinarily pleased to set to his severities in dealing with his own people, it will be proper for us to consider the good as well as the evil things in our condition; fairly to compare our grounds of complaint with those of others of God's people, either in our own times or in past times; and to remember that the *'end of a thing is better than the beginning thereof.'* Nor ought we ever to forget, that, whatever grounds we have for humiliation under the mighty hand of God, for confession of sins, for fasting, or speedy reformation of every thing amiss in our tempers and conduct, these do not affect the grounds of our faith in God through Christ Jesus, nor supersede the duty of glorifying the Lord in the evil day, by the patient enduring of his will, and by expressing our faith and joy in the Lord. David, in the days of his troubles, though conscious that he had provoked the divine displeasure against himself, did not despair of seeing the face of God again with joy.*'Why are you cast down, O my soul and why are you disquieted within me? Do you hope in God, for I shall yet praise him.'*

Verse 21. – *I went out full, and the Lord has brought me home again empty. Why then do you call me Naomi, since the Lord has testified against me and the Almighty has afflicted me?*

'The Lord gives, and the Lord takes away.' When he gives he is under no necessity of securing to us the possession of what he gives. We may soon provoke him, by our sins, to bereave us of all that he has given us; but however careful we may be to please him, we cannot merit the continuance of his favours, and, without any special provocation on our part, he may have good reasons for impoverishing us, and placing us in conditions quite the reverse of those to which we have been accustomed. Millions have found reason to say in the course of their early pilgrimage, that once they were full, but the Lord has emptied

them. And one great reason why God so frequently changes men's prosperous condition into misery is, to teach us the folly of trusting to our present enjoyments. *'But this I say, brethren, the time is short. It remains that both they that have wives be as though they had none, and they that weep as though they wept not, and they that rejoice as though they rejoiced not, and they that buy as though they possessed not, and they that use this world as not abusing it, for the fashion of this world passes away.'*

That Naomi was once full and was now empty, we can easily believe. But what does she mean by saying, *I went out full, but the Lord has brought me home again empty?* Was she not so empty when she went out, that she was forced to leave her native land for bread? And had she not now at her return the prospect of finding bread in her own land? Why then does she make herself so much richer at her departure than at her return?

It is natural for men under depression of spirit to make unfair and invidious comparisons, both of their own condition with that of others, and of their own former, with their present condition. When we look back on the past period of our life, if it has been on the whole prosperous, we forget those little vexations and disgusts that mingled themselves with our enjoyments, and fondly fix our review on the pleasant things that sweetened our former days. But when we consider our present condition, if we have been afflicted by the hand of God, and felt his chastisements, we are ready to mistake the comfortable parts of our condition; and, while our minds are occupied with former and present pains, we fondly imagine that if we could recover all the pleasures of our former life, we would be superlatively blessed; but when this cannot be expected, we seem to be fallen into an abyss of misery from which we can never be raised up. Thus we often, by our folly, make our present days miserable, when they might be enjoyed with some degree of comfort. The lies which our fancies invent, we believe at their report, although we might easily know the deception.

But Naomi could with propriety say that she had gone out full, although her family was impoverished when she left the holy land. Although she was destitute of silver and gold, and of the conveniences, and almost of the necessaries of life, she was rich in the possession of her husband and children. At that time, when she compared her present condition with her former, she thought that she was poor; but when she now compared it with that condition in which she returned to the land of Israel, destitute of those riches which she thought far more valuable than gold and silver, she says, *I went out full.* She was now sensible that she might have been happy and thankful at that time, although it may be questioned whether she thought so when the necessity of a voluntary exile damped her spirit. Too often our vexations cause us to forget our mercies. When everything is not agreeable to our wishes, we sink in one disquiet the sense of an hundred mercies. We are unhappy, because we want one or two of the many things which we think necessary for our comfort. God deprives us of one or two more of the ingredients of our felicity, of far more consequence than the former, and this convinces us that we had formerly much more reason to be thankful than we could then believe.

A little reflection might convince us, that we still have reason to be thankful. *'It is of the Lord's mercies that we are not consumed.'*

Consider these words of Naomi, you who have your familes yet spared, although you find it difficult, in the present distress,[1] to provide for them. *'Is not the life more than meat, and the body than raiment?'* Bless God for the life of your friends, when your cupboards are empty. Do not say that you are bereaved of every thing that makes life comfortable, if you enjoy the sweet society of those whom you love, or ought to love, as parts of yourselves. If you thanklessly bemoan your condition, as if God had bereaved you of all the fruits of his mercy, the time may come when you will think that you were full, although you thought yourself empty; and ought to have blessed God for what he gave and preserved, when you were giving a loose to useless wailings for what he had taken away.

But if any of you are in Naomi's condition, bereaved not only of your substance, but of your friends, which are more precious to you than your substance; amid your humiliation of spirit under the rebukes of God, remember that the mercy of God is not clean gone. Ruth was left to the good woman when her sons were lost, and she was as good to her as ten sons. Had she not great reason to be thankful for the daughter whom she had borne in her exile? for Ruth was not only the daughter-in-law of Naomi according to the flesh, but her spiritual daughter in the Lord.

If no friends of any kind are left to you on this earth, have you not a friend in heaven? Is not Christ the friend of our race? and does he not call unto you from heaven to come unto Him, that you may find in him that rest, that satisfaction, which nothing earthly can give?

Why then do you call me Naomi, since the Lord has testified against me and the Almighty has afflicted me? Afflictions are a testimony against men that they are sinners but they are not always a testimony that the sufferer is guilty of some particular sins for which God chastises him (Job 2:3). Yet, when our calamities are chastisements, they are testimonies of God's displeasure on account of our offences; (Psalm 107:17). Those who are broken in their spirit, are disposed to think of their sins under their afflictions, and to acknowledge that they are testimonies against them, the fruits of a just quarrel that God carries on with them. They know that they need corrections, and confess that they have deserved all that comes upon them, and a thousand times more.

Yet we must not judge our neighbors because they are sorely afflicted; for although they well deserve all that comes upon them, we may deserve as much, and more. And if we are not corrected by God when we offend him, we are so far from having any reason to magnify ourselves against God's afflicted people, that we have reason to tremble lest we are found *'bastards, and not sons; for what son is he whom the Father does not chasten?'*

And the Almighty has afflicted me. Naomi dwells upon the consideration that all her calamities came from almighty God. If it is God that smites us, then let us not slight our troubles, or overlook any part of the operations of God's hand; for none of his works are unfruitful works of darkness. But let us not faint when we are rebuked of him. *'It is the Lord, let him do what seems him good.'* He who afflicts you, believers, is your God, and your Father. Learn from your Redeemer to say, *'The cup which my Father has given me, shall I not drink it?'*

LECTURE VI.

RUTH GOES TO GLEAN, AND MEETS WITH BOAZ.

CHAPTER 2:1-4.

Verse 1. – *And Naomi had a kinsman of her husband's, a mighty man of wealth, of the family of Elimelech. And his name was Boaz.*

Some allege that all men ought to be equal in wealth; but God makes rich, and makes poor. He gives to some men power to get wealth, and withholds that power from others. He enables some to leave wealth to their families, while the families of other men are left to struggle with all the inconveniences of poverty. *'Who shall say to God, What do you do?'* or, Why do you dispose so unequally of your benefits? *'The earth is the Lord's, and the fullness thereof.'* He has given the earth, indeed, to the children of men, but he was not bound to give to every one of them equal portions of it. If he has given us any portion of it for our necessary subsistence, we ought to be content and thankful. Still more, if he has given us an ordinary portion of the comforts of life. If we are displeased because he has not given us so much as he has given to some of our neighbors, *'our eye is evil because he is good.'* What have you given to God? Verify your claim, and you shall be recompensed. God will be in no man's debt.

Naomi was very poor, and she had a kinsman by affinity who was very rich. Nothing is more common than for the rich to have poor, and the poor to have rich relations. Let a man exert all his activity, let his labors be attended with all the success he can wish, let him have the comfort of seeing his children becoming rich while he yet lives with them, yet it is not to be expected that many years will elapse till some of his posterity feel the inconveniences of poverty. Elimelech was probably, as well as Boaz, of the princely race of Nahshon; yet Boaz was a mighty man of wealth, when Elimelech was under the necessity of leaving his country to seek bread in a foreign land. Our happiness is very precarious if it is placed either in our wealth or in our children. What multitudes of Abraham's posterity are now in a wretched condition, although he abounded in wealth while he lived in this world! But he sought his happiness in God, and in the better country.

Boaz is said to have been a mighty man of wealth. The meaning is, that he possessed a very large portion of riches. But the expression may remind us of the power that is ordinarily conferred by wealth. Rich men can do much, although not so much as many think they have it in their power to do. How many excellent things were done by Job! By the wise and charitable distribution of his wealth, *'he was eyes to the blind, feet to the lame, an husband to the widow, a father to the fatherless; and many blessings of them that were ready to perish came upon him.'* Yet let us not envy the rich. They have power to do hurt as well as good; and they can do themselves much more hurt than they can do to any one else. We trust too much to ourselves, if we think that we would certainly make a good use of riches if we possessed them. Even Solomon, with all his wisdom, found that his wealth was, in many instances, a snare. He did much good, but he also did much evil which would not have been in his power if he had been a poor man.

Naomi had a kinsman of her husband's. Marriage makes the husband and wife one flesh. The kinsman of the one ought therefore to be accounted the kinsmen of the other. It is wisely ordered by the great Lawgiver, that men should not marry the nearest of their own kindred, that various families might be connected by means of this institution. Let every man, therefore, and every woman, learn to show that respect and kindness to their relations by marriage, which they owe to their relations by blood. If we admire the behaviour of Naomi and Ruth, why do we not follow their example as far as our circumstances are like theirs?

Verse 2. – *And Ruth of Moab said to Naomi, Let me now go to the field and glean ears of grain after him in whose sight I shall find grace.*

Ruth is again called the Moabitess. It was her honour that, when her birth and her nativity were of the land of Moab, her behaviour was that of an Israelitess indeed. There are fools who upbraid men or women of virtue with their parentage or their country. It is mentioned to the honor of Ruth, not that she was a Moabitess, but that, being a Moabitess, she was a woman of virtue and piety. It will be the condemnation of many, that, when they were born in the church of God, they behaved as if *'their father had been an Amorite, and their mother a Hittite.'* It will be the praise of others, that they forgot their father's house, and their own people, to join themselves unto the Lord.

She said to Naomi, Let me go and glean. It was necessary for her to think of some way of obtaining a livelihood for herself and for her mother-in-law, who had returned empty to Bethlehem. Some women in Naomi's condition would have thought themselves entitled to a decent support from their rich relations; but the good woman did not wish to be troublesome to her friends. It does not appear that she had even spoken of them to Ruth, and Ruth knew no way of obtaining bread but by her own industry. As long as we can live by the labour of our own hands, why should we be a burden to others? This the apostle Paul declares, that *'if any man will not work, neither should he eat.'*

But why does Ruth propose such a mean employment as that of gathering ears of corn wherever she could find a man that would give her leave? Should not a woman, connected by marriage with an illustrious family in Judah, have sought out a more honorable employment? It is to be considered, that the land of Israel was not a commercial country like ours, and afforded much less choice of employment to the poor. Besides, the refinements of our age and country were never thought of in those ancient times. We find that Boaz was far from being ashamed of the employment chosen by his kinswoman, if she could be said to have made such a choice where choice was perhaps not in her power. She and her mother needed bread; and no time was left her for seeking out another way of life, till present wants were supplied.

'*When you reap the harvest of your land,*' said God to his people, '*you shall not wholly reap the corners of your field, neither shall you gather the gleanings of your harvest. And you shall not glean your vineyard, neither shall you gather every grape of your vineyard; you shall leave them for the poor and stranger: I am the Lord your God.*' (Lev. 19:9,10). In these words, God gives to the poor and stranger a right to glean in the fields of the Israelites. Ruth was both poor and a stranger. The same God who gave the field to the proprietor, gave the gleanings to the poor and strange. She had the same right to glean in the fields, which the disciples of Jesus had to pluck the ears of corn in another man's field; and even the malicious Pharisees did not question their right to do it on a labouring day, because the law had said, '*When you come into the standing corn of your neighbour, then you may pluck the ears with your hand, but you shall not move a sickle into your neighbour's standing corn.*'

Yet Ruth, who was probably ignorant of the law, was willing to accept as a favour what she might have claimed as a right. '*Let me go and glean in the man's field in whose sight I shall find grace.*' The poor are often too bold in their claims. They have a title, by the law of God, to their necessary food from the rich; yet they ought to be thankful to the rich when they are willing to allow their claim. The rich should be ready to distribute; yet they must be judges of their own ability to distribute, of the persons that have a claim upon their charity, and of the share that these claimants ought to have of the fruits of their liberality. The modest and thankful among the poor will be most cheerfully and liberally supplied; nor will they be despised for their poverty by any Christian who remembers that our Lord was once so poor for their sakes, that he accepted of the ministrations of the substance of many women from Galilee. Impudence and greediness will expose poor persons to contempt and neglect, but honest poverty will always meet with respect.

Let me go to the field and glean ears of grain after him in whose sight I shall find grace. She is willing to employ herself in this mean occupation, rather than return to the land of Moab, where she might perhaps have found a more plentiful substance, without incurring obligations to strangers. She was a true daughter of Abraham, although she sprung from Lot. When Abraham came into the land where Ruth had now come to dwell, there was a famine; but Abraham never thought of returning to the country of his kindred, which he had left in obedience to God. He would rather risk his own life, and what was dearer to him than his life, among strangers, than return to the country which God had commanded him to leave. Ruth would rather have been a gleaner of the ears of corn in the land of Israel, than a lady in the land of Moab. She had come to trust under the shadow of the wings of Naomi's God; and the meanest estate in the land where He was known was preferable in her eyes to the highest station in a land of idolaters.

Ruth does not propose that Naomi should go with her to the field. She wished her honored mother to enjoy the rest and ease suited to her time of life, while herself was exposed to the troubles and inconveniences of her humble occupation in the fields of strangers. Young persons should be cheerfully willing to bear fatigues and troubles for the sake of their aged parents, that they may enjoy such ease as the infirmities of age require. Let those who are in the vigour of age, if their parents are feeble, remember what their mothers endured for them in infancy or in sickness; how they willingly suffered anxiety of mind, the want of sleep, and many fatigues of body, that their beloved offspring might enjoy pleasure, or be relieved from distress. How selfish are the spirits of those young persons, who grudge toil or expense for their parents in that time of life when they can enjoy little pleasure but what arises from beholding the affectionate attachment of their children! The charities of the heart sweeten life. A young woman cheerfully laboring for aged parents, is far happier than a fashionable lady spending in idleness and dissipation the fruits of the industry of her ancestors.

David, the great grandson of Ruth, showed a like regard to his parents with that which Ruth showed to her mother-in-law. Jesse needed no provision to be made by his children for his old age; but he found himself under a necessity of becoming an exile, to avoid the rage of the tyrant, whose hatred to the son of Jesse extended to all his friends. David was unwilling that his aged parents should share in the toils and dangers of his wandering life; and therefore he supplicated the king of Moab to afford them protection till he should know what God would do for him. In his distresses he wished not his parents to share, but resolved that they should share in his prosperity if they were spared to see it.

Verse 2. – *And she said unto her, Go, my daughter.* Naomi was blessed with the same humble and kind disposition with her daughter-in-law. Doubtless, it was a great grief to her that she could not place Ruth in a more comfortable and respectable condition among her own people; but since it was the will of God that they should live in poverty, and subsist by the humblest of occupations, she readily submits to His pleasure. Why should we repine at God's dealings with either ourselves or our friends? If God has humbled them by his providence, we ought to be thankful if he has given them a spirit suited to their lot. If he has given them little, let us be thankful for that little. If he has given them nothing, let us be thankful if he has given them hands and a heart to work. Every thing that God gives any of us, and every opportunity of obtaining what we need, are undeserved mercies from the Giver of all good.

Go, my daughter! The affection of Ruth to Naomi was not unmerited. Naomi loved and treated Ruth as a daughter. The law of kindness was in her mouth, and transfused gratitude and love into the heart of her daughter-in-law. Mothers often complain, with reason, of the ingratitude of their children: yet one of the reasons is frequently to be found at home. If there were more Naomis, we might expect to see more Ruths. Undoubtedly, children owe affection and honour to their mothers, in whatever manner they behave. The relation, independently of every other consideration, demands filial duty. But why should parents, by coldness or rudeness to the fruit of their own bodies, provoke them to break the first commandment with promise, to the prejudice of both themselves and their children? If it is the duty of children to honour their parents, it must be the duty of parents to behave in such a way as to procure honour from their children.

Some parents do much for their children, and put themselves to a great deal of trouble on their account, and after all, lose the thanks which they might have, by the coldness, the bitterness, the repulsive manner, with which they often speak to them. *'Is not a word better than a gift? but both are with a gracious man.'* Our Lord tells us, that by our words we shall be justified or condemned; and there is no place where our tongues ought to be better governed than in our own houses. It is delightful to visit those families where the various members appear, from their mutual behaviour, intent upon making one another happy. It is painful to observe sons and daughters, fathers and mothers, wives and husbands, turning their common dwelling into a house of correction to one another.

Verse 3. – *And she went. And she came and gleaned in the field after the reapers. And she happened to come upon a part of the field of Boaz, who was of the kindred of Elimelech.*

There are some whose virtue and industry lie only in their tongues. They say, and do not. But Ruth was no less diligent in business, than wise in her resolutions. When she obtained Naomi's leave, she went forth immediately to the field, and asked leave of a certain steward whom she met with, to glean and gather after the reapers among the sheaves. This leave being readily granted her, she entered with cheerfulness upon her work, in which she continued till the heat of the day compelled her to make use of a shelter.

Although Naomi had several relations at Bethlehem, she did not desire Ruth to go to any of their fields. Not that she wanted confidence in their kindness. She was, at least, sensible that Boaz had been a kind friend before she went to the country of Moab; but she knew that her poverty gave her a right to send Ruth to glean in the field of any of the Israelites, and she seems not to have wished to appear troublesome to her relations. Those are most likely to meet with kindness from their rich friends, who are least intrusive.

It was the hap of Ruth to come into the field of Boaz; and her coming into his field, brought her into acquaintance with the man who was to be her husband, and by whom she was to become one of the mothers of our Lord. The misery or happiness of our life is often derived from accidents that appear quite trivial. *'Time and chance happens to all men,'* and no man can tell what consequences the slightest accident may have. Connections happy or pernicious, riches or poverty, life or death, may be the consequence of a walk or a visit intended for the amusement of a single hour.

It is plain that divine Providence was her conductor to the field of Boaz. Nothing is accidental to God. When the lot is cast into the lap, the disposing, the whole disposing of it, is of the Lord. We are ever in His hands, and he can bring the richest benefits, or the sorest chastisements, out of causes from which we formed no apprehension, either of good or evil.

'The steps of a good man are ordered by the Lord, and he greatly delights in his way.' The same God that brought Ruth from Moab to Bethlehem, led her to the field of Boaz for her good. He led her to the land of Israel, that she might be fully instructed in righteousness. He led her to the field of Boaz, that her virtue might become conspicuous to a man who had it in his power and in his will to reward her. When Abraham's servant went to take a wife to his son from among his kindred, Abraham told him that the God before whom he walked would send his angel to conduct him; and the faithful servant thankfully acknowledged that he had not been amused with vain hopes. *'I being in the way, the Lord led me to the house of my master's brethren.'* All who are wise enough to observe the agency of Providence in the various accidents of their lives, will find like reason with Abraham's servant to praise God for his goodness. We may indeed recollect a variety of accidents that have proved hurtful, as well as others that have turned out beneficial to us. But to those who are taught to make a due improvement of what befalls them, nothing is eventually hurtful. *'There shall no evil happen to the just.'* The things that are evil to others are good to them. *'All the paths of the Lord our God are mercy and truth to them that remember his covenant and his testimonies.'*

Verse 4. – *And behold, Boaz came from Bethlehem and said to the reapers, The Lord be with you. And they answered him, The Lord bless you.*

Boaz was an old man, and he had a steward set over the reapers. Yet he came from Bethlehem to see with his own eyes how his work was performed. When our Lord says, *'Take no thought what you shall eat or drink,'* or, as the words ought rather to have been rendered, Take no anxious thought what you shall eat or drink, he does not recommend indolence or carelessness about our worldly business. We must seek first the kingdom of God and his righteousness, and then all other things shall be added to us; but they shall be added to us while we are using warrantable means to obtain them. *'Be diligent,'* says Solomon, *'to know the state of your flocks, and look well to your herds.'* Slothfulness may be the ruin of men of princely fortunes, *'for riches are not for ever, and does the crown endure to all generations?'*

Although Boaz was a rich man, he despised not his men-servants nor his maid-servants. He did not look upon his reapers with a supercilious eye. He did not come unto them with words of pride or reproach, but with a blessing in his mouth. *'The Lord be with you!* He was a good man, and there is no place where real goodness will more display itself than in a man's own family, not only to his wife and children, but likewise to his servants. A good master will be a father to his servants when they faithfully perform their work. Such even Naaman, when he was a heathen, appears to have been; and happy was it for himself that he had taught his servants to look upon him as a father. Few parents have derived such benefits from the most dutiful children as Naaman derived from the confidence and duty of his servants, when they advised him to comply with the prophet's advice.

Good men will pray for the best blessings to their neighbours around them, and especially to those of their own house. It has been often the happiness of masters to be blessed with praying servants, and often the happiness of servants to have masters whose prayers brought down the blessing of heaven upon those who dwelt under their roof.

The Lord be with you! This was a real prayer from the mouth of Boaz. It is too common with men to say, *'God be with you!'* when God is not in their thoughts. The name of God is profaned when it is used without consideration. It is reported of the great philosopher Boyle, that he never mentioned the name of God without making a visible pause in his discourse. Most certainly none of us ought to mention such an awful name without thinking of Him who is called by it, or to seek any thing from him for ourselves or others without earnest desires to obtain it, and without a becoming sense of our dependence upon him for all those good things which we wish ourselves or others to enjoy.

All good things are requested in this prayer, *The Lord be with you!* God's presence and favor will satisfy our souls; will supply every want; will turn sorrow into joy, and the shadow of death into the morning. But without God's presence and blessing, the richest confluence of sublunary blessings will leave us wretched and miserable, poor, and blind, and naked. The laborious reapers, whose toils ended only with the sun, and were every day renewed, were happy beyond expression if their master's prayer was heard. The kings who reign over many lands know not what happiness means, if they have nothing but what earth can bestow. *'Many say, Who will show us any good?'* but few know what that good is which they should constantly seek to obtain. *'Lord, lift up the light of your countenance upon us!'* and our hearts will be filled with that gladness which the men who their portion in this life never taste, in the richest abundance of their corn and wine.

The Lord bless you! said the reapers to Boaz. They loved their master; they were grateful for his kindness; they prayed for the same blessings to him which he requested for them. Masters often complain of the selfishness of their servants, and the complaint is often too just. But they must be very depraved men who are not faithful servants and sincere friends to such masters as Boaz. *'Even publicans,'* says our Lord, *'love those who love them.'*

The Lord be with you! – The Lord bless you! Such were the petitions which the Israelites were taught by God to present to his throne, for themselves and for one another. The priests were commanded to pray for all the people in these words, *'The Lord bless you, and keep you. The Lord make his face shine on you, and be gracious to you. The Lord lift up his countenance on you, and give you peace.' 'Grace be unto you, and peace,'* &c., or, *'The grace of our Lord Jesus Christ be with you all!'* is the prayer of Paul for all the churches. Christians are called to inherit a blessing, and therefore they must bless and not curse. They ought to bless even those who curse them. It is God alone who can give the blessings that we need; but we are both required and abundantly encouraged to ask His blessings, not only for ourselves, but for our friends and neighbours, our kindred and servants. He is the fountain of blessings. He sent His Son into the world to purchase for us the best blessings. He has promised that *'men shall be blessed in Him, and that all generations shall call him blessed.' 'Ask, and you shall receive.'* Ask for your friends and dependents. You are not straitened in Him, who gives liberally and upbraids not. Ask his blessings when you are upon your knees in your stated devotions. Seek them by earnest aspirations when you are on your beds; when you are sitting in the house; when you are walking by the way; when you are employed in the businesses of life. Never approach irreverently to the Divine Majesty. But where the fear of God habitually governs the heart, prayer need not, and will not, be confined to stated times. Such requests as these of Boaz and his servants, if they are offered up to God in the name of Christ, meet with a gracious audience, when the most ostentatious devotions of the formalist are despised and abhorred.

LECTURE VII.

BOAZ SPEAKS KINDLY TO RUTH IN THE HARVEST FIELD.

CHAPTER 2:5-14.

Verse 5. – *Then Boaz said to his servant who was set over the reapers, Whose girl is this?*

A great man's house is different from an ordinary man's. There are servants in it of different stations. Boaz was a mighty man of wealth, and he had not only reapers, but a man set over the reapers. Servants commonly need the eye of a master, or of one in the place of a master, to direct their work, to stimulate industry, to prevent or to remedy dissension. Good servants will be pleased with proper superintendence, and bad servants need it.

Although Boaz had a faithful steward to govern his reapers, he went himself to the field to see how his work went on, and he was one of those happy masters whom the servants were happy to see.

When he saw the fields covered with plenty, he no doubt thought of the goodness of God, who had now visited his people, and blessed them, after nine years of famine, with fruitful seasons. But his attention was soon engaged by a beauteous stranger whom he saw employed in gleaning the ears of corn. He asked the steward who she was, not with an intention to check, but with an intention, if he found she deserved it, to give her encouragement.

Verse 6. – *And the servant who was set over the reapers answered and said, It is the girl from Moab who came back with Naomi out of the country of Moab.*

The first thing required in stewards is, *'that a man be found faithful'* to his employer; but it is also a good property in a steward to be humane towards his lord's servants, and towards all that have any dependence upon him for employment or favours. The man that was set over the reapers of Boaz had already shown such favour to Ruth as it was the part of a steward to do; and, by his answer to his master's question concerning her, he was a means of procuring her such favour as a steward could not confer without permission. Words fitly spoken may do much good; and indicate good sense and good dispositions in the speaker.

It is the girl from Moab who came back with Naomi. She was a Moabitess, but she was well entitled to all that respect which was due to the females of Israel, when she came with Naomi from the country of Moab. The Moabites were not to enter into the congregation of the Lord until the tenth generation. Yet the children of Israel, when they came out of Egypt, were taught to respect the Moabites as the children of Lot, the friend and disciple of Abraham. They had exchanged the God of their father for Chemosh, but Boaz might reasonably pity them for their unhappy apostasy, when he considered that his own people were reclaimed from many like apostasies by such extraordinary means as had not been employed with any other nation. But whatever might be thought of the degenerate race of the righteous Lot, Ruth was entitled to high praise, when she had left the gods of Moab to worship no other god but the God of Israel.

It is the girl from Moab who came back with Naomi. Boaz was related to Naomi. He knew her worth; he pitied the unhappy reverses of her fortune; and it was to be expected that he would look with a kind eye upon that girl from Moab who had been her son's wife, and who testified such uncommon attachment to her mother-in-law, when the relation between them seemed to be dissolved.

It appears from these words of the steward, that Boaz had heard of this girl from Moab that came to Bethlehem with her mother-in-law. It is not to be doubted, likewise, that he knew the poor circumstances in which they returned. Why, then, did not Boaz, before this time, visit Naomi, and endeavour to console her in her afflictions, and to alleviate them? We cannot give a positive answer to this question. We can easily say, it was not owing to want of generosity and kindness in Boaz; verse 20. Reasons might have hitherto hindered him which are not mentioned, and which there was no occasion to mention. Perhaps Boaz, though full of good intentions, might be too dilatory in executing them.

He certainly would not have suffered either Naomi, or the girl from Moab, to be oppressed with the extremes of poverty, while he was able to supply their need; but good men have sometimes been too slow in executing their good intentions.

Verse 7. – *And she said, I pray you, let me glean and gather after the reapers among the sheaves. So she came, and has kept on even from the morning until now, but that she stayed a little in the house.*

The steward informs his master, that the girl from Moab did not presume to enter the field without leave asked and obtained. Nor did he apologize to his master for granting her the liberty of gleaning. He did nothing but what the authority given him by his master warranted him to do. As it is a sin for a judge to countenance a poor man in his cause, it would be no less criminal in a steward to bestow favors upon the poor, without the consent of his master expressed or understood. But this steward knew that Boaz did not wish any poor person to be excluded from gleaning in his fields, and least of all a poor stranger from the land of Moab, who had showed so strong an attachment to Naomi, and to Naomi's God.

She has kept on even from the morning until now, but that she stayed a little in the house. The steward commends her industry in these words. She had continued busy at her work from the morning, till the heat, or some other cause, constrained her for a little to take shelter in a house or shed, where it is probable the reapers rested at noon. The heat of the weather in the land of Israel would render it almost impossible to continue in harvest from morning to night, exposed, without a shelter, to the beams of the sun. Ruth had spent no more time under cover, than was absolutely necessary for enabling her to return to her labours. Some of the most ancient translations differ from our copies of the Bible, and say that she had continued all day at her labour, without returning to her house, or enjoying any rest. She was a true daughter of Jacob, who was so careful of the flocks committed to him, that without repining, he suffered himself to be consumed in the daytime by the heat, and in the night to be pierced by the chilling frosts.

'It is vain to rise up early and sit up late, to eat the bread of sorrows.' We ought to consult our health in carrying on labours, and not to make them a burden too heavy for us to bear. When covetous desires of gain induce men to overwork their powers, they sacrifice their health to Mammon, whom they have chosen for their God. But Ruth was labouring for her mother as well as herself. Her love to Naomi would give her spirits and strength to endure the heat of the climate. A reaper or a gleaner in the field, sustaining toil or inclement weather to support her aged parent, is worthy of more praise than a victorious general, who exposes himself to all the perils of battle, if his chief view is to gather laurels for himself.

Verse 8. – *Then Boaz said to Ruth, Do you not hear, my daughter? Do not go to glean in another field, neither go away from here, but stay close by my maidens.*

Boaz was glad to meet with the girl from Moab that came with Naomi. He had already, we may presume, intended to show her the kindness of God; and now, when Providence brought her into his presence, he addresses her in the language of kindness, *'Hear me, my daughter.'* Ruth had left her father and her mother. She lost nothing. Naomi was become her mother, and Boaz now speaks to her and treats her as a father. We may, without hesitation, leave those relations that are dearest and kindest to us for God. *'He that leaves father or mother for me,'* says Christ, *'shall receive an hundred fold more in this world, fathers and mothers, brothers and sisters.'* That loss must be great indeed which infinite Goodness cannot compensate.

Do not go to glean in another field, neither go away from here. This prohibition is full of love. The expression signifies, that Boaz would take it highly amiss if she went to glean in any other field but his own. But it implies a promise, that she should find it her interest to glean in his field. The tenderest love may be expressed in the language of command, of prohibition, or even of threatening. Many of God's commandments and prohibitions are expressions of his excellent loving-kindness. What can be more full of grace than the first commandment of the moral law, *You shall have no other gods before me?'* or Hosea's comment upon it, *'I am the Lord your God from the land of Egypt; and you shall know no God but me, for there is no Saviour besides me?'* When God commands us to trust in himself alone, and threatens us with his displeasure if we place our confidence any where else, does he not tell us that we shall find it our highest interest to trust in him?

Stay close by my maidens. Young women, if they are wise, will ordinarily choose their companions from among their own sex. Ruth was a modest woman, and would be glad to find a virtuous woman with whom she might associate in the field of Boaz. There were men employed with them in the labours of the harvest, but Ruth had nothing to apprehend either from the male or female servants of this good man, who ruled his family in the fear of the Lord.

Verse 9. – *Let your eyes be on the field that they reap, and go after them. Have I not commanded the young men that they shall not touch you? And when you are thirsty, go to the vessels and drink of that which the young men have drawn.*

While Ruth was to keep by the young women, and go after them, she had no reason to dread the young men. Young men, in any station of life, are often, by their rudeness or licentiousness, the terror of modest young women; but Boaz would allow of no indecency in words or conversation among his servants. A good man will not only refrain from doing or speaking evil, but will restrain all that depend on him from licentious or rude behaviour. Paul will have none to be admitted to the office of elders in the church, who do not rule well their own houses. Not that it is a duty incumbent on elders only, to keep their families in due subjection, but because elders must be exemplary in every thing worthy of praise. We are all accountable for those evils which it was in our power to have prevented.

Have I not commanded the young men? says Boaz to Ruth. He knew the heart of a stranger. She might think that she stood exposed, as a sojourner from Moab, to those insults to which a stranger from Israel might be exposed in her own country. *'We have heard of the pride of Moab. He is exceeding proud;'* and, as wickedness proceeds from the wicked, insolence and abusive treatment may be expected from the proud. But if Ruth had any fears of this kind, Boaz put an end to them. It is an office of humanity to comfort those that are cast down, and to dispel every uneasy apprehension from the modest and timorous. A man of sensibility knows, in some measure, what is passing within the breast of his poor neighbour; and will, by his words, uphold him that is falling, and confirm the feeble knees.

We do not live in a country so fruitful as the land of Israel. Our fields are not like the field of Bethlehem or Ephratah, which received their names from the fruitfulness of the soil. Yet every place has its advantages, as well as its disadvantages. We are better stored with water than that land which flowed with milk and honey. It was no small favour to Ruth, that Boaz invited her, whenever she was thirsty, to go and drink of the water which his young men had drawn. Thirst would sometimes be almost intolerable to labourers in the field under the scorching heat of the sun in Palestine. When Ruth felt the heat of noon, she might say, as one of her descendents did on another occasion, *'O that one would give me to drink of the water of the well of Bethlehem!'* But her wishes are anticipated. Her considerate friend gives her a general invitation to drink, whenever she found it necessary, of the water provided for his own servants; or, if they had any thing better than water to quench their thirst, she was welcome to share.

Verse 10. – *Then she fell on her face and bowed herself to the ground, and said to him, Why have I found grace in your eyes, that you should take notice of me, since I am a stranger?*

What had Boaz done for Ruth that she falls down on her knees, and thanks him for his favours in language expressive of such warm gratitude? He had assured her of his protection. He had invited her to gather the gleanings of his corn, and to drink of his water. What would she have said had he invited her to partake, as he afterwards did, of all his wealth? And what thanks do we give to Him who invites us to come and buy wine and milk from him, without money and without price? Boaz made Ruth welcome to drink of the water of one of the wells of Bethlehem. Jesus says, *'If you knew the gift of God, and who it is that says unto you, Give me to drink, you would ask, and he would give you living water; the water of which when a man drinks he shall thirst no more.'*

Ruth thought herself greatly honoured by the attentions of Boaz. She was a stranger and foreigner, an alien to the commonwealth of Israel, and did not reckon herself entitled to any kindness from the people of the Lord. Perhaps she did not yet know how kindly the laws of Israel required them to treat strangers. The children of Israel had themselves been strangers for many generations in the land of Egypt; and were required to show that kindness to strangers which they would have gladly received from the people among whom they sojourned. Boaz, above all other Israelites at that time, might be expected to treat foreign women with favour; for his own mother had been not only a stranger, but one of the accursed nation of Canaan; and yet there was not an Israelitess entitled to more respect, for she was famous, and deserved to be famous to all generations, both for her faith and her good works.

Most men and women entertain too high notions of themselves, because they think with complacency on those qualities that seem to entitle them to consideration, but overlook those which diminish their own value. Ruth almost forgot her own virtues. She thought she had done no more than it was her duty to do, if she did so much, when she attended Naomi into the land of Israel: but she remembered that she was a stranger; that she had been hitherto a worshiper of strange gods, and might have continued so till the end of her life, if God had not sent some of his people to guide her feet into the way of truth.

Remembering what she had been, she received ordinary favours with a warm sense of gratitude. The humble are always disposed to be thankful, and therefore they are always happy. When men are swelling with such a sense of their own merit that they think themselves entitled to every thing, they will never be pleased. If you give them small presents, they will think you defraud them of their due, because you do not give them rich presents; if you give them rich presents, they think that they are entitled to all that they have received, and much more. But you can scarcely displease the humble man, because he thinks any thing better than he deserves. He enjoys peace in his own bosom, because his expectations are seldom disappointed. He acquires the good-will of all around him, because he is thankful for the smallest favours, and not dissatisfied when he meets with none.

Verse 11. – *And Boaz answered and said to her, It has been fully shown to me all that you have done to your mother-in-law since the death of your husband, and how you have left your father and your mother and the land of your birth, and have come to a people whom you did not know before now.*

'Let another praise you, and not yourself.' Ruth showed no disposition to praise herself. She did not claim a right to glean from what she had done for Naomi, but wondered that such kindness should be showed by Boaz to her who was a stranger; and she hears the voice of praise from the mouth of one whose commendations were a very great honour. No saying was oftener in the mouth of Jesus than this, *'He that exalts himself shall be abased, and he that humbles himself shall be exalted.'*

Nothing can be meaner than flattery addressed either to the rich or poor, but it may frequently be proper to praise those who deserve to be praised. Our Lord praises his disciples, when he tells them that they were the men who had continued with him in his temptations. Paul often commends the Christians to whom he wrote his epistles, although he never failed to remind them that they were indebted to the grace of God for all that was worthy of praise in their conduct or temper. Boaz commended Ruth, not to inspire her with vanity, but to animate her resolution, to comfort her dejected spirit, and to encourage her to use those freedoms which he wished her to use with himself, and with other Israelites.

It has been fully shown to me all that you have done to your mother-in-law. Ruth little expected that her behaviour would be reported to any great man in the land of Israel. She did no more than she apprehended to be her duty to such a kind and pious mother-in-law. If her behaviour pleased God, and her own conscience, and Naomi, she was well satisfied, although no other person ever heard of it. As some men's sins are open, going before-hand unto judgment, so are the good works of others. *'Take heed,'* says our Lord, *'of the leaven of the Pharisees, which is hypocrisy; for there is nothing covered that shall not be revealed, nor hid that shall not be known.'* Although we are not to do our works to be seen or to be reported by men, yet we ought to provide things honest in the sight of all men that see, or that may hear of, our behaviour. Our works will all be known at the last day, and more of them, perhaps, than we think, before the last day. Let us beware of any thing in private, that would dishonour our name and our profession if it were known to the world. Ruth found, at this conference with Boaz, the truth of what one of her descendants teaches us, that *'a good name is better than precious ointment, and loving favour better than silver and gold.'*

It has been fully shown to me all that you have done to your mother-in-law since the death of your husband. Many who are connected by affinity, think that no more duties remain to be performed, when the bond of connection is broken by the death of that husband or wife on whom the relation depended. Naomi and Ruth were of a different spirit. Naomi never could forget Ruth's kindness to her son. Ruth testified her regard to the memory of her deceased husband, by her attentions to his mother. She not only did *'good, and not evil,'* to her husband, *'all the days of his life,'* but she did all the good she could to him when he was dead, by performing those services to his mother which he would gladly have performed, if he had been still alive. This part of her behaviour endeared her to Boaz. He was charmed with the amiable manners of Ruth, and thought himself highly indebted to her for her goodness to the mother of his friend Mahlon. The apostle John testified his affection to his departed Lord, by taking his mother to his own house, and treating her as a mother. There are kindnesses due to the dead as well as to the living; and in these, a generous spirit will be careful not to fail.

Verse 12. – *May the Lord repay your work, and may a full reward be given you from the Lord God of Israel, under whose wings you have come to trust.*

Ruth's kind and good behaviour to her mother-in-law deserved much praise, but there was another part of her behaviour entitled to still higher commendation. She came to trust under the wings of the Lord God of Israel. Her humanity was consecrated by piety; her kindness to her friends was sanctified by her faith in God. Those labours of love are truly acceptable to God, which proceed from a regard to his own name; Heb. 6:10.

The living God was exhibited to the faith of his ancient people, as the God who dwelt between the cherubim that spread their wings over the mercy-seat, the throne of his grace. It was perhaps in allusion to this symbol of God's residence among his people, that those who sought protection from him were said to trust under the shadow of his wings. *'He that dwells in the secret place of the Most High, shall abide under the shadow of the Almighty. His feathers shall cover you; under his wings you shall trust; his faithfulness shall be your shield and buckler.'*

By a figure less elevated, but not less significant and consolatory, our Lord teaches us the happiness of them that trust in Him, and the riches of his own grace and condescension. *'How often would I have gathered you, as a hen gathers her chickens under her wings!'*

Ruth came to trust under the wings of the Lord God of Israel. She had heard of him in her own country, and left it to dwell in another where he was well known, and where he gave his people signal proofs of his protection. The name of the Lord was so dear to her, that she left her kindred, and her father's house, to enjoy a place among his people. How inexcusable are we, if we do not make the Lord our refuge, when we were born in a land blessed with the knowledge of him, baptised in his name, and trained up to know and serve him! If a Moabitess came to trust under the wings of the Lord God of Israel, how shameful was it in Israelites not to know and trust the God by whose name they were called! And *'is he the God of the Jews only? is he not the God of the Gentiles also,'* who justifies the uncircumcision through the same faith in Christ by which he justified the circumcision?

May the Lord repay your work, and may a full reward by given you from the Lord God of Israel! The Lord God of Israel is the God and Father of our Lord Jesus Christ, in whom he is well pleased. Through him he accepts our persons; through him he accepts our works, and records them with testimonies of his favour worthy of his rich grace. Our best works have no merit in them. We are but unprofitable servants when we have done all that is commanded us; but we serve a liberal Master, who takes pleasure in uprightness, and beholds our meanest endeavours to serve him with a pleasant countenance.

Those acts of kindness which we perform to men with no higher views than their or our own advantage, cannot be accepted of God as services to himself. When no regard is entertained for His will and his glory, there is an essential defect in our performances. If men are the highest object of our regard in the good things we do, from men let us expect our reward; but God is not unrighteous, to forget our works and labours of love done for the name of Christ. He will reward them above what we can ask or think.

Boaz prays to God for the gracious reward of her works of love, and by this prayer encourages her to persevere in that confidence which was to be crowned with a full recompense. *'Cast not away your confidence,'* says Paul, *'which has great recompence of reward.'* To have respect to the recompense of reward, was not unworthy of the faith of Moses, or even of the faith of Christ himself, *'who, for the joy that was set before him, endured the cross, despising the shame.'*

'It is our desire,' says the apostle, *'that whether present or absent, we may be accepted of him.'* And we desire not only that our own works, but that the good works of our friends and brothers, may be rewarded. Boaz intended to reward the work of Ruth by his own generous treatment of her, but great as his power was, her good works went beyond it. The rewards that the richest and greatest men can confer for services done to themselves or to their friends, are not to be compared with the gracious rewards bestowed by God on the meanest of his servants, for the meanest service. *'Whosoever,'* says our Lord Jesus Christ, *'bestows but a cup of water on a disciple in the name of a disciple, shall in no wise lose his reward.'*

Verse 13. – *Then she said, Let me find favour in your sight, my lord, for you have comforted me; for you have spoken kindly to your handmaid, though I am not like one of your handmaidens.*

Ruth was so far from thinking herself entitled to any recompense from God, that she thought it an act of unmerited goodness in Boaz to take any notice of her. The Lord has respect to the lowly, and he usually gives them favour in the sight of men also. Ruth did not reckon herself like one of the handmaidens of Boaz, and Boaz thought her worthy of his bed. Happy are they who are disposed to think their neighbours better than themselves. They are free from those stings of discontent and envy which torture the hearts of the vain and proud. They preserve themselves from those variances and strifes which are the bane of social life. They endear themselves to those with whom they are connected in society. They procure many favours and kindnesses which are doubly pleasant to them, because they did not think themselves entitled to them. *'By humility, and the fear of the Lord, are riches, and honour, and life.'*

Let me find favour in your sight, my lord; for you have comforted me; for you have spoken kindly to your handmaid. Pleasant words are like an honey-comb, sweet to the soul. Those words which at once indicate friendship and nourish piety, are doubly pleasant. Boaz had not only expressed his affection and esteem to Ruth, but raised her views to the Lord God of Israel, from whom he encouraged her to expect her reward. His words were no less valued by her than his gifts. Words are cheap to ourselves, and they may be very precious to those to whom they are addressed, especially to those who need our sympathy. Job, by his words, instructed many, and strengthened the weak hands. Let us follow his example; but remember that we ought to do it, not only in the words of our mouth, but in the temper of our minds and in the works of our hands. We must *'love, not in word and in tongue only, but in deed and in truth.'* Such was the love of Boaz to Ruth. Such is the love of all the followers of Him who loved us and gave himself for us.

Verse 14. – *And Boaz said to her, At mealtime come here and eat of the bread and dip your bit in the vinegar. And she sat beside the reapers. And he handed her parched grain, and she ate and was satisfied, and left.*

All that Ruth expected or requested, was leave to glean; but she was invited, when she was labouring for herself, to eat of the master's bread, and to dip her morsel in the vinegar provided for the reapers. In the house of Boaz, there was bread enough, and to spare. His reapers were not so stinted in their provision, as to have nothing to afford to an unexpected visitant. Boaz was none of those men who say, *'Shall I take my bread and my water, which I have provided for my shearers,'* or my bread and vinegar which I have provided for my reapers, and give them to a stranger? He had a large estate, and a large heart. He truly enjoyed the liberalities of Providence, because he took pleasure in distributing what God had given him.

Boaz was not ashamed to eat his morsel with his reapers. He made them happy in his company, and himself happy, by diffusing cheerfulness around him. We must not judge of Boaz by those laws and customs of society, which regulate the behaviour of such as do not wish to appear singular among ourselves.

He gave to Ruth of the parched corn with his own hands, and she did eat and was satisfied. Ruth wondered at his goodness to her who was a stranger, and not like one of his own handmaidens; but she was not happier in receiving than Boaz in giving, since our Lord spake truth when he said, *'It is more blessed to give than to receive.'*

Let us do good to all men, especially to them that are of the household of faith, and most of all to those of the household of faith who stand in greatest need of our kindness, to whom we are bound by particular connections to show our friendship, and to those who are most disposed to be thankful to God and man for the favours they receive. At the day of judgment we will find, that every office of love performed to the meanest of the followers of Christ, has been performed to himself.

LECTURE VIII.

BOAZ'S DIRECTIONS TO HIS REAPERS TO TREAT RUTH KINDLY – HER SUCCESS IN GLEANING, etc.

CHAPTER 2:15-23.

Verse 15. – *And when she had risen up to glean, Boaz commanded his young men saying, Let her glean even among the sheaves, and do not rebuke her.*

'In the sweat of your face,' said God to fallen man, *'you shall eat bread.'* For our sins we must toil; but, through the mercy of God, our toil in sweetened by intervals of rest, and of refreshemnt from food and sleep. Ruth eats her meal, and then rises to glean till the evening, when she goes home to enjoy the rest and sleep of the night, made doubly pleasant to her by the labours of the day. Let not labourers complain; but let them confess, that the toils they endure are too well deserved; and let them bless God that their days do not pass on in an uninterrupted labour.

She rose up to glean. In the morning she came with, perhaps, an anxious mind to the field, uncertain what reception she might meet with, either from the master of the field, or from his servants. She rose to her new labours with pleasure, when she found herself not only allowed to glean, but commended for her virtuous conduct, and recommended to the mercy of the God whom she came to serve, by the prayers of such a venerable man as Boaz. Let us hold the path of duty, whatever it is. If it is attended with toils and anxieties, comforts will spring up when we are not expecting them, to solace our labours. Boaz did every thing that he promised to Ruth, and more than he promised. He gave a charge to his young men to allow her to glean among the sheaves, and forbade them to reproach her for her country, her poverty, her mean occupation; or to insinuate any suspicions of her honesty, while she was gleaning among the sheaves.

The permission of gleaning among the sheaves would not have been granted to Ruth, if her character had not raised her above suspicion. Are you poor? take care to avoid every appearance of dishonesty. A good character is the estate of the poor. A reputation for honesty will procure you employment and bread. Are you rich? do not causelessly suspect the poor, that you may not deprive them of that which is no less valuable to them than to yourselves – a good name. It is of more importance to them than to you, because their subsistence depends upon it. Why should you deprive your indigent brother of his only resource?

Do not rebuke her, said Boaz to his servants. Ill-taught servants are too often disposed to sport with the feelings or the character of strangers, or of their own indigent countrymen. Why should they who are themselves in a dependent condition, add to the distress of those who are still lower in condition than themselves? It affords them amusement, perhaps, to make those uneasy who cannot avenge themselves; but would it not give them more pleasure to alleviate distress by words of kindness, than to aggravate it by scorn and petulance? Is it more pleasant to us to make our poor neighbours unhappy, than to gladden their hearts? How then dwells the love of God in us?

Verse 16. – *And also let some of the handfuls fall on purpose for her, and leave them so that she may glean them, and do not rebuke her.*

Why did not the good man rather make her a present at once out of his floor and wine-press, than order handfuls of barley to be dropped for her gleaning? He delighted to behold her industry, and wished to encourage it. Charity, wisely directed, will not tempt the poor to be idle. Habitual idleness is not consistent either with virtue or happiness.

Let some of the handfuls fall on purpose for her. The servants of Boaz could not have left handfuls to be gleaned by the poorest person in the country, without dishonesty, unless their master had commanded them. When they received commandment, it would have been dishonest not to have done it. The Lord, who hates robbery for burnt-offering, will not allow servants in great houses to give away what is not theirs to the poor. They must have the permission of their masters or mistresses to do good to the poor, unless they do it at their own expense; and, having received this permission, it would be injurious both to the poor and to their masters, to withhold what is allotted to those who need.

And do not rebuke her. Boaz was very careful to prevent any insult from being offered to the virtuous stranger. He no doubt knew, that masters were in some degree accountable for the conduct of their servants, and that they shared in the guilt of those faults which they did not care to prevent or to correct.

Do not rebuke her, as if she used too much freedom. Wound not her feelings, by reproaches of that poverty which I wish to relieve. God gives liberally, and upbraids not. Let us be followers of him as dear children.

Verse 17. – *So she gleaned in the field until the evening, and beat out what she had gleaned. And it was about an ephah of barley.*

'Man goes forth to his labour, until the evening.' The day is the season of labour, and the night of repose for our race; except that part of mankind who choose rather to follow the example of the beasts of prey, whose season of action and enjoyment is the night because their works must be in the dark.

When you are fatigued with the labours of the day, consider that the night is not far distant, when you may hope to enjoy that delicious sleep, which is almost a recompense for your toils. Idle men, though they feed upon dainties, toss upon their beds from night till morning; but *'the sleep of the labouring man is sweet, whether he eat little or much.'*

Ruth, no doubt, longed to see Naomi after her conversation with Boaz, that she might gladden the heart of her beloved mother, and pour her own grateful sensations into her bosom. But there is a time for going forth to labour, and a time for returning from labour; and the wise will endeavour to do every thing in its proper season. Their reason, and not the impulse of the moment, will regulate their hours.

In the evening, she beat out what she had gleaned, and it was about an ephah of barley; about a firlot of our measure.[1] The Lord blessed her industry, by disposing Boaz to show kindness to her. Labourers are not ordinarily to expect such uncommon interpositions of Providence in their favour; but when they are able, by their industry, to procure the necessaries, and a few of the comforts of life for themselves, and for their beloved relations, it will be owing to their own thankless dispositions if they are not happy. If riches were necessary to happiness, the Almighty must have doomed to misery the greatest part of mankind. But we are the makers of our own misery, when we prescribe to the Most High what he shall do for us.

Verse 18. – *And she took it up and went into the city. And her mother-in-law saw what she had gleaned. And she brought it forth, and gave to her what she had kept after she was satisfied.*

It is no less necessary to be careful of the fruit of our labors, than to labor with diligence. Christ himself, who could multiply bread at his pleasure, commanded the fragments of the barley loaves and fishes to be gathered up, that nothing might be lost. *'In all labour there is profit,'* says the wise man; yet there are some that *'labour for the wind.'* They lose what they have wrought, because they allow it, through their carelessness, to slip through their fingers. This folly, however, is much less frequent in things relating to the body, than in those which relate to the soul. There is a greater number of persons who deserve reprehension for immoderate solicitude to secure their property, than of that slothful generation who *'will not be at the trouble of roasting what they have taken in hunting,'* or of carrying home what they have reaped in the fields. Yet some need admonition to manage their worldly affairs with discretion; but it is far more needful to be careful that we *'lose none of those things which we have wrought'* in the service of God, for the benefit of our souls, *'but that we receive a full reward.'*

Her mother-in-law saw, and saw with joy, *what she had gleaned.* Doubtless, it was a feast to the heart of Ruth to observe the pleasure which brightened Naomi's countenance, when she saw how God had blessed her industry. Young persons! be industrious, frugal, virtuous, if you desire to give pleasure to the father that begat you, and to her that bare you. In their declining years they need such comfort. If you withhold it, the time will come when the pain which you gave them will be doubled to yourselves.

And she brought it forth, and gave to her what she had kept after she was satisfied. When Boaz gave her a liberal portion of the food prepared for himself and his reapers, it was not expected that what she left should be returned, but it was to be carried home for future use; and now she brought it forth for the use of Naomi, between whom and Ruth every thing was common. The poor stranger had now, by the blessing of God, and the kindness of Boaz, bread enough and to spare. Happy changes can soon be effected by the good providence of God, in that condition which appeared forlorn. *'The Lord gives food to the hungry,'* and he gives it in such quantities, and of such a kind, and in such ways as he pleases. *'Those who trust in Him, and do good, shall dwell in the land, and verily they shall be fed.'*

Verse 19. – *And her mother-in-law said to her, Where have you gleaned today? And where did you work? Blessed is he who took notice of you. And she told her mother-in-law with whom she had worked, and said, the man's name with whom I worked today is Boaz.*

The friendly converse of those members of a family, whose hearts are knit together in love, affords a pleasure which sweetens a dinner of green herbs, and renders it more delicious to the taste, than *'a stalled ox, where love is wanting.'* Naomi asks of Ruth where she had wrought, that she might have the pleasure of knowing who the friendly man was that had taken knowledge of her beloved daughter. Ruth had no reason to conceal that kindness which had been showed her beyond her expectation. They enjoyed the feast of friendship, and the flow of soul, with a keener relish than the gayest and wealthiest domestic circle in Bethlehem.

Blessed is he who took notice of you! Naomi desired to know where Ruth had wrought, that she might know her benefactor, and make such recompenses to him as were in her power, by prayer to God on his behalf. Before she knows his name, she prays for blessings to him. Her heart overflowed with gratitude, and out of the abundance of her heart her mouth spake. This is one reason why we ought to do good to those especially, who are of the household of faith. They are all praying persons, and their prayers are heard by the God who loves them. *'He is a prophet,'* said God to Abimelech, concerning Abraham, *'he is a prophet, and he shall pray for you.'* Abimelech thought his presents well bestowed upon a man who could pray for him with acceptance. But, through the name of Christ, all believers, though they are not prophets, have confidence towards God; *'for whatsoever,'* says our Redeemer, *'ye ask in my name, I will do it for you.'*

Naomi was told that the man's name was Boaz, and immediately called to mind what kindness her family had received from him in times past:

Verse 20. – *And Naomi said to her daughter-in-law, Blessed is he of the Lord, who has not left off his kindness to the living and to the dead. And Naomi said to her, The man is near of kin to us, one of our near kinsmen.*

Blessed is he of the Lord! Naomi had already prayed for a blessing upon him, without knowing who he was; and she prays again for a blessing to him from the Lord, when his name was mentioned. It put her in mind of former favours, which she had not forgotten, although her distresses, engrossing her mind, had hindered her from thinking of them. A grateful heart will never forget kindnesses received from men; far less will a truly thankful soul forget the former loving-kindnesses of the Lord. *'Bless the Lord, O my soul; forget not any of his benefits!'*

He has not left off his kindness to the living and to the dead. He had been a steady friend of Elimelech's widow, to the mother and relict of Mahlon. Nothing is more common in the world than fickleness in friendship, but that man only deserves the name of a friend, who loves at all times, in adversity as well as in prosperity, in death as well as in life. We sin against God, as well as against men, when we causelessly forsake our own or our father's friend. All our professions and promises are marked in His book.

One great cause of our grief for the death of our friends is, that they are removed beyond the reach of our kindness. But they are not wholly incapable of receiving testimonies of our friendship, if they have left beloved relations behind them, to whom we can show our regard. David could recompense Jonathan's kindness to himself, when his generous friend was in heaven with the angels of God. Although our Lord left our world almost eighteen hundred years ago, we can still testify our love to Him by our kindness to his brothers and sisters on earth.

Blessed is he of the Lord; for he has not left off his kindness to the living and to the dead. Naomi could not reward Boaz, but she knew who could and would reward every act of kindness done to her. Her prayers to God for Boaz were worth more than all that it was either in his heart or in his power to do for her.

And Naomi said, The man is near of kin to us, one of our near kinsmen. The relation in which Boaz stood to Mahlon was probably one of the reasons that induced him to be so kind to Ruth. God has made of one blood all nations of men, and therefore we ought to look upon all human creatures as our brothers and sisters, the children of the same common progenitors, by the ordination of their common Creator. But those who are related to us by immediate parents, or by progenitors not far removed from us, have a special claim to our kindness. *'A brother is born for adversity.'*

Yet the poor ought not to make themselves burdensome or troublesome to their prosperous relations. Naomi sought nothing from Boaz, and, till this time, does not seem to have expected new favours from him. He had formerly been kind, and she did not wish to tax his goodness by applications for new favours. God is never weary of conferring his blessings. Those petitioners are most welcome to him that come most frequently, and ask most importunately. But the richest of men may soon be impoverished, and the most bountiful may soon be wearied, by giving.

Paul thanked God in the behalf of the Philippian Christians, that their care of him had flourished afresh. Naomi considers it as a token for good, that the care of Boaz for her family was now again flourishing and bringing forth fruit. With joy she informs Ruth, that the man whose kindness so deeply affected her, was a near relation. What might they not expect from a near relation so rich and so kind? What may we not expect from him, who, being in the form of God, made himself our near kinsman, that he might redeem us to God?

Verse 21. – *And Ruth of Moab said, He said to me also, You shall keep close by my young men until they have ended all my harvest.*

Grateful souls take pleasure in hearing and in speaking of their benefactors, and of the favours which have been done or promised them. How constantly ought we to remember, and how ready should we be to speak of, the mercies of God! He has done great things for us, and gives us every encouragement to hope that he will still grant us all that is good for us.

Verse 22. – *And Naomi said to her daughter-in-law Ruth, Good, my daughter. You go out with his maidens so that they do not fall upon you in any other field.*

Naomi asked Ruth where she had been, and desired particular information of the treatment she had met with, that she might give her such advice as might be useful for the direction of her future conduct. Old persons may be expected to have collected, by reflection and experience, more wisdom than the young, and should be ready to communicate instruction to those that need it. An ostentatious display of their requirements, where it can be of no use, or where there is no disposition to profit by them, would only expose them to contempt. But they hide their talents in a napkin if they do not make those wiser by what they know, who are disposed to learn, and those especially whom divine Providence has placed under their care. Young persons, on their side, should be ever ready to listen to the instructions of the aged, and especially of aged parents, or relations that stand in the place of parents. Ruth profited much by the instructions and advices of Naomi; and it was one of the great comforts of Naomi's declining years, that she could be useful to Ruth, by giving her the counsels of experience. Let the young have their hands prepared for the service of the old; and the old may recompense them abundantly by the words of their mouth. Happy would it have been for Rehoboam, and for all his people, had he known what respect is due to the wise counsels of the aged. What numbers of young persons take rash steps in the journey of life, which cannot be retraced, because they rather choose to follow the impulse of their own passions, than to ask and follow the advices of those who brought them into the world!

*Good, my daughter. You go out with his maidens.*Ruth had said that Boaz had invited her to keep fast by his young men. Naomi perhaps meant to insinuate in this advice, that, while she accepted the invitation, she ought to consider the maidens as her best companions. She was not bound to avoid all intercourse with the young men. Boaz had taken care that none of them should behave rudely to her; but her chosen companions were to be of her own sex. Ruth needed little admonition on this subject. Boaz observes, to her praise, that she had not followed young men, whether poor or rich.

Good, my daughter. You go out with his maidens, since he invites you to glean in his field. Although Naomi would not be troublesome to her relations, nor solicit favours from them when necessity did not compel her, she was not so high-minded as to reject a favour that was offered. Poor persons, who have seen better days, are sometimes too nice and scrupulous in receiving obligations. It is good to be as independent in the world as our circumstances will allow; but to be absolutely independent is impossible: and to have a spirit above the acceptance of favours, when our circumstances render the acceptance of them needful, is a proud resistance of our spirits to that Providence which manages our concerns, and which manages them with wisdom and kindness when it lays our pride in the dust.

That they do not fall upon you in any other field. If they had met Ruth in any other field, their master might have been offended to find that his bounty was undervalued, or his sincerity distrusted, or that his kinswoman chose rather to receive obligations from another than from himself. A generous man takes pleasure in being trusted. Nothing will more displease him than want of confidence in his kindness and professions.

If we ought to express our gratitude to earthly benefactors, by showing a readiness to be obliged to them, and a firm confidence in their favour, how readily ought we to accept of the precious gifts of God, and how ungrateful is it to act as if His gracious professions and promises were unworthy of our trust! Is not the saying, that *Christ Jesus came into the world,* a faithful saying, and worthy of all acceptation? Why then does any of us refuse with thankfulness to receive his unspeakable gift? Or why should we be found vainly searching among creatures for what is to be found only in God?

Verse 23. – *So she kept close by the maidens of Boaz to glean until the end of barley harvest and of wheat harvest. And she lived with her mother-in-law.*

Her mother-in-law's word was a law to her. According to her advice, she gleaned in the field of Boaz, and associated with his maidens. Obedience to parents, is obedience to Him who says, *'Honour your father and your mother.'* We will, however, soon have occasion to observe, that there are limits to be set to this obedience. God must in all things be obeyed. The commandments and counsels of parents are to be followed, as far as they do not interfere with the will of God.

Ruth not only entered upon a course of useful, though humble industry, but she persisted in it. She did not weary of her mean occupation, but persisted in gleaning till the end both of barley and of wheat harvest. Her relation to Boaz did not inspire her with vain conceits that she was entitled to greater favour from him than a permission to glean after his reapers. Such aspiring thoughts would have greatly impaired, or destroyed at once, her virtues, her reputation, and her happiness. She was well content with her present low condition, and thankful for the small favours that were done for her, and waited patiently on that God, under the shadow of whose wings she came to trust; and, in his own time, he exalted her to possess the fields which she now gleaned.

And she lived with her mother-in-law. 'Changes and war are against me,' said Job. This language is not uncommon with those who have lost their nearest relations and most beloved friends. But few have so much reason to speak this language as that patient sufferer. Changes in his condition robbed him of every comfort. Naomi was now deprived of her husband and her two sons. Ruth was deprived of her husband. But each of them had a kind and pleasant friend left, in one another. Their religious converse, their kind attentions to one another's comfort, compensated, in a great measure, the loss of other friends. They were not so rich as they had once been; but the goodness of Providence to them in their destitute circumstances, would probably give them more pleasure, than the rich taste in their abundance. They loved one another, and dwelt together in peace and unity. And where virtuous love is found, pleasure is not absent; for *'better is a dinner of green herbs where love is, than a stalled ox and hatred therewith.'*

Many are reduced to a more solitary condition than Naomi. Deprived of their best friends, they have none else to supply their place, or none from whom they can derive much comfort. But let them not repine at the providence of God, whose ways are always mercy and truth to them that love him. Although you should be forsaken by father and mother, by wife and children, remember that there is a Friend who cannot be lost. Job's children were all destroyed. He had one near relation left, whose behaviour gave him pain instead of pleasure. But his spirit was not crushed by his afflictions; for he knew that his Redeemer still lived. Seek fellowship with the Father, and with His Son, Jesus Christ, and your joy shall be full: (1 John 1:3,4; John 14:20,21).

RUTH, AT THE INSTIGATION OF NAOMI, LAYS HERSELF DOWN AT THE FEET OF BOAZ, AND REQUESTS HIM TO CAST HIS SKIRT OVER HER.

CHAPTER 3:1-9.

Verse 1. – *Then her mother-in-law, Naomi, said to her, My daughter, shall I not seek rest for you so that it may be well with you?*

Naomi was happy to find Ruth so well satisfied with her mean condition, but earnestly desired to have her placed in more comfortable circumstances. She was herself an old woman, and wished not, at her departure from this world, to leave her daughter-in-law friendless. Her thoughts were often employed in consulting how she might best promote and secure the happiness of such a beloved friend. She had now, no doubt, given up all thought of much earthly comfort to herself, except what she found in the love of Ruth. But she was full of solicitude for her daughter-in-law, that she might have no temptation to regret the sacrifice which she had made to herself and to her religion, of the pleasures of her father's house.

Shall I not seek rest for you, my daughter? It is our common practice to insist upon the duties owing to us from our friends, and not to give ourselves much trouble about what we owe to them. There are some parents so foolish as to think that their children owe every thing to them, and that they owe nothing to their children. For this reason, they are full of complaints concerning their children's undutiful behaviour, when, if their consciences or their reason were awake, these might tell them that the fault was originally in themselves. If they had been more attentive to the happiness of their children, their children, out of grateful affection, might probably have been disposed to return the obligation.

Shall I not seek rest for you so that it may be well with you? For this end, Naomi wished rest for her daughter-in-law, *'that it might be well with her.'* When young persons become widowers or widows, the relations of the deceased husband or wife often attend more to their interest in the deceased, than to the happiness of the survivor, although those who have left the world can receive no more benefit from them; and the best proof which they can give of their affection to the friend whom they have lost, is to show a proper attention to the happiness and comfort of the persons dearest to them while they were upon the earth. Naomi doubtless thought, with as much regret as other mothers do, upon her beloved son now in the grave; but she did not think it would be any advantage to his soul, or to his memory, to keep his widow unmarried. Death dissolves the marriage relation; and at the resurrection, there will be no reclaiming of husbands or wives that were left in this world; (Luke 20:35).

Naomi had no thoughts of marriage for herself, because she was too old to think of it, chap. 1:12; but she thinks of marriage for her daughter-in-law, who was not yet too old to have an husband, and to entertain the hope of children. Thus Paul, who advises persons in certain circumstances not to marry, or to renew that nuptial bond from which they are loosed, gives an opposite advice to other virgins or widows. *'The younger widows refuse,'* says that apostle to Timothy. Admit them not to those offices or trusts which would render marriage inconvenient, or which would be a temptation to them to wax wanton in the unmarried state, and then to enter into marriages with such persons, or into marriages attended with such circumstances, as would bring guilt, and reproach, and danger upon them; but *'I will,'* adds he, *'that the young women,'* or the younger widows, *'marry, bear children, guide the house, give none occasion to the adversary to speak reproachfully.'*

Naomi was not one of those old women who grudge to the younger those comforts and advantages which themselves are too old to enjoy or to relish. *'We are glad,'* says Paul, *'when we are weak and you are strong.'* Thus Naomi will be glad to see her beloved daughter-in-law enjoying rest in the house of an husband, although herself was constrained by old age to live in perpetual solitude. Perhaps her daughter-in-law, when married, might find it convenient to have her mother-in-law with her; but if not, still Naomi wished her to be happily married. The comfort of her daughter-in-law was chiefly in view in the advice she gave her. And whenever any person pretends to give an advice to another, he must lay aside all considerations of himself, and have in his view nothing but the advantage of his neighbour; or, if he wishes to serve himself by his advice, let him fairly avow it, that he may preserve the consciousness of integrity. We may very honestly request a favour to ourselves, but we must not steal it by false pretences of regard to the interest of those from whom we desire it, when we have only our own in view.

Parents, in particular, ought to have solely in view the happiness of their children in those advices which they give them about entering into the marriage state. They ought to consider the happiness of their children as their own, and to choose for sons and daughters-in-law, not those persons who are most agreeable to themselves, but such as, all things considered, are most likely to render their own children happy. It is vain to hope that we shall be able to force the inclinations of our children into a similarity with our own. Gentle persuasions and serious advices may frequently be of good use. Compulsion belongs, not to a parent, but to a tyrant.

'That it may be well with you. An augmentation of happiness is that which all men and women seek in entering into the state of marriage. And marriage, contracted with due deliberation, may be reasonably expected to yield such happiness as earthly things can afford. *'It is not good,'* said God, *'that the man should be alone; I will make him an help meet for him.'* It is to be remembered, however, that the woman made to be an help meet for him was made in his own image, as he was made in the image of God. Both men and women have lost their integrity, and therefore married persons may expect trouble in the flesh. Thorns and briars have sprung up in all the relations and connections of life, as well as on the face of the ground. Yet the pleasure and advantages of marriage are likely to counterbalance, by many degrees, the sorrows that attend it, when the parties are equally yoked. If we are blessed with partners renewed in knowledge and holiness, after the image of our Creator, not only will our present comfort be greatly promoted, but our eternal interests likewise; and we will have reason to bless God for the happy connection, not only during the few years that we may live together upon earth, but through endless ages.

If wise persons enter into this relation that it may be well with themselves, they will consider that their partners entertained the same views. We must be over-run with selfishness, and with a foolish kind of selfishness which disappoints its own views, if we hope to receive, without endeavouring to communicate happiness. Even an Abigail could not make such a churl as Nabal happy. But half her sense and virtue might have made a man happy, whose dispositions were like her own.

Shall I not seek rest for you so that it may be well with you? It might serve a good purpose, if persons joined together in marriage would seriously consider these two things – whether their happiness is increased by their change of state – and whether the happiness of their partners is increased by it. If we are rather miserable than happy in this connection, there must be a great fault on one, and probably on both sides. Nor is it the less likely to be on our own side, that we are disposed to lay all the blame on the other. Most persons might find much happiness in marriage, if they uniformly persisted in endeavours to do the duty of the relation for their own part, whatever their companions in life do, and at the same time endeavoured, to the utmost of their power, to impress religious sentiments on the minds of their partners. Religion is the solid basis of morality in all its branches. *'A woman that fears the Lord, she shall be praised,'* for her conjugal and other social virtues, as well as for her piety.

Verses 2,3,4. – *And now is not Boaz of our kindred, he with whose maidens you were? Behold, the winnows barley tonight in the threshing-floor. Therefore wash yourself, and anoint yourself, and put your clothing upon you, and go down to the floor. Do not make yourself known to the man until he has finished eating and drinking. And when he lies down, you mark the place where he lies, and you shall go in and uncover his feet and lie down. And he will tell you what you shall do.*

Hitherto we have found nothing in Naomi's conduct that does not gain our approbation; but imperfection is the attendant of humanity in its present state, and Naomi appears, in that part of her conduct which we now consider, to have erred. Her views were good, but the means she took to accomplish them were unwise. They were, indeed, followed with success; but for the success we are to praise Boaz, or rather that gracious Providence which over-ruled ill-contrived means to accomplish its own ends. God, in his mercy, often prevents those errors in our conduct to which the darkness of our own minds would lead us, and often prevents those errors into which we fall from being attended with the pernicious consequences which would otherwise attend them.

And now is not Boaz of our kindred, he with whose maidens you were? A kinsman among us is a person with whom we reckon ourselves entitled to use some freedom; but, to understand the words of Naomi, we must remember that there were laws concerning kinsmen given to the Israelites, by which they were encouraged to expect relief from them in their distress. The kinsman was to be a redeemer to those Israelites that were in bondage. Estates sold by the poor, might be recovered by their interposition, and children might be given to the dead by the marriage of his widow with his kinsman. Naomi knew the tender affection of Boaz for his kindred, his compassion for their afflictions, his regard to the law of God. Shebelieved that he needed only to be put in mind of the duties of a kinsman, to do everything for Ruth that she could reasonably desire; and we are here told how she proceeded in this important business.

Behold, he winnows barley tonight in the threshing floor. Barley must be winnowed that it may be used; but will Boaz himself take part in such a mean employment? What should hinder Boaz from taking part in it? He lived in the days of ancient simplicity. Modern refinements and etiquette cannot give more pleasure to the fashionable gentleman, than honest industry gave to this grandson of a famous prince of the children of Judah. We do not withhold our admiration from Camillus, or Fabricius, or other famous consuls and dictators of the ancient Romans, because they held the plough with those hands which destroyed the enemies of their country.

Wash yourself, and anoint youself, and put your clothing upon you. Anointing the head was customary as well as washings, among persons of ordinary condition in the land of Israel; where they were highly expedient on account of the heat of the climate, and where they are still much practised.

And put your clothing upon you. Naomi does not advise Ruth to procure new clothes for the occasion, which she might have perhaps been enabled to do by the profits of her labour. Her '*adorning was not that of putting on of apparel, but the ornament of a meek and quiet spirit.*' Yet it was proper, when she went to a feast, that she should put on the best clothes in her possession. If decency of apparel is not a virtue, slovenliness is at least an approach to vice. It is our duty to treat with becoming respect our inferiors and equals, and still more our superiors, when they honour us with their kindness.

Do not make yourself known to the man until he has finished eating and drinking. And when he lies down, you mark the place where he lies, and you shall go in and uncover his feet and lie down. She was to discover nothing of her intention to Boaz when she went to the feast, but rather to avoid any particular notice, that he might entertain no suspicion of what was to follow. Concealment of intentions may be very proper, and very consistent with uprightness, in some cases. But we must beware of doing any thing that will not bear the light, or using those arts of concealment in transacting lawful affairs that may be attended with bad effects upon our character. It was perfectly consistent with uprightness in Samuel to conceal his chief intention when he came to Bethlehem to anoint David; and in Solomon, when he commanded a sword to be brought, and his guards to slay the living child about which the two harlots contended. But it was not wise or safe in Ruth to conceal her intentions from Boaz, when she came to his feast. Friendliness, and openness of dealing, is in general better policy than those arts of concealment which, if they are not evil in themselves, are often bad in their consequences.

Naomi seems to have considered Boaz and Ruth as married persons; otherwise it is scarcely conceivable what end she could propose in advising Ruth to mark where he lay, and place herself at his feet. She either did not know, or did not recollect that there was a kinsman nearer to them than Boaz, or knew that the nearest kinsman would not perform the kinsman's part to Mahlon. However good her intentions were, she greatly erred in attempting to form a connection between them in secret. Marriage transactions ought to be openly published to the world. There may be just impediments to a marriage, which neither the parties nor their witnesses know. Naomi might probably think that their ancestor Judah plainly considered Tamar as the wife of Shelah, before she was given to him. He would not have required her to be burnt when he heard of her pregnancy, if he had not considered it as the fruit of adultery. If Boaz and Ruth stood in the same relation as Shelah and Tamar, why might they not agree about living together, without any new ceremony? or, if any thing more was necessary to be done, Boaz would take care of it upon himself, after this plain indication of Ruth's willingness to become his wife. Such were probably the thoughts of this good woman, for many even of the thoughts of the wise are vain.

Whatever apologies may be made for Naomi or Ruth, none can with any appearance of reason be made for clandestine marriages among ourselves. If even the wise and pious Naomi acted so unwarily, when the laws and customs of the country seemed to favour her plan, what can be said for those who wilfully violate a plain law of their country, instituted for the prevention of the most abominable crimes? What adulteries or incestuous conjunctions would be the natural consequence of the abolition of the laws requiring publicity in marriage transactions! The transgression of laws absolutely necessary for the prevention of any vice is an attempt to remove the barriers by which it has been restrained. Important circumstances necessary to be known and attended to, appear to have been overlooked by Naomi, when she gave directions to Ruth about her marriage. If Boaz, and other friends, had been duly informed of her views, they would have secured Ruth against that danger of disgrace, or of something worse, which was evidently incurred; though God, in his mercy, prevented the mischief.

Verse 5. – *And she said to her, All that you say to me I will do.*

Ruth, we may suppose, felt some repugnance at the thought of lying down at the feet of Boaz; but she believed her mother-in-law to be a wiser woman than herself, and better acquainted with the laws and customs of Israel. She therefore promised to comply exactly with her advice. We are pleased with her humility, her deference, and her obedience to her mother-in-law; and yet it is to be wished that she had consulted her own judgment more than she did. The holy writers often advise children to obey their parents, but their obedience must be *'in the Lord.'* Faults that lean to virtue's side are still faults. As none ought to call that unclean which God has sanctified, nothing can sanctify what is contrary to the revealed will of God.

The blame, however, if we must blame Ruth, was not so much her own as Naomi's.Let all parents, and all whose office it is to command or to advise, be careful to furnish themselves with clear views of sin and duty, that they may not cause those who pay, and should pay, a great deference to their judgment, to err out of the way of understanding. One great end of the writing of the book of Proverbs was, that we might be furnished with stores of wisdom, enabling us to give sound counsel to our neighbours. *'A man of understanding shall attain unto wise counsels;'* (Prov. 1:5).

Verse 6. – *And she went down to the floor and did according to all that her mother-in-law had told her.*

There are some who say and do not. There are some who will not say, and yet will do what they are commanded by their parents. Ruth both says and does what her mother-in-law advised her to do. Both in word and deed we ought to testify our reverence for parents, and for all that possess a just title to our obedience. Exceptions must be made, because none but God can claim an unlimited right to our submission. Ruth might err by excess of complaisance to her mother-in-law; but the errors of young persons are commonly of an opposite kind.

Verse 7. – *And when Boaz had eaten and had drunk, and his heart was merry, he went to lie down at the heap of grain. And she came softly and uncovered his feet and lay down.*

'Go your way, eat your bread with cheerfulness, and drink your wine with a merry heart, when God accepts your works,' and gives you special testimonies of his goodness. *'Every creature of God is good, and nothing to be refused, being sanctified by the word of God and prayer.'* Although wine, as it is used by the sons of riot, *'is a mocker, and strong drink is raging,'* yet it is a good creature of God, given to cheer the heart of man. Christ himself turned water into wine for the entertainment of a company met together at a marriage-feast.

Boaz did not think it below his dignity to eat and drink with his servants, nor did he think it inconsistent with the laws of sobriety to take a moderate share of that pleasant liquor which *'cheers the heart of God and man.'* He would observe God's faithfulness, as well as goodness, in the provision of his table, when he enjoyed the blessing of his father Judah, to whom it was promised that *'his teeth should be white with milk, and his eyes red with wine.'*

Think not that Boaz had gone beyond the bounds of moderation, when his heart was cheerful through wine. He had drunk away no part of his understanding, as you will see by his behaviour. Drunkenness is the introduction to other sensual impurities, when the devil can find means to present a suitable temptation. *'Your eyes,'* says Solomon to the drunkard, *'shall behold strange women, and your heart shall utter perverse things.'* But when Boaz found that there was a woman lying at his feet, he was ashamed, and on his guard against every appearance of evil.

He went to lie down at the end of the heap of wheat, in his clothes. This was another instance of the simplicity of manners in his age. Why should we wonder that people of ancient times had manners different from ours? There is no law of reason or religion that binds the men of other nations to adopt the British laws. There was as little reason why the ancients should observe those modes of conduct which are thought proper to be observed in our days.

She rose softly and uncovered his feet, and lay down. Neither of them was undressed. Yet we can by no means justify Naomi or Ruth. We ought to *'abstain from all appearance of evil,'* and to *'make straight paths for our feet, that that which is lame may not be turned out of the way.'* No woman can plead Ruth's example as an excuse for similar conduct, not only because no bad examples, even of good men or women, are to be imitated, but because the circumstances of those who might plead such example, cannot be the same, unless the Jewish laws, concerning the marriage of the near kinsman, were to be restored to their force.

Verses 8,9. – *And at midnight the man was afraid and turned himself. And behold, a woman lay at his feet. And he said, Who are you? And she answered, I am Ruth your handmaid. Therefore spread your skirt over your handmaid, for you are a near kinsman.*

Boaz was startled when he awaked out of sleep and felt one lying at his feet. He was amazed when he cast his eyes on the person who had used the freedom, and saw that it was a woman. Had he intoxicated himself at the feast, when his heart was merry with wine, he would now have been exposed to one of the most dangerous snares of the devil. But he was in full possession of his reason. What was still better, his virtue or his grace was awake to preserve him from the power of temptation. By the grace of God he kept himself, and the wicked one troubled him not.

Who are you? he said. He could perceive by the little light he had, that it was a woman that lay at his feet; but what woman it was he could not discern, and it was natural to suppose that it must have been one of the foolish women, who came with no good intentions, to place herself so near him. We must have no fellowship with the unfruitful works of darkness, but rather reprove those who evidently sin, and call those to account whose conduct is suspicious, when they will expose themselves to our censure.

I am Ruth your handmaid. Therefore spread your skirt over your handmaid. Ruth does not now hesitate to make herself known to Boaz. She tells him who she was, and solicits him to spread his skirt over her, and thus to acknowledge himself her husband. A woman may, in some extraordinary cases supposable among ourselves, solicit or demand marriage from a man, without violating the laws of delicacy or reserve which nature or custom enjoins. But the law of Moses allowed a woman to request marriage from the brother of her husband who died without children, and to put him to open shame if he refused to comply. Boaz was not a brother-german of Mahlon; but either the law, it appears, was this age understood to comprehend the nearest relations, when brothers by fathers or mothers were wanting; or a custom, founded on the spirit of the law, was introduced to extend its benefits.

Women, in ordinary cases, would greatly err and expose themselves to shame, were they to show an eager desire of marriage; but they may likewise err by affected refusals of an husband, or by obstinately continuing in the single state when they ought to marry. *'I will,'* says an apostle, *'that the younger widows marry.'* He does not will them all to marry. There are circumstances in which they who do not marry, do better than those who marry; but there are others in which they would expose themselves to needless temptations, or to useless vexations, by continuing single. In this, as in every important step of life, let men and women attend to the directions of the word of God, and acknowledge Him by prayer, and he will direct their steps in the way of peace and holiness.

Spread your skirt over me, for you are a near kinsman. The near relation of Boaz to Ruth by Mahlon, was her encouragement to seek and to hope that she should be covered with his skirt. May we not much more take encouragement from the near relation of our blessed Lord, to hope that he will not disdain to receive us into a marriage-relation? Why did he take part of our flesh and blood? Was it not that he might betroth us to himself? In his grace and pity he *'was in all things made like unto us, that he might be a merciful and faithful High Priest, to make reconciliation for the sins of the people.'* He is the great pattern of conjugal love, for he gave himself for his destined spouse, *'that he might sanctify and cleanse her by the washing of water through the word, and might present her to himself a glorious church, not having spot or wrinkle, or any such thing.'* Why does he send forth his servants, the ministers of the gospel, to declare his name to us? Is it not that they may *'espouse souls to one husband, and present them as chaste virgins unto Christ?'*

LECTURE X.

BOAZ PROMISES TO RUTH TO MARRY HER, IF HER HUSBAND'S NEAREST KINSMAN DID NOT INSIST UPON HIS PRIOR RIGHT. HE DISMISSES HER WITH A PRESENT TO HER MOTHER-IN-LAW, WHO EXPRESSES GREAT SATISFACTION WITH HER KIND RECEPTION BY BOAZ.

CHAPTER 3:10-18.

Verse 10. – *And he said, Blessed are you of the Lord, my daughter; for you have shown more kindness in the latter end than at the beginning, in that you did not follow young men, whether poor or rich.*

Ruth, no doubt, felt much anxiety in her mind, when she thought of the reception with which she might meet from Boaz, as the whole colour of her future life depended upon it; but his former kindness gave her hope, and she was not disappointed.

Some men meeting with such an application from a young woman, would have taken advantage of her imprudence to draw her into the snares of the devil. Others would have treated her with asperity, as a presuming wench divested of the modesty belonging to her sex. Boaz knew Ruth and Naomi too well to entertain any injurious suspicion concerning Ruth's present conduct. He saw that she was acting according to Naomi's direction, and that their views were pure, whatever might be thought of the manner in which they endeavoured to accomplish them. Actions are often to be estimated from the character of the actor. Virtuous women may be found in situations that might justly expose them to suspicion, if their former behaviour did not give them a just title to have that conduct ascribed to mistake, or to some unknown cause, which at first view appeared almost inexcusable.

Blessed are you of the Lord, for you have shown more kindness in the latter end than at the beginning, to your husband's family. She had no doubt made an excellent wife to Mahlon. Since his death, she had fulfilled all the offices of an affectionate daughter to Naomi. Her desire of becoming the wife of Mahlon's near kinsman, was considered by Boaz as an instance of her kindness to the deceased, that deserved still greater praise. Boaz was an old man. A young woman of Ruth's beauty and character might have expected an husband among the young men of the country, better suited to her taste, and more likely to make her happy through life, if her happiness had not consisted to a great degree in showing respect to the memory of the dead, and to the comfort of her living friends.

You have not followed young men, whether poor or rich, Some might have supposed, that a mean and covetous spirit had induced Ruth to seek an alliance with Boaz, rather than with a man near her own age. But nothing could have been more unjust, than to entertain such an opinion of a woman of approved virtue. None but a woman fit to be a prostitute for hire, would marry a man for his riches, when she would have preferred another man to him if he had not been poor. Ruth's contentment with her low condition, her conjugal affection to Mahlon, still apparent in her filial behaviour to his mother, her modesty, her piety, were proofs that she could not act upon motives so unworthy to come into the mind of an Israelitess. An Israelitess she may with propriety be called. She was so by choice if not by birth; and from a pious regard to the God and to the people of Israel, she preferred widowhood, or the meanest connections in the Holy Land, to any prospects she could form among her friends in Moab.

God has made of one blood all nations of men, to bind them in the connections of a common brotherhood. And he has parcelled out men into particular kindreds and families, to bind them closer in friendship with those to whom they may communicate, or from whom they may receive, the kindnesses due from men to their own flesh. Boaz, entertaining a warm regard to his own kindred, thought himself indebted to Ruth for that affectionate regard which she had showed to his friends. He gave her due praise for her behaviour, and promised that he would take care of her interests.

Verse 11. – *And now, my daughter, do not fear. I will do to you all that you ask. For all the city of my people knows that you are a woman of virtue.*

Blessings of the tongue are cheap, and very readily given by some who have nothing else to give. Boaz prays that the Lord might bless Ruth, and at the same time undertakes to do what she required, if he found it consistent with the rights of a still nearer kinsman.

He calls her his daughter, and yet is very ready to take her for a wife. Equality of age is very desirable in the marriage relation, but not indispensable. If a young woman find that she cannot love an old man, she cannot, without sinning, and without exposing herself to great temptations for the time to come, enter into that relation, the duties of which cannot be rightly performed without that conjugal affection which ought to be maintained between those who are *'no more two, but one flesh.'* Nor can parents, without unnatural cruelty, urge their daughters to marry men, to whom they cannot cheerfully promise that love and reverence which are indispensably requisite in Christian wives. But Ruth found no difficulty in the matter. She entertained a cordial love to Boaz as a good man, as the best friend of her family, and her own friend. Boaz neither thought, nor had any reason to think that she wished from any improper motives to become his wife, for she was well known to be a virtuous woman.

If she had not been a virtuous woman, Boaz would not have thought of making her his wife. Neither beauty, were it equal to that of our first mother in her first estate, nor wit, nor any qualification, however brilliant, or however engaging, can supply the place of virtue. Without virtue, the most attractive qualities are very likely to become incentives and temptations to vice; (Prov. 31:30).

All the city of my people knows that you are a woman of virtue. This was a great recommendation of Ruth to Boaz, that her virtue was well known and acknowledged by all his fellow-citizens. All young women ought not only to behave well, but to keep at a distance from every thing that may render their character doubtful. What wise man will ever pay his addresses to a woman, however virtuous, unless she entertain a due regard to her own character? It cannot even be said that a woman is unexceptionable in virtue, when she is not duly careful of the appearance, as well as of the reality of virtuous conduct. Whatsoever things are lovely, and of good report, must be thought upon and practised by Christians of both sexes. Female delicacy requires particular attention to this rule of conduct from the weaker sex.

Although Boaz was charmed with the behaviour, and pleased with the character of Ruth, yet he would take no unfair methods to obtain her for himself. *'A virtuous woman is a crown to her husband.'* But an honest man will not use unjustifiable methods to obtain the best crown which this earth can afford.

Verses 12,13. – *And now it is true that I am your near kinsman. However, there is a kinsman nearer than I am. Stay tonight, and in the morning if he will perform to you the part of a kinsman, it shall be good. Let him do the kinsman's part. But if he will not do the part of a kinsman to you, than I will do the part of a kinsman to you, as the Lord lives. Lie down until the morning.*

When Alexander the Great took Tyre, he was informed of a young prince who had obtained a high character for virtue, and offered him the crown. The young prince refused it, because he had an elder brother, who had a better title than himself to the royal dignity; for they were of the ancient blood of the Tyrian kings. Boaz deserves no less praise than this Tyrian prince. Such a wife as Ruth would have been preferred by Boaz to a royal diadem; yet he would not take her to himself to wife while there lived another man who had a preferable claim to her, if he was willing to make use of his right. We ought to *'look every man not on his own things only, but every man also on the things of others.'*

And now, it is true that I am your near kinsman. Purse-proud men are ashamed of their poor relations, but Boaz takes pleasure in being accounted the near kinsman of such a virtuous woman as Ruth. If we are ashamed of virtuous and godly friends because they are poor, we would have been ashamed to acknowledge Jesus as a friend, when he lived in poverty upon earth.

However, there is a kinsman nearer than I. There are different degrees of relation, all of which have their respective duties and their respective rights belonging to them. We sin either by neglecting any of the duties of these relations, or by arrogating the rights peculiar to nearer relations. A brother or an uncle are near relations; but neither of them can claim the authority of a father, except in extraordinary cases, when particular circumstances have devolved the authority of a parent upon them. Boaz would do every thing to serve Ruth that became her nearest relation, but one; and this one thing he declined, because he had no right to do it. He would not intrude into the rights of another man, till they were voluntarily surrendered. As every man ought to abide in his own calling, so we all ought to keep our own places in society. Much of the unhappiness, and many of the sins of social life, originate in that assuming and meddling disposition, which renders some people a pest to their neighbours, and still more to themselves.

Stay tonight, and you shall know whether your nearest kinsman chooses to do the part of kinsman to you. Although we must not be busy-bodies, yet we act a kind part to our friends when we take an interest in their affairs, and, at their desire, understood or expressed, transact such of them as they cannot so well transact for themselves. Ruth might have gone to her nearest kinsman, and required him either to marry her or renounce his right; but Boaz saves her the trouble, and we may say of him as he said of Ruth, that his kindness in the end was greater than at the beginning. It was a great pleasure to him to *'cause the widow's heart to sing for joy.'*

Stay tonight, and I will transact the business in the morning. Boaz would do with his might what his hand found to do. He would not cause Ruth to wait in suspense a single hour beyond what was necessary for bringing the most important business of her life to a conclusion. One of the English kings was called Ethelred the Unready, because he was always too late with his preparations to oppose the enemies of his country. O that men could know and attend to their duties in the proper season! Then would they be like trees planted by the rivers of water, whose leaf fades not, and whose fruit does not fail. Christ has redeemed us from all iniquity, that we might be ever ready for every good work.

If he will perform the part of a kinsman, it shall be good. Let him perform the part of a kinsman. But if he perform the part of a kinsman, Boaz must give up all thoughts of marrying the woman who stood so high in his estimation, and in the opinion of all his fellow-citizens. True; but if he is disappointed of a virtuous wife, he keeps a good conscience. A good wife is a good thing, but a good conscience is better. If you could obtain the best wife in the world by injustice, you make a very foolish bargain.

'We are glad,' says Paul to the Corinthians, *'when we are weak, and you are strong.'* If Boaz must see Ruth the wife of another man, he will rejoice in his happiness, and in the happiness which he hoped Ruth would enjoy in his house. We should learn to rejoice with them that rejoice, when we have reason on our own account to mourn.

But if he will not perform the part of a kinsman, I will perform the part of a kinsman to you. You see he does not think the worse of Ruth for lying down at his feet. He was governed by that charity which thinks no evil.

As the Lord lives. Oaths are not to be sworn on trifling occasions. Boaz accounted the present an occasion of sufficient importance to justify his taking the name of God into his mouth. His words might very well have been believed without an oath; but he wished to give full satisfaction to Ruth about his intentions, that her mind might be set perfectly at ease, and that she might patiently wait the event without putting herself to any farther trouble.

It is a sign of profane spirit not to fear an oath. It is vain, scrupulously to be afraid of an oath when we are called to swear.

Lie down until the morning. Boaz probably wished that she had not come to lay herself down; but since she was laid at his feet, he did not think it safe for her to leave him till the morning. He did not wish her to expose herself to the fears and perils of the night, nor did he think it prudent either to go with her, or to send one of his servants to attend her, in the darkness of the night, to her mother's house. In considering what is fit to be done in particular businesses, it is often necessary to attend to existing circumstances. Certain situations and circumstances may render it necessary and wise to do those things which, in different situations, it would be very unwise to do; as you see in Paul's direction about those points, concerning which the Corinthian believers consulted him by letter; (1 Cor. 7:10).

Verse 14. – *And she lay at his feet until the morning. And she rose up before one could know another. And he said, Do not let it be known that a woman came into the floor.*

Let us endeavor to do nothing that will not bear the light. But if we have done any thing that may expose us to unjust suspicions if it were known, it is not inconsistent with integrity to conceal it, provided it can be done without falsehood or dissimulation. Although Boaz was fully persuaded that Ruth came with no evil intention to the floor, and was conscious that their mutual converse was innocent, he did not know what ill-natured constructions might be put upon the conduct of either of them by some of their neighbors. *'All men do not have faith,'* says Paul; and we know too well that all men have not charity.

It is necessary for us at all times to cut off occasions from those who would speak reproachfully. It was necessary especially that a stranger and proselyte should be careful of her character, and above all, a stranger to whom a respectable citizen might claim for a wife. If matters had been so conducted, that Ruth's behaviour had excited suspicions against her, how could Boaz have proposed a marriage with her to her nearest kinsman? It might have been supposed, that he only wished for a refusal. that he might take her to himself. But, highly as he esteemed Ruth, he would take no steps to obtain her, on which he could not reflect with pleasure.

Verse 15. – *Also he said, Bring the veil that you have upon you, and hold it. And when she held it, he measured six measures of barley, and laid it on her. And she went into the city.*

This, some may say, was a strange present. Who ever laid a load of barley upon the shoulders of a young woman whom he wished to marry, as a proof of his affection? Might he not have given her rings, or nose jewels, or some Babylonish garment, rather than a load of grain fit to be laid on the shoulders of a beggar?

It may be answered, that Boaz could better judge than we, what presents were fit to be made to Ruth. Such questions will be asked by those only, whose acquaintance reaches not beyond the manners of their own time, or of their own people. If you have read the most ancient of uninspired books, you will find that it was not, in the days of old, accounted inconsistent with the dignity of heroes and kings to kill and roast their own meat. If you read the accounts of recent travellers to the East, you will find that great men think they pay a compliment to strangers of distinction, by sending them presents of provisions, even of the kind that is most common and cheap.

Lovers among us, it is true, do not give presents of barley to their mistresses; yet barley is more precious than any of the trinkets which the customs of modern times have introduced, as proper testimonies of regard to the objects of love. When our Lord fed a multitude with barley loaves, he multiplied them, but he did not change them into loaves of fine wheat. Ruth, and her mother Naomi, had learned by poverty to set a value upon those kinds of grain which fulness of bread, and abundance of idleness, dispose too many to despise. Those who must live on barley bread are monsters of ingratitude, if they do not receive their portion of the good things of this world with thankfulness to the Author and Preserver of their being. The apostle Paul was often not so well supplied with food as the poorest of our cottagers, and yet his heart was warm with gratitude to Him who gives us all things richly to enjoy; (1 Tim. 6:17).

He laid it on her, and she went into the city. – She received the barley in her veil, and carried it to the house of her mother-in-law. She disdained not the present. She did not think herself too fine a lady to carry it, although she hoped soon to be the wife of *'a mighty man of wealth.'* God had given her health and vigor, and she was not ashamed to use her strength in those useful employments, which may perhaps appear too mean to some of the lowest class of society among us. It is said of a certain Spanish king, that one of his attendants, seeing him one day employed in a piece of mechanical work, took the liberty of observing, that such employments were fitter for a carpenter's apprentice, than a king. 'Nature,' replied the monarch, 'has given hands to kings as well as to other men, and I know no law that should hinder me from using them.'

Verse 16. – *And when she came to her mother-in-law, she said, Who are you, my daughter? And she told her all that the man had done to her.*

Naomi doubtless waited with impatience the time when Ruth might be expected to return, but was surprised to see her come at a time she was not expecting her, when the light began to appear in the heavens. The present, too, which Ruth carried, increased her wonder, which she expressed in these words, *'Who are you, my daughter?'* We sometimes use a like expression, 'Is this you?' when a friend pays us an unexpected visit.

And she told her all that the man had done to her. Ruth used to hide nothing that was interesting to herself from her affectionate mother-in-law; and was, no doubt, happy to inform her of any thing that would give her satisfaction.

Let no young woman deal in secrecy and concealment. Beware of doing any thing that you would not wish your affectionate mother to know; and, if you have done any thing unfit to be known, make not falsehood your refuge. Ruth had no reason to be afraid of telling her mother-in-law what passed between her and Boaz. *'He who does truth, comes to the light,'* for he is not afraid to have *'his works made manifest.'*

Verse 17. – *And she said, These six measures of barley he gave to me, for he said to me, Do not go empty to your mother-in-law.*

Ruth could not conceal the bounty of Boaz, for her heart overflowed with gratitude; and she mentions it to Naomi in language that would highly gratify the good old woman. Although Naomi had Ruth's happiness only in view, as her own connection with the world was nearly at an end, yet she must have been pleased with the attention paid to her by her friends. You cannot restore youthful vigor to your aged friends. You cannot give them a relish for youthful enjoyments. Yet you may console them by those kind attentions to which they are well entitled from those young friends whom they love.

Verse 18. – *Then she said, Sit still, my daughter, until you know how the matter will fall. For the man will not rest until he has finished the thing this day.*

'There is a time to speak, and a time to be silent;' a time to act, and a time to sit still. Ruth had now done all that her mother thought necessary. She may now sit still, for her affairs are in the hand of one who will take care to manage them in the most expeditious manner, and to bring them to a happy conclusion.

Some cannot be persuaded to act when activity is necessary; others cannot be induced to sit still when they have done all that is fit to be done. Their anxiety keeps them in a constant bustle. They neither can be at rest, nor suffer others around them to rest. *'It is vain for men to rise up early, and sit up late, to eat the bread of sorrow,'* and to refuse to their minds and bodies their necessary repose. Let us not neglect our duty about our secular as well as our spiritual interests. Slothfulness is reprobated both by reason and religion; but let us still remember our Lord's gracious injunction, *'Take no thought,'* or rather, Take no anxious thought, *'for the morrow.'* We ought never to say to our souls, *'Take your rest, eat, drink, and be merry;'* but we have too often reason to say, *'Why are you disquieted within me? Hope in God.'*

Sit still until you know how the matter will fall. Ruth might well be supposed to entertain uneasy thoughts about a business that was to determine the fortune of her future days. She did not know whether she was to be the wife of Boaz, or of her nearer kinsman. But what could she do by the indulgence of disquieting thoughts? She could not alter the laws or customs of the country. She could not do any thing more than she had already done, to procure for herself that alliance which she desired. What could she now do better than to sit still, resigning herself to the providence of God. Things that will happen, cannot be prevented by our utmost solicitude. Things not appointed will never take place, if all the care and all the toil of men and angels were jointly employed to bring them about. For *'who is he that says, and it comes to pass, when the Lord does not command it? Out of the mouth of the Most High proceeds not evil and good.'*

For the man will not be in rest, until he has finished the thing this day. Naomi knew Boaz to be a man of wisdom and activity, a generous and honest man, who would not rest till he had accomplished the business in hand. Ruth, having such a friend to transact her business, had no occasion to give herself any more trouble. A faithful friend is the most precious blessing which this world can afford. *'He that sends a message by the hand of a fool, cuts off the feet, and drinks damage;'* but *'as a cloud of dew in the heat of harvest, so is a faithful messenger to them that send him,'* for he refreshes the soul of his employers.

Do you profess to be a friend? Show yourself friendly in your conduct. Do not be backward to engage in the concerns of your friend, when you are qualified to manage them to better advantage than he can do, or to give him friendly assistance to manage them for himself. When you have undertaken the management of any affair, make no needless delays; for *'hope deferred,'* though not crushed, *'makes the heart sick.'* It was the known character of Boaz that inspired Naomi and Ruth with such confidence in his good offices. Why should you forfeit the things of the services you mean to do, by wearying out the patience, and perhaps disconcerting the plans, of those who trust to your friendship? Defer nothing till tomorrow that may as well be done to day, either for yourselves or for your friends. *'Who knows what a day will bring forth?'* It is said of

Richard II., king of England, that he lost his crown and life by being a day too late in coming to join his army in Wales.

When you have tried friends, trust their friendship as far as men can be trusted. David was not afraid to put his life into Jonathan's hands, when Saul, for Jonathan's interest, was seeking his destruction.

Have you no friends to manage your troublesome affairs, or to direct your management of them? Say not so, as long as you are permitted to say concerning Christ, '*This is my beloved, and this is my friend!' 'Commit your works unto the Lord, and your thoughts shall be established. Be not anxiously careful about any thing; but in every thing, by prayer and supplication, with thanksgiving, let your requests be made known unto God, and the peace of God, which passes all understanding, shall keep your hearts and minds through Christ Jesus.*'

LECTURE XI.

BOAZ, IN THE PRESENCE OF TEN ELDERS OF BETHLEHEM, PROCURES THE CONSENT OF RUTH'S NEAREST KINSMAN TO HIS MARRIAGE WITH HER.

CHAPTER 4:1-10.

Verse 1. – *Then Boaz went up to the gate, and sat him down there; and behold, the kinsman of whom Boaz spake came by; unto whom he said, Ho, such a one! turn aside, sit down here. And he turned aside, and sat down.*

'*Marriage is honorable in all,*' but some make it dishonorable to themselves, by being unequally yoked, or by reprehensible methods of entering into the state of marriage. By dishonest means they gain the affections of their partners, or transgress the good and necessary laws of their country by clandestine engagements. Surely there is no business in life which ought to be transacted with a closer attention to the revealed will of God, than one on which so much of the happiness or misery of life depends. We are so far from acting like Christians, that we proceed upon atheistical principles, if we expect any more joy from changing our condition than God is pleased to give us. We will find satisfaction or disquiet, happiness or misery, in marriage, according to the will of our Maker; and therefore in this, and in all our ways, let us acknowledge Him, and he will direct our steps. '*If a man's ways please the Lord, he makes even his enemies to be at peace with him.*' If a man's ways do not please the Lord, he can set his friends at variance with him, and poison the streams of his felicity with bitterness, lamentation, and woe.

Boaz proceeds with candour and openness in the business of his marriage. He would not move a step in it, without letting his intentions be known to the only man that had a right to throw obstructions in his way; and transacts the matter with him in the presence of ten of the most respectable men in Bethlehem. Thus he '*provides for things honest, not only in the sight of God, but in the sight of all men.*'

He goes to the gate of the city. The gate was the place of concourse in ancient times. It was the place where courts were held, and where the most important affairs were discussed. The near kinsman seems to have been called off his way by Boaz, after he took his seat at the gate. The Lord brought him to the place where Boaz wished to meet with him. Thus, when Abraham's servant '*was in the way, the Lord led him to the house of his master's brothers.*' Things the most accidental to us, are regulated by God.

Ho! such a one. Did not the sacred writer know the man's name? Undoubtedly. But he seems to have concealed it from us, with the design of burying it in oblivion. The man appears to have been more solicitous than he ought to have been about the preservation of his own name, and it is allowed to perish. He would not raise up a name to Mahlon, that he might not mar that inheritance by which his own name was to be preserved. But the name of Mahlon comes down to the latest posterity, with the name of Boaz; while none can tell what was the name of the man who was so anxious to avoid any thing that might impair the lustre of his family.

And he turned aside, and sat down.

Verse 2. – *And he took ten men of the elders of the city, and said, Come sit down here. And they sat down.*

Whether he sent for them before or after he sat down, we are not told. He did not proceed to business till he had abundance of witnesses to attest the proceedings, and of counsellors or judges to determine difficulties, if any should occur. *'In the mouth of two or three witnesses,'* says the law, *'shall every word be established.' 'In the multitude of counsellors,'* says the wise man, *'is safety.'*

Verse 3. – *And he said to the kinsman: Naomi, who has come again out of the country of Moab, sells a parcel of land which was our brother Elimelech's.*

Naomi was a poor widow, and yet she had a parcel of land to sell. It was doubtless so encumbered, that hitherto she could not derive any benefit from it since her return from the land of Moab. It was her interest to sell it, that she might draw from it some help to her present subsistence; and it was highly proper that the first offer of it should be made to that kinsman, to whom the office of redeeming inheritances belonged, according to the law. *'He that has friends must show himself friendly'* when he has the power and opportunity; and, when he is in distress, may reasonably expect succor from his friends.

'This land pertained to our brother Elimelech,' said Boaz. All near relations were called brothers among the Israelites. By calling Elimelech their brother on the present occasion, Boaz insinuates the obligation lying upon them to deal kindly with Naomi. When she was compelled to sell the land of her deceased husband, it was to be expected that his surviving brothers would give her better terms than strangers. If they did not give a larger price, they might soften the necessity that urged her to sell, by attentions and favors of no great cost to themselves.

Verse 4. – *And I said I will tell it in your ear, saying, Buy it before those who live here, and before the elders of my people. If you will redeem it, redeem it. But if you will not redeem it, then tell me so that I may know. For there is none to redeem it besides you. And I am after you. And he said, I will redeem it.*

Boaz plainly intimates his intention of buying Elimelech's land, if his nearest kinsman found it inconvenient for himself to do it; but he felt it his duty to give advertisement, in the first place, to him who had the best right to do it if he chose. The money of Boaz was as good as his friend's money; but it might be an advantage to possess the land, although the full price were given for it, and it seemed agreeable to the Jewish law that the nearest kinsman should have his option. We must not go beyond, or defraud our brother in any matter great or small, nor do any thing that has the appearance of taking an advantage of him. When land is to be set in tack, artful and clandestine means to obtain possession of it are suspicious. The master is under no obligation to let it to the former tenant. He may have justly incurred his landlord's displeasure. He may be less qualified to make the land productive than some of his neighbors, or he may be unwilling to give a reasonable advance in the rent. But let no unfair advantage be taken of him by his neighbors. If they find themselves at liberty to enter in bargain with his master, they ought not to behave towards the former tenant in any other way than they would think it reasonable for their own neighbors to behave towards themselves in similar circumstances. Fair proceedings seldom need concealment. *'Whatsoever you would that men should do unto you, do even so unto them.'* We ought not to account ourselves upright men, if this maxim does not regulate every part of our behavior.

There is none to redeem it besides you, and I am after you. There was none nearer in relation than this kinsman, but Boaz was next in degree. *'There is a friend that sticks closer than a brother.'* Such a friend was Boaz to Ruth, and yet he would not claim the rights of the nearest kinsman, but was in readiness to perform his duties, if he declined the performance. We ought to invade no man's rights, but to perform the duties belonging to every man in his place and relation. Nor are we always to confine ourselves, in performing the duty of relations, to those which in ordinary cases belong to our degree of relation. An uncle may be called, by existing circumstances, to perform the duty of a father, or a nephew to perform the duty of a son. There are some to whom it is a great loss to have near relations careless of their duty, or not well qualified to perform it. They are neglected by other relations, who would be kind to them if they did not trust the care of them to those who are more nearly connected; or perhaps they are glad to have a pretext from the nearer relationship of others, to excuse themselves from troublesome duties. Boaz was ready, either to redeem the inheritance of Mahlon, or to leave it to be redeemed by a nearer kinsman.

And he said, I will redeem it. His meaning was, that he would give the money necessary for the purchase. But, when he heard the conditions of the bargain, he declined it.

Verse 5. – *Then said Boaz, That day you buy the field from the hand of Naomi, you must buy it also from the hand of Ruth of Moab, the wife of the dead, to raise up the name of the dead upon his inheritance.*

When a man dies, his wife must lose his society, and the benefits of his industry; but let her not lose what she has a right to claim, her portion of the common goods, and the friendship of his relations. The rights of the widow are protected and her injuries are avenged by Him who is '*the judge of the widow, and the father of the fatherless, in his holy habitation.*' Whatever necessity Naomi was under of selling the land of Elimelech, she would not deprive Ruth of her just claim upon it. He who buys the land, must marry Ruth, to raise up the name of her deceased husband.

'*The dead know not any thing, neither have they any more a reward; for the memory of them is forgotten, and their love, and their hatred, and their envy, is now perished: neither have they any more a portion for ever in any thing that is done under the sun.*' Yet their memory is to be respected by surviving relations; and the respect due to their memories is to be held the more sacred that they have no more a portion in any thing. When they have lost every thing earthly, let them not be bereaved of what may still be reserved, the esteem to which their memory is entitled. They cannot hear the voice of friendship: but it was their wish, while they were with us, to be remembered with kindness, when they would no longer enjoy our company. And, when we must die, it would aggravate our affliction to have reason to think that our memory will perish with us. God provided, by a law, for the preservation of the name of those who died childless. '*If brothers dwell together, and one of them die, and have no child, the wife of the dead shall not marry a stranger. Her husband's brother shall go in to her, and take her to him to wife, and perform the duty of an husband's brother to her; and it shall be, that the first born which she bears shall succeed in the name of his brother which is dead, that his name be not put out of Israel.*' (Deut. 25:5,6).

The law was not exactly applicable to the case in question. The next kinsman of Elimelech was, probably, not his own brother, nor did he live in the house together with him. But a custom, founded on the spirit of the law, seems to have given the nearest kinsman a right, by proscription, to the refusal of a childless widow; and to the widow, a right to expect the nearest kinsman in marriage, unless some considerable objections, from her former behavior, or from particular circumstances, rendered the connection ineligible.

This law was peculiar to Israelites. Those who die childless among us, must remain so for ever. But we enjoy clearer revelations than the ancient church, of the felicities of the other world. We need not greatly wish to have our names registered in the records of any city upon earth, or in the genealogy of any house. It will be sufficient for us to have our names '*written among the living in Jerusalem;*' and if we have begotten any children by the gospel, they '*will be to us for a name and a crown of rejoicing in the day of Christ.*' This honor is to all those saints who turn any sinner from the error of his way, though not invested with the ministry of the gospel; (James 5:19,20).

Verse 6. – *And the kinsman said, I cannot redeem it for myself, lest I mar my own inheritance. You redeem my right to yourself, for I cannot redeem it.*

Unless we knew more than the sacred historian has thought it necessary to tell us concerning the circumstances of this near kinsman, we cannot say whether his objection to the marriage with Ruth was founded in truth and reason, or whether his dislike to the match prompted him to make use of an evasion. It is likely that he had a family by another wife, and that he was afraid of injuring it, by laying out money on a possession that would not descend to them.

Young persons should not enter into the marriage relation without serious consideration. This is still more necessary for widowers with young families. By rashness in entering anew into the married state, they may bring great disquiet to themselves, and may incapacitate themselves to do for their families what they had a right to expect. Yet it is to be feared, that too many decline the married state through distrust of divine Providence, or through unwillingness to forego some of those gratifications which the expense and care of a family would oblige them to relinquish. Paul speaks of a time, when, *'for the present distress,'* it was not good to marry; and, at any time, some are in circumstances which make it expedient for them to continue in the single state. But when men find the temptations of a single life dangerous to their souls, and yet abide in it to avoid the expenses of the reduction in their style of living, which marriage would render necessary, they expose themselves to the snares of the devil, by neglecting those precautions against sin which human corruption renders necessary. What sins and sorrows to young men might often have been prevented by prudent marriages!

You redeem my right to yourself, for I cannot redeem it. Although this kinsman did not choose to marry Ruth, he was so honest as not to wish to hinder her marriage with another. He was unlike to some persons, who, while they are undetermined about marrying the objects of their attachments, use indirect means to hinder them from marrying other persons with whom they might be happy. Nothing can be a greater indication of a selfish and grovelling mind, than for a man to work himself into the affections of a young woman so far as to hinder her from listening to the addresses of others, while he is balancing in his own mind whether he will marry her or not, and behaves in such a dubious manner, that expectations are raised, while positive engagements are avoided. Let all young women guard against such insidious enemies of their peace. A man cannot be truly in love with a woman, when his self-love is so strong, that he attends only to his own conflict and interest, and cares not what pain he inflicts upon her to whom he pretends a regard.

Verses 7,8. – *Now this was the custom in former times in Israel concerning redeeming and concerning changing, in order to make all things sure. A man plucked off his shoe and gave it to his neighbor. And this was a testimony in Israel. Therefore the kinsman said to Boaz, Buy it for yourself. So he drew off his shoe.*

This ceremony is evidently different from that which was prescribed in the law of Moses, concerning the man who refused to marry the childless widow of his brother that had dwelt in the house with him. In that case, the widow herself was to pluck off the man's shoe, and to spit in his face as a reproach upon him for refusing to raise up seed to his brother. A distant relation was not under the same legal obligations, nor subjected to the same reproach.

Significant ceremonies are still used among men in transferring the property of land from one to another, as well as in many other transactions of importance. They are useful for authenticating transactions, and preventing disputes for the time to come. The kinsman of Boaz not only expressed his resignation of his right in the ears of witnesses, but presented a visible sign of it to their eyes, that all possibility of doubt or contention might be obviated. *'Here is my shoe,'* said he to Boaz. *'He who wears this shoe, has a right to buy and use the ground in question. Let this be a witness, that what was formerly mine, is become yours with my consent.'*

The use of visible signs for establishing bargains may call to our minds the wonderful condescension of our blessed Redeemer, in granting us visible signs of his grace for the confirmation of our faith. As certainly as the shoe of this kinsman was in the possession of Boaz, the land which that kinsman had the prior right to redeem now belonged to

Boaz. As certainly as we are cleansed by water, and nourished and refreshed by bread and wine, (the symbols of the body and blood of the Lord,) are our souls cleansed, nourished, and invigorated, by the blood and body presented by them. We may say of such visible signs of a covenant, what Paul says of oaths, that they *'are for confirmation, to put an end to all strife.'*

Verse 9. – *And Boaz said to the elders and to all the people. You are witnesses this day that I have bought all that was Elimelech's and all that was Chilion's and Mahlon's from the hand of Naomi.*

Boaz was not afraid of marring his own inheritance, nor did he seek any pretexts for declining that generous bargain which the kinsman refused. It is a happy thing, not only for a rich man himself, but for all around him,when he is disposed to use his substance for the purposes for which Providence bestowed it.

When Boaz makes the bargain, he calls not only upon the elders, but upon all the people present, to be witnesses. He followed the example of his father Abraham. He never bought any land but a burial-place, and he took all possible care to obviate any contentions about the purchase to himself and to his heirs. *'The field of Ephron, which was in Machpelah, which was before Mamre, the field and the cave which was therein, and all the trees which were therein, were made sure unto Abraham for a possession in the presence of the children of Heth, before all that went in at the gate of his city;'* (Gen. 23:17,18). *'A good man will guide his affairs with discretion.'*

I have bought all that was Elimelech's, and all that was Chilion's and Mahlon's. You see how changeable earthly property is. Men think they can secure it almost against death. By purchasing land, and using legal methods for transmitting it to the offspring of their own bodies, they can possess it in the person of their second selves, after they go down to the grave. But although you have both children and friends, you can be secure of no dwelling, but the house appointed for all living; of no larger estate, than that quantity of ground which is sufficient to cover your bodies. In the course of ten years sojourning in the land of Moab, Elimelech and all his sons died, and now his estate came into the possession of Boaz. Here you have no continuing possession. Seek a place in the better country. All believers in Christ receive a kingdom which will not pass to others; but *'the world passes away, and the lust thereof.'*

Verse 10. – *Moreover Ruth of Moab, the wife of Mahlon, I have purchased to be my wife, to raise up the name of the dead upon his inheritance, so that the name of the dead may not be cut off from among his brothers and from the gate of his place. You are witnesses this day.*

Boaz was now, in all probability, far advanced in years, and yet he scruples not to bring a wife, and even a young wife, into his family. It is certainly not, in most cases, advisable for an old man to marry a young wife; and yet we must not reproach men for doing what the law of God does not forbid. It is probable that Abraham married a wife when he was old; (Gen. 25:1). A woman past the flower of her age is not prohibited by the apostle to marry, provided she marry in the Lord. Men and women must judge for themselves in cases where the law is silent. *'Do not be unequally yoked,'* is a law which prohibits the marriage of believers with unbelievers, or of virtuous with profane persons. It may be extended, in the spirit of it, to other inequalities which might render the marriage state uncomfortable or ensnaring to either of the parties; which a very great inequality of age would in most cases do. But it could not have applied to the case of Boaz, although it had been found in that part of the Bible which was given to Israel. The inequality of age was so richly compensated by similitude of disposition and mutual attachment, that it made little or no abatement of happiness to either party.

Moreover Ruth of Moab. He was not ashamed of her extraction. She was a descendant, not of Abraham but of Lot, according to the flesh; but she deserved so much the more respect when she was a daughter of Abraham and Sarah in faith, in well-doing, in patience, and in courage. She forgot her own people, and her father's house, and the eternal King greatly desired her beauty.

The wife of Mahlon, I have purchased to be my wife. Ruth was a widow, but not the less desirable for a wife on that account in the esteem of Boaz. From the duty she performed to Mahlon, living and dead, he concluded that she would make the best of wives to himself. She had this advantage above virgins, that her own works, as a wife and a widow, praised her in the gate, and all the children of his people knew that her virtue had stood the test of many trials.

I have purchased her to be my wife, or acquired a just right to her. It was necessary for him to redeem her estate, that he might marry her; but he made an excellent bargain, although the land was to go to the legal posterity of Mahlon, for *'the price of a virtuous woman is above rubies.'* Houses and lands are the inheritance of parents, but *'a prudent wife is from the Lord.'*

To raise up the name of the dead upon his inheritance, so that the name of the dead may not be cut off from among his brothers, and from the gate of his place. Although the happiness that Boaz expected to enjoy in his connection with a woman so virtuous and amiable, could have been a sufficient inducement to him to marry Ruth, yet it was not his only motive. He made no vain boast of his kindness to Mahlon when he expressed his desire of perpetuating the name of the dead. It was for the sake of the dead that Ruth desired him to take her into the marriage relation, and he showed all that readiness to comply with her desire which could consist with the rights of a nearer relation. It is mean and dishonest to pretend that you do any thing for the benefit or credit of your friends, when you are actuated only by self-love. *'He that boasts of a false gift, is like clouds and wind without rain.'* It is base to boast of your friendly offices to others when vanity dictates your words; but Boaz professed his friendly intentions to the dead with a view to the credit of him whose place he was to occupy.

But how did Boaz know that his marriage with Ruth would keep up the name of the dead in his inheritance? He certainly was not ignorant that God alone is the creator of man, and that the fruit of the womb is from him. But he believed that God would give him seed by Ruth, because he was taking that method which God had authorized for raising up children to the dead. He married Ruth in the faith that God would make his own appointed means effectual, if he saw it good, for the end in view. Although the letter of the law (Deut. 25) did not require him to raise up seed to Mahlon, he acted on the principle on which the law was founded. His expectation of seed by this marriage is the more observable, as Ruth had been hitherto barren, and Boaz himself was well stricken in years. Perhaps we should not err, if we alleged that, like his father Abraham, he received a son by faith; although his faith had not the same difficulties to surmount.

The men of ancient times seem to have entertained more ardent wishes than the people in our days, to have their names preserved after their death by real or legal descendants. A name after death will be of little use to us, if we are not found *'written among the living in Jerusalem.'* It is certainly however our duty, to endeavour to leave a good name behind us, by doing those works that will deserve it. *'The memorial of the righteous is everlasting.' 'A good name is better than precious ointment; and the day of death* (to persons entitled to a good name) *is better than the day of their birth.'* Christ requires us to make our *Light so to shine before men, that they, seeing our good works, may glorify our Father which is in heaven.'* When our works commend themselves to the consciences of men, they will glorify God on our account, not only while we are yet alive, but as long as our names and virtues are remembered. Remember your rulers and other good men, now with God, who once conversed with you on earth; and follow their faith, *'considering the end of their conversation,'* and then it may be expected that some will follow your faith, when you have obtained the end of it – the *'salvation of your souls.'*

LECTURE XII.
RUTH'S MARRIAGE. AND THE BIRTH OF OBED.
CHAPTER 4:10-22.

Verse 10. – *You are witnesses this day.*

Verse 11. – *And all the people that were in the gate, and the elders, said, We are witnesses. May the Lord make the woman who has come into your house like Rachel and like Leah, for these two built the house of Israel. And may you be blessed in Ephratah, and be famous in Bethlehem.*

You are witnesses this day. It was highly proper that Boaz should call the elders and the people to bear witness to the purchase of Elimelech's land. It was still more necessary to have witnesses of his marriage-contract. Many of the female sex would have been rendered miserable for life by a clandestine entrance into the prevention of general licentiousness of manners. And those who break the good laws Belial, in opposition to the interests of the kingdom of Christ.

We are witnesses, said all the people. They gladly came forward to bear their part in that generous transaction, by which the family of Elimelech was to be rescued from oblivion, and, in some sense, raised from the grave in which it lay buried. It was a grief to the people who entered in by the gates of Bethlehem, that a family once honored among them, was now on the point of extinction; and with joy they declared themselves the witnesses of a marriage which gave them hopes that it would be again built up among them.

May the Lord make the woman who has come into your house like Rachel and like Leah, for these two built the house of Israel. The fruit of the womb was greatly desired by the ancient Israelites. It was one of the blessings promised to them in the Sinai covenant, if they obeyed God's testimonies. *'I will have respect to you, and make you fruitful, and multiply you, and establish my covenant with you.'* The children of Judah would value this blessing the more, in the hope of giving birth to the Messiah, who was to spring from Judah. The men of Bethlehem did not yet know that their city was to be honored above the other cities of Israel, or that the family of Nahshon was to be honored above all the families of Judah, by giving him birth; but they cordially prayed that Boaz might be blessed with a numerous progeny, as the fruit of his marriage with Ruth.

May the Lord make the woman who has come into your house like Rachel and like Leah, the general mothers of Israel. Leah was more fruitful than Rachel. She was the mother of the men of Bethlehem. She was the elder sister; and yet they put the name of Rachel before hers, because she was the wife whom Jacob chose, and who had the best right to the bed of the patriarch. Perhaps they might have another reason for mentioning Rachel without distinction. Her history was a standing memorial of the power of God, in giving or withholding the fruit of the womb. She was for a time barren; but God, in answer to her prayers, gave her two sons, who were to be the fathers of a great multitude of descendants. The blessings requested for Boaz correspond to the prophecy of Jacob concerning the posterity of Joseph: *'In you shall Israel bless, saying, God make you as Ephraim, and as Manasseh!'*

Like Rachel and Leah, who built the house of Israel. Why is it said that Rachel and Leah built up the house of Israel? Did not Bilhah and Zilpah, share with them in this honor? Yes. But the children of Bilhah were accounted the children of Rachel, and the children of Zilpah were Leah's children. This is a comfort to the poorest mother among us, that she possesses undivided the comfort of her relation, both to her children and to her husband.

May the Lord make the woman who has come into your house like Rachel and like Leah, which built the house of Israel. Boaz brought the woman into his house to build up the house of Elimelech, but his townsmen prayed and hoped that this worthy action would be rewarded by the enlargement of his own family. He that does good shall receive blessings from men, and shall be well rewarded by God. *'To him that sows righteousness shall be a sure reward.'* And he may expect a reward in kind, if God sees it will be good for him. *'The Lord give you seed of this woman,'* said Eli to Elkanah, *'for the loan which you have lent to the Lord.' 'He that forsakes father and mother, and other relations, for my sake,'* says Christ, *'shall receive an hundred-fold, fathers, and mothers, and brothers, and sisters.'* Nothing is lost, but every thing is more than saved, that is from proper motives bestowed on those men to whom God gives a right to our benefactions.

And may you be blessed in Ephratah! He had done worthily, and they hope and pray that he may still do worthily. It is not enough for us to have done what is good; we must still continue to do what is well-pleasing to God. Are there not twelve hours of the day? none of them are intended for sleep. Let us work during the hours of day the work of our divine Master, and it will be pleasant for us to fall asleep, and to rest from our labors. Boaz was now an old man. He must still do worthily. Although he cannot, perhaps, do what he was once able to do, he may do works no less useful to men and pleasing to God. *'The trees planted in the house of the Lord, and flourishing in the courts of our God, shall bring forth fruit in old age.'*

And be famous in Bethlehem! He was already highly esteemed, and they wished his fame to continue and increase by well-doing. A great name is not greatly to be coveted, but *'a good name is better than precious ointment.'* The possession of a good name, acquired by doing worthily, fits us for doing much good to men, and for answering the end of our life in glorifying God; 1 Peter 2:12.

Ephratah and Bethlehem are two names for the same town. It is situated, as the name signifies, in a fertile spot of the earth. It more than doubly deserved this name, when *'the man whose name is the Branch'* grew up out of this place; that blessed man who *'gave his flesh to be the life of the world.'*

Verse 12. – *And let your house be like the house of Pharez, whom Tamar bore to Judah, of the seed which the Lord shall give you of this young woman.*

Who could have expected that Pharez, the son of Judah, should be blessed with an offspring so numerous, that in him should Israel bless, saying, *'The Lord make you like Pharez in the fruit of your body'?* Pharez was the son of Judah by his daughter-in-law. The punishment denounced against some incestuous practices is, that the persons guilty of them should be childless; (Lev. 20). Judah's sin was not intentional incest, but exceedingly blameable; and yet God, who is rich in mercy, made him, by Tamar, the father of a numerous seed, of which were many illustrious saints and heroes, and of which was Christ himself according to the flesh. When Er and Onan died, and no sons were left to Judah but Shelah, whom he was afraid to give unto Tamar, he would probably despair of ever having a great name among the tribes of Israel. But though his beginning was small, his latter end greatly increased. Benjamin had ten sons, and yet his tribe was the least of Israel. Judah had only three sons left after the destruction of the two oldest, and the birth of two of them was his shame and sorrow. Yet *'Judah was he whom his brothers praised'* for the multitude and the glory of his race.

The Ephrathites discover great ardour in their prayers for a numerous family to Boaz. We know that their prayers were answered in the glory of many of his descendants; (1 Chron. 3), and in their great number.

Whom Tamar bore to Judah. We all know that she was a Canaanitess, and that she brought upon herself, and upon Judah, much guilt; but God pardons iniquity, transgression, and sin. Her name was perhaps mentioned by the Ephrathites, because she was of heathen extraction, and of a race of heathens of a worse name than the countrymen of Ruth. That God, who made a Canaanitess whose name was blackened by the vices common in her nation, the mother of many in Israel, might be expected to bestow a like blessing upon the virtuous Moabitess.

Which the Lord shall give you of this young woman. The ancient Israelites used to speak of their children as a gift bestowed upon them by God, and a gift much more precious than gold or lands. There are thankless men, who account their children a burden. Large families, indeed, may expose poor men to much toil, and to much anxiety in thinking what they shall do to find provision for so many eaters; but *'the Lord will provide,'* and has commanded us to cast all our care upon him, because he cares for us.

Of this young woman. Ruth was yet young, although her husband, whom she married in her youth, was in his grave. This is one great advantage of equality of years in the married state, that the parties may hope to live together for a greater number of years, than those who marry husbands or wives much older than themselves. But this hope, like all others not founded on the word of God, is precarious. More persons die in youth than in old age. Boaz, it is probable, lived longer with Ruth than Mahlon had done.

Verse 13. – *So Boaz took Ruth, and she was his wife. And when he went in to her, the Lord made her conceive. And she bore a son.*

He took Ruth, and she became his wife. He did not rashly promise to spread his skirt over her; but that conditional promise which he made was faithfully, and with all convenient speed, performed. It is much better to be speedy in performing than in promising. We may easily ensnare ourselves by well-meant words. Works are the surest proof of real kindness.

And the Lord made her conceive. These words of God to Eve, *'I will greatly multiply your sorrow and your conception,'* were a merciful threatening. God remembered mercy to our race, when he denounced the just punishment of our sin. Men's brows were to sweat with toil, but in the sweat of their brows they were to eat bread. Women were to feel bitter sorrows, that they might learn how evil and bitter a thing it was to sin; but they were to enjoy the comfort, in their sorrows, of conceiving and bearing children. When it is said that the Lord gave conception to Ruth, it is not a punishment but a mercy that is spoken of. She felt the sorrows of other women, but she blessed God for these sorrows that were to bring her the joys of a mother in Israel.

It is not said that she bore any children to Mahlon, the husband of her youth; but to Boaz she conceived, and bore a son, for the Lord gave her conception. *'He makes the barren woman to keep house, and to be a joyful mother of children: Praise the Lord, who forms our bodies fearfully and wonderfully,'* and who creates the spirit of man within him.

Verse 14. – *And the women said to Naomi, Blessed be the Lord, who has not left you without a redeemer, so that his name may be famous in Israel.*

The birth of Obed brought gladness not only to his mother and father, but to Naomi and all her neighbours. They loved her, and therefore they rejoiced in her joy. It was the praise of Naomi that she gained their love, by the virtue, the piety, the mildness of her manners; and those who behave as Naomi behaved, will, for the most part, gain the affections of some of their neighbors. If the poorest women are destitute of friends, let them examine their own conduct, and they will probably find that the fault is partly in themselves. That place must be very destitute both of piety and virtue, where an unblemished conduct, joined with sweetness of manners, will procure the affection of few or none.

Our joy in the prosperity of our friends and neighbors should be expressed in thanksgivings to God, the giver of all good. *'Blessed be the Lord!'* said Naomi's neighbors, *'who has not left you this day without a kinsman.'* Paul expected that many thanksgivings would be presented to God on account of the mercies bestowed upon himself, and he abounded in thanksgiving to God on account of the mercies bestowed on his friends.

Blessed be the Lord that has not left you this day without a kinsman. Whatever joy men give us, praise is due to God who makes them the instruments of his benefits. In the good-will of Boaz, as well as in the birth of his child, Naomi's neighbors saw reasons to bless the Lord for his goodness. Her nearest kinsman would not perform the duty of the kinsman; but God left her out without a kinsman. When one friend behaves in an unfriendly manner, God can easily find us, or make us, a better friend. Let us never be dejected by the unkindness of those from whom we expected favors. All hearts are in the hand of God. When David found no favor with his own father-in-law, the king of Israel, he found much favor with the king of Gath, many of whose people he had killed in the quarrels of the king of Israel.

He has not left you without a kinsman, that his name may be found in Israel. What fame would be acquired in Israel by the kindness of Boaz to Ruth and Naomi? Was it to be hoped that his goodness and bounties to them would be known and praised among all the tribes? It is natural for men to think that the actions which they admire, should be known and admired by all. The hopes of these good women were perhaps more sanguine than the case could justify; and yet they were more than realized. The name of Boaz became famous through all Israel, and will continue famous among the Gentiles also while the world lasts, because it is mentioned with honor in the book of God. Both bad and good actions are often published to a greater extent, and continue longer to be known, than the doers or any of their friends expected. Single actions have often become the seed of everlasting praise or censure in the world. Little did the woman, who poured the box of ointment on the head of Jesus, expect, that, wherever the gospel was preached, that which she has done would be *'spoken of for a memorial of her throughout the whole world.'* Our good or bad actions never die. They are written in the book of God. Our bad actions may, indeed, be blotted out by pardoning mercy. If they are not forgiven, they will appear to our shame in the next world, and perhaps in the present. If our good actions are not remembered by men, they will be brought to remembrance by the Lord. The nearest kinsman of Naomi lost an opportunity of being renowned in Israel, because he would not raise up seed to Mahlon. The name of Boaz will live in the church, and what he did will, at the last say, be published before men and angels.

Verse 15. – *And he shall be to you as one who gives you back your life, and one who cheers your old age. For your daughter-in-law who loves you, who is better to you than seven sons, has borne him.*

'For your daughter-in-law has borne to him (a son.' So some understand these words, and refer them to Boaz. Our translation is indeed the obvious meaning of the words, and agrees with others of the most celebrated versions. The verse seems, according to this way of reading it, to express the hope of Naomi's neighbors concerning the son that was now born to Ruth; that he would be a comfort to Naomi's declining years, and would, by his virtues, by his kind attentions to Naomi, as well as by the tender affection which Naomi would bear to him as the only remnant of her family, make her last days as pleasant as her former had been sorrowful.

Boaz was already, and, they hoped, would continue to be, the nourisher of her old age, and the restorer of her life. What he was, they expected his son would be. Good men have not always the comfort of seeing their children walk in their ways. But it is very natural for friends and kind neighbors to hope well of the children of those, who they know will be careful to train them up in the nuture and admonition of the Lord.

Blessed be the Lord, who has not left you without a redeemer, that his name may be famous in Israel. Some refer these words, not to Boaz, but to his son, of whom the following words are spoken. But the word which we render kinsman, is generally, if not universally, to be understood in a sense not applicable to the child; and there does not appear any absolute necessity to understand the same person as the subject of discourse in both these verses: *'And he shall be to you a restorer of your life;'* or, *'You shall have a restorer of your life, and a nourisher of your old age.'* The God, they thought, who had showed her so much mercy, in goving her a kinsman-redeemer, had now given her a new proof of his goodness in the son that fondly hoped that her grey hairs would go towards the grave with joy, from the good behaviour and kindness of Obed. Nothing earthly is certain. Naomi had been already greatly disappointed in her hopes concerning her family. She had bitterly lamented the change in her condition, when she came a poor desolate widow to Bethlehem. Her spirits sunk within her, when she compared her former with her present condition. But now God smiled upon her by his providence. She had as good reason, at least, as her neighbors, or as any old person could have, to hope that her last days would be comfortable.

The time of old age is a time of heaviness to a great part of mankind. It is the time of which it is ordinary for men to say, that have no pleasure in it. For this reason, the children, or grand-children of old persons, ought to do all they can to sweeten to them the bitterness of that period. If you could restore again the life of your dead parents, would you not do it with joy? You cannot bring them again from the grave, where *'the worm is spread under them, and the worms cover them.'* But you may give them new life before they go to the grave, by your dutiful and religious behavior. *'Now we live,'* said Paul to the Thessalonians, *'if you stand fast in the Lord.'* Their steadfastness in faith was life to Paul. Such a life the women of Bethlehem expected would be given to Naomi, by the child born to her by Ruth. How little do those deserve life, that will not suffer those who gave them life to live with comfort! No punishment is reckoned too severe for them who are murderers of their fathers or of their mothers; but what is life, without comfort, but a lingering death? and nothing so effectually destroys the comfort of the aged, as the bad behavior of children. If any thing can restore that pleasant life which they enjoyed in youth, it is the sight of virtuous, dutiful, and happy descendants.

He shall be the restorer of your life, and the nourisher of your old age. He was to be the mourisher of her old age, not merely by supplying her wants, but by those kind regards which give far more pleasure to the mind than food gives to the taste. *'Pleasant words are like an honey-comb, sweet to the soul, and health to the bones.'* But pleasant words are doubly pleasant when they come from the mouth of a beloved child.

Naomi was not the mother of this child, nor even his grandmother, in the common sense of the word; but she was his grandmother-in-law, and therefore had the same title to dutiful behavior from him as other mothers or grandmothers. It is not to immediate parents only, but to remote parents likewise, whether they are our relations by blood, or by law, or by parental offices, that we owe filial regard. *'But if any widow have children, or nephews,'* says Paul, *'let them learn first to show piety at home, and to requite their parents, for that is good and acceptable before God.'* Grandchildren are here meant by nephews. The word has changed its meaning since our translation of the Bible was made. Yet other aged relations are likewise entitled to that honor and duty which their degree of relation demands, especially when they want nearer relations. When rich friends want heirs of their own bodies, we hope to profit by them when they die. If they are poor, should they not derive some advantage from us while they live? If it is not in our power to supply their wants. it is in our power to pay them the respect due from the nearest of their kinsmen.

Although Naomi was not a relation by blood to the young child, she was his relation by a friendship that sticks closer than that of blood. Dearly she loved Ruth, and Ruth loved her with no less warmth of affection. *'Ruth, your daughter-in-law, which loves you, which is better to you than seven sons, has borne him.'* *'Your own friend, and your father's friend, forsake not,'* says Solomon. He speaks as if we were bound to regard our father's friend no less than our own. Naomi could not but love with a fond affection the child of Ruth. This consideration, independently of her own legal relation to the babe, must have endeared him to her heart. But he must have been endeared to her likewise as the son of Mahlon, no less than if he had been the offspring of his own body, as love to that deceased husband was one of Ruth's great inducements to desire that marriage of which he was the fruit.

Your daughter-in-law, which is better to you than seven sons, has borne him. Children of the youth are compared by the Psalmist to arrows in the hands of a mighty man, and that man is said to be blessed who has his quiver full of them. Seven children were esteemed by Hannah one of the richest of earthly blessings. *'She that is barren has borne seven, and she that has borne seven languishes.'* But the good behavior, the filial affection, and dutiful condition of children, is a far greater comfort to the parents than the number of them. Naomi had only two sons, both of whom were dead, and yet she was as happy as Ruth, as other women were in the enjoyment of seven children. Great were her afflictions, but her happiness was likewise great, and it was not lost to her in the remembrance of those children that were not. Those persons are not always the least happy, who have experienced the bitterest trials. Their comforts may counterbalance or exceed their afflictions. If we are wise, we will not think more frequently or more intensely on what we have lost, than on what we have; and if the comforts left to us are few in number, we will consider whether the value of them does not make abundant compensation for their paucity. God has taken from you many children, and perhaps left you but one, while he has spared the whole family of some of your neighbors. But if your one son, or daughter, excels in virtue, you may find more pleasure in your one child than your neighbors find in all of theirs. A certain Duke of Ormond, who lost a virtuous son, the Lord Ossory, said, that he would rather be the father of the dead Ossory, than of any living nobleman in England. Naomi would rather have been the mother-in-law of Ruth, and the grandmother-in-law of Obed, than the mother and grandmother by blood of any woman and child in Bethlehem, or in Israel. Her soul was melted at the remembrance of Mahlon and Chilion, but it was cheered by the virtue and happiness of Ruth.

Verse 16. – *And Naomi took the child, and laid it in her bosom, and became nurse to it.*

The infants of our race are feeble and helpless beyond most of the young of the animal creation; but divine Providence has not left us without a protector for our years of infancy. *'Why did the knees prevent us? Why the breasts that we should suck?'* Because a gracious God infused maternal love into the hearts of our mothers. Why did we find tender compassions in the breasts of those women who assisted our mothers to rear us up to a firmer age? All the care employed about us in these first years of life, we owe to Him who took us safely from the womb. That love of children which naturally arises in the minds of those who have the care of them, is wisely appointed as a recompense for their pains. Naomi laid the newborn babe in her bosom, and became the nursing mother. She did not reckon it a burden, but a delicious pleasure, to have the care of that precious infant which was now the only remnant of her family.

Some make themselves unhappy, by viewing only the gloomy circumstances of what befals them; and others live content and thankful to Providence, under many adversities, because they view everything in its most favorable light. Naomi's sorrows would have fretted her mind, had she considered the child of Ruth only as the son of a distant relation, by one from whom she once expected heirs to her own family. A peevish woman in her place would have said to herself, This child is my son's only in name; whatever right he may possess to our estate, there is no natural relation between him and Mahlon. But Naomi loved the child, not only for the sake of Ruth and Boaz, but for her son's sake, whose name was called upon him. She expected from him, in maturer years, all that tenderness of regard which a dutiful child can have to his mother, and felt an exquisite pleasure in those painful offices which the feebleness of infancy requires. Such was her attachment to it, that her neighbors spoke of it as if it had been her own child.

Verse 17. – *And the women, her neighbors, gave it a name, saying, There is a son born to Naomi. And they called his name Obed. He is the father of Jesse, the father of David.*

It belonged to the parents to give new-born children their names. The first child born into the world received his name from his mother. John Baptist received his name from his father, when other friends wished to give him a different name. Jesus received his name from both his real and supposed parent, by the direction of an angel. The neighbors of Naomi gave a name to the child that was born to her, and both she and the parents acquiesed in their wishes. It adds greatly to the pleasure of life, when neighbors are real friends, and when the freedoms of friendship are taken kindly on both sides.

Obed signifies a servant. The reason why they gave this name to the child seems to have been, that they hoped he would cherish Naomi, and be obedient to her will in all things as a servant. Children ought to serve their fathers all the days of their life; and in childhood especially they ought to honor and be ready to serve, not only their parents, but other friends of mature age. Little hope is to be entertained of those pert children, that will rather do what they please than what they are commanded or required to do, by those to whom nature has given authority over them. The women of Bethlehem could not believe that the son of Boaz and Ruth would be one of those unnatural children, who refuse to their parents, immediate or remote, that honor to which they are entitled. *'The eye that despises his father, and refuses to obey his mother, the ravens of the valley shall pick it out, and the young eagles shall eat it.' 'Honor your father and mother,'* and all that stand in the place of parents to you, *'and your days shall be many.'* We have no reason to doubt that Obed fulfilled the hopes of the women of Bethlehem, and the following genealogy gives us reason to think that he lived very long upon the land which the Lord his God gave him:

He is the father of Jesse, the father of David. If there is no omission of names in the following genealogy, Obed's grandfather was one of the princes who came into the promised land with Joshua; and his grandson, David, lived within four years of the time when the temple of Solomon began to be built. We are told, 1 Kings 6, that the temple began to be built four hundred and eighty years after the coming up of the children of Israel from the land of Egypt. Four hundred and thirty-six years must, therefore, have intervened between the entrance into Canaan, when Nahshon, the father of Salmon, was dead, and the death of David, who was the fifth from him in descent.

Verses 18-22. – *Now these are the generations of Pharez: Pharez fathered Hezron, and Hezron fathered Ram, and Ram fathered Amminadab, and Amminadab fathered Nahshon, and Nahshon fathered Salmon, and Salmon fathered Boaz, and Boaz fathered Obed, and Obed fathered Jesse, and Jesse fathered David.*

As this genealogy terminates in David it appears to have been written in his time. Although he was anointed with holy oil, he was not ashamed to have it known that his great grandmother was a Moabitess, and that she had once been a gleaner of corn after the reapers. The family of David was of princely extraction, and yet several of them seem to have been remarkable for their humility. Salmon married Rahab the Canaanitess. We have seen how Boaz married a poor Moabitess, and was content with the name of Obed for his son. David was the greatest and best of them all, and no less eminent for his humility than for his other virtues. *'What am I, and what is my father's house, that you have brought me hitherto?'*

From this pedigree of David, we may guess for what reason he committed his father and mother to the king of Moab. Jesse's grandmother was a Moabitess. It is not, however, probable that his parents were well treated by that prince. When he was forced out of the land of Israel, he chose rather to go to Gath, whose mightiest champion he had killed, than to go to the land of Moab.

Ruth not only became a mother in Israel, but the mother of the best and greatest men in Israel. I question whether there ever was a line of kings of whom such a large proportion were both good and great men as the line of David.

Infidels have no just pretence for alleging that it was impossible there could be so few generations as five between the departure from Egypt and the building of the temple, at the distance of four hundred and eighty years. The life of man was, indeed, shortened before the days of David, and even from the time of Moses, to its present period. What then? *'Is the arm of the Lord shortened?'* He can, if he pleases, give as many years to us as to Methuselah. It is very probable that many of our Lord's ancestors were eminent for corporeal vigor and longevity as well as for better qualities.

But how are infidels sure that there were no more generations than five? Five only are mentioned here and in other places of Scripture, where we find the names of these illustrious men. But it is well known that the Jews did not reckon themselves under any necessity to omit no names in their genealogical tables. Four kings are omitted in Matthew's genealogy of our Lord. I mention their dignity as an evidence that the evangelist, although he had not been infallibly guided by the Holy Ghost, could not be ignorant of their history and lineage.

It was the glory of Ruth to have David, *'the man who was raised on high, the anointed of the God of Jacob, the sweet singer of Israel,'* mentioned among her descendants. The lineage of this good woman here ends in this greatest and best of kings; this eminent pattern set before all kings that are blessed with the knowledge of God, for their model.

But it is a far greater glory that we find not only her husband's name, but her own, expressly mentioned among the ancestors of our Lord. A rich recompense was given her by the Lord God of Israel, under whose wings she came from the land of Moab to trust. Yet we have no reason to envy her glory among mothers. We are related to Jesus by a more endearing and a closer connection, if we do the will of his Father. *'He that does the will of my Father which is in heaven, the same is my mother, and sister, and brother.'*

INTRODUCTION
TO
DISCOURSES ON ESTHER.

Every word of God is precious. Let no man, therefore, pretend that there are some parts of the Bible from which he can derive little instruction. The blame is in yourselves, if you do not find treasures more precious than gold, in that inexhaustible mine of sacred knowledge, the Holy Scripture.

But you will perhaps say, We find little mention of the name or attributes of God, and still less mention of Christ and of salvation, in some books, or portions of books, in the Old Testament. In the whole book of Esther, for instance, the name of God does not once occur. Can that book come from God, or give us instruction in the knowledge of Him, that does not once make mention of his name?

The first question here to be considered is, Whether we have any good proof that this book is a book of God? If we have not, let us hold it only in that estimation which it appears to us, after reading it, to deserve. If we have, we ought to be assured, that it is *'profitable for doctrine, for reproof, for correction, for instruction in righteousness;'* and, in short, that it is every way worthy of its divine Author, and of the gracious design for which he causes his Word to be published to the sons of men.

That it is divinely inspired, you know and confess. You have the same reason, indeed, for believing that it comes from God, that you have for believing the divine inspiration of the other books of the Old Testament. To the Jews, says Paul, were committed the oracles of God. From the Jews, who lived in the days of Christ and of his apostles, we are authorized to receive as authentic whatever books were acknowledged by their church as parts of the divine oracles. They have put into our hands the book of Esther, as well as the books of Moses: And although some have pretended, that the Jews treat this book with less respect than their other Scriptures, because the name of God is not found in it; yet learned men, better informed on the subject, assure us, that no book of Scripture, after the books of the lawgiver, is held in higher estimation by the Jews, than the book of Esther.

Is the name of God not in this book? If *'the wonderful works of God declare his name to be near;'* it is written in large characters in the book of Esther; which gives us an account of one of the most wonderful interpositions of God in ancient times, for the salvation of his people.

Is the name of our Lord Jesus Christ not to be found in this book? Are we not taught very plainly by Moses, and the prophets who followed him, that the Son of God, the Angel of his presence, in whom his name is, was the Saviour of Israel in every age? (Exod. 3:2,6,15; Gen. 48:15,16; Psalm 68:17-20; Compare Eph. 4:8-10). Was he not, then, the Author of the great deliverance wrought for his people in the days of Esther? and do we not learn the glory of his grace, and wisdom, and power, from this work of his hand?

For what end did God cause his ancient oracles to be written? Asaph informs us, (Psalm 78:5-8). And do we find any of the books of the Old Testament better fitted for the important purpose there mentioned? Do we not learn from this book, if we are not absolutely unteachable, to *'set our hope in God, and not to forget the works of God, but to keep his commandments?'*

But let us read this book with attention. Let us consider the instructions plainly conveyed in it to our minds. Let us meditate upon the glorious works recorded in it. Let us supplicate God to open our eyes, that we may see the wonderful things of his law. Then shall we know whether this book is from God or not. In the mean time, we need not trouble ourselves with the question, Why the name of God is not to be found, in the letters of it, in this book? It is found in it in such a form, as will strike with admiration, and inspire with holy affections, all who have learned that *'the Lord is known by the judgments which he executes.'*

DISCOURSE I.

AHASUERUS'S FEAST.

CHAPTER 1:1-9.

Verse 1. – *Now in the days of Ahasuerus (this is the Ahasuerus who reigned from India even to Ethiopia, over an hundred and twenty-seven provinces),*

It is the opinion of those who seem to have considered the matter with most attention, that the Ahasuerus here mentioned was Artaxerxes Longimanus, one of the most humane and most prosperous of the kings of Persia, of a quite different character from the Ahasuerus spoken of in the fourth chapter of the book of Ezra.

This prince was lord of a great part of the world. He reigned over an hundred and twenty-seven provinces, some of them large enough to have made powerful kingdoms. What rich gifts has God often bestowed on men who know him not! Think not, however, that God is more liberal to his enemies than to his friends. Some of the vilest of men possessed all the great and large dominions of the Persian empire. But if God has bestowed on you the least measure of true faith, of unfeigned love, of unaffected humility, he has bestowed on you treasures of inestimably greater value than all the possessions of Artaxerxes Longimanus, or of Nero. It would be unreasonable and impious to think, that his donations to such men as the last mentioned prince, the disgrace of thrones, could bear any proportion in value with his gifts to the poorest and meanest of the objects of his special love. The richest of earthly blessings are but curses to those who are not enabled to make a good use of them. Some of the objects of the love of God in Christ Jesus are naked, and destitute of daily food, till they are supplied by the hand of charity; but they are *'blessed with all spiritual blessings in heavenly things in Christ.'*

Ahasuerus reigned from India even to Ethiopia: A vast extent of country, much larger than the dominions of David or Solomon, when they reached *'from the river to the ends of the earth,'* or of the land. Why, then, did God so often speak of the vast extent of dominion given to these princes, as a testimony of his special favor, when he has given much larger dominions to many who did not call on his name? The extent of the dominions of David and Solomon was a pledge of his kindness to them, as kings of his own people, to whom God showed forth his covenant-faithfulness, not only in giving them the large inheritance promised to their fathers, but in making them *'the head, and not the tail,'* among their neighbors. David and Solomon were blessed in the great extent of their dominions, because the sphere of their usefulness and virtues was thereby enlarged. A curse is mingled with all the prosperity of sinners, because they know not how to use or to enjoy, but are disposed, by their corrupt tempers, to abuse everything which they possess. But it is chiefly to be observed on this subject, that the extent of the dominion given to David and Solomon is to be considered as a shadow of the vast extent of dominion which was to be given to the true Son of David, whom all people, and nations, and languages, were to obey. Ahasuerus reigned from India to Ethiopia. David, in the person of his glorious Son, was to be *'the head of all the heathen.'* of all the nations *'from the rising of the sun to his going down.'*

Verses 2, 3. – *That in those days, when king Ahasuerus sat upon the throne of his kingdom, which was in Shushan the palace, in the third year of his reign, he made a feast unto all his princes and his servants. The power of Persia and Media, the nobles and princes of the provinces, were before him:*

This prince did not sit quietly on the throne of his kingdom in the beginning of his reign. By the wicked artifices of Artabanus, who had killed his father, he was persuaded to kill his own brother, Darius; and he was under the necessity of disputing the throne with another brother, whom he subdued, after detecting and punishing the wickedness of Artabanus, who wished to destroy him, and seize his throne. When he obtained the peaceable and secure possession of his throne and kingdom, he made a feast, that his princes and servants might rejoice with him.

'A feast is made for laughter:' And we do not blame the prince for calling his ministers and princes to celebrate a festival on an occasion happy for himself, and for his kingdom. Yet it would have been more honorable for him to have feasted less, and to have testified his joy in thanksgivings to Him *'by whom kings reign;'* and at the same time his grief, that the death of two brothers should have been found or supposed necessary to his own security, and to the peace of the empire. It can scarcely be supposed, that a prince so humane would ever entirely forgive himself for the death of his elder brother, when he found that there was not the least ground for those reports which induced him to consent to his destruction. *'But the heart knows its own bitterness;'* and often the policy of the great obliges them to conceal it under the appearance of joy.

Verse 4. – *When he showed the riches of his glorious kingdom and the honor of his excellent majesty many days, a hundred and eighty days.*

Many days, even an hundred and eighty days! What intolerable feasting was this! Did not the king see that he was turning a pleasure into a burden too heavy to be borne? Who would not rather be condemned to work in the gallies for a whole year, than to perpetual feasting for the half of that time? Solomon said in his heart, *'Go to now, I will prove you with mirth; therefore enjoy pleasure.'* But (possibly before half a week elapsed) he said, *'This also is vanity.'* He *'said of laughter, It is madness; and of mirth, What does it?'* I believe all those princes, who had the honor to partake of Ahasuerus's feast, said so in their hearts, whatever language flattery might dictate to their lips.

Epicurus himself, who placed happiness in pleasure, enjoined temperance as a necessary means of pleasure. An author of our own nation justly observed, that, when a great multitude of alluring dishes are set upon a table, a wise man may see palsies, apoplexies, and other grievous or mortal distempers, lurking among them. What disorders of the head, of the stomach, of the bowels, of the spirits, must have been the effect of an half year's gormandizing and drunkenness (for the Persians piqued themselves in their strength to drink wine, and mingle strong drink)! Dearly did they pay for their entertainment.

Poor men, who are unable to provide for themselves any thing beyond the bare necessaries of life, are apt to envy those who have it in their power to fare sumptuously every day. Be persuaded, if you desire to be content with your condition, that happiness does not lie in the abundance of the things which a man possesses, or in the rich entertainments which he is able to furnish out for himself or his friends. A person of quality[1] observes in his works, that *'the rich, if they do not in many things conform to the poor, particularly in temperance (sometimes even abstinence) and labor, will be the worse, and not the better, for their riches.'* This remark he makes as the result of his own large compass of observation; for he had been frequently in foreign countries, and had an extensive acquaintance with the great. Could not Jesus have furnished out as elegant an entertainment for those whom he fed by miracles, as Ahasuerus to his noble guests? And yet he fed them only with barley-loaves and fishes. Could not God have brought wine, as easily as water, out of the rock for the refreshment of his people?

But, do you think that you would be really happy. if you were admitted to a banquet as rich, and of as long continuance, as that of Ahasuerus? Well, you shall have a feast far richer, and of far longer continuance, if you will believe the words of Solomon, and follow his directions: *'He that is of a merry (or cheerful) heart, has a continual feast.'* *'Wisdom has builded her house, she has hewn out her seven pillars, she has slain her oxen, she has mingled her wine.'* Surely the feast which wisdom has provided, the eternal, the personal Wisdom of God, is as much richer than this magnificent feast of Ahasuerus, as the heaven is higher than the earth. True, you will say; of this there can be no doubt: but where are the happy men that are invited to this feast? – You are invited. You shall partake of this precious entertainment, if you do not turn a deaf ear to the voice of the eternal Word: *'Whoso is simple,'* says the Wisdom of God, *'let him turn in hither: Come, eat of my bread, and drink of the wine which I have mingled;'* (Prov. 9:4,5).

When he showed the riches of his glorious kingdom and the honor of his excellent majesty. – Poor man! little did he know wherein true riches, and glory, and royalty consisted. Happy were those kings that lived in Solomon's days, and heard his wisdom. If Ahasuerus had enjoyed this advantage, he would have learned, that the land is to be pitied *'whose princes eat in the morning,'* and that the land is happy *'whose princes eat in due season, for strength, and not for drunkenness.'*

It is said of the father of Louis XV. King of France, that when his preceptor one day was speaking of this feast of Ahasuerus, and wondered how the Prince of Persia could find patience for such a long feast, he replied, that his wonder was, how he could defray the expense of it. He was afraid that the provinces would be compelled to observe a fast for it. On another occasion, the same prince said, that he did not understand how a king should taste unmingled joy at a feast, unless he could invite all his subjects to partake; or unless he could be assured, at least, that none of them would go supperless to bed. Had this prince lived to reign, and retained such sentiments, he would have taught his people, by their happy experience, wherein the true glory of a king consists.

Verse 5. – *And when these days had expired, the king made a feast to all the people who were present in Shushan the palace, both unto great and small, for seven days in the court of the garden of the king's palace.*

This generous prince did not despise the poor of his people; but wished them to taste, for once, of his bounty. For small and great, in the royal city, he ordered a feast of seven days to be prepared. All that were wise among them would think seven days enough, or too much, to be spent in eating and drinking. Job thought one day at a time was rather too much than too little, to be employed in feasting. In the days of his sons' feasting, he was afraid that in their mirth they might lose their reverence for God, and provoke him to anger against them; and therefore, while they were eating and drinking, he was praying for them, that they might be preserved from sin. Christ himself sometimes attended feasts in the days of his abode on earth; and therefore it cannot be unworthy of his followers, on proper occasions, to partake of a feast. But, whatever heathens might do, let the followers of Christ endeavor, on festival or on other occasions, to behave as Christ did.

As the king of Persia could not furnish a house for so many guests as were invited to his entertainment, pavilions were prepared for them in the palace-garden.

Verse 6. – *There were white, green, and blue hangings, fastened with cords of fine linen and purple to silver rings and pillars of marble.*

Learned men are not agreed about the exact meaning of the words which we render *'red, and blue, and black marble.'* Certain it is, that every thing on this occasion was suited to the state of the king, and fitted to give high ideas to the people of his riches and magnificence. The guests would reckon themselves happy to be admitted to the view of such splendor, and to take their seats on beds of gold and silver. Yet it is questionable, whether their pleasure would be very great at the end of the first, or of the second day. Every day we behold a more glorious scene in the canopy of the heavens, spread over our heads. The roses and the lilies which adorn our gardens, are more beautiful than any of the productions of art which royal wealth can call forth. *'The earth is full of God's riches. The heavens show forth his glory.'* Those who delight to have their eyes and their minds at once entertained, can be at no loss, though they are far from royal palaces, when the earth displays her beauty, and the stars their glory.

An ancient father, when he first set his foot in Rome, at that time the mistress and the wonder of the world, made this pious observation: *'If an earthly kingdom is so glorious, how glorious must the New Jerusalem be!'* If you account those men happy who were feasted in the royal gardens of Shushan, how blessed must those be, who are admitted to an eternal feast in Christ's Father's house! Gold, and silver, and pearls, are but poor emblems of its celestial splendor.

Verse 7. – *And they gave them drink in vessels of gold (the vessels being different from one another), and royal wine in abundance, according to the state of the king.*

A certain king, asking a philosopher's advice how he should behave, was counselled by him, *'always to remember that he was a king.'* Ahasuerus remembered that he was a king in his feasts. His wine was royal; his wine-vessels were of gold: every thing was *'according to the state of the king.'*

Blessed are they that shall drink new wine with Christ in his Father's kingdom! Every thing there is according to the state of the King of kings. His entertainments are worthy of his infinite grandeur and love. If all wise princes make it their rule to be like themselves in every thing they do, it is not to be feared that God will ever deny Himself.

Verse 8. – *And the drinking was according to the law. No one compelling, for so the king had commanded all the officers of his house that they should do according to every man's pleasure.*

None was compelled to drink less or more than he pleased. The king's officers had positive orders to leave all his guests, poor or rich, to please themselves in the quantity and quality of the wine. This heathen prince behaved better than many Christian landlords; if we can call those men Christians, who tyrannize over the will and consciences of their guests, by forcing them to make themselves brutes, and to expose themselves to the damnation of hell. Are not men made brutes, when they are compelled, by importunate solicitations, to drink away their reason? Is not drunkenness one of those *'works of the flesh which bring the wrath of God on the children of disobedience'*? What Habakkuk says to the king of Babylon, in figurative language, is true in the literal sense: *'Woe to him that gives his neighbor drink, that puts your bottle to him, and makes him drunk also, that you may look on their nakedness;'* (Hab. 2:15).

Wise men will not be forced by any consideration to eat or drink more than the laws of temperance allow. They will not be teazed to destroy their own health, or their souls, by drinking the healths of the greatest men in the nation. The man who would compel them to wound their own souls, by sinning against God, they will view in no better a light than a barbarian, who puts a sword into their hands, and requires them to sheathe it in their own bowels.

It was the law of the Persians, that no man should be compelled to drink more than he pleased; and the king ordered this law to be observed in his feast. Did an absolute prince pay such regard to the laws of his country, and to the liberty of his subjects? and shall not Christians pay an equal regard to the laws of their religion? Are these laws less obligatory upon us at feasts, than on other occasions? Shall we requite the liberal Giver of all good things with insults on his authority, at the very time our table is covered by his bounty? No; in eating and drinking, and in every thing we do, we should remember the chief end of man.

In one thing we ought to go farther than the Persian prince. He would suffer no man to be compelled to drink: We should allow no man to drink too much in our houses without compulsion; otherwise, we are accessory to the guilt and ruin of our neighbor. If we saw him, through heedlessness, in danger of falling over a precipice, and breaking his neck, would we not reckon it an act of charity to hold him back by force? If we saw him about to swallow some deadly poison, would we not seize upon the vessel which contained it, and cry aloud to him to do himself no harm? Perhaps we may be made the song of fools for refusing to drunkards the means of gratifying their intemperate appetites. But better to be the song of fools, than to offend God by neglecting to strive against sin. If we exercise liberality when it is our duty, we are in no danger of being reputed misers for exercising our authority in our own houses, in matters wherein it ought to be exerted.[1]

Verse 9. – *Also Vashti the queen made a feast for the women in the royal house which belonged to king Ahasuerus.*

The king did not grudge to his queen, and to the women of Shushan, the pleasures which he allowed to himself and to his male subjects, as far as they could be enjoyed without indecency. It would have been dangerous to morals, and inconsistent with received usages, for the queen and the ladies of Shushan to have associated with the other sex in their banquet; but they had a feast by themselves, in which they doubtless respected the laws of decorum and temperance.

It has been justly accounted an instance of grievous tyranny among the nations of the East, that the women are excluded from society with men. But every thing may be carried to excess. How many mischiefs does the unrestrained intercourse of the sexes occasion in many public diversions! Let not women be locked up in their chambers, as if they were criminals that must be held under close restraint; but let them not use their liberty for an occasion to the gratification of idleness, or a spirit of dissipation. Let them beware of that society that would corrupt their morals, or stain their character. Let them keep at a distance from those scenes of riot and festivity, where *'foolish talking and jesting, which are not convenient,'* are likely to be heard. They are not obedient to Christ, speaking by his apostles, if they are not *'keepers at home,'* and if *'shamefacedness and sobriety'* are not better *'ornaments'* in their estimation *'than gold, and pearls, and costly array.'*

DISCOURSE II.

THE DISOBEDIENCE AND DIVORCE OF VASHTI

CHAPTER 1:10-22.

Verses 10,11. – *On the seventh day, when the heart of the king was merry with wine, he commanded Mehuman, Biztha, Harbona, Bigtha, and Abagtha, Zethar, and Carcas, the seven officers who served in the presence of Ahasuerus the king, to bring Vashti the queen before the king with the royal crown, in order to show the people and the princes her beauty – for she was beautiful to look upon.*

'Wine is a mocker, strong drink is raging; and whosoever is deceived by it is not wise.' Ahasuerus formerly behaved like a king. His wine, and the vessels in which it was drunk, were royal, according to the state of the king; but now his behaviour is like one of the vain fellows. He boasts of the extraordinary beauty of his wife. In defiance of the laws of decency, he will now have her brought into a drunken assembly of princes and peasants for a public show. What is it that has thus degraded the great king? An honest peasant, that knows how to guide his affairs, and to govern his family with discretion, is more truly royal than Ahasuerus, exposing his shame before his people. Wine has transformed him from a king to a clown, or something below a clown. It is said, that the Spartans used to compel their slaves to intoxicate themselves, that they might show them in their cups to their children, and thus produce in their minds a perpetual detestation of this worse than beastly vice. You have no occasion to bring drunken men into the presence of your children. Scripture gives you pictures of this vice, sufficient for your admonition and theirs. It is plain, from the instance before us, that a sober slave is more respectable than a drunken king.

'The crown of the wise is their riches; but the foolishness of fools is folly.' The foolishness of rich and great fools is folly in its exaltation. The great king sends not a menial servant on the foolish business of bringing Vashti before him; but he sends seven of his high lords, in all the pomp of state, to conduct the queen; and she must come with the crown-royal upon her head, that not only Vashti, but royalty itself, might be disgraced in her person, when she was made a gazing-stock to the people with her royal ornaments.

She was beautiful to look upon; – and all the princes and the people must, for once, be gratified with a sight of her charms, that they might admire the king's happiness in the possession of such unrivalled beauty. Vain man! Did he not know, that the most glorious beauty of the human face is but a fading flower? Still less did he know, that this beauty, in a day's time, would be no longer his property, and that he would lose the possession of it by his own folly. Let those who have wives, however beautiful, be as though they had them not; for the fashion of this world passes away.

Verse 12. – *But the queen Vashti refused to come at the king's command by his officers. Therefore the king was very angry, and his anger burned within him.*

Learn from this part of the history, that *'favor is deceitful, and beauty is vain; but a woman that fears the Lord, she shall be praised.'* A beautiful woman, destitute of virtuous principles, will, by the frowardness of her temper, and her rebellion against those whom she is bound to obey, discover a soul more deformed by pride and selfishness, than her body can be beautified by nature and art combined: but a woman that fears the Lord will cultivate humility and self-denial. She will show a ready disposition to give honor and obedience to whom honor and obedience are due; because she makes the will of the Lord the rule of her conduct.

Vashti had good reason to beg to be excused from appearing in a company where too many were merry with wine; and it is probable, that if she had sent her humble request to the king to spare her modesty, he might have recalled his orders. The king's word was not, like the laws, sealed with the king's seal. But Vashti gave a flat and unqualified refusal to the king's orders, announced by his honorable princes. She very probably thought she was supporting the decorum of her sex. But in the judgment of the king's wisest counsellors, she was exposing herself by her disobedience to just punishment; and she was really acting under the influence of pride, covered with the appearance of modesty. The king's command was foolish; but her disobedience was not wise. She was in no danger of being insulted by indecent words, or wanton glances, in the presence of her royal husband, whose frown was death to his subjects. She thought she was supporting the honor of her sex. But did she not see that she was affronting her husband, and her king, not only before his chamberlains, but before all his people? If he suffered his own family to trample upon his authority, his respectability among his other subjects must have been greatly lessened. The queen is the first subject in the kingdom; she ought, therefore, to go before all the other subjects, in showing a becoming deference to the king's pleasure. In like manner, the wives of other men who have servants or children to govern, are utterly inexcusable, if they do not, by such obedience as is required from wives, render the authority of their husbands respected in the family. This is a matter of such importance, that Paul will not allow those men to be chosen to rule in the church, who have not the power to govern their own houses: *'For if a man,'* says he, *'know not how to rule his own house, how shall he rule the church of God?'*

I will not come, said Vashti; and all the persuasions of the great men sent to conduct her could not prevail upon her to give satisfaction to the king. She is too often imitated by women who have promised obedience to their husbands. They will allege, that the meaning of their promise was, that they were to obey their husbands in all reasonable things. If by reasonable things they meant things in which they could give obedience with a good conscience, the limitation would be very proper. But a more frequent meaning which they have for the expression is, things which please their own humors. If these only are the matters in which they are disposed to yield obedience, the promise ought never to have been made; for whenever they conform themselves to their own humor, rather than to the known will of their husbands, they break a solemn promise; and thus, in the course of their lives, heap guilt upon guilt by many violations of the covenant of their God.

Let us not, however, overlook another observation suggested by the words before us, for the admonition of husbands. If they expect due obedience from their wives, let them be always reasonable in their commands; otherwise, half the guilt of the disobedience of their wives will remain with themselves. You see, that all the authority of the greatest king in the world could not make Vashti obedient to a foolish command. She will rather encounter the king's wrath; and *'the wrath of a king is like messengers of death.'* She will rather risk the loss of her royal dignity, than come into a drunken company, at the order of Ahasuerus himself. Never impose a burden upon your wife, which either female delicacy, or her particular temper, which you ought to know, will render too heavy for her to bear.

Therefore the king was very angry, and his anger burned in him. – He was confounded and shocked at the unexpected disappointment. He hoped to show to all his princes and people in Shushan how happy he was, and only showed them his misery. He boasted of his wife's beauty; and she showed how little respect she entertained for her husband and her king. When he expected the readiest obedience. he met with avowed rebellion. The person most indebted to him in all his dominions, was the first to set an example of opposition to his will.

Let husbands and wives remember, that there are no persons in the world from whom they have received more decisive testimonies of esteem and affection, than from one another; and therefore, that there are no persons from whom any instances of disrespect will be taken in worse part, unless they have obtained a great command of their temper. Husbands! provoke not to anger your wives, who have placed such confidence in you, that they have given you themselves. Wives! do not dishonor those husbands, who have chosen you from among all the rest of your sex, to commit to you the care of their comfort and their honor.

Beware of being too easily provoked by the behavior of your husbands or wives. They have not treated you, you say, as they ought to have done. It may be so. But, perhaps, if you duly consider your own conduct, you may find that a part of the blame is your own. Was Vashti ever wont to treat Ahasuerus as she now did? No. He had never treated her before as he now treated her, and her resentment was kindled at the indecent proposal of being made a spectacle to all the people in Shushan. She could not be justified; but if Ahasuerus had considered how much of the blame lay upon himself, he might have moderated his anger, and turned a great part of it upon himself.

Verse 13. – *Then the king said to the wise men who knew the time for so was the king's manner toward all who knew law and judgment:*

It was good advice given to Augustus Caesar by the philosopher Athenadorus, when he found himself angry never to speak or act under the influence of this passion, till at least he had repeated the Greek alphabet. By the time when he had done so, the philosopher thought his passion would be so far calmed, that his judgment would have liberty to operate. Ahasuerus was wise in taking the advice of his wise men, when his anger burned within him, before he would inflict any punishment on Vashti. He would have acted still more wisely, if he had delayed the matter till his passion was abated, and till he considered how much himself was to blame.

'In the multitude of counsellors is safety,' says Solomon. Not only kings, but also private persons, often need wise counsels, especially when they are hurried away by their passions. But our loss is, that at such times we are more unfit than usual to receive counsel. Anger has been justly said to be a short madness; and yet we never think ourselves so wise as when this fit of madness is upon us.

Every man is not fit to be a counsellor. Ahasuerus took advice with his wise men, who knew the times, and who knew laws and judgment. *'Times'* sometimes signify the events that fall out in different periods; (1 Chron. 29 ult.) Those who in this sense know the times, are eminently fit to give good counsel, because, from what has been, and from what has been done, we may form a good conjecture of what is likely to be, or to be done; (Eccles. 1:9,10). But by men that know the times, it will perhaps be better to understand those who know what is fit to be done on any occasion. The princes of Issachar, in the days of David, are said to have been *'men who knew the times, what Israel ought to do.'* No kind of knowledge is more important than the knowledge of the times, and of the duties proper to them. *'Because man knows not his time,'* says Solomon, *'he is like fishes taken in an evil net, and like birds caught in a snare, when it falls suddenly upon them.'* Our Lord greatly laments the ignorance and inconsideration which made the people of Judea, in his days, careless about the signs and the duties of the times. *'O that you had known, you at least, in this your day, the things that belong to your peace!'*

For so was the king's manner toward all that knew law and judgment. – It was customary with the king to treat with high respect men of knowledge in the laws, and to consult them in the management of his affairs. Happy is the land that is governed by kings who trust not to their own understanding; who highly respect the laws, and make use of wise men learned in the laws, as their counsellors! Such was Solomon's disposition. Although he was the wisest of men, he had old counsellors, whom he consulted in all his affairs. And it was the folly of his son Rehoboam, by which he brought unspeakable mischief on himself, and upon his people, that he forsook the old counsellors who had stood before his father, and hearkened to those young counsellors, that paid much more regard to their own passions, and the king's, than to laws and judgment.

It was one great loss, however, to the Persians, and to all the heathen nations, that they were unacquainted with the laws of the Bible. There were, doubtless, many good laws among them; but there were bad laws likewise; such as that made by Darius, that no god or man (save the king only) should have any supplication presented to him, for the space of thirty days. It was the distinguishing advantage of the people of God, that their laws were the perfection of wisdom; (Duet. 4:6-8). Let us make the laws of God the subject of our meditation day and night; so shall we attain more true wisdom, than the wisest heathen sages by a thousand years of the most diligent study. The laws of the Bible will direct our own feet in the paths of peace, and enable us to give the best counsels to our neighbors. *'Have I not written to you,'* says one of the inspired writers, *'excellent things in counsels and knowledge, that I might make you know the certainty of the words of truth; that you might answer the words of truth to them that send unto you?'*

Verse 14. – *and the next to him was Carshena, Shethar, Admatha, Tarshish, Meres, Marsena and Memucan, the sevan princes of Persia and Media, who saw the king's face and who sat the first in the kingdom*

The kings of Persia did not allow themselves to be seen by their people promiscuously. They wished to be accounted superior to other mortals, and would not put themselves on a level with the rest of mankind, by exposing themselves to the eyes of the multitude. Thus they gratified their pride at the expense of their happiness and usefulness. They could not enjoy the comforts of society, nor procure the information which they needed, of the state of their subjects and kingdom, while they secluded themselves from their people.

But there were seven princes of Persia and Media who had a right by law to see the face of their sovereign. It was highly necessary that these men should exceed their fellow-subjects in wisdom, from whom the king was to receive the greatest part of his information, and by whose counsels he was to regulate his measures. But it cannot be reasonably supposed, that the happiest selection should always be made of men intrusted with such privileges. Those who wish to raise themselves above the rank of mortals, are likeliest of all others to fall below it. Few men in Persia were likely to know less of the real state of the kingdom, than a king whose grandeur rendered him inacessible to the greater part of his subjects.

Verse 15. – *What shall we do to the queen Vashti according to law, because she has not done the commandment of the king Ahasuerus, by the officers?*

Inflamed as the king was with rage, he wishes not to inflict any punishment upon the queen, but such as the laws warranted. Absolute princes, in their anger, commonly make their will their law; but this humane prince makes the law his will. The laws of kingdoms may be unjust; but it is far better to be governed by fixed laws, than by the capricious wills of men.

This pagan prince sets us in some degree an example for the government of our passions. In the heat of his rage, he seeks advice, according to the laws. Are you angry at your wife, or at any body else? Before you give vent to your displeasure, inquire what you may do to the offender, not according to the dictates of your anger, but according to the laws. The laws of Persia might mislead Ahasuerus, although they were less likely to do so than his own passion. You have for your direction the law of Christ, which cannot mislead you. Do you ask, what ought to be done, according to this law, to a disobedient wife? Endeavor to reclaim her in the spirit of meekness. It does not permit you to banish her from your bed and house. It requires you still to love her as your own body; to temper all your admonitions with love; and to overcome evil with good.

Verse 16. – *And Memucan answered before the king and princes, Vashti the queen has not only done wrong to the king, but also to all the princes, and to all the people who are in the provinces of the king Ahasuerus.*

There is one malignant circumstance in open sins, which is not generally considered to the extent it deserves; what is the influence which our conduct is likely to have upon other persons? Are there many who are likely to follow our example? then we must share in their guilt. We are their tempters to sin. You know under what infamy the name of Jeroboan, the son of Nebat, lies, because he made Israel to sin. *'Woe to the world,'* says our Lord, *'because of offenses! Offenses must needs come; but woe to that man by whom the offense comes!'*

Vashti's offense was likely to be hurtful to all the princes and people of all the great and large dominions of King Ahasuerus. So extensive might the influence of the queen's example be expected to prove. The great are under strong obligations to be circumspect. The greater they are, the greater will the influence of their good or bad behavior be, and therefore, if they behave ill, their grandeur will be the occasion of their greater condemnation. Yet, let not persons of a low rank in life conclude that they may take liberties to themselves which their superiors ought not to take. We have all our sphere of influence. If we are possessed of Christian charity, we will endeavour to do good to all, and hurt to none; (Rom. 13:10).

Verse 17. – *For this deed of the queen shall become known to all women, so that their husbands shall be despised in their eyes, and it shall be reported that the king Ahasuerus commanded Vashti the queen to be brought in before him, but she did not come.*

It has been observed by heathen authors, that all the world regulates itself by the example of the king. It is to be lamented that the maxim holds too much even among Christians, who have an infinitely better model for their behavior than the example of princes. If any man says that he is a Christian, he says that he abides in Christ; and *'if any man says that he abides in him, he ought himself to walk even as He walked.'* And yet, how common is it for those who call themselves Christians, to be conformed to this world, and to think that they can never degrade themselves, if they follow the example of the great! Read carefully the history of the bad kings of Israel and Judah, whose example their people followed. Did God count it any extenuation of their abominable indolatries, that their kings led the way in their wickedness? *'Ephraim was oppressed and broken in judgment, because he willingly walked after the commandment,'* and after the example, of his princes. The Jews, in a subsequent period, brought calamities upon themselves, greater than any nation had ever suffered, because they followed the example of their rulers in crucifying Jesus, and rejecting his gospel. We are ready to follow the bad examples of others, chiefly in those evil things to which we are most prompted by our own prevailing corruptions. Submission to those whom God has placed over us, is a duty not pleasant to our corrupt natures. Our pride continually tempts us to raise ourselves to an equality with our superiors. For this reason we see so many undutiful sons, so many disobedient wives. And those who do not willingly subject themselves to their superiors, are glad to find examples to patronize them. If queen Vashti refused obedience to her husband, why might not the ladies of Persia and Media refuse subjection to their husbands also? And if both the queen and inferior ladies refused this subjection, why might not women of low rank follow an example so gratifying to their love of independence? Can any husband in the king's dominions expect greater submission from his wife than the king himself?

Verse 18. – *The ladies of Persia and Media shall say the same unto all the king's princes who have heard of the deed of the queen. So there shall be too much contempt and wrath.*

The ladies of Persia and Media shall say the same. – The king's nobles and princes trembled for their own dignity and authority. They dare not trust the good sense of their wives, but expected that Vashti's disobedience would by all of them be made a pretext for disobedience to themselves. Their fears were probably too just. What could be expected from women held in the chains of ignorance and slavery, as the women of the East generally were, but that they would embrace every opportunity and seize every pretext, for disentangling themselves from their fetters? Better things may be expected from women in our land, who are trained up in the knowledge of the true religion, and indulged with all reasonable liberty. They ought to know better things than to plead the example of the great, as if it were the rule of their duty. Our gracious queen has always set a good example of conjugal duty; but were it otherwise, what excuse would her example give to those who have been taught, that God requires them to be obedient to their husbands in all things, as the church is unto the Lord? If the great should take the road that leads to damnation, will the sight of their misery in the regions of punishment alleviate our torments? Or will it be any comfort to the damned, that they have for companions in misery those heads that were once encircled with crowns? If so, then it will lessen their torments that they are to be associated with the devil and his angels, for these malignant spirits were once greater than the kings of any land.

So there shall be too much contempt and wrath. – This would be the natural and necessary consequence of wives despising their husbands, that there would be fierce wrath and endless disputes between them. When authority is not acknowledged in a kingdom, there must be wars and seditions without hope of any termination; and when in a family honor is not given to the husband and father, the house is divided against itself, and peace and comfort are banished.

Wives! be obedient to your own husbands, if you value your peace and happiness above the gratification of a foolish unhallowed pride. Think not that you can ever find satisfaction in the indulgence of a perverse, rebellious, and imperious disposition. Your husbands know that you have no title to domineer over them, and must be provoked at that insolence which prompts you to usurp their place. Perhaps they may rather yield to your authority than live in perpetual war, but their tempers towards you will be soured. Their love will be turned into terror and aversion. You will no longer be considered by them as their dear and amiable companions, but as their tyrants. Is it not far better to engage their love, than to be feared by them? You cannot blame them for requiring obedience from you, because you have promised it. But when you require subjection to your government, it is impossible that they should not be aggrieved, when your conduct is so directly the reverse of your promises, and of the known will of God?

Contempt and wrath in families is an evil of such magnitude, that the princes of Persia thought it necessary to use the most vigorous and severe measures to prevent it.

Verse 19. – *If it please the king, let there be a royal command from him, and let it be written among the laws of the Persians and the Medes, so that it may not be changed, that Vashti come no more before king Ahasuerus. And let the king give her royal state unto another who is better than she is.*

What a happy difference is there between the Christian law and the laws of the Persians, if Memucan's advice was conformable to them! It is true, divorce for disobedience might serve the purpose which he had in view. It would greatly strengthen the authority of husbands. But that authority in husbands which is founded in terror, cannot contribute to the happiness of the conjugal life. What pleasure can it give to a man to find that his wife is careful to obey him, because she dares not behave otherwise? Or, why should laws be made to secure the authority of men, by the depression and misery of their wives and daughters? The Christian law, which does not allow of divorce, *'saving for the cause of fornication,'* is acknowledged by the best writers, even of those who little regard the authority of Christ, to be exceedingly conducive to the peace of families. Wives, if they be not very inconsiderate, will see it necessary to submit to that authority from which they cannot be set free but by death: On the other hand, husbands, if they are not fools, will use their authority with mildness, when they know, that if they provoke their wives to give them disgust, by opposition to their will, they must bear all the miseries of a warfare which can be terminated only by the death of one of the parties.

The Persians and most other nations, were careful to support the authority of men over women. But they paid little regard to the rights of women, who have as good a claim to kind usage, as men have to authority. And it will always be found, that where selfishness leads us to maintain our own claims, without any regard to the just claims of others with whom we are connected, the oppressed will find the means, one way or other , of retaliating upon their oppressors. Tyrants may find submission in those who are compelled to be their slaves; but the submission prompted by fear is attended with aversion or discontent. And what man can be happy in seeing misery around him, the fruit of his own lawless pride? Or, what pleasure can he take in the submission of a human creature, whom oppression may provoke to return his injuries by some methods which he cannot forsee nor prevent?

Let Vashti be deposed from her royal dignity, and her royal estate given to another who is better than she is. – In the eyes of Ahasuerus, Vashti was more beautiful than any woman that could have been put in her place; and her beauty was probably the cause of her elevation. But let men who have wives to choose know, whatever they think at present, that they will soon be convinced from experience, that there are qualities in women of far greater importance than a fine set of features, or a blooming complexion. In the married state, that woman who is best disposed to perform her duty will be found the most agreeable companion; and the beauty of her mind will soon render her more lovely to the eye than any outward form would do.

Verse 20. – *And when the king's decree which he shall make shall be published throughout all his empire (for it is great), all the wives shall give their husbands honor, both the great and small.*

This decree was, indeed, likely to inspire all the wives with fear of their husbands. But was it not as likely to make all the husbands tyrants? If the king tyrannizes over the queen in this wide-extended empire, and announces his own example as their model, will not all husbands, great and small, learn to rule their wives with a rod of iron? The wives will, of consequence, be obedient slaves while the eyes of their husbands are upon them, but will not cordially promote their interests and comfort. Let your wives be sharers in your happiness, if you wish that they should contribute to it. Let them be treated with tenderness, if you expect sympathy from them in your distresses. Let not their faults be punished with rigor, until you can say, that your behavior has never tempted them to commit such faults.

Verse 21. – *And the saying pleased the king and the princes. And the king did according to the word of Memucan.*

We do not wonder that the king was pleased with a proposal which gratified his pride and his anger. The princes, too, were pleased with a law which flattered their vanity, and sanctioned their domestic tyranny. Had they been taught to love their neighbor as themselves, no law would have appeared equitable to them which favored the tyranny of the one-half of the human race over the other. It was, indeed, highly proper that the laws should secure the authority of men in their own houses; but this might have been as effectually done by a milder punishment. *'And the king did according to the word of Memucan;'*

Verse 22. – *For he sent letters into all the king's provinces, into every province according to the writing of it, and to every people in their language, so that every man should bear rule in his own house, and that it should be published according to the language of every people.*

Great care is taken by this prince to prevent the bad effects which might result from the disobedience of Vashti. He not only divorces her, but publishes a decree through all his dominions, that every man should bear rule in his own house. He was afraid that a spirit of independence among the female sex would soon spread disorder through the kingdom, if he did not take strong measures to counteract the bad example set by the queen. It is certainly the duty of all princes to do what they can to promote good order in their dominions, and to prevent or suppress every immorality. The safety and honor of a prince is in the virtue, as well as in the multitude, of his people.

So that every man should bear rule in his own house. – This is the law of God, as well as of Ahasuerus. Let every wife willingly submit to the authority of her husband in all lawful things. Consider what miseries you may bring upon yourselves by refusing compliance with that order which God has settled for the peace of families. What did Vashti think of her own conduct, when she lost a royal diadem by one act of disobedience? Did she not curse that pride, which a little before she had considered as an instance of female delicacy?

You cannot lose a diadem by disobedience. Your husbands cannot divorce you; but they can embitter your lives, by their resentment of your conduct. For this reason you ought to behave well in the married state, because nothing but death can dissolve it, and therefore the whole or the best part of your days are likely to be poisoned by discord, if you do not contribute your part to maintain that mutual love which alone can render it happy.

You will not lose a crown of gold by your disobedience; but you may lose a crown more precious than gold. '*The hoary head,*' either in man or woman, '*is a crown of glory, if it be found in the way of righteousness.*' '*A virtuous woman is herself a crown to her husband.*' Whether would you choose to be a diadem of beauty to him, or to be '*rottenness in his bones*'? God grant us peace to behave in such a way, in every situation of life, that some of the wise heathens may not rise up against us to condemn us in the day of Christ!

DISCOURSE III.

EXTRAORDINARY METHOD USED TO SUPPLY THE PLACE OF VASHTI.

CHAPTER 2:1-11.

Verse 1. – *After these things, when the wrath of king Ahasuerus had calmed down, he remembered Vashti and what she had done, and what was decreed against her.*

Absolute kings are envied by their inferiors, because they can do whatever they please, without contradiction. For this very reason they ought to be pitied. A man who may do what he pleases, will often do what will be very displeasing to himself in the recollection. Was Alexander the Great to be envied because his dominions were great, and his power absolute? He did not think so himself, when in his pride and drunkenness he had killed his faithful friend Clitus, and would next have killed himself, if he had not been forcibly restrained. When the fury of Ahasuerus against Vashti was cooled, did he rejoice in that absolute power by which he was enabled so easily to take severe vengeance on her disobedience? Did he not envy persons of a private condition, whose actions are placed under such restraints that they cannot expose themselves to such terrible remorses, as those which have often embittered the days of kings?

When the wrath of king Ahasuerus had calmed down, he remembered Vashti. – He thought upon the happy days he had enjoyed in her society; upon the proofs she had formerly given him of her affection and obedience; upon the folly of his own conduct, which had tempted her, for once, to dispute his orders; upon the cruel punishment inflicted on her: upon the impracticability of reversing the sentence passed against her, upon a thousand circumstances which added to the disgust of his mind. Remorse now punished him almost as severely as his imperious device had punished the unhappy queen.

Verses 2-4. – *Then the king's servants who served him said, Let beautiful young virgins be sought for the king. And let the king choose officers in all the provinces of his kingdom, so that they may gather together all the beautiful young virgins unto Shushan the palace, to the house of the women, unto the hand of Hege the king's officer, keeper of the women. And let their ointments be given to them. And let the young woman who pleases the king be queen instead of Vashti.*

'He that reproves a man shall afterwards find more favor than he that flatters with his lips.' If the king's seven counsellors had advised him to moderate his anger against Vashti, to require and accept from her such acknowledgments of her fault as might have prevented the bad effects of her example, and to suffer her to retain her royal station, he would have thanked them, when his anger was appeased. They seem to have been apprehensive, that when he was restored to himself his anger would be turned upon them. What method must be taken for their security? It would be inconsistent with the fundamental laws of Persia and Media, to restore the degraded queen to her rank. Besides, her vengeance, in case of her restoration, might prove fatal to the authors of her disgrace. On the other hand, the queen's beauty was so highly admired by the king, that he is not likely to forgive the advisers of the divorce, unless he can find a wife equal in beauty. For this reason, his servants (among whom his great counsellors were the chief) advised him, by means of proper offices, to collect all the fairest virgins in the various provinces of his dominions, and to put them under the care of Hege, the officer, to prepare them by proper purification for converse with the king, that he might choose out of them, as his queen, the fairest woman in all his dominions, or (which was the same thing perhaps) in all the world.

This advice appears to us very strange and barbarous. Must the king engross all the beauty of his dominions, by taking to himself, as his queen or concubines, all the beautiful young women that could be found in all his provinces? Are women born for nothing else, but to be the property of any man that can purchase them by his money, or tyrannize over them by his power? Are a thousand of the most beautiful women to become the property and the prisoners of one man? If the king is so fond of female beauty, he should remember that other men feel the same desires, and claim the same right to gratification with himself.

The king's behavior, however, was such as might have been expected in a country where men thought they had a right to multiply wives to themselves, if they had the means of procuring and supporting them. Where no regard is paid to equity and purity of conduct among a people, their prince will naturally think that his power and affluence entitle him to superiority in the inordinate gratification of his sensual appetites. Where reason and the law of God do not set limits to the desires of men, they will be carried beyond all bounds.

How much are we indebted to the Bible for present as well as expected happiness! We learn from it, that God has created one man for one woman. We could not value its discoveries too highly, were it only for the accounts that it gives us of creation, and of the great law of marriage resulting from it. The knowledge of the divine authority of this law, that a man ought to have only one wife, is equally essential to the happiness of both sexes of the human race. Why then do not both men and women resent every attempt made by the enemies of religion to weaken the authority of a book, which so effectually secures the natural rights of the male as well as of the female part of human kind?

The thing pleased the king, and he did so. – He did so, because it pleased him; but he ought to have considered, not only his own wishes, but the laws of justice and equity. He was not blessed with the knowledge of divine revelation; but did not his own heart tell him, that we ought to do nothing to please ourselves that is oppressive to those who are made of the same materials, and have the same feelings with ourselves? If Ahasuerus had not been a king, but a subject, would he have thought it reasonable that kings should inclose all the beautiful women of the country in their seraglios? Would he have thought it reasonable, in that case, that his own sisters, or daughters, should have been immured for life within the walls of a palace, to minister occasionally to the pleasures of a prince, if he should think of sending for them; or to live and die forgotten by their capricious lord?

We enjoy the inestimable advantage of knowing our Lord's will by divine revelation. We are very unworthy of that benefit, if we do what comes into our own minds, or what is suggested to us, merely because it pleases us. The first question with us ought to be, How we are to walk so as to please God? Nothing is a surer sign of reigning depravity, than to prefer the pleasing of our flesh to the pleasing of Him who made us; of him by whom we must be judged at the great day. If we make it our great business to *'fulfil the desires of the flesh and of the mind,'* we *'walk according to the course of this world, according to the prince of the power of the air.'*

Verses 5,6. – *Now in Shushan the palace there was a certain Jew whose name was Mordecai, the son of Jair, the son of Shimei, the son of Kish, a Benjamite; who had been carried away from Jerusalem, with the captivity which had been carried away with the Jeconiah king of Judah, whom Nebuchadnezzar the king of Babylon had carried away.*

The greatest objection against the opinion that Ahasuerus was the same prince who is called Artaxerxes in the books of Ezra and Nehemiah, is taken from this passage, in which Mordecai is said to have been carried captive with Jeconiah king of Judah. If he was then carried captive, he must now have been more than a hundred and fifty years old, although he was afterwards capable of exercising the office of Prime minister to the king of Persia.

It is, indeed, improbable, though not impossible, that Mordecai might live, and be fit for business at this great age. We have often heard of a Countess of Desmond, who lived and enjoyed health for one hundred and fifty years. She lived during the reigns of Edward V. and his successors, to the reign of James I. In the reign of Charles I. John Par lived to the age of one hundred and fifty-two; and, in the following reign, Charles Jenkin to the age of one hundred and sixty-nine. Scripture itself informs us of a man who was a prime minister in the end of his life, although he died at the age of one hundred and thirty years; (2 Kings 12).

But, perhaps, it is more to the purpose to observe, that in the time of Artaxerxes Longimanus, Ezra often speaks of the people of the Jews as if they had been captives in Babylon, although it is certain that very few of them had ever seen that land of captivity. *'Thus were assembled unto me,'* says that inspired historian, *'every one that trembled at the words of the God of Israel, because of the transgression of them that had been carried away captive.'* These words refer to an event that happened in the very year when Esther became queen of Persia, if Ahasuerus was the same with Artaxerxes; and yet the people are said to have been carried away captive. They certainly were not carried away captive in their own persons, but in the persons of their ancestors. Why may we not suppose, that the writer of the book of Esther uses the same mode of expression in speaking of Mordecai?

A still easier solution has been given of this difficulty, by referring what is said in the beginning of the 6th verse, not to Mordecai, but to Kish, his progenitor.

But why was Mordecai in Shushan the palace, when the Lord had turned again the captivity of his people? Why did he not rather reside in the Holy Land, that he might be near the house of the Lord? Was he not of a very different spirit from David, whose great desire was to dwell in the house of the Lord all the days of his life? We cannot, without rashness, condemn the good man for this part of his conduct. Even Daniel continued in Babylon after the proclamation of liberty to the Lord's captives. Both these men, doubtless, loved the habitation of the Lord's house; but they might have reasons which entirely justified their continuance in a foreign land. It was love to the habitation of the Lord that fixed Daniel at a distance from it, where he could perform services to Jerusalem, which he could not have performed at Jerusalem itself. This, too, was Nehemiah's motive for residing at the king's court; and the same, in all probability, was the motive which induced Mordecai to dwell in Shushan.

Verse 7. – *And he brought up Hadassah, that is, Esther, his uncle's daughter. For she had neither father nor mother, and the young woman was fair and beautiful – whom Mordecai, when her father and mother were dead, took for his own daughter.*

Hadassah, otherwise called Esther, was daughter to an uncle of Mordecai. It is uncertain whether she was the immediate daughter, or more remote descendant of Mordecai's uncle, for it is well known that the word *daughter* may, with equal propriety, be taken in either of these senses. She must, at least, have been much younger than Mordecai, who took her not as a companion, or a wife, but as a daughter, her father and mother being dead. He performed a kind and laudable action to this poor orphan; and was well rewarded for it by the gratitude of Esther, and by the liberality of divine providence.

It is lamentable for poor infants, especially of the weaker sex, to be bereaved of both their parents. But, blessed be the Father of the fatherless! they often find friends no less kind, and no less useful, than fathers or mothers. Let young persons deprived of their parents learn to say, '*Though my father and mother both should leave me, the Lord will take me up.*' Esther, through the favor of Providence, was well educated by a cousin; and was advanced to the highest dignity which could be conferred on her sex, although she neither expected, nor perhaps desired it.

Verse 8. – *So when the king's commandment and his order was heard, and when many young women had been gathered together unto Shushan the palace, into the hand of Hegai, Esther was also brought unto the king's house, into the hand of Hegai, keeper of the women.*

Poor Esther, who had been so kindly cherished by Mordecai, was now led away from his house to be the slave, or the beloved wife, of the great king, as his caprice should determine. Her consent was not asked; the consent of Mordecai, her adoptive father, was not asked. They were both slaves to a despotic master. Blame not Esther, therefore, but pity her, when you hear that, like so many other maidens, she was led away to the house of the king's women. Think not that she sets an example of entering into marriage-connections with a partner of a false religion. She was not an actor, but a sufferer. Had she been left to her choice, it is probable she would have chosen the poorest Jew that was faithful to his religion for her husband, in preference to the great king.

Some young women may think it hard to be under the authority of parents, and under the necessity of paying great deference to their counsels in the choice of a husband. Be thankful that you are under the direction of such affectionate friends, rather than under the command of an unfeeling lord. How glad would Esther have been to be left under the direction of her second father! The time has been when, even in England, many young women were under the control of haughty lords, who disposed of them in marriage at their pleasure.

Verse 9. – *And the young woman pleased him, and she received kindness from him. And he quickly gave her the ointments for herself, with such things as were set aside to her, and seven young women who were fit to be given her, out of the king's house. And he moved her and her maids to the best place in the house of the women.*

Esther's singular beauty, her modesty, her unaffected simplicity of dress and behavior, appear to have engaged the affection of all that conversed with her. It was God that gave her these lovely endowments which captivated all hearts. It was God that gave her favor in the eyes of beholders. She was, no doubt, deeply affected with the thought of separation from her beloved father, to be put under the government of strangers, and to enter into involuntary competition with so many beauties for the possession of the king's heart. She was certainly of the temper of the Shunamite who said to Elisha, '*I dwell among my own people;*' but God, for gracious ends, permitted her not to enjoy her wishes. He consoles her, however, by the favor that he gave her in the eyes of the man to whose care she is committed. His respect and attention made the change of her condition less painful to her. Every thing was done for her that she could wish, to make her confinement easy. She had her things for purification given her. She had seven maids given her to wait upon her. She had the best apartments in the house of the virgins. All the presents allowed by the king to his women were readily given her by Hegai with a good grace, and without any means used on her part to obtain them. This favor of the chamberlain might be considered by her as a pledge of the care that divine Providence took of her comfort, and a presage of the favor that she might expect from the king himself, when the year was expired.

Verse 10. – *Esther had not revealed her people, nor her kindred, for Mordecai had commanded her that she should not show it.*

We must never be ashamed of our people, or our kindred, especially when we have the honor to be related to the godly. Yet it may be, on many occasions, a part of prudence to say little or nothing of our connections. We must never be ashamed of our religion, if we desire that Christ may not be ashamed of us at the day of his appearance. Yet there is a time to be silent, as well as to speak, of that blessed name by which we are called. Mordecai knew that many hated the Jews and their religion, and that Esther, by publishing her connection with them, might procure malevolence to herself, without serving the cause of her people. *'A wise man's heart discerns both time and judgment.'*

Esther's obedience to Mordecai is no less worthy of attention and imitation, than Mordecai's prudence. Let young women learn from her to pay a due deference to the instruction of their parents, not only when under their eyes, but when they are removed from them. What miseries to young people might be prevented, what happiness might they enjoy, would they but cease from their own wisdom and humor, and obey those whom God commands them to obey!

Verse 11. – *And Mordecai walked every day in front of the court of the women's house in order to know how Esther did and what was to become of her.*

Mordecai, though the adoptive father of Esther, was not permitted to visit her. How much better are our laws calculated than those of the eastern nations, for the comfort of human life! Let us be thankful for our advantages of free intercourse with our friends, and *'not use our liberty for a cloak of licentiousness.'*

Mordecai did not forget his favorite cousin, when she was taken from him. He took care to be informed daily of her health and welfare. Our friends ought not to be out of our mind, when they are removed from our sight. We may be useful to them by our prayers, and by other means, when we cannot see them. When Paul was distant from the Christians whom he loved, he was always desirous to know their circumstances, and to inform them of his own; (Eph. 6:22).

DISCOURSE IV.

ESTHER MADE QUEEN OF PERSIA – BY HER MEANS MORDECAI DISCOVERS TO THE KING A CONSPIRACY FORMED AGAINST HIS LIFE.

CHAPTER 2:12-23.

Verse 12. – *Now when every maid's turn had come to go in to king Ahasuerus, after she had been twelve months, according to the law of the women (for so the days of their anointing were done – six months with oil of myrrh, and six months with sweet odors, and with other things for the purifying of the women),*

The pleasures of sensuality were carried to the highest excess by those men who ruled over the Persian empire. The women designed for their embraces were obliged to undergo a wearisome purification, to render them the more agreeable to their pampered lords. Their eyes and their nostrils must be at once regaled by the presence of their beauteous companions. Voluptuousness must be turned into an art, and a toil, to gratify their senses. Had they never learned, that they who devote themselves to pleasure destroy it? Moderation in the pleasures of sense is necessary for the enjoyment of them; and those who can relish pleasure only in excess, prepare for themselves satiety, disappointment, or chagrin. If we will not regulate our enjoyments by the laws of God, made known to us by reason, religion, and experience, our pleasures will end in the worst of pains.

Verses 13,14. – *Then indeed the young woman came to the king. Whatever she desired was given her to go with her out of the house of the women to the king's house. She went in the evening, and on the next day she returned to the second house of the women, into the hand of Shaashgaz, the king's officer who kept the concubines. She did not come in to the king any more, unless the king delighted in her, and she was called by name.*

Such was the fate of those wretched beauties that were collected for the king's pleasure. They were gratified with rich presents. They might have what jewels or what ornaments they desired, when they were first admitted to the king's presence. But when they became his concubines, or secondary wives, and were committed to the custody of Shaashgaz, to be held in captivity for life, they were not so much as admitted into the king's presence, unless he was pleased to call them by name. How much better was it to be the wife of a peasant, than to be a concubine to the great king? And the peasant who loves his wife, and is beloved by her, enjoys pleasures which princes who love none but themselves cannot taste.

Verse 15. – *Now when the turn of Esther, the daughter of Abihail the uncle of Mordecai, who had taken her for his daughter, had come to go in unto the king, she asked nothing but what was chosen by Hegai the king's officer, the keeper of the women. And Esther had favor in the sight of all who looked upon her.*

Esther had no wish to set off her beauty by such ornaments. She asked nothing from Hegai, although she had the complaisance to put on the ornaments which he gave her. Vanity very often disappoints itself: and no women are so beautiful in the eyes of beholders, as those that discover the least desire of admiration. Esther obtained favor with her unaffected ornaments in the eyes of Hegai, in the eyes of all beholders, in the eyes of the king himself.

Verse 16. – *So Esther was taken to king Ahasuerus into his royal house in the tenth month, which is the month Tebeth, in the seventh year of his reign.*

For the space of four years Vashti's place was unoccupied. It is not surprising that the king, who divided his love (if it may be called love) among so many women, should so long want a partner to his crown. He knew not the true pleasure of the conjugal life. He discerned, however, other qualities besides beauty, in Esther. He found her mind still more charming than her face.

Verse 17. – *And the king loved Esther above all the women, and she received grace and favor in his sight more than all the virgins. So much so that he set the royal crown upon her head, and made her queen instead of Vashti.*

What a surprising revolution took place in the fortune of this orphan daughter of Abihail! Among so many hundreds of competitors, she could have but a poor prospect of rising above the rank of concubine. But the king was charmed with her beauteous countenance, the indication of a virtuous mind; and set the crown-royal upon her head.

We are not, however, to ascribe this change in her circumstances so much to the king's admiration either of her person or mind, as to the over-ruling providence of God; in whose hand are the hearts of kings, to be more easily turned by him whithersoever he wills, than the rills of water in a field can be turned by the husbandman to water his ground. The same gracious providence which exalted Joseph to be lord over Egypt, that he might be *'the shepherd and stone of Israel,'* raised Esther to the dignity of a great queen, that she might be the protector of the race of Jacob in a time of extreme danger.

While we regret the unmerited fate of Vashti, who was degraded for a pardonable offense; while we deplore the effeminacy of a great king, who was a slave to the love of pleasure, and the unhappy fate of those ladies who were sacrificed to his vanity or lust; let us adore that all over-ruling providence, which managed the vices and weaknesses of the king of Persia in a subserviency to the interests of his despised people, and to the glory of that wisdom by which he brings safety and felicity to his chosen. out of those events which appeared to have no relation to them. *'Our help is in the name of the Lord of hosts, who is wonderful in counsel, and excellent in working.'*

Verse 18. – *Then the king made a great feast unto all his princes and his servants, Esther's feast. And he ordered a release for the provinces, and gave gifts, according to the state of the king.*

The king appears to have taken much delight in feasts. It was well that he did not take delight in something worse. A feast on occasion of his marriage with the accomplished queen whom he espoused, cannot expose him to blame. We find marriage-feasts common among patriarchs and judges in Israel. Jesus himself, and his disciples, attended a marriage-feast, where he performed the beginning of his public miracles. *'A feast is made for laughter;'* and we may partake of it without sin, if we are careful to glorify God in eating and drinking, and in whatever we do.

The king, at the same time, gave a release to the provinces from their usual imposts, and bestowed gifts, according to the state of the king. His heart overflowed with joy at the acquisition of a queen so beautiful, and possessed of so many virtues. He wishes his subjects to rejoice with him; and endeavored, by his liberality on Esther's account, to procure for her the good-will and the blessing of his people. That man must be selfish to an uncommon degree, who can confine his joys to himself. The man of a truly generous spirit would have all around him, if possible, as happy as himself.

Verse 19. – *And when the virgins were gathered together the second time, then Mordecai sat in the king's gate.*

The virgins that had been collected for the king, were first put under the care of Hegai. They were now collected together, as secondary wives, under the care of Shaashgaz, to be left in perpetual solitude, or to be sent for by the king to share his bed, as his humor should direct him. Such was their unhappy condition; and such the condition of Esther would have been, if God had not given her favor in the sight of her lord. Esther was, doubtless, penetrated with gratitude to God, when she considered the condition of her rivals, who were buried alive by a perpetual seclusion from the pleasures of society. And have not the poorest of European women reason to thank the great Disposer of human affairs, when they consider the slavery imposed upon women in the East? How precious are those laws of Christ, *'Let every woman have her own husband – Husbands, love your wives, even as Christ loved the church'*! What happiness has been diffused by them over all those places of the earth, where they have been received as the commandments of the Lord!

Mordecai sat in the king's gate at the time when Esther was made queen, and the other ladies of the king were collected into the house of the concubines. What was Mordecai's office at the king's gate, we cannot precisely say. It was probably not so mean as that of a common porter, nor so high as Mordecai might have expected, if it had been known that he was the queen's adoptive father. But his eyes were not lofty, nor his heart haughty, nor did he seek a great place for himself in the palace. He had even taken measures to prevent the knowledge of his relation to the queen.

Verse 20. – *Esther had not yet revealed her kindred nor her people, as Mordecai had commanded her. For Esther obeyed the command of Mordecai as she did when she was brought up with him.*

Esther was far from being ashamed of her people or of her kindred. She rejoiced more that she was the daughter of Abihail, than in her royal dignity. She was far from being unwilling, when occasion should require it, to solicit needful favors for her people and her kindred, whose welfare, we will afterwards find, was preferred by her to her life. But she did not choose to be needlessly troublesome to the king with her petitions; and, at the same time, she was under restraints by the commandment of Mordecai, who had charged her to say nothing about her kindred or her people.

But did not Esther forget her rank, when she would obey Mordecai as she had done when she was a child? Shall the wife of the great king be held under pupilage upon her throne? Esther is more truly great in the obedience she still yielded to Mordecai, than in the honors conferred on her by Ahasuerus. Her gratitude, her humility, her filial obedience, ennoble her more than a hundred diadems of the brightest gold could have done.

The woman, as well as the man, that enters into the state of marriage, must leave father and mother. But think not that your change of life sets you free from the obligations of honoring your parents, or even of obeying them, as far as obedience to them is compatible with your new duties. You must honor your father as long as he lives; and you must not despise your mother when she is old, and stands in more need than ever of the comforts which she will receive from your attentions.

You that have been left orphans, and have found parents in other friends, are bound, whether in the single or married state, to testify your respect and gratitude to them as if you were their children. In some respects you are more indebted to them than children to their parents. They took you under their protection when you were in a destitute condition, and when they were not constrained by such powerful obligations as natural parents.

Let no change in your condition be a pretext for forgetting the duties you owe either to parents, or to friends who have treated you with the tenderness of parents. Esther, when she was a queen, paid the same deference to Mordecai, as when she was a dependant upon his bounty. Our Lord Jesus Christ was more highly raised above his mother from the very beginning of his mortal life, for he was the Son of God; and yet he was subject to his parents while he lived with them; and when he was upon the cross, provided another son for his mother to comfort her, when he should leave the world.

Verse 21. – *In those days, while Mordecai sat in the king's gate, two of the king's officers, Bigthan and Teresh, of those who kept the door, were angry and tried to lay a hand on king Ahasuerus.*

It was not the design of the writer of this book to give us the history of king Ahasuerus, or of his wicked servants, but to give us the history of a wonderful salvation wrought for God's scattered people. But events of many different kinds are combined, and co-operate under divine direction for accomplishing his gracious purposes to his people. Who would have thought that the conspiracy of Bigthan and Teresh, fatal only to themselves, had any relation to the salvation of Israel? But if their conspiracy had not been formed, it would not have been detected; and by detecting it, Mordecai gained that favor with the king which afterwards proved fatal to the great enemy of Mordecai and of Israel.

Bigthan and Teresh were angry, and tried to lay a hand on king Ahasuerus. – You may envy kings, and think they are more fortunate than other people, because they were born to be great. But greatness ensures neither safety nor happiness. If kings were immortal, when other men must descend to the dust, or if their loyalty would protract their lives to the age of Methuselah, there would be some plausible pretense for looking up to them with an envious eye. But they die like men, although they are honored with the title of gods. They are even exposed to dangers from which men of lower ranks are exempted. The father of Artaxerxes was treacherously destroyed by one of his own servants. One of his descendants and successors was killed by a favorite eunuch, and had his flesh given to the rats. This prince himself, one of the best that swayed the Persian sceptre, had his life sought by the treachery of those who did eat of his bread, and who had doubtless given him many assurances of their attachment to his person and government. The life of European princes, in our time, seems to be less precarious than that of many ancient princes, because their governments are so constituted as to obviate the hopes of ambition in their subjects. Yet, in our own days, we have seen two sovereigns cut off by the hand of violence, and the life of our own sovereign (whom may God long preserve!) exposed to danger from the hands of madmen.[1]

Bigthan and Teresh were angry with king Ahasuerus; and therefore they sought to lay hands on him. Kings are often ill informed of the real disposition of their subjects towards them. Flatterers assure them, that whatever they do pleases all the people; and there are few, or none, that choose to wound their ears with painful truth. But none are more exposed to ill-nature and dislike. It was the saying of Louis XIV. of France, that when he bestowed any office, he made ninety-nine men discontented, and one thankful (meaning the person to whom he gave the office). What were the grounds of the wrath of Bigthan and Teresh, we cannot tell. But in the management of the affairs of a large empire, there must be many things daily done which will awaken the wrath of selfish and ambitious men. What man was ever so fortunate as to dispense a thousand favors, without giving disgust to some of those who did not share in them? and perhaps not less to those who have shared in them; for it is difficult to make a proud man believe that he is respected according to his merits.

Mortify all your corrupt passions, and never let them be suffered to regulate your conduct. How often has the passion of anger involved men in blood and treason! Most justly does our Lord explain the sixth commandment to include the prohibition of anger.

Beware of speaking a word, or entertaining a thought, inconsistent with that high respect which is due to princes; *'for a bird of the air shall carry the voice, and that which has wings will tell the matter.'* Bigthan and Teresh afford but one of many thousands of instances in which the secret thoughts and speeches of traitors have been unexpectedly brought to light, by the providence of him who *'gives salvation unto kings.'*

Verse 22. – *And the thing was known to Mordecai, who told it to Esther the queen. And Esther told the king of it in Mordecai's name.*

We are not told how the thing came to the knowledge of Mordecai. But we know that, whatever was the means, God was the author of the discovery. It was by his good providence that the life of the king was preserved, that he might be useful to the Israel of God. It was by his good providence that Mordecai the Jew was the discoverer of the treason, that the king's favor might be conciliated to Mordecai, and to Esther, and to their people. May we not add, that the wicked designs of these traitors, Bigthan and Teresh, were permitted by the providence of God, that the detection of them might contribute to the advancement of his gracious purposes? He permits no more wickedness to take place, that he knows how to over-rule for good. *'The wrath of man shall praise him, and the remainder of his wrath shall he restrain.'*

As soon as Mordecai came to the knowledge of the plot formed against the king, he took the best measures to prevent its execution, by revealing it to the queen, and by her to the king. If we forbear to deliver those that are drawn unto death, and those who are ready to be slain, we are partners in the guilt of their blood. We are bound especially to contribute our best endeavors, as we have opportunity, to preserve the lives of princes, those ministers of God for good, under whose protection we enjoy life and its comforts. Mordecai was under special obligation, as a servant of his king, who sat at his gate, to be careful of his life. But all the subjects of a king are under powerful obligations to seek and to promote, by all proper means, his life and welfare. Abishai procured to himself great honor, and yet did no more than his duty, when he put his life into his hand, and encountered a mighty giant, to save the life of David.

Esther certified the matter to the king in Mordecai's name. Here she appears to have acted without commandment from him. It was sufficient for Mordecai to do his duty, and to save the king's life, without seeking either praise or reward for a service which he could not neglect without baseness and treachery. But Esther, on the other side, wished not for those rewards and honors from the king which more justly pertained to another She had now an opportunity of recommending to the king's favor her affectionate friend and father, and she did not allow it to pass neglected. Never let us assume to ourselves the praises that belong more justly to another; but let us be ever ready to procure for our friends and brothers those honors and rewards to which they are entitled.

Verse 23. – *And when the matter was searched into, it was found out. Therefore they were both hanged on a tree. And it was written in the book of the chronicles before the king.*

The king Ahasuerus would not by his absolute authority deliver up to punishment even men who had conspired against his life, till he had good proofs of their guilt. Happy would it have been for him and for his subjects, if he had never departed from this principle, that proof should go before punishment. Grievous and dangerous as the crime of idolatry among God's people was, he would not have it punished till proper inquisition was made about the fact; (Deut. 13). What safety can any man enjoy, if accusation is to hold the place of evidence?

Both traitors were hanged. Their punishment was just and necessary, and more moderate than punishments often were among the Persians. Ahasuerus would not allow his enemies to escape vengeance, although he was a humane prince. And think not, you who are enemies and traitors to the Prince of the kings of the earth, that you shall escape the vengeance merited by your wickedness? *'Those my enemies,'* he will say, *'who would not have me to reign over them, bring forth and slay before my face.'* Earthly princes are terrible in their wrath against the enemies of their crown or life; but all that they can do is only to kill the body. The King of heaven has power to kill both soul and body, and to cast both into hellfire.

And it was written in the book of the chronicles before the king. – It was a wise institution in Persia, that secretaries should commit to registers every remarkable action of the king, and every event of his reign. It was a great encouragement to well doing, and a powerful discouragement from evil doing, to know that what was done would not be forgotten. Suppose you knew that a register was kept by some invisible scribe of all that you think, or speak, or act, what manner of persons would you endeavor to be in the exercise of every virtue? Know, then, that none of your actions ever can be forgotten; that even your most secret thoughts are written in durable registers. The Lord hearkens and hears all that is spoken by us. He observes all that we think or do, and a book of remembrance is written before him, which will one day be opened, to the praise of them that do well, and to the confusion of the wicked.

Mordecai was not presently rewarded by the king for the eminent service which he had done him. No matter. It was marked down in the king's register. He may one day find, that it was a good thing patiently to wait the king's time. At present he wanted nothing. The time may come when the king's favor may be more valued by him than life itself. If he had never been rewarded by the king, the testimony of his conscience, and the assurance of divine approbation, were more to him than all that the king could bestow.

It was possible that the king of Persia might forget the services done to him, though they were recorded in his books. But let none of those who perform any services, in the fear of God, to God or to man, to kings or to beggars, be afraid of losing their reward. *'God will not be unrighteous to forget any works or labors of love'* done for the name of his dear Son. *'A cup of cold water given to a disciple shall in no wise lose its reward; and whatever good thing any man does, the same shall he receive of the Lord, whether he is bond or free.'*

DISCOURSE V.

THE ELEVATION OF HAMAN – HIS PRIDE, AND RESOLUTION TO REVENGE FANCIED INDIGNITIES, RECEIVED FROM MORDECAI UPON THE WHOLE NATION OF THE JEWS.

CHAPTER 3:1-6.

Verse 1. – *After these things king Ahasuerus promoted Haman the son of Hammedatha the Agagite, and advanced him, and set his seat above all the princes that were with him.*

A thousand years before this time, the family of Agag was renowned in the world. *'His king,'* said Balaam concerning Israel, *'shall be higher than Agag.'* The generous spirit of Ahasuerus might probably feel sentiments of compassion for the poor representative of a family once so glorious, and endeavor by his favor to make him some compensation for the fallen grandeur of his house and people; but why did God allow a man to be raised high above the princes of Persia, who was to make such a bad use of his grandeur, as we will soon find Haman did? *'Promotion comes not from the east, nor from the west, nor from the south. But God is the judge. He puts down one, and sets up another.'* Why, then, is the basest and proudest of men set so high, that all the princes of Persia must bow to him? It is needless to answer the question at present. We will find it sufficiently answered in the course of this history; which will teach us, that *'when the wicked spring up as the grass, and when all the workers of iniquity do flourish, it is that they shall be destroyed for ever; because you, Lord, are most high for evermore;'* (Psalm 92:7,8).

Verse 2. – *And all the king's servants who were in the king's gate bowed and worshipped Haman, for the king had so commanded concerning him. But Mordecai did not bow nor worship.*

Many of the king's ministers had their stations in the king's gate, where, it is probable, convenient apartments were provided for them; and all of them honored him whom the king delighted to honor. *'Where the word of a king is, there is power.'* All will bow to the man on whom the king is pleased to smile. If the favorites of earthly kings are so highly respected, ought we not to honor those who are the favorites of Heaven? The mind of Christ is not in us, if we do not *'honor them that fear the Lord.'*

Why did the king command his servants to pay such distinguishing honors to Haman? Did he not believe that his own known affection to Haman, and the high honors conferred upon him, were abundantly sufficient to ensure to him all that honor to which the highest subject could be entitled? From this command it appears probable that the king desired greater honor to be given to Haman, than was usually given even to kings' favorites; and this was probably the reason why Mordecai refused to perform that homage to Haman, which he expected from the royal command in his favor. Many authors attest, that honors of a religious king used to be given to the kings of Persia, by those who came into their presence; and some share of the like honor was, it is likely, required by the king for his favorite and friend.

This, at least, we may safely say, that Mordecai did not decline the required homage to Haman, either from motives of envy, or from narrow scruples of conscience in a matter where conscience was not concerned. He well knew that Abraham made no scruple of bowing himself to the ground before strangers who came to his tent; that Joseph accepted of the homage of the Egyptians, which (if our translation of Gen. 41:43, is just) amounted to no less than bowing the knee before him; and that when the people of Israel worshipped the Lord and king David, they did nothing inconsistent with their religion. It was only civil homage that they performed to their fellow men. But, in all appearance, something more was understood to be signified by that homage which was required for Haman; and Mordecai would not in the least instance violate his duty, to please the greatest of men.

Verse 3. – *Then the king's servants who were in the king's gate said to Mordecai, Why do you transgress the king's commandment?*

The king's servants thought his commands entitled to implicit obedience. Whatever he said was a law to them. He was an image of God upon earth; and obedience of an unreserved kind seemed to them a part of their duty. Christians have not so learned to regulate their practice. There is one King whose commands must ever be a law to us: For *'why call we Christ, Lord, Lord, if we do not the things which he says?'* (Luke 6:46). The commands of earthly princes are to be done likewise, out of conscience towards God, when they do not oppose his commandments. But when any thing is enjoined us contrary to the honor of God, and to the duty which we owe to Him, we must obey God, and not man; *'for whether it be right in the sight of God to obey God or man,'* it is not difficult to decide.

Why do you transgress the king's commandment? Mordecai professed, and practised on former occasions, strict loyalty. He had recently saved the king's life, and might hope for a good reward, if he continued to satisfy the king by his obedience. Why, then, does he now act in express opposition to his declared will? Did he not know that kings must be obeyed, and will not suffer disobedience to their orders to pass unpunished?

Confessors of the truth, who exposed themselves to reproach and punishment for their fidelity to God, have been the wonder of the world in every age; especially when their opposition to the public laws seemed to turn upon small matters. The heathens who saw the Christians expose themselves to a cruel death, because they would not throw a few grains of incense into the fire, nor worship the genius of Caesar, believed that they had lost their reason. The like notions were formed concerning Protestant and Presbyterian martyrs by their enemies. But surely true wisdom will direct us to choose the greatest sufferings, rather than the least sin. God can easily recompense our worst sufferings in his cause; but who can compensate the damage of the least sin? Remember the words of Jesus, – *'Whosoever shall break one of the least of these commandments, or shall teach men so, he shall be called the least in the kingdom of heaven;'* (Matt. 5:19).

Verse 4. – *Now when they spoke daily unto him, and when he did not listen to them, they told Haman, to see if Mordecai's matters would stand. For he had told them that he was a Jew.*

They spoke daily unto him.– This they understood to be the office of friends; for Mordecai, they thought, was risking his life for a trifling scruple about his religion. They did not think it the part of a man of sense to throw away his life for the punctilios of religion; and used all their eloquence to persuade him to change his conduct. But their friendship to him was of the same kind with Eve's friendship to Adam, when she persuaded him to eat the forbidden fruit; or with Delilah's friendship to Samson, when she insisted upon a proof of his love that was to be fatal to his own life. Those are our true friends who warn us against declining the cross of Christ by sinful compliances. Those are our worst enemies, who persuade us to prefer our life and comfort to our duty. Our Lord Jesus Christ taught us this lesson when he said to Peter, *'Get behind me, Satan!'* Peter's offense was, that he would not have his Lord to suffer. This he accounted an expression of his friendship; but Christ esteemed it an expression of enmity worthy of Satan, the great enemy of God and men.

When they spoke to him day by day, Mordecai was still the same man. He laid it down as a principle, that he would do his duty, be the consequence what it would; and that no intreaties, no persuasions, no dangers, should induce him to violate the commands, or to sacrifice the honor, of his God. To what purpose do we enter into the way of righteousness, if we do not persevere in it? The importunities of those who would turn us aside from the path of duty, are to be considered as temptations of Satan by his emissaries; and shall they be set in opposition to the commands of God, or to the dictates of our own consciences? Would we listen to any man, if he persuaded us to inflict deadly wounds upon our bodies? But our bodies are less precious than our souls, to which every wilful sin gives a deadly stab. At length;

They told Haman, to see whether Mordecai's matters would stand, and whether he would not at last be constrained to yield to their advices. They appeared to be his friends when they exhorted him to obey the king's commandment; but now they discover themselves to be his enemies, when they expose him to the vengeance of the haughty favorite. There are too many whose friendship is but little removed from enmity. They will show you great kindness, if you allow them to be your masters: but if you think it necessary to judge for yourselves what you are to do, they reckon themselves affronted. If you follow their example, they will praise your understanding; if you act in opposition to it, they consider your conduct as a libel on their own, and care not what mischiefs may be the consequence.

For he told them that he was a Jew. – And it seems they desired to see whether the Jews would be allowed to observe, with impunity, their singular customs.

It was high time for the Jews to be strict in observing the laws of their God; those laws, especially, which prohibited the alienation of religious worship from their own God. They had already smarted severely for idolatry, and now it was necessary for them, unless they wished for utter extermination, to stand at the utmost distance from this fatal crime. We find in the Grecian history, that the Jews were not the only people who refused to give that homage which was required by the kings of Persia. The Athenians put Timagoras, one of their citizens, to death, for saluting the king of Persia in the Persian mode; and some of the soldiers of Alexander the Great rebelled against him, when he demanded from them the honors usually given to the kings of Persia. But these blind heathens acted rather upon the principle of honor, than of religion. They might have performed religious homage to the Persian monarchs as reasonably and innocently as to the ordinary objects of their worship; But the Jews were taught of God to worship himself alone. Shadrach, Meschach, and Abednego, chose to give their bodies to the burning fire, rather than worship any other god than their own God: and Mordecai chose to run every hazard, rather than prostitute to a creature those honors which belonged exclusively to God his Maker.

Mordecai would not comply with the solicitations of the king's ministers: but he gave them a good reason why he would not do it, when *'he told them that he was a Jew;'* and that the laws of his fathers prohibited his compliance with their wishes. He forbade Esther to tell her people or her kindred: but, when occasion required, he was not ashamed to tell his own people, and kindred, and religion. Here he followed the example of David, *'who would speak of God's testimonies before kings, and would not be ashamed.'* Why should any fearer of God, any follower of Jesus, be ashamed openly to avow his profession before the greatest of men? Nothing can be more shameful, than to be ashamed of our Creator and Redeemer. The followers of the Lamb *'have their Father's name written on their forehead.'*

Verse 5. – *And when Haman saw that Mordecai did not bow nor worship him, then Haman was full of wrath.*

Mordecai did not bow nor worship him. – Was not Mordecai too full of scruples? Might he not have bent his body in civil homage, to which Haman was entitled by his station? He might then have been overlooked; the difference between his mode of paying homage, and that of the other servants of the king, might have been unobserved, and thus he might have escaped the danger that threatened him.

Mordecai would not, surely, have withheld civil homage from the king's favorite, although he was of the race of Agag, if he could have performed it without being supposed to give to him that religious respect which was paid to him by others. But he would have preferred peace to truth, and his own life to a good conscience, if he had rendered to him any kind of homage that would have been generally understood to contain the lowest acts of religious worship. It is a necessary duty to *'abstain from all appearance of evil.'* We must give no offence to any man, even by doing those things that are in themselves lawful. But when, without practising any acts of idolatry, we do those things which may lead weak brothers into idolatry, we sin against our brothers, and against Christ who died for them. It is an excellent story that is told of old Eleazar, (2 Mac. 6), who refusing to eat swine's flesh at the commandment of the king, his pitying, but weak friends, proposed to bring some other kind of flesh to him,that he might eat it as swine's flesh, and thus escape the torments prepared him. But the good man would by no means sully his old age with the reproach of simulation to save his life; nor lay a stumbling-block before the younger Jews, by giving them any appearance of reason to think that he had done a thing so contrary to the laws of his fathers. He chose rather to bear the cruel effects of the royal indignation, than to flinch, even in appearance, from that good profession which he had maintained for ninety years; and Mordecai would rather encounter all the rage of a haughty favorite, than do any action which might prove a stumbling-block to any of his brothers of the children of Israel.

Haman was full of wrath, when he heard and saw that Mordecai refused him that homage which was given him by every other man, without excepting even the highest of the king's princes. How dreadfully this wrath flamed in his bosom, we learn from the method which he took to express it. We may observe, at present, what misery pride, by its own nature, and its inseparable consequences, brings upon men! No proud man ever received all that respect, or was treated with all that delicacy of regard, which he thought his due. Now pride, mortified by neglect or contempt, kindles a fire in the soul, which burns, and torments, and destroys. What man can be more miserable than he who burns for vengeance upon the objects of his displeasure, but torments himself in the first place by a fire which he is constantly feeding within his own bowels?

A wise man would have overlooked the supposed injury, and respected, or at the worst pitied, scruples that appeared to him unreasonable. Haman's master would have probably smiled at the singularity of Mordecai's behavior. It is said that Darius, grandfather to this prince, was once, on a journey, solicited by one of his attendants to give him his embroidered robe, which happened to be torn. The king, knowing that it was a capital crime, by the laws of Persia, for any subject to wear the king's robe, gave it to the man, with a strict prohibition from wearing it. He no sooner received it, than he dressed himself in the gorgeous robe. When the king's other attendants were filled with indignation, the king said, *'I give him leave, as a woman, to wear the embroidery; and as a madman, to wear the robe.'* If Haman had passed over the supposed indignity with such a jest, he might have saved himself from much misery, and would have lost none of his honors. But none are so proud as men raised from a dunghill to a seat near the throne. Cyrus, Darius, and Artaxerxes, whom we suppose to be the king Ahasuerus of this book, had Jews in their courts, who certainly did not give them honors unfit for men to receive; and yet those princes showed them great favor. But the upstart minion thought no punishment too severe for a man that would not honor him as a god. May God preserve us all from unexpected heights of prosperity; or give us grace to bear such dangerous changes in our condition as becomes saints!

Verse 6. – *And he scorned to lay hands only on Mordecai, for they had revealed to him the people of Mordecai. Therefore Haman sought to destroy all the Jews who were throughout the whole kingdom of Ahasuerus, the people of Mordecai.*

Pride thirsts for the blood of those by whom it is wounded. And this is certainly enough, and too much, for its gratification. When the Pharisees and priests were hurt by the fame and by the testimony of Jesus, they sought to destroy him; and his own blood would have been sufficient, while he lived among them, to satiate their fury. When they sent a band of men with Judas to apprehend him, they gave them no commission to apprehend his disciples along with him. But the wound given to the pride of Haman was too sore and deep to be healed by the blood of Mordecai alone. The blood of a thousand, the blood of ten thousand men, was not sufficient. The whole nation of the Jews must be sacrificed to his revenge. In some barbarous nations, atrocious crimes are punished, not with the death of the malefactor only, but with the death of every member of his family, or of all his kindred. The fury of Haman is not satisfied with the destruction of Mordecai, and of all his father's house; all the Jews throughout the wide-extended empire of Ahasuerus were no more than a sufficient sacrifice to his revenge. They were;

The people of Mordecai. – This was his quarrel with them. Was this a reason for their destruction? Let Mordecai be the worst of men, it does not follow that all his countrymen must be wicked. If a whole nation were to be extirpated when a single atrocious criminal is to be found among them, all the nations of the world must have been long ago rooted out of the land of the living, and the earth left one large desert for lions, and tigers, and bears, and wolves, to prey upon the weaker animals. But the wrath of man cannot hear the voice of reason and justice. It wants ears; but it has a loud voice, crying, Blood! blood! If you desire to hold your innocence, give no ear to its clamors. Make it to appear that you have learned the truth as it is in Jesus, *'by putting off the old man with his deeds, which is corrupt, according to the deceitful lusts.'* Among other lusts, *'put away all malice and envies'* – *'Be angry and sin not – Let not the sun go down upon your wrath; neither give place to the devil.'* Your wrath may prove very troublesome to the persons against whom it is directed; but it will be beyond comparison more troublesome to yourselves. The wrath of Haman drew many tears and sighs from Mordecai: but it drew down fearful vengeance upon Haman himself, and upon all his family. God give us all that *'wisdom which is from above, which is first pure, then peaceable, gentle, and easy to be entreated, full of mercy and good fruits, without partiality, and without hypocrisy;'* (James 3:17).

DISCOURSE VI.

HAMAN OBTAINS FROM THE KING A DECREE FOR THE DESTRUCTION OF THE JEWS.

CHAPTER 3:7-15.

Verse 7. – *In the first month, that is, the month Nisan, in the twelfth year of king Ahasuerus, they cast Pur, that is, the lot, before Haman from day to day, and from mouth to mouth, to the twelfth month, that is, the month Adar.*

The meaning plainly is, that on the twelfth day of the month Nisan, the cast lots with reference to all the days and months of the year, to know what would be the lucky month for the business in agitation. The Vulgate translation runs thus: – "On what day, and in what month, the Jews ought to be slain.' And the twelfth month, which is called Adar, came forth.

It was the reproach of some of the Jewish Kings, that they observed times. But it was common among the heathens to make a distinction between lucky and unlucky days. By this superstitious distinction, they sometimes suffered opportunities to be lost which could never be recalled, and thereby exposing themselves to great losses, or to extreme dangers.

The business which Haman had now in contemplation was important, and might prove dangerous. He therefore endeavors to discover the will of the gods by the use of the lot, concerning the most proper time for executing his purpose. But there was surely another point which ought previously to have been determined, whether he should attempt to execute his purpose, or forbear. It might have occurred to him, that possibly there was no time at all in which it would be safe to undertake an enterprise so full of horror. But his passions blinded him. The enterprise must be undertaken. He cannot enjoy life unless his enemies are destroyed. The time only is referred to the lot; and, through the good providence of God, it directs him to a very distant day, at the end of not less than eleven months.

Little did Haman know that the whole disposing of lots belonged unto the God of that people whom he proposed to exterminate from the earth, and that of consequence the season pointed out by the lot was likely not to be the best season for executing his purpose, but the most proper season for preventing the execution of it, and for turning the meditated vengeance upon his own head. *'The wicked is snared in the work of his own hands.'* While he crouches and humbles himself, and uses every artifice that the poor may fall by his strong ones, he is, in effect, spreading snares for himself.

Verse 8. – *And Haman said to king Ahasuerus, There is a certain people scattered abroad and dispersed among the people, in all the provinces of your kingdom. And their laws are different from all people, neither do they keep the king's laws. Therefore it is not for the king's gain to allow them to live.*

It is surprising that it could ever come into the mind of any man, to seek the destruction of a whole nation for an offense given him by one man. But it is far more surprising that Haman could ever have the audacity to propose it to his sovereign, and to a sovereign known to be of a humane disposition. He stood high in the favor of his prince; but did he not risk the total loss of that favor by a proposal so evidently unjust and inhumane? Why did he not dread the wrath of the king, which is *'as messengers of death?'* Might he not have heard such words as these, in answer to his proposal? 'Audacious wretch! what have you seen in me that you should hope to make me the murderer of my people? Man of blood! you scruple not to seek the destruction, at one blow, of thousands of my subjects, upon a vague unsupported charge which you bring against them! Will you not another day follow the example of Bigthan and Teresh? Will you be more afraid to lay your hand upon one man, though a king, than upon many thousands of my subjects, who have done you no wrong?'

But Haman had his reasons to justify his strange proposal to the king. The people whose destruction he sought were a contemptible people, scattered through every province of the king's dominions. They had laws peculiar to themselves, and they were not observers of the king's laws.

They were scattered through every province of the king's dominion. He speaks as if they had no country which deserved to be called their own. This, however, was not a fact, for the nation of Israel was now brought back to its own land; and although many of them still continued to dwell in foreign lands, were they therefore to be marked out for slaughter? Was Ahasuerus to make his name infamous among all nations, and to all posterity, by imitating the example of the tyrant Busiris, whose custom it was to sacrifice all strangers that he found in the land of Egypt, where he reigned? If the Jews must die because they dwell not in the land of their fathers, let Haman himself, and all the remnant of Amalek, perish. They have been brought, by the revolutions of time, or by the providence of God, into a condition still more contemptible than that of the Jews.

And their laws are diverse from all people. – True. But is this a reason why they should be destroyed, before it is considered whether these laws are better or worse than the laws of other people? Let this be considered before this people is condemned for having such laws. Have they laws to authorize murder, treason, hatred of mankind, robbery, or adultery? Then let them be compelled to adjure such laws, or be rooted out of the land of the living: But if their laws are found to be the best in the world, let it be acknowledged that this nation is a wise and understanding people; unless they are found careless about their own laws, and disposed rather to observe other rules of conduct.

But this was another charge against them, that they were too observant of their own laws, and did not regard the laws of the king. It is, indeed, a great crime, in most cases, to disobey the laws of the country where we dwell, and of the king under whose protection we live. Unless the king's authority is respected, good order cannot be maintained; nor can men be secured in their life, property, and honors, where kings do not enforce obedience to their good laws. Yet there are cases in which it is a virtue to transgress the laws of the greatest king. What if the laws of God are contrary to them? Kings themselves are but subjects to the everlasting King; and as subjects are bound to disobey their superior fellow-subjects when they require them to do things inconsistent with the laws of the king, so all subjects are bound to respect the will of God, in opposition to the will of an earthly sovereign. Nothing, indeed, can be more wicked then to violate good laws under pretense of conscience towards God. But wise princes themselves will respect those men most among their subjects who are least disposed to sacrifice their highest duties to complaisance for princes. The Emperor Constantius, father to Constantine the Great, once commanded all his Christian servants to offer sacrifices to the gods of Rome. If they refused to obey his command, they were to be dismissed from his service. Many of them obeyed; others did not, and accordingly were dismissed. But in a day or two he turned out all who had complied with his orders, and recalled those whom he had expelled; saying, that those would be most faithful to their prince, who were most faithful to their God; and that he would not trust men who were false to their religion.

Verse 9. – *If it pleases the king, let it be written that they may be destroyed. And I will pay ten thousand talents of silver to the hands of those who have charge of the business, to bring it into the king's treasuries.*

If it pleases the king, let it be written that they may be destroyed. – Why? They are a worthless people, *'for they are scattered over all the king's dominions, and live according to their own singular laws, without observing the king's laws; and therefore it is not for The king's profit to allow them to live.* And must the lives of hundreds of thousands be sacrificed to a vague, unproved accusation? If the Jews are a scattered people, that is their misfortune, rather than their sin. If they have singular institutions derived from their fathers, are they to be blamed for observing them, before it is proved that they are wicked, or inconsistent with the safety of other men's lives and property? It was commonly held among the heathens to be a virtue, rather than a vice, for men to respect the laws of their fathers. If they did not observe the king's laws, let them be punished for it, unless they can prove that their consciences required them to act as they did; but let them be punished according to the nature of their offense. The king's laws were not the laws of Draco the Athenian; which were said to be written in blood, because he made every fault capital. He thought that the smallest faults deserved death, and for the greatest crime he could find no greater punishment.

It is not for the king's gain to allow them to live; and therefore let them be put to death. But will it be profit to the king to put them to death? Will he derive much pleasure or advantage from the guilt of an hundred thousand murders; from the execrations of all his surviving subjects, and of all generations of mankind; from the horrors of self-accusing conscience; and from the prospect of the vengeance which the Creator of mankind may be expected to inflict on the destroyers of the work of his hands?

But the profit of which Haman chiefly thought, was the flourishing state of the royal revenue. This nation was so poor, that the revenue would not be lessened by its destruction. If, however, the king was under any apprehensions that his revenue would suffer damage, Haman proposes to make a full equivalent by paying into the king's treasuries ten thousand talents of silver; which make several millions of our money. This sum he probably intended to raise in part out of the effects of the condemned nation, and to make up what was wanting from his own private estate. His revenge was so dear to him, that he would not only hazard the king's favor by the horrid proposal of murdering a whole nation, but expose himself to a severe loss in his fortune, rather than allow the hated race to live. What liberal sacrifices will men make to their passions! They will give a great part of the substance of their house for the gratification of their hatred or their lust. Why then should we think it an hard matter to give a part of our substance to God? If our desires are as eager for the advancement of virtue and purity; if we are as earnest in our wishes to have the wants of the poor supplied, and the afflictions of the unfortunate relieved, as revengeful men, like Haman, are to gratify their ill-nature; it will give us pleasure to honor the Lord with our substance, and to minister to the necessities of our fellow-men.

Verses 10,11. – *And the king took his ring from his hand, and gave it to Haman the son of Hammedatha the Agagite, the Jews' enemy. And the king said to Haman, The silver is given to you, the people also, to do with them as seems good to you.*

Here we see the danger of despotism, and the value of liberty. Ahasuerus was none of the worst of princes. Humility appeared to characterize his government; yet we find him, in an unguarded hour, and in the effusions of his friendship to an unworthy favorite, giving his consent to a massacre, which, if it had been perpetrated, must have ranked him with the most odious tyrants that ever lived. What tyrant ever consigned a whole nation of subjects to destruction by a single decree? Caligula, it is said, wished that the whole Roman people had but one neck, that he might cut it off at a single blow. Yet we do not read that he ever attempted to destroy at one blow any of the numerous nations that were subject to the Roman empire. But Ahasuerus compliments Haman with the lives of a whole nation scattered through all his dominions, without putting himself to the trouble of asking what proof Haman had of the crimes, if they could be called crimes, that were laid to their charge. The mischief of arbitrary power and of slavery in nations, lies not chiefly in the insecurity of life, and of property, but in the tendency which they both have to corrupt the hearts and the morals of men. Could any man, not invested with unlimited power, have ever thought of making such a horrid present to one of his favorites? When men are taught that the may do what they please, they must be exempted from the weaknesses and vices incident to human nature, if they always confine their pleasure within the limits which men must prescribe to themselves who are limited by laws. Bondage under masters of unlimited power, has, on the other side, a strong tendency to debase and vitiate the soul. No wise man will wish to possess the power of doing evil. Every subject of a free government is no less bound to be thankful to God for that precious blessing, than for food and raiment.

Ahasuerus appears to have been a man of an easy temper, and ready to confer the greatest obligations, without deliberation, on those whom he loved. But there is no true virtue without judgment and steadiness. A thoughtless man, of an easy temper, is more likely to turn out a vicious than a virtuous character; because, in a world where so many more bad than good men are to be met with, he is likely to give himself up to the guidance of those who will lead him out of the way of understanding; or if he should be led in the right path by some of his friends, there are others that will lead him out of it. Ahasuerus would have heaped favors upon the Jews, if Mordecai had been to him at this time what Haman was. If he was the prince whom we take him to have been, he had already conferred very high favors upon the Jews in the seventh year of his reign; (Ezra 7). And now, at the distance of five years, he signs a death-warrant for the whole nation, without knowing or thinking what he was doing. He does not appear to have so much as asked what that nation was which Haman solicited him to destroy. For all he knew, he was giving consent to a decree for the destruction of his beloved queen, and of Mordecai, to whom he was indebted for his life. He now takes his ring, and gives it to Haman, to sign what decrees he pleased to make. How did he know that Haman would not sign a decree for his own deposition or death? Some say that Semiramis obtained her husband's permission to reign for five days, and in that time ordered her husband to be slain, that she might get perpetual possesion of his throne.

Many have not duly distinguished between an easy and a good temper. An easy temper is a very dangerous one, when it is not under the powerful restraints of wisdom. It is vain to boast of a ready compliance with every good motion suggested to us, if we are equally ready to comply with bad motions. If we surrender ourselves to the direction of our friends, we may soon find that we have given up ourselves to our enemies, He is not our friend who desires to be our lord. A true friend will wish us to behave like men, and like Christians; and if we are Christians, we must not be slaves of the best of men on earth. *'You are bought with a price – Be not the servants of men, but of the Lord Christ – Please men for their good to edification.'* Be always ready to grant reasonable requests, and to follow good counsels. But you must judge for yourselves by the light which God has given you, what requests are lawful to be granted, and what counsels are worthy to be followed.

The silver is given to you, and the people also, to do with them as seems good to you. – Observe in what light this prince viewed his people. He considered them as a part of his goods and chattels, of which he was at liberty to dispose at his pleasure. Unhappy the people whose kings are trained up in such notions! Still more unhappy the princes whose minds are swelled, and their hearts vitiated, by such conceits of their own powers! And yet, if the people had been as entirely the king's property, as cattle are the property of the husbandman who rears them, would he have been justified in transferring his right to an avowed butcher? The husbandman incurs no blame by giving up to the slaughter those animals that may be used as food; but if he should give up the slaughter those beasts that are used in work only, would he not greatly abuse his power, and incur the just charge of wanton cruelty? A good man regards the life of his beast. A proud man little regards the life of his fellow-men in the lower ranks of life.

Verse 12. – *Then the king's scribes were called on the thirteenth day of the first month, and there was written according to all that Haman had commanded to the king's lieutenants, and to the governors who were over every province, and to the rulers of every people of every province, according to the writing of it, and to every people according to their language. It was written in the name of king Ahasuerus and sealed with the king's ring.*

The wickedness of the intended massacre does not rest with Ahasuerus and Haman. Great multitudes of the king's subjects must participate in the guilt. The governors and rulers of every province, and the people under their command, have letters written to them, sealed with the king's seal, to contribute their part to the massacre. Let the great consider what they do. If they are wicked, they are not wicked alone. They make others sharers with them in their guilt; and while they make their inferiors sin, they may expect to bear their execrations in hell for bringing them along with themselves to that place of torment.

These men were greatly to be pitied who lived under an absolute government, because, in many instances, they would find it necessary either to sin against their own souls, or to offend a prince whose frown was death. We ought to bless God that no man has power to require us to do any thing but according to the known laws of the land: And yet men of true virtue will not comply with the will of the most absolute monarchs, when it is not consistent with the laws of justice and of mercy. At the famous Bartholomew massacre, when the King of France sent his orders to the commanders in the different provinces to massacre the Huguenots, one of them returned him this answer: 'In my district your Majesty has many brave soldiers, but no butchers.' That virtuous governor never felt any effects of the royal resentment. It is to be feared that few of the Persian governors would have given such proofs of virtuous courage, if the king's edict had not been reversed. We find none of all the governors of the provinces of the Babylonian empire, that refused to bow their knees to the graven image of Nebuchadnezzar the king set up. The subjects of princes who rule with unlimited dominion, are for the most part slaves both in body and in soul. They are taught from their earliest days, by the examples which they see around them, to consider their princes as gods on earth, whose will must not be disputed.

Verse 13. – *And the letters were sent by postal riders into all the king's provinces, to destroy, to kill, and to cause to perish, all Jews, both young and old, little children and women, in one day, upon the thirteenth day of the twelfth month, which is the month Adar, and to take what they owned for a prize.*

Malice must have blinded the eyes of that wicked man to a strange degree. He gives as the reason why he would have the hated nation destroyed, *'That they did not keep the king's laws;'* but in the edict against them are comprehended many thousands who could not possibly break them. The little children, who could neither do good nor evil, may reasonably be supposed to make a fourth or fifth part of the whole nation. There might be supposed, at least, as many in the whole nation of the Jews as at Nineveh in the days of Jonah, *'who could not discern between their right hand and their left.'* The king's humanity must have revolted at the thought of shedding the blood of so many innocents, as soon as he reflected calmly on this horrible decree. It is said, that one of the hardened bigots who killed many of the Protestants in the Irish massacre, found his conscience tormented as long as he lived with the thought of some babes whom he had stabbed in the heat of his zeal. Their images often presented themselves to his fancy, and inflicted severer pangs than the gibbet could have done. What then, must a prince, naturally of a clement disposition, have thought in his moments of reflection, concerning a favorite who had, in an unguarded moment, persuaded him to give a death-warrant against the poor babes of a whole nation, who could not in any manner offend him; as well as against their fathers and mothers, who had done nothing to offend him, but by observing the laws of their fathers? Although Providence had not so wonderfully interposed to turn Haman's mischief upon his own head, it is very probable he would not long have escaped the vengeance of his misguided prince; who could not have forgiven himself nor his favorite the guilt of so many causeless murders.

The Jews are the people expressly mentioned as the unhappy objects of this edict. Haman did not know that Esther herself, no less than Mordecai, was included in this intened proscription. Had any one drawn his sword against the queen s life, what punishment could justly have been inflicted upon him by the king, when he could produce a warrant sealed with the king's seal?

But there was another point of still more importance unknown to this enemy of the Jews; that they were a nation which could not be extirpated, because they were under the special protection of the God of heaven. The malice of Haman could no more frustrate the ancient oracles related to the Jews, than it could pull the sun out of the firmament, and deprive the world of the light of day. *'The sceptre was not to depart from Judah, nor a lawgiver from between his feet, till Shiloh should come.'* The Shiloh was not yet come. Judah must therefore continue a distinct nation, under governors that proceeded from himself. Haman's malice will be so far from finding the means of extirpating Judah, that the glory of that people, though eclipsed, must again shine forth as the morning.

Verse 14. – *The copy of the writing, for a commandment to be given in every province, was published unto all people so that they should be ready for that day.*

Nebuchadnezzar gathered the governors of all his provinces to Babylon, that they might witness the honors done to the graven image that he had set up. But the event was very different from his expectation. They all saw the disgrace of the worshippers of graven images, and the glory of the God of Israel, who preserved his faithful servants in the midst of that fire which consumed the king's servants that cast them into the furnace. Thus Haman caused the edict against the Jews to be published in the language of every people, that they might all be prepared to bear their part in the destruction of the Jews. But the enemies of Israel had one thing in view, and the God of Israel quite another. Haman intended to make the destruction of Judah as sure as possible, but God intended to make all nations attentive witnesses of his power and wisdom displayed in counteracting the designs of their enemies, and accomplishing their salvation. The effect of such an edict would be the fixing of all men's attention on the event; and the event was to make it evident that there was no god like the God of Israel; nor any people on the earth so much the care of Heaven, as that nation which was held in abhorrence by Haman.

Verse 15. – *The posts went out, being hurried by the king's commandment, and the decree was given in Shushan the palace. And the king and Haman sat down to drink, but the city Shushan was perplexed.*

Haman was in great haste to publish the decree through all parts of the king's dominions, though it was not to be executed till eleven months were elapsed from the time when it was enacted. His intention was, that everything should be in readiness for the execution on the proper day. But did he not outwit himself? Would it not have been much better to have kept it a profound secret till it could be a secret no longer? Had he no reason to think that there might be some one or other in the king's large extended dominions that might befriend the oppressed nation, and make the king sensible how much he had been imposed upon? What if some one of the king's noble princes, envying Haman's credit, might take the advantage which the atrocious cruelty and injustice of the decree gave him, of opening the king's eyes to the wickedness of his conduct? The Jews themselves, at least, might be expected to adopt some measure, either to preserve themselves, or to sell their lives dear. What if despair should inspire them with courage to aim a deadly blow at the head of this oppressor? They could make the attempt without risking their lives, when they were already under sentence of death. Their losing their lives a few months sooner than the time fixed would be a relief to them from so many months of anguish.

In the folly of Haman's conduct, we see the wisdom of God over-ruling the counsels of the wicked, to serve his own purposes; and infatuating them, that he might destroy them. The Jews have time to pray, and confess their sins. The terror into which they were thrown, would put them in mind of Him who was *'the Hope of Israel, and the Saviour thereof in the time of trouble.'* God himself was in the meantime *'whetting his sword, and making it ready. He was preparing for him the instruments of death, that the violent dealing'* of the wicked Haman, *'might come down upon his own head.'*

Haman, in the meantime, gives up himself to pleasure and jollity, in which he had the honor to be companion to the king. He will soon find that *'the end of this mirth is heaviness.'* The city Shushan was perplexed, when the king and Haman were enjoying this merriment. What heart could be free from perplexity on such an occasion? The Jews were known to be as innocent as their neighbors. Many of them resided in the city of Shushan. The prospect of their miserable and unmerited fate was terrible. Who could tell where such mischiefs were to end? Haman might next day petition his deluded master to compliment him with a like sacrifice of other lives. The people of Shushan at this time would be in much the same state of mind with a Persian minister of state in later times, who said that he never left the king's presence without putting his hand to his head, that he might feel whether it was still standing on his shoulders.

We have reason to bless God that most men in civilized nations feel an abhorrence at bloody crimes. Many who scruple not to lie, or to cheat, would be struck with horror at the guilt of murder in themselves or others. Many and gracious are the methods used by God for the security of the life of that favorite creature which he made after his own image. May we spend those lives to his glory, which are protracted by his goodness!

DISCOURSE VII.

THE GRIEF OF MORDECAI AND THE OTHER JEWS AT HEARING OF THE BLOODY EDICT – MORDECAI SOLICITS ESTHER TO INTERCEDE WITH THE KING ON THEIR BEHALF.

CHAPTER 4:1-11.

Verse 1. – *When Mordecai understood all that was done, Mordecai tore his clothes and put on sackcloth with ashes and went out into the middle of the city, and cried with a loud and bitter cry.*

Mordecai was watchful over the interests of his people, and deeply affected with all their concerns; (Chap. 10:3). Judge, then, what must have been his feelings, when he was informed that an edict had passed for their destruction! But what was still more distressing to him was the consideration that himself was the occasion of it. He could not reflect upon his own conduct, indeed, as the proper cause of the mischief. He had done nothing but what his conscience approved, and what he still resolved to do in similar circumstances; (Chap. 5:9). And who could ever have imagined that the revenge of Haman would have extended farther than his own life? But still he must have been penetrated with bitter anguish at the thought that the sanguinary decree originated in Haman's revenge against his own conduct. And, as David told Abiathar that he had been the occasion of the death of all the persons of his father's house, so he might be reflected on by the Jews as the death of every person of their nation. With cutting reflections he would think on the day when he first entered into the king's service. If he had not been one of the men that sat in the king's gate, he might never have seen Haman's face; and the decree would never have been thought of. Why did he still reside in a foreign land, when he might have been a dweller in the Holy Land, with his brothers who had returned from their captivity? Why had he not rather chosen the meanest condition, which would have kept him at a distance from kings and courts, than a situation which had so unhappily involved himself and all his people in the danger of utter extermination? Had a sentence of death been pronounced upon himself; and his beloved Esther and all the persons of his father's house been comprehended in the sentence; his grief would have been very great, but in no wise comparable to what he felt from the present danger of all his people.

Poor Mordecai had it not in his power to confine his anguish to his own bosom, or to his own house. He published it through all the city of Shushan. You need not ask for what reasons persons overwhelmed with grief do not inquire what purpose the publication of their grief may serve. The strong impulse often makes them publish their complaints to the winds or to the trees. Yet who knows what good end it might serve to announce the unmerited calamity of the Jews through the whole city of Shushan? There might be some compassionate hearts among the people that would be interested by such a dire calamity: and though the people had no direct access to the king, yet they could present their supplications to the counsellors who saw his face; or if nothing could be gained, nothing could be lost by men already doomed to death.

We are not, after all, to suppose that Mordecai's sorrow was altogether hopeless. His faith in God might be shaken, but it was not destroyed. He could not be ignorant of the many precious promises concerning the Lord's redeemed captives, which were to be found in the prophecies of Isaiah, of Jeremiah, of Ezekiel, and of many other prophets. The Jews, restored to their land, or scattered among the nations, might be sore vexed, but they could not be utterly destroyed. God's promise could not fail forevermore. *'Deliverance,'* said Mordecai, *'shall rise up to the Jews.'* Yet he did not know how or when it would arise. He did not know but many might lose their lives before deliverance came. He mourned sore, although he did not mourn like one that had no hope.

Verse 2. – *And he even came before the king's gate – for none might enter into the king's gate clothed in sackcloth.*

Mordecai might go where he pleased with his sackcloth and ashes, excepting only to that place where his duty required his attendance. Not those who are clothed in garments of heaviness, but those who wear gay clothing, are in king's palaces. Within the gates of the palace of Shushan, badges of sorrow were criminal. The king could not banish trouble of heart; he could not banish sickness, or vexation, or death from his palace; but he banished all those ordinary signs by which grief is expressed. The maker of this law was certainly of a different judgment from a much wiser king, who advises men to go to the house of mourning rather than the house of feasting; (Eccles. 7:2). We have heard of princes that forbade death to be mentioned in their presence. How terrible must the harbingers of death have been to those great personages! Since the last enemy must be encountered by the greatest as well as the least of our race, is it not far better to be prepared for meeting him, than to banish him from our thoughts?

Verse 3. – *And in every province, wherever the king's commandment and his decree came, there was great mourning among the Jews, and fasting, and weeping and wailing. And many lay in sackcloth and ashes.*

'In this day did the Lord God of hosts call to weeping and to mourning, and to baldness, and to girding with sackcloth:' and the call was so loud and awful that it commanded compliance. All that loved their lives, all that loved their friends and brothers, mourned bitterly, and refused to be comforted. All that had any impression of religion among the Jews, joined religious fasting to their expressions of grief, that they might pour out tears unto God. And there is reason to believe, that religious impressions would be now felt even by those who had forgotten God in their days of prosperity.

If a sentence of death pronounced by an earthly sovereign produced such grief, such anxiety, such cries for deliverance, what impression ought to be made on the minds of sinners by that sentence which is passed against them in the court of heaven – *'Judgment is come upon all men to condemnation!'* We are still under that sentence of condemnation, if we are not in Christ Jesus. Surely we believe neither law nor gospel, if we can enjoy peace in our own minds, without the humble hope of mercy through our Lord Jesus Christ unto eternal life.

Verse 4. – *So Esther's maids and her officers came and told her. Then the queen was exceedingly grieved, and she sent clothing to clothe Mordecai, and to take away his sackcloth from him. But he did not receive it.*

Esther was advanced to the highest station which a woman could fill. She dwelt in a magnificent palace, where she might fare sumptuously, if she pleased, every day. Her wardrobe was filled with a rich profusion of raiment embroidered with gold. She was attended by maids and officers devoted to her will. But did she find happiness in that magnificence which surrounded her, or in the riches which she might use, or abuse, at her pleasure? She might, indeed, be thankful that her condition was such as it was, when she considered the humiliating condition of the other ladies of the king. But her palace was a prison. She could not enjoy the society of her former friends, or even of her beloved Mordecai. She was, at this time, ignorant of the pitiable condition of her nation. She was cut off from her wonted sources of pleasure, and the man to whom she must now devote her life seemed almost to have forgotten her. The happiness of men and women is by no means proportioned to their station, their riches, their power, or their manner of living. There are vexations annexed to greatness, of which the poor have little apprehension; and there are comforts within the reach of the poor as little known to the great. Those who know the world will see little reason to envy their superiors; and the great have no reason to look down with disdain upon the lowest ranks.

Esther, in her elevation, and in her separation from her friends, was far from forgetting them. She was deeply afflicted when she heard of the mourning habit and sore affliction of Mordecai. She was vexed that he should appear at the king's gate in a dress in which he could not enter it, and therefore sent to him change of raiment. But she knew not the sources of his distress. Grief so firmly rooted, and so well founded, could not be removed without a removal of its cause. To send him change of raiment was like singing songs to a heavy heart. Mordecai was doubtless pleased with her kind attention: but she must do something of a very different nature to banish his sorrows.

Verse 5. – *Then Esther called for Hatach, one of the king's officers whom he had appointed to attend upon her, and gave him a commandment to Mordecai to know what it was and why it was.*

If we weep in sincerity with those that weep, it will be our desire, if possible, to remove their sorrows. But to this end it is necessary to know their cause. Physicians cannot administer proper medicines to their patients, unless they know the causes of their diseases. They may palliate the symptoms, the root of the distemper remains if the cause is not removed. So, we may soothe the minds of persons laboring under grief, and cause them for a time to forget their sorrows; but if they are rooted in the mind, they will soon recover their force, and hold the soul in misery, unless the causes are removed: And these cannot be removed but by a change in those outward circumstances which occasioned them, or by a change in the state of the mind, when it is convinced that the supposed causes do not exist, or that they are not sufficient grounds for the sorrows they occasioned, or that relief or consolation may be found, or virtue sufficient to counteract their force.

Esther could not now visit Mordecai, or call him to her palace, and therefore, conversing with him by means of a third person, inquires into the causes of his distress, with a sincere intention to do everything in her power to set his heart at ease.

Verses 6,7,8. – *So Hatach went forth to Mordecai, to the street of the city which was in front of the king's gate. And Mordecai told him of all that had happened to him, and of the sum of the money which Haman had promised to pay to the king's treasuries for the Jews in order to destroy them. Also he gave him the copy of the writing of the decree which was given at Shushan in order to destroy them, to show it to Esther and to declare it to her, and to command her that she should go in to the king to make supplication to him, and to seek help for her people.*

It is unpleasant to be the messenger of bad tidings. It is, however, often useful. If a physician saw you laboring under a mortal distemper, and insensible of your danger, he is the preserver of your life, when, by warning you of the peril of your condition, he rouses your fear, and excites to apply the proper remedy. Esther must have been shocked beyond measure at hearing of the sentence of death pronounced against her dearest friends, against her whole people, against herself, by the man who had raised her to a share in his bed, and in his throne, without a crime proved against any one of them. But it was better to hear of it at present, than ten or eleven months afterwards, when it would be too late to provide a remedy.

There are some who cannot bear to hear of any bad tidings, however true; and think those men their enemies who tell them the truth. They consider those friends or preachers as their enemies who speak to them of their sins, and of the judgments of God denounced against them. But was not Esther under deep obligations to Mordecai for informing her of the danger of her people, and urging her to exert her influence for preserving them? Whether was Ahab most indebted to those prophets who told him that the Lord was with him, and would give him victory at Ramoth-Gilead; or to him who told him that he would fall in the battle? By following the counsel of the former, he lost his life; he might have preserved it, if he had believed the latter.

It is indeed cruel to distress men by false or doubtful intelligence of calamities that have not happened, or, if they have happened, cannot be remedied. Mordecai was far from wishing to disquiet the mind of his royal friend by uncertain rumors. But he had too good intelligence to be mistaken; and he puts into her hands decisive proofs of the danger of her people, and of Haman's activity in procuring their ruin. Nor did he give her this intelligence to torment her before the time. If nothing could have been done to avert the danger, he might have permitted her to enjoy tranquillity till it could be concealed no longer. But who could tell what might be the result of supplication to the king, especially from a queen who was understood to be the object of his warmest love? He therefore desires, or rather requires, her to go in and make intercession to the king for her people, and for her own life.

Mordecai uses authority in his language to the queen, and does her great honor by using such language. He dare not have charged her to do her duty, if he had not known her humbleness of mind in her greatness. She was as much disposed as in her youngest days to give him the authority of a father; and this he knew so well, that he uses it without scruple or apology. Happy are those on whom prosperity makes no change but for the better!

He charges her to make intercession to the king. The knowledge of that dreadful situation in which the Jews were placed, was to be improved by all the Jews as a call to fasting and intercession with the God of heaven, on whom their hope was to rest. But it was to be improved by the queen in particular, as a motive to the exertion of all her influence with the king. All, according to their places and stations, are bound to do what they can to avert threatened miseries from their nation. But some are bound to do much more than others, because they have peculiar opportunities, which, if they are not improved, must render them in some degree accountable for the mischiefs consequent on their neglect. Those who can do nothing by their own power, may do much by their influence with others. In the reign of the bloody Jehoiakim, the princes of Judah saved Jeremiah from his hands. If these princes had not used their influence for this purpose, they must have shared in the guilt of his blood.

Verse 9. – *And Hatach came and told Esther the words of Mordecai.*

'A faithful messenger refreshes the soul of him that sent him.' Hatach was a faithful messenger, and yet he stunned his employer. But refreshment to her soul was the consequence in due time of his fidelity, and of Mordecai's firmness.

Verse 10,11. – *Again Esther spoke to Hatach, and gave him commandment to Mordecai – All the king's servants and the people of the king's provinces know that whoever, whether man or woman, shall come to the king into the inner court, who is not called, there is one law of his to put him to death, except such to whom the king shall hold out the golden scepter so that he may live. But I have not been called to come in unto the king these thirty days.*

Esther was not unwilling, but she was afraid, to go in unto the king. She does not absolutely refuse; but she objects against compliance with Mordecai's charge. If Mordecai can find out no other probable means of safety, she will undertake the business: but she earnestly desires to be excused, if some other can be found to undertake the cause, whose interest with the king may be greater than hers.

Some are too ready to undertake services for which they are unqualified. But dangerous services are too often declined by those who are both called to undertake them, and best qualified to execute them. Moses was eminently qualified by God to be the deliverer of Israel from Egypt, and clearly called; and yet he earnestly desired God to excuse him; and this he did again and again on various pretenses, till he saw God's anger kindled against him. Let us never trust to ourselves, as if we are able of ourselves to think so much as a good thought. But let us never distrust God, as if he would *'send us a warfare on our own charges.'* If we can believe, *'all things are possible to him that believes'* – *'when he is weak, then he is strong.'*

Danger of death is one of Esther's objections against undertaking this business. This, too, was one secret reason that made Moses so unwilling to undertake the work of delivering Israel. There is a strong love of life implanted in us by God, and it is not easy to give up life even to Him that gave it. There are few so courageous as Paul, who was moved by nothing that is grievous to other men; and who *'counted not life itself dear to him, that he might finish his course with joy.'* But when we compare Paul's courage with the fears of Moses or Esther, or other Old Testament believers, let us remember the advantages that Paul enjoyed above them, by living in that happy period when Jesus *'had abolished death, and brought life and immortality to light by the gospel.'*

But why was Esther so afraid of her life, if she should make intercession to the king for the life of her people? Was it so criminal in the court of Persia to present a supplication to the king? Or, if it was a crime in others, was it a crime even in the queen? Yes; it was universally known, says Esther, and Mordecai could not well be ignorant of it, that if any person should venture, uncalled, to approach the king in the inner court of his palace, he must be put to death, unless the king was pleased graciously to pardon him; nor was the queen herself excepted from the penalties of this law. The laws of the Persians were strange indeed! No man was allowed in a mourning-habit to enter into the king's gate; and no man in any apparel was allowed to come near the king in the inner court. Did these kings ever consider for what end they were elevated above their fellow-men? Was it not to defend the poor and the afflicted, and to do judgment and justice to all their people? How could they do the duties of princes, if they were inaccessible to their people? But if it was a crime to intrude into the private apartments of the palace, and to disturb the privacy of the prince, was it one of those atrocious crimes that can be justly punished with death? Could no milder punishment assuage the wrath of a proud mortal, who wished to make himself invisible like his Maker? Surely it may be said of a law that punished an offense like this with death, that it was written in blood; and of a government which would establish such laws, that Daniel had too good reason to represent it by the emblem of a bear; (Dan. 7:5).

Blessed be God, the laws of heaven are not like those of the Persians! Our King *'who dwells on high,'* is at all times accessible to the afflicted mourner. The poor and the afflicted had ready access to Jesus while he was upon the earth; nor is He less accessible in his state of glory. At all times we may come near to God, even to his throne of grace, that we may obtain mercy, and find grace to help in time of need.

Esther was believed by Mordecai to be a great favorite with the king; and doubtless, there was a time when she was very dear to him. But Esther was afraid that this time was past, and questioned whether Mordecai would insist upon the charge he had given her, when he was informed, that for thirty days past she had not been called to go in unto the king. This she considered as a sign that his affection was alienated, and that it was questionable whether the golden sceptre would be held out to her, if she should presume to enter the king's apartment. What reason the king had for this coldness to his virtuous queen, we know not. This is plain, that it was a providential trial appointed for Esther, by which it would be known whether she had the courage to serve her people and her God at the risk of her life. It was a severe trial of her faith and charity. She felt the force of the discouragement; and expressed her sense of it to Mordecai, that she might receive further directions from him.

To whatever difficult duty we are called, we may lay our account with trials. If you desire to serve the Lord, look for temptation. But remember, that *'the man is blessed who endures temptation; for when he is tried, he shall receive of the Lord the crown of life which he has promised to them that love him.'* Those who have held on in the path of duty, under sore temptation, shall at last *'stand before the throne of God with white robes, and palms in their hands'* – *'But the fearful and unbelieving shall have their portion in the lake of fire burning with brimstone, which is the second death.'*

DISCOURSE VIII.

MORDECAI INSISTS ON THE CHARGE TO ESTHER TO GO IN UNTO THE KING – SHE COMPLIES WITH HIS DESIRE; BUT REQUIRES HIM TO PROCURE FOR HER THE HELP OF THE SOLEMN PRAYERS OF ALL THE JEWS IN SHUSHAN.

CHAPTER 4:12-17.

Verses 12,13. – *And they told Mordecai Esther's words. Then Mordecai commanded them to answer Esther, Do not think within yourself that you shall escape in the king's house more than all the Jews.*

It is necessary for those who desire to be useful to the souls of their neighbors, not only to tell them, as occasion requires, what it is their duty to do; but to repeat their admonitions, to enforce them by reasons, and to obviate those objections which rise up in their minds against the performance of it. Those who desire a good increase from the seed sown in their fields, must plow the ground over and over, if it is stiff; must root up the weeds; must cover the seed with the harrow. In like manner, instructors must often repeat their good advices, and enforce them by arguments, and make it to appear how weak those reasons are which our slothful dispositions set in opposition to our duty. Eli admonished his sons to repent; but he did not follow up his admonitions with new reproofs, and warnings, and corrections. For this reason the Lord reproved Eli himself as an accessary to the sin of his children. Mordecai charged Esther to go in unto the king; but when Esther wished to be excused, he did not satisfy himself with what he had already done, as if he had already discharged his part of the duty. He renews his charge, he enforces it by powerful arguments, and he prevails. He was but a poor subject of that king who had made Esther his queen. But the grandeur of her station did not hinder him from using all freedom in dealing with her. He was her father. She was still his daughter in her heart as much as ever. He knew her modesty, her veneration for himself, her contempt of earthly grandeur; and makes use of his influence with her to excite her to her duty. Happy are those friends who freely make use of their mutual influence for such purposes!

Esther was afraid for her life if she should go in unto the king. Mordecai shows her, that if she valued her own life, she ought to go in unto him, and to make supplication to him for her people. Her safety lay not in shunning, but in doing, a duty so needful. She might risk her life in venturing to do a thing which was prohibited by the unreasonable laws of Persia; but she must lose it by refusing to obey the commandment of God, which requires us to use all lawful endeavors to preserve our own life, and the life of others.

It was natural for Esther to think that her own life was in no danger from the bloody decree. Her husband had unknowingly signed a warrant for her death: But who would venture to lift up his hand against the queen? Or what would it avail her murderers to allege the king's law, when the king himself, who was above the law, would consider the cause as his own? We must not, however, entertain such a mean opinion of Esther as to think, that she would be less zealous in the cause, because she might apprehend herself to be safe. Yet Mordecai hopes to quicken her zeal, by letting her know that she was not more safe than other Jews. God would find some means to free them from their danger; but Esther, though in the king's house, must not expect to escape if she deserted the cause of God, and of his people in their extreme danger.

Human probabilities were on her side. The king, though perhaps alienated from her, would not allow himself to be insulted by a murder perpetrated upon his queen, and in his own palace. Even Haman himself would not dare to arm an assassin against the queen. But we are not to trust to human probabilities. God is the author and the preserver of our lives. When He withdraws his protection, we are undone; and how could Esther expect his protection, if she refused, at the loud call of his providence, and at the pressing admonition of Mordecai, to seek the life of her people? *'If you forbear to deliver them that are drawn unto death, and them that are ready to be slain; if you say, Behold, we knew it not, does not He that ponders the heart consider it? and He that keeps,'* or He that observes, *'your soul, does not He know it? and shall not He render to every man according to his works?'* Are we worthy of have our lives preserved, if we show no concern for the lives of our fellow-men? Are we not in some measure chargeable with those deaths which we do not endeavor, if it is in our power, to prevent? Let it be remembered, that the life of the soul is infinitely more precious than that of the body, and that we have more frequent opportunities of contributing to the salvation of souls, than to the preservation of natural life; though we have more opportunities of the latter sort than we carefully improve, or perhaps think about. When we see men wasting their bodies, and shortening their days, by idleness, by intemperance, by the indulgence of those bitter passions which are as rottenness to the bones, we may contribute to the life of both soul and body, by good advice, by earnest expostulation, by our prayers to God. By our prayers, by our holy example, by well-timed and well-advised reproofs and exhortations, we may save souls from death. If we do not what God enables us to do for the salvation of perishing souls, are we not accessory to their perdition?

Do not think that you shall escape in the king's house. – It is vain to trust in kings, or in the sons of men, in whom there is no confidence. Kings die. *'In that day their breath goes forth, and their thoughts perish.'* Kings are changeable creatures, like other men. The kings were not like the laws of the Medes and Persians, which could not be altered. He that was in the morning their favorite, might, before the evening, be hanged by their orders. Herod, king of Judea, dearly loved his wife Mariamne, and yet he ordered her to be put to death without any crime, but what was committed in his own dark imagination. Monima was a beloved wife of Mithridates, the great king of Pontus, and yet, when he lost a battle against the Romans, that she might not fall into other hands than his own, he commanded her to die; and the only favor he showed her, was to give her the choice of her own death. Her choice was, to strangle herself by her royal tiara, which had long been hateful to her. But even in this she was disappointed, and her last, or nearly her last words were, 'Poor bauble, can you not do me even this mournful office?'

Jesus forbids us to fear them that have power only to kill the body. Still less, if possible, are we to trust them; for they have no power even to save the body. God is to be trusted and feared. He is the Lawgiver, who is able to save and to destroy; (Psalm 146:3-6).

Verse 14. – *For if you are completely silent at this time, then relief and deliverance shall arise to the Jews from another place, but you and your father's house shall be destroyed. And who knows whether you have come to the kingdom for such a time as this?*

What evidence had Mordecai to go upon, in alleging that deliverance and enlargement should arise from some one place or another to the Jews at this time? He had as good evidence as the word, and even the oath of God, could give him. The Lord had made a covenant with Abraham, to be a God unto himself, and to his seed after him. *'This covenant he ratified by his oath unto Isaac, and confirmed the same unto Jacob for a law, and to Israel for an everlasting covenant.'* Haman's malice, and, what was more formidable than Haman's malice, the sins of God's people, could not make void the promise of God, nor make his oath and his covenant of none effect. We are sure, even in this age of the world, that no Haman will ever be able to extirpate the natural seed of Abraham: For *'the gifts and calling of God are without repentance.'*

There were many prophecies published by Isaiah, by Jeremiah, by Ezekiel, by Daniel, and the other prophets, concerning the restoration of the captive Jews; concerning God's care of them in their own land, or in their dispersion; and concerning that Saviour who was to *'come to Zion, to turn away ungodliness from Jacob.'* These prophecies were, doubtless, well known to Mordecai. They were the life of his soul, and the joy of his heart.

The Lord had, in every age, been *'the hope of Israel, and the Saviour thereof in the time of trouble.'* He had given enlargement to his people when they were shut up between rocks and seas, and the sword of an enraged enemy, who was much too strong for them; and he who had delivered his people from so great deaths, had assured them that he would still deliver them: *'The Lord said, I will bring again my people from the depths of the sea, and from Bashan hill.'*

The hearts of the unbelieving Jews would sink within them in their present perilous condition; but believers in the word of God would not be confounded. They knew that the honor of God was as deeply interested in the event, as were their life and welfare; and that he who had so often wrought for his name's sake, would still work for his people. There were many and strong enemies; but they had the Almighty God for their friend.

Mordecai was one of those believers who, in the days of Israel's distress, *'remembered the years (or the changes) of the right hand of the Most High;'* and in the words before us, he expressed his full assurance that God would frustrate Haman's plot. Blessed are they that trust in the Lord! God *'will keep them in perfect peace,'* and enable them in the darkest days to express their joyful hope, that *'at evening-time it shall be light.'*

But why did Mordecai mourn so bitterly, if he was assured that deliverance would arise from some place to the Jews? Because *'in that day did the Lord God of hosts call to mourning and to weeping.'* In such a dark day the people of God were called to pour out their hearts like water before the face of the Lord, for their life, and for the life of their children. The faith of God's people does not interfere with the exercise of affections suited to mournful dispensations of providence. Faith encourages us to come before God with tears and cryings, because it assures us that he knows all our distresses, and puts our tears into his bottle.

Relief and deliverance shall arise to the Jews; to the Israel of God, under the gospel, as well as under the law. Amid all the distresses of the church, we may rest assured that she cannot perish. Particular churches may be destroyed, but the church universal is *'built by Christ upon a rock, and the gates of hell shall not prevail against it.'*

If Jews according to the flesh were blessed with the assured hopes of deliverance to their nation in every danger, however dreadful; those who are Jews in the noblest sense, may at all times expect help from God. *'He is not a Jew who is one outwardly, but who is one inwardly: neither is that circumcision which is outward in the flesh; but circumcision is that of the heart, in the spirit, whose praise is not of men, but of God.'* If its praise be of God, he will be its almighty protector. He may *'sift Israel as corn is sifted in a sieve,'* but one grain shall not be allowed to fall upon the ground.

If you are completely silent at this time, then relief and deliverance shall arise to the Jews from another place. – Esther, though warmly solicited to interpose in the behalf of the Jews, must not imagine that their safety depends on her. If she succeeds, she will have reason to bless God for making her the honored instrument of their deliverance; and the Jews will have great reason to bless her, and to bless God for her. But she will have no reason to be proud. She is assured, that whether she had any hand in their deliverance or not, their deliverance was sure. It by no means depended upon her exertions; for if she had never been born, if she had never been a queen, or if she had been a base apostate to the religion of the court, Israel was safe under the protection of the God of Israel. The safety of the church depends not on her best friends on earth; nor can her deliverance be prevented, either by the coldness of her friends, or by the power of her enemies. All, therefore, who perform eminent services to the church, ought humbly to thank the Lord for choosing to employ them rather than others; for He is never at a loss for servants to his work. The life of Moses might have been thought by the Israelites so necessary for them when they were delivered from Egypt, that they could have little hope, without him, of obtaining possession of the promised land; and yet he died when they were come to the borders of it. But God could put a sufficient portion of Moses' spirit in Joshua to bring his people into the land of which he had sworn unto them; and when they were both in heaven, he could raise up other saviours to his people, to deliver them from their enemies.

But you and your father's house shall be destroyed. – Why? Because Esther neglected to do what she ought to have done for the salvation of Israel. It is a common, and not a false maxim. That sins of omission are less heinous than sins of commission. But let us not mistake the maxim; the meaning of it is, that sins of omission, as such, are not so atrocious as sins of commission. On other accounts, they may be criminal above most sins that you can name. It is worse to do what God plainly forbids, than to neglect doing of what he requires; because (when other things are equal) it is a token of a more rebellious disposition, to be active in doing what is sinful, than through negligence and inattention, to omit a duty required from us. Yet, if you saw a man drowning in the water, and did not attempt to save him from the danger, would not your sin be no less than murder, and consequently worse than an officious lie, or even than an instance of fraud? But if Esther had neglected to interpose in the present case, she would have suffered the whole nation to perish. If she did not so interpose, she had at least the guilt of not doing what she could to prevent it, and thus she exposed herself and her father's house to destruction from the anger of God.

But what had her father's house to do with her sin? Is it not said, that *'the son shall not die for the iniquity of the father, nor the father for the iniquity of the son?'* This is a law which the universal Lord has prescribed for men, and not for himself. We know that God destroyed even whole families for the sins of their heads. Only we must remember that the whole world is guilty before God. He can, without injustice, destroy a whole family when one member has sinned, and when the rest had no participation in the guilt, because guilt of another kind can be justly charged upon them. The punishment is therefore, properly speaking, the punishment of the single offender made ten-fold more heavy, by involving with him so many dear objects of his regard. His relations were chargeable with sins which exposed them to death when God pleased to require their souls; and they have no more reason to blame the righteousness of the divine procedure, than the debtor has to find fault with the creditor for demanding the money due to him, when he finds occasion to use it.

If you are silent at this time, you and your father's house shall be destroyed. – But was it the exclusive duty of Esther to take this business upon herself? Where was that law to be found which imposed a burden upon this good woman, from which all the rest of the Jews were exempted? Was there a special commandment given to her, which she could not disobey without exposing herself and all her father's house to destruction? Esther was certainly under the same laws which bound all the rest of the Jews, and under none else. There was no special precept given to her, like that which was addressed by Jesus to the young man, who was commanded to sell all that he had, and give to the poor. Yet Esther, by that common law, had a special duty enjoined on her. All were bound to use the means competent to them to preserve their nation from destruction. Petitioning the king was a means of safety necessary to be used, and the providence of God plainly pointed out Esther as the petitioner most likely to succeed. The law of God is the only rule of our duty: but the providence of God often points out to individual persons, duties which the law requires especially from themselves. Those things may be necessary duties at one time which are not duties at another; or to one person, or to one class of persons, which are not required from others: and the neglect of those duties which are required from us, and not from others, or of those duties which are rendered so only by a particular train of providences, may involve us in deep guilt, and in great danger. A man who knows a particular remedy for a certain disease, of which others are ignorant, would be chargeable with the fatal consequences that may arise from the general ignorance, if he locks up his knowledge in his own breast. If Providence furnish us with talents which are not granted to others, we must account for our use of them. If we have opportunities of doing much good which others have not, and make no use of them, we make ourselves guilty of a crime which can be charged upon none but ourselves. The law is the same to all; but particular circumstances place us under the obligation of particular precepts, which take no hold of persons in different situations.

And who knows whether you have come to the kingdom for such a time as this? – The circumstances which led Esther to a throne were wonderful, either in themselves, or in their combination. The daughter of Abihail the Jew, was astonished to find herself the wife of the great king Ahasuerus; and doubtless must have thought, that the providence of God, which shone so wonderfully in her exaltation, had some design in view, of which she was hitherto ignorant. When Joseph was raised to be lord over all the land of Egypt, God was making provision for the support of Jacob's family. When Esther was elevated to the dignity of a great queen, and when a sentence of death had gone forth against her whole nation, it appeared highly probable to Mordecai that God designed her to be the preserver of her people. It was, therefore, in his judgment, her necessary duty to make the attempt, that she might not be backward to second the designs of Providence. To hide our talent in a napkin is criminal and dangerous.

If God has done remarkable things for us, we have reason to believe that he expects some services from us suited to the situation in which he has placed us, and to the means of service with which he has furnished us. We ought, therefore, when we consider what God has done for us, to consider at the same time what he requires from us. If our circumstances are peculiar, it is likely that some peculiar services are required; or if we cannot find out any particular service to be done at present, let us wait a little, and we may find calls to services suited to our condition. *'The Lord has made all things,'* and he still does all things, *'for himself.'*

What if you are come to the kingdom for such a time as this? – It is at least highly probable. But the duty itself is certain: and if we do not improve particular dispensations of providence for the purposes for which they are intended, we walk contrary to God, and provoke him to walk contrary to us. *Whoso is wise to observe the doings of the Lord, even he shall understand his loving-kindness.'* But when men do not know their times and opportunities, their misery is great upon them.

Verses 15, 16. – *Then Esther told them to return to Mordecai this answer – Go, gather together all the Jews who are present in Shushan, and fast for me, and neither eat nor drink three days, night or day. My maidens and I will also fast in the same way. And so I will go in unto the king, which is not according to the law. And if I perish, I perish.*

Esther highly respected Mordecai; and she respected him not the less, but the more, because he continued to use the freedom of a father with her. She doubtless thought herself blessed in a friend who took the liberty to remonstrate with her concerning duties which she felt an aversion to perform. He that rebukes and admonishes, will be far more valued by us, if we are wise, than he that flatters with his lips.

Esther never intended to decline the perilous service recommended by Mordecai, when she should find it to be a necessary duty. Being now convinced that it was, she promises to go in to the king, let the consequence be what it would. But, as her hope of success was in God, she requires all the Jews in Shushan to fast for her three days. The Jews in other places would have been required to give her the same help, if it had been practicable to give them seasonable information of her wishes and intentions. Paul frequently seeks the help of the prayers of the church. Esther seeks the help, not only of the prayers of the Jews, but of all the devotional exercises of a solemn fast of three days continuance. The situation of the Jews was critical and dangerous in the extreme. Esther's hopes from her influence with the king were faint. If God did not pity his people, they were undone. Never did God more loudly call for fasting than at this time; and a single day observed in fasting was thought by her too little to be employed in the exercise. Perhaps she called in mind the example of the Ninevites, and the happy success of their devotion. They observed a strict fast of three days, and cried mightily to God, and turned from their wickedness; and *'the Lord repented of the evil which he thought to do unto them, and did it not.'* Esther would justly think that the Lord, who showed such favor to an Assyrian city, infamous for its former wickedness, would not turn a deaf ear to his own people in the day of their distress.

It would be folly to think that Esther placed the least dependence upon mere abstinence from food, when she required the Jews to fast. All her expectations of advantage from this fast were founded upon God, who had instituted this duty, and promised happy consequences to it, when it was observed according to his will. We have, therefore, no reason to say that the name of God is not to be found in this book, which speaks of his worship (a part of his name). The name God, or Lord, is not in it. But who does not know, that the exercise of fasting here enjoined by Esther, is a part of His service, and that no advantage can be expected from it but through divine mercy accepting this service, and hearing the supplications of his people? Esther, indeed, does not speak of the prayers, of the self-examination, of the confessions, of the reformation, that were to accompany this abstinence from food. The exercises proper to a day of fasting were already known to the Jews; or they would learn them from the history of Jonah, to which the similarity of the present danger of the Jews with that of the Ninevites would lead their minds; of if they needed any further information on the subject, Esther believed that Mordecai was better qualified than herself to give them proper directions. She insists, however, upon one thing, that they should neither eat nor drink three days, day or night; but observe the fast with strictness, like persons so deeply concerned in the business, that they would deny the strongest cravings of nature, and bear the extremes of hunger and thirst, that they might express the deepest humiliation of spirit before God, and pour forth their hearts before him. There are too many among us who would think it an intolerable hardship to be deprived of their food for a single day, or for half of a day, when they have the loudest calls to solemn fasting. How would such persons have acted in the time of Esther's fast? Would not the remedy have appeared to them almost as bad as the disease? Was it not as good to die by the sword of their enemies, as to starve themselves to death? Yet we do not find that any of the Jews in Shushan refused to comply with Esther's desire. The fear of death before their eyes made their ordinary food a matter of indifference to them. What though they should deny themselves the ordinary comforts of life for three days, when their object was to obtain a reversal of a sentence of death given forth against them?

We are not, however, to understand the words so strictly as to make them a prohibition of all sorts of food for three days, even to those men, women, or children, whose bodies could not sustain such a long fast. Doubtless there were some among them who, through sickness or weakness, could as little bear a complete privation of food for three whole days and nights, as that Egyptian slave whom David relieved from mortal weakness, contracted by a fast of three days, when he was marching against the Amalekites that had burnt Ziklag. Esther did not think that it was any man's duty to destroy his body by a voluntary fast. She knew that God would have mercy and not sacrifice. Her desire was not to destroy, but to save the lives of her people. Her words may be reasonably understood to mean, that the Jews were not to take any regular meal, nor any other supplies of food, but such as might be necessary for the preservation of health and vigor. Perfect abstinence for three days and three nights would have been inimical, rather than favorable, to the great purpose of the fast. Paul said to the mariners that sailed with him to Rome, '*This day is the fourteenth day that you have tarried, and continued fasting, having taken nothing.*' Surely they did not want food during two complete weeks; yet they are said to have continued fasting, and taken nothing, because, amid the agitation of fear and hope, they were incapable of taking any regular meal.

Fast for me, and neither eat nor drink for three days. – They were not called with Esther to go in unto the king. A service attended with no danger was required from them. But what they can do, and are called to do, they must do as conscientiously as Esther. There are many great works which are beyond our strength, or out of the line of our calling; and yet we may and ought to take a part in them, by strengthening the hands of those who are called to undertake them. Paul had many helpers in his work of the gospel, even among those who could not, or to whom it would not have been allowed to, speak in the church. We all ought to be fellow-helpers to the truth. While many go abroad to spread the gospel among heathens, we find it our duty to continue in the land of our nativity; but, without removing from it, we may promote the work in which they are employed, by our contributions, or at least by our prayers.

There are some who beg the prayers of others, and yet pray little for themselves. Esther, who requested the Jews to fast for her, told them that she also would fast, and would abstain as strictly from food as she desired them to do. She had been accustomed to a well-furnished table; but she was not thereby disqualified from afflicting her soul by fasting when she saw it to be her duty. She no doubt observed the annual fasts prescribed to the Jews; and she determined to observe this extraordinary fast which she herself prescribed. She hoped to obtain mercy from the Lord, that she might escape death by the laws of Persia, and might be the instrument of the salvation of her people. But if she miscarried, her fasting and prayer would be proper acts of preparation for her latter end.

I and my maids will fast. – Some, it is probable, of Esther's maids, were heathens when they came into her service; (Chap. 2:9). Yet we find her promising that they would fast. She can answer for them, as Joshua for his household, that they would serve the Lord. If mistresses were as zealous as queen Esther for the honor of God, and the conversion of sinners, they would bestow pains upon the instruction and religious improvement of their female servants. If women may gain to Christ their own husbands by their good conversation, may they not also gain the souls of their servants? and if they are gained to Christ, they are gained to themselves also. Esther expected much benefit from the devotional exercises of her maidens. Paul expected much from the prayers of his converts. Those whom we convert from the error of their ways, will probably be our joy and helpers upon earth; they will certainly be our joy and crown of rejoicing in the day of Christ.

I and my maids will fast. – Esther could not join in the public prayers of the Jews, when they met together out of many families to strive together in their prayers to God. But she will fast at home, not only by herself, but with her maidens. There are public fasts in which all are expected to join. There ought likewise to be secret and family fasts observed by us, according to the calls of providence, and the situation of our affairs, or the condition of our souls; (Matt. 6:16-18).

And so I will go in unto the king, which is not according to the law. – She would not go in unto the king, till she made her supplication to the Lord, and till the Jews had given her the assistance of their prayers. She was sensible, that though *'all men will intreat the ruler's favor, every man's judgment comes from the Lord;'* and that the hearts of kings are turned by him according to his pleasure. What, therefore, she desires in the first place is that she may obtain comfortable assurance of the divine favor. If the Lord is on her side, she is safe. If the Lord favors her suit, she need not fear the coldness of Ahasuerus, or the mortal enmity of Haman. *'The floods may rage.'* They may lift up their voices and make a mighty noise: but the Lord on high is mightier than the waves of the sea, or the voice of their roaring.

But when the fast is over, she will go in unto the king. She will not think that her duty is done, when she has prayed and fasted. She will seek, by the use of proper means, to obtain that blessing which she has been asking. The insincerity of our prayers is too often discovered by our sloth and cowardice. We ask blessings from God, and, as if he were bound to confer them, not according to his own will, but according to ours, we take no care to use those means which he has appointed for obtaining them, or we do not use them with requisite diligence. Esther will go in unto the king, although she could not go in without violating the laws, and risking her life.

I will go in unto the king, which is not according to the law. – Who will keep the king's laws, if the queen herself does not observe them? Did not Esther know that Vashti lost her crown, and her husband, for disobeying the king in a matter of less consequence than a standing law deliberately enacted by the king's authority? True; but necessity has no law. She will keep the king's laws as far as she can keep them and the laws of God at the same time. But in the present case, she must be a betrayer of her country, of her own life, of the laws of Heaven, if she hesitate any longer to go in unto the king, although it is not according to the law. We must obey princes, *'not only for wrath, but also for conscience sake.'* But, for conscience sake, we must stop short where the law of God interposes; (Acts 4:19).

Esther may lose her royal dignity. She may be expelled from the king's bed. She may lose her life for disobeying the laws. But *'if I perish,'* she says, *'I perish.'* It is not necessary for me to live, but it is necessary for me to do my duty. If I perish in obeying the will of God, it is better than to live in disobedience.

If I perish, I perish. – Our lives are not our own; they cannot be long preserved by us. They will be of little value to us without a good conscience. That life which is purchased by neglect of duty, is shameful, bitter, worse than death. Whosoever shall save his life in this manner, shall lose it in this world, as well as in the next. His life will be but a lingering death: for the dissatisfaction and painful reflections which fill it up are far less tolerable than the bodily pain which usually precedes death. But to lose life for the sake of Christ and a good conscience, is truly to live. A day of life employed in the most hazardous duties, by which we show that our love to God is stronger than death, excels a thousand days of a life spent in the service and enjoyment of the world.

Verse 17. – *So Mordecai went his way and did according to all that Esther had commanded him.*

Mordecai commanded Esther, and she obeyed him. Esther commanded Mordecai, and he obeyed her. They served one another in love. It would be happy for us if we knew how to command and how to obey in our turns, being *'subject one to another,'* in the fear of God.

Mordecai required the Jews to fast three days according to Esther's orders; and we have no reason to doubt of their ready and grateful compliance. They would not think it hard, but necessary and useful, to be called to afflict their souls to an extraordinary degree, when their lives and the lives of all their people were in question. And yet the present life of all the many thousands of Judah was not of equal importance to the eternal life of one precious soul. What, then, are we to think of ourselves, if the sentence of eternal death denounced against every sinner, has never induced us to devote as many hours to fervent prayer, as these Jews employed days in prayers and fasting to obtain deliverance from temporal death? Is it not to be feared, that we do not really believe what the Scripture tells us about that judgment which is come upon all men to condemnation, if we think it too much trouble to spend some hours or days in considering our condition, and pouring out supplications for that mercy which we so greatly need? The Jews fasted. Esther went in to the king, uncertain about the event, but pressed by hard necessity. Necessity is laid upon sinners, yea, woe unto them if they do not obtain mercy! But great encouragement is given them to come to the throne of grace to obtain mercy. God himself puts words in their mouths, and will He not hear those prayers which are dictated by his own Spirit? (Hos. 14:2-4; Jer. 31:18-20).

DISCOURSE IX.

ESTHER GOES IN UNTO THE KING, AND FINDS FAVOR IN HIS EYES - HAMAN, INFLAMED BY REVENGE, PREPARES A GALLOWS FOR MORDECAI OF FIFTY CUBITS HIGH.

CHAPTER 5:1-14.

Verse 1. – *Now on the third day Esther put on her royal clothing, and stood in the inner court of the king's house, across from the king's house. And the king sat upon his royal throne in the royal house, across from the gate of the house.*

Esther was not one of those who resolve and promise well, but do not perform. How ready are we, like the disobedient son in the parable, to say, We will go and work in the vineyard, and after all go not! But what excuse will we have for breaking our promises through the mere power of laziness, when Esther kept her word at the risk of her life? She deserves to be ranked with the noble army of confessors, if not of martyrs. She went in unto the king when a law faced her which declared it to be death for any subject, not excepting the queen, to go in unto the king's private apartments without his leave.

Nor did she linger in doubt whether she should go in unto the king or not. If she had, new temptations, dangerous to her virtue, might have assaulted her. Her resolution had been already formed; and she makes haste, and delays not to do the commandment of Mordecai, which she considers as a commandment from God. On the third day, she went in unto the king. Her fast did not, it seems, consist of three complete days and nights. In the language of the Jews, *'three days and three nights'* might mean one whole day and a part of two others. Jesus is said to have been *'three days and three nights in the heart of the earth,'* and yet he is said to have risen *'on the third day.'*

She observed her fast, and it was no sooner over than she went in unto the king. It was wise in her, when she had finished her supplications, to present her petition to the king. When Hannah prayed in the bitterness of her grief, her heart was eased; she was no more sorrowful. We have reason to think that Esther's anxieties, too, were banished by her devotion. She had been lifting up her soul to the Lord. She had been, doubtless, *'remembering her song in the night,'* and *'the wonderful works of former times'* would inspire her with the hope of a happy event to her present enterprise. Thus she was able to approach unto the king with all that composure of mind, and cheerfulness of countenance, which were necessary for the occasion.

She put on her royal apparel when she went in to the king. She cared not for the distinction of her rank, and placed not her delight in the outward adorning of gold and pearls and costly array. But it was necessary to lay aside her mourning apparel, and to put on her beautiful garments, when she went in to the king. Good wives will endeavor to please their husbands by a decency in dress, as well as other things that may appear little when they are not considered as means to gain an important end. *'The married woman cares,'* and ought to care, *'how she may please her husband;'* and those women do not act as becomes saints, whose dress, or any part of their behavior, naturally tends to produce disgust. Esther had a peculiar reason for dressing herself with her beautiful garments, when she went into the king's presence. But all women are bound to please their husbands in things lawful and innocent, because the law of Christ binds them to reverence their husbands: and their husbands, if they are not fools, will not desire them to transgress the laws concerning dress, which two apostles have thought it necessary to record for their direction; (1 Tim. 2:9; 1 Peter 3:3-6).

She stood in the inner court of the king's house, across from the king's house; that is, across from the king's private apartment in the palace. The word rendered house may signify either a large pile of building, or particular apartments in it. In the first of these senses it is to be understood, when it is said *'she stood in the inner court of the king's house'* or palace. In the second, when it is said that she stood *across from the king's house.* She stood within his view as he sat upon his royal throne, waiting for the intimation of his will, either to leave her to the penalty of the laws, or to save her alive. We have already seen that Esther was a courageous woman. She would venture her life for the salvation of her people. It is probable, however, that she felt great agitation of spirit in this critical moment, when the sentence of life or death was in effect to be pronounced upon her. Her busy imagination would call up her fears, by setting in her view the cruel law, the coldness of her king, the severity exercised upon Vashti. But, in the multitude of her thoughts within her, it is to be presumed, that God's comforts delighted her soul.

Verse 2. – *And when the king saw Esther the queen standing in the court, she received favor in his sight. And the king held out to Esther the golden scepter that was in his hand. So Esther drew near and touched the top of the scepter.*

The countenance of Esther at this critical moment was highly interesting to the king her husband. Grief, anxiety, pity, painted in her beauteous face, awakened his pity, and attracted his love. She found favor in his eyes, and he held out to her the golden sceptre, the sign of grace and pardon; which Esther touched, in thankful acceptance of the offered mercy.

'As a prince,' said God to Jacob, *'have you power with God; and with men also shall you prevail.'* Esther had been weeping and making supplication, like her father Jacob, and had prevailed, and saw the face of the king as if it had been the face of God, and her life was

preserved; and, what was still better, she had the happy presage of the preservation of the life of all her people, in that favor which was extended to herself. What wonderful favors from men may fervent supplication to God obtain! *'If He be for us, who can be against us?'*

Verse 3. – *Then the king said to her, What do you desire, queen Esther? And what is your wish? It shall be given to you even to half of the kingdom.*

The heart of the king, if it was formerly alienated from Esther, was now most effectually turned to favor her. He not only held out to her the golden sceptre, but addressed her with expressions of the tenderest love, and of the richest bounty. She may now confidently seek from him the life of all her people; for she was assured that she should receive the richest boon which discretion could allow her to ask.

Our Lord teaches us to draw a comfortable instruction from the bounty of parents to their children: *'If even you, being evil, know how to give good gifts unto your children, how much more shall your heavenly Father give good things to them that ask him?'* May we not with equal assurance draw the same instruction from the kindness of Ahasuerus to his queen? A man who would wantonly devote a whole nation to destruction, and a nation to which his queen belonged for aught he knew, will nevertheless give her what she pleases to ask, when she comes to him as a humble petitioner, although her coming to him was not according to the law. When we come to the throne of the eternal King, we have the law of grace on our side. *'Come boldly unto the throne of grace – Ask, and you shall receive.'* The King whom we approach is *'rich in mercy to all that call upon Him.'* He will not withhold from us the desire of our lips. He will *'do for us above what we can ask or think.'* We have perhaps come into his presence under discouraging apprehensions of his displeasure, but *'He will not contend forever, neither will he be always wroth – He has heard the desire of the humble – You will prepare their heart, you will cause your ear to hear.'*

Verse 4. – *And Esther answered, If it seem good unto the king, let the king and Haman come today to the banquet which I have prepared for him.*

Esther had surely a good opportunity to present her request to the king, when he was so well disposed to grant it. But the importance of it was far more than life. Her timidity was not entirely removed by all the kind words which the king had spoken. He might take it kindly to find a rich banquet prepared for him by Esther. She hopes that his heart would be warmed with friendship, and inspired with generous and pleasing sentiments, by a banquet to his taste; and she wished for some more time of recollection, preparation, and prayer, before she made known her great request to the king. All, therefore, that she requests at present is that the king and Haman might come to the feast which she had prepared for their entertainment.

A feast is, especially in the eastern countries, a seal of friendship; and therefore, it may appear strange that Haman was invited along with the king, although Esther had it in view to present a petition to the king against him. But necessity was laid upon her, if she invited the king, to invite Haman also, who was as inseparable from him at this time as his right hand. The fault was in the king, and not in Esther, if any wrong done him by cherishing those proud imaginations that were soon to be humbled to the dust. She was not in a situation to act with the delicacy of Saladin, sultan of Egypt, who gave a draught of refreshing liquor to his thirsty captive, Guy, king of Jerusalem; but when the king handed the cup to his companion in bonds, Arnold, lord of Brescia, the sultan desired him to observe, that it was not he, but the king of Jerusalem, that gave him the cup. The reason of this behavior was that Saladin had justly doomed Arnold to death for barbarities treacherously perpetrated by him against his people. No man, however, can say that Esther dealt unfairly with Haman. His presence was expedient at the presenting of the petition, that there might be no pretense to complain of injury. He was to be charged with the worst of crimes, and there was nothing unfair in giving him an opportunity, by being present, to exculpate himself, if that had been possible.

Verse 5. – *Then the king said, Cause Haman to hurry so that he may do as Esther has said. So the king and Haman came to the banquet which Esther had prepared.*

The king was not displeased at the timidity of Esther, but considered it as a mark of the profound reverence which she entertained for him. He was pleased with the respect showed to him in inviting him, with his friend Haman, to a banquet. He knew that Haman would reckon himself highly honored by the invitation, and sent for him to come in all haste to share in the entertainment. Thus far things went well with Esther. She was assured of the king's kindness, and furnished with an opportunity of ingratiating herself still more with the man to whom, under God, she must look for the life of her people.

Verse 6. *And the king said unto Esther at the banquet of wine, What is your petition that it shall be granted unto you? And what is your request? It shall be performed even to half of the kingdom.*

We find, in the second chapter, that the beauty and modesty of Esther gained the hearts of all who saw her. Doubtless, when the king, at the banquet of wine, had an opportunity of conversing with Esther, and of observing those lovely graces that appeared in every part of her behavior, his love was inflamed, and he thought he could not give her too great proofs of his kindness. The pleasure he enjoyed in the entertainment, and in the society of those whom he most loved, opened his heart to liberality; and he again desires Esther to present her request before him, with the repeated assurance that it should be granted her to the half of the kingdom. The fears of Esther, however, seem not yet to have been altogether extinguished, although hope predominated.

Verses 7,8. – *Then Esther answered and said, As to my petition and my request, if I have found favor in the sight of the king, and if it pleases the king to grant my petition and to perform my request, let the king and Haman come to the banquet which I shall prepare for them, and I will do tomorrow as the king has said.*

It was a great favor that she had already received, that the king honored her banquet with his presence, and all that she will venture to ask more at this time is that this favor may be repeated. But the great object of her desire for which she entered into the king's presence, she dares not yet to produce. She lays herself, however, under an obligation to vanquish her fears, and to acquaint the king with her wishes, if he will favor her with his presence tomorrow. The king would not take it amiss that Esther discovered such timidity in his presence. He loved her, and wished to be loved by her; but he wished likewise to be feared with a reverence greater, perhaps, than is due to mortals.

But, could Esther have a better opportunity than the present to present her chief request to the king? She could not, perhaps, prudently publish it in the king's apartments, where some of the princes might be present, who would be ready to declaim against the request, as a petition for the overthrow of the fundamental laws of the empire. Here none but the king and Haman were to be present, and Haman must be her enemy whenever the petition is presented. The king was now in the best humor imaginable, and nothing but courage in Esther seemed to be wanting to complete the business.

It is to be considered, however, that there was no occasion for great haste in the business, because more than ten months still remained of the time set for the destruction of the Jews; and if the queen had gained much this day upon the king's affection, she might gain still more by the entertainment and converse of the next. It is to be remembered that there were difficulties almost insurmountable in the way of granting her request. It might seem to demand the overthrow of a fundamental law of the kingdom, that laws ratified by the king's authority, and sealed with his seal, should not be altered. It might even have been supposed that the king's right to the throne was exposed to question, if he should attempt unconstitutional innovations in the government, by granting such a petition. We all know that a race of our own kings forfeited the throne by such attempts.[1]

The king's kindness to Esther was a great encouragement to her to present her request. But his attachment to Haman might well render it doubtful whether that favorite or the queen would prevail. It is not, therefore, strange that Esther desired another day before she presented her request. She trusted in God, but she must likewise use the utmost prudence. Paul believed God that he should be saved from the hands of the Jews, to testify concerning Christ at Rome; (Acts 23:11); and yet he made application to the chief captain to protect him from their snares. The use of the best means for obtaining what we desire ought to accompany our hope in God.

It is good always to avoid undue delays in doing what is right; yet precipitancy is likewise to be avoided. We know not what a day may bring forth, when we wait for a proper season. Esther seems plainly to have been directed by the Divine Providence in deferring her petition to the following day. Very unexpected events fell out in the interval, which greatly favored her request.

Verse 9. – *Then Haman went forth that day joyful and with a glad heart. But when Haman saw Mordecai in the king's gate, that he did not stand or move for him, he was full of fury against Mordecai.*

Unhappy are they whose chief happiness lies in the favor of princes, or in any earthly object. Haman thought himself happy in the king's favor, which he enjoyed. He thought himself happy in the queen's favor, which he did not enjoy. He was soon to know that he was equally deceived in both. The queen was already plotting his destruction, and the king's favor was soon to be converted into deadly hatred.

Vain are the joys of them that have their portion in this life. Double vanity is in the joys of the proud. They are exposed to misery no less by their own capricious fancies, than by the changeable nature of external objects. Although Haman had been able to secure the king's favor to the end of his life; although he had been no less the favorite of Esther than of Ahasuerus; what good would all have done him, when such a trifle as the stiffness of Mordecai's knees could make him unhappy? He must every day have met with something to deprive him of the possession of his own soul. A man who cannot be happy unless every person give him all the respect which he may think his due, will never be happy till the Almighty resign to him the government of the world.

Mordecai was as far as ever from bowing the knee to Haman. He acted on a principle of conscience, and no circumstances could alter the settled purpose of his soul. Haman can procure a sentence of death against him, and against his people; but he cannot turn sin into duty: and let death or life come, it was Mordecai's resolution to be found in that good path which leads to life and peace. – *'Haman was full of fury against Mordecai.*

Verse 10. – *But Haman held himself in. And when he came home, he sent and called for his friends and Zeresh his wife.*

When proud men are seeking glory from others, they are often secretly ashamed of themselves. Haman was ashamed to disclose that secret rage which boiled in his bosom, when Mordecai bowed not his knees to him. He had indeed good reason to be ashamed, that a man so great, and blessed with such affluence of worldly comforts, should be a slave to his own vanity, and dependent on every man he saw for his happiness. What man is more to be pitied than he who cannot enjoy any comfort without the consent of all his neighbors, without excepting those whom most of all others he hates and despises? Such is the proud man. He despises all around him, and yet cannot taste of happiness if any of them think fit to deny him that homage which he wishes to enjoy. Let him hear the praises or the flatteries of nine hundred of his neighbors, his heart may be swelled with joy; but that joy is dependent for its continuance upon the next man he meets. The meanness of such a man's spirit must cover him with shame, when it is disclosed. Haman would not disclose his chagrin in the presence of Mordecai, but he could not conceal it from his friends. *'When he came home, he sent and called for his friends, and Zeresh his wife.'*

Verses 11,12. – *And Haman told them of the glory of his riches, and the multitude of his children, and all the things in which the king had promoted him, and how he had advanced him above the princes and servants of the king. Moreover Haman said, Yes, Esther the queen let no man but me come in with the king unto the banquet that she had prepared. And also tomorrow I am invited to her banquet with the king.*

Haman gives his friends an inventory of his happiness. He was immensely rich. He had many children to preserve his fame in the world. He was the unrivalled favorite of the king; and he was no less so of the queen, who honored him almost as much as the king did. Among all the king's noble princes, none was admitted to the queen's royal banquet with the king but himself. Not one of the brothers or cousins of the king, not a relation of the queen, was called to the feast. Haman, must, therefore, be considered as the second man of the kingdom.

Riches are good. The favor of kings and of queens may be very useful, and give great pleasure. But, unhappy is the man whose chief happiness lies in any of these things, or in all of them together. Riches soon make to themselves wings, and fly away; and during the time of their continuance, they cannot ease the body afflicted with the slightest disorder; far less can they produce that tranquillity of soul, without which men must be miserable were they in paradise itself. Children are no less mortal than their parents, and their life is often more grievous than their death would be. Princes may shower down favors upon us, and their smiles may gratify our vanity. But they may smile to-day, and frown to-morrow. To-day they may invite us to their banquets, and, if they are absolute princes, may to-morrow pronounce the sentence of our death. Besides, we know not the hearts of princes, and we may deceive ourselves with fond opinions of their friendship, which a short time will discover to have been illusions of our own imagination. Haman's fate ought to be a lesson to those who boast themselves because they are become exceeding rich, and because they are blessed with every thing that the heart of a man of the world can wish. We know not what a day may bring forth. On the morrow after Haman boasted to his wife and friends of his unequalled prosperity, his honor was laid lower than the dust. His great friends appeared to be his deadly enemies. His wealth became the property of one of the nation which he had devoted to destruction. His ten children were left unprotected, to feel the dismal effects of their father's crimes. How well-founded is the precept of the apostle! – *'Let them that have wives (or any relation) be as though they had them not; and they that rejoice, as though they rejoiced not; and they that buy, as though they possessed not: for the fashion of this world passes away.'*

Verse 13. – *Yet all this avails me nothing as long as I see Mordecai the Jew sitting at the king's gate.*

Haman himself confesses the vanity of his high-swelling words. Why does he talk of his riches, of his children, of the favor of the king and queen, of the grandeur of his condition? That his friends might congratulate him as the happiest man in the king's dominions. Yet with the same breath he declares himself unhappy. He confesses that all that confluence of blessings which swelled him with pride, were not blessings to him, because a certain man whom he despised did not bow the knee to him.

There are few who will confess so plainly as Haman the weakness of their own spirit. Men are ashamed to say that trifles disturb their minds and deprive them of self-enjoyment. But it is certain, that numbers, like Haman, are miserable amid the means of happiness, because they want a disposition for enjoying happiness. They are so unreasonable, that a thousand enjoyments lose all their relish for the want of something else which they cannot obtain. *'A good man is satisfied from himself;'* and he that is not satisfied from himself will not be satisfied from anything without him. He is like a sick man surrounded with the richest dainties. He cannot relish them. He starves in the midst of plenty.

Give a whole world of pleasure to a man who loves the world, and the things of it, he will soon find that something is wanting, though perhaps he does not know so well as Haman thought he did, what it is. He finds some gall and wormwood that spread poison over his pleasures. All his abundance cannot compensate for the loss of some one thing or other that he deems essential to his happiness. The fact is that the world cannot give a right constitution to his disordered soul, or be a substitute for that divine favor in which lies the life of our souls. Habakkuk, Paul, and the other good men, could be happy in the want of every earthly enjoyment; nor could all the miseries which are the objects of aversion to the generality of mankind greatly disturb their tranquillity; (Hab. 3:17,18; 2

Cor. 2:14); for God was the portion of their inheritance, and in him they had what a thousand worlds could not give. But those who know not God, and his Son Jesus Christ, in whom are the light and the life of men, know not the way of peace. Whatever they have, they want the one thing needful, without which all things else are vanity and vexation of spirit.

'I have all things, and abound,' said an apostle, who was often in hunger, and thirst, and nakedness; and who, at the time when he wrote these words, was a poor prisoner, that had newly received a temporary supply from his friends. This man had nothing, and yet possessed all things. Ten thousand talents were but a small part of Haman's wealth; and yet he is miserably poor, for all that he had could avail him nothing. The believer in Christ must be rich in the midst of poverty; for he is possessed of *'gold tried in the fire.'* The man who knows not Christ, is poor though he is rich, because he is utterly destitute of *'the true riches.'*

Verse 14. – *Then Zeresh his wife and all his friends said to him, Let a gallows fifty cubits high be made, and to-morrow speak to the king that Mordecai may be hanged on it. Then go in merrily with the king to the banquet. And the thing pleased Haman, and he caused the gallows to be made.*

Miserable comforters were all those friends of Haman. They were all physicians of no value. What though Mordecai had been hanged, and, to make his ignominious end the more conspicuous, upon a gallows of fifty cubits high? Haman's disease lay deep in his heart. A day would not have passed till some other vexation would have disquieted him. He would have rejoiced for a moment at Mordecai's downfall; but the joys of murder cannot be pure. The bitterness of hatred, and the reflections of conscience, must have polluted and embittered his pleasure. His pride would have raised up other Mordecais. Some, through inadvertency, others through envy, would soon have disquieted his soul with new instances of disrespect, which to him would have been insufferable insults. Or if fear had constrained every man in the Persian dominions to give him all the honor he desired, yet it was not to be hoped that it would be rain and sunshine at his pleasure; that dogs, and horses, and bulls, would always regulate their motions by his humor. He was not less proud than Xerxes, the father of his lord Ahasuerus, who exercised his impotent vengeance upon the winds and the seas, when they took the liberty to break down his bridge over the Hellespont!

If a proud man make his complaint to you of his unhappiness, you but make him more unhappy if you advise him to gratify his pride by unreasonable and sinful means. You might as well advise a man dying of a dropsy to pour into his throat large quantities of water. Advise him to mortify his pride, and to learn of Him who was meek and lowly in heart to deny himself; to prepare himself for bearing the cross; to take upon himself the yoke of Christ, which is easy. The humble man is always happy. The proud man never can be happy till he is effectually humbled. It is not consistent with the nature of things, nor with the will of the high and lofty One, who abhors the proud, that the gratifications which pride requires should ever give pure or lasting pleasure to the soul.

Haman was pleased with the advice of his friends, and began to put it in execution. But he found too soon, that *'he who flatters a man spreads a net for his feet.'* Haman prepared for Mordecai in intention, but for himself in reality, a gallows of fifty cubits high. Remember and believe the instruction of the wise man, – *'He that digs a pit shall fall into it, and whoso breaks an hedge, a serpent shall bite him.'*

DISCOURSE X.

HAMAN IS COMPELLED TO CONFER A SINGULAR HONOR UPON MORDECAI, WHICH HE HOPED TO PROCURE FOR HIMSELF.

CHAPTER 6:1-13.

Verse 1. – *On that night the king could not sleep, and he commanded to bring the book of records of the chronicles. And they were read before the king.*

The king could not sleep, any more than we, when he pleased. Of what use, some will say, is royal dignity, if it cannot procure sleep to the wearied eyelids? A king, by the wise administration of government, may procure sleep to his people; on the contrary, by his oppression, he may cause many wearisome nights to his subjects, in which their sorrows will not suffer them to sleep. But the regal dignity will not insure sleep to him who enjoys it. It is more likely to debar his eyes from rest by those anxious cares which attend it; or by those uneasy reflections which attend the abuse of power. Labor, and a good conscience, will procure sweeter sleep than all the riches in the world.

On that night the king could not sleep. – On what night? The night preceding the decisive day on which Esther was to present her petition, and the morning on which Haman had a petition of an opposite kind to be presented to the king. Observe how divine Providence kept sleep from the eyes of Ahasuerus, to serve his own gracious purposes. It is said that *'God gives his beloved sleep.'* But he sometimes, too, withholds sleep from them for good purposes; and he sometimes has withheld sleep from other persons, or disturbed it with strange dreams, for their benefit. A dream was sent to Pharaoh, that Joseph might be delivered from his prison and exalted to power. Another dream was sent to Nebuchadnezzar, to procure the exaltation of Daniel and his friends. Ahasuerus was kept from sleep, that he might not allow Mordecai to be hanged.

It is of great use to know how to improve those moments of the night in which we are debarred from sleep. Ahasuerus, it seems, thought he could not employ his waking moments better than by hearing the chronicles of his reign. Here, too, we may observe the superintending care of providence. Why did not a prince, who delighted in pleasure, rather call for the melody of the harp and viol, than for the chronicles of his reign? It was the will of God that he should be put in mind of what Mordecai had done for him, because now the fit time was come that he should receive the reward of his fidelity.

Verse 2. – *And it was found written that Mordecai had told of Bigthana and Teresh, two of the king's officers, the keepers of the door who tried to lay a hand on the king Ahasuerus.*

How came this part of the records to be read at this time, rather than the celebrated exploits of Cyrus, or some other passage which might be expected best to entertain the wearied king? Such was the appointment of Providence, which regulates the minutest events. *'The footsteps of a good man are ordered by the Lord'* in wisdom and love; and the footsteps of other men are ordered by Him in wisdom and love to them that love God, *'to them that are the called according to his purpose.'*

Mordecai might think that he had good reason to complain of the disregard showed to his eminent services. The king was a liberal rewarder of others who had done little, but seemed to have forgotten the man who had done so much in his service; the man to whom, under God, he owed his life. Yet Mordecai had this to comfort him, that his name and his services were recorded in the book of the chronicles, and therefore were not likely to be always forgotten. May not all God's faithful servants, when they think He has forgotten them, comfort themselves with the assurance, that a book of remembrance is written before God, in which not a cup of cold water given to a disciple, in the name of a disciple, is omitted; and that infinite wisdom will choose out the time of their reward?

Verse 3. – *And the king said, What honor and dignity has been done to Mordecai for this? Then the king's servant who served him said, Nothing has been done for him.*

The king did not doubt but some honor and dignity had been conferred upon Mordecai for saving his life. He could not believe that he had been so thoughtlessly ungrateful, as never to requite for such a length of time a service so eminent as that which Mordecai had performed; and was astonished to hear his servants say that nothing had been done for him.

Let us take a review of our lives, and consider what we have done, or not done. If our memories are good, we shall be surprised at many instances of our conduct, or of our forgetfulness. Have we showed all that sense of gratitude to our benefactors, to which we must acknowledge them to be entitled? Have we not often intended to do what we have never done, although we must blush at the thought that we have not done it? And can we forget, that among our benefactors are to be reckoned our parents, and, most of all, God our Maker?

We are taught, likewise, by this question of Ahasuerus, not to impute to intention what may be the effect merely of inadvertence. We are apt to make louder complaints than we have any reason to make, of the ingratitude of those to whom we have performed good offices. Perhaps they have forgotten that they did not requite them. Perhaps their neglects have not originated in depravity of heart, or insensibility to benefits; but in thoughtlessness; or, it was occasioned by the many avocations of other affairs. We cannot, indeed, justify those who do not with the first opportunity requite benefits received; but we must not aggravate real evils. Who will say that David did not retain a grateful remembrance of what Jonathan had done for him? And yet several years seem to have elapsed, after he was advanced to the regal dignity, before he inquired who were left of the house of Saul, that he might show them the kindness of God for Jonathan's sake; and several more years passed away, before he brought the bones of that beloved friend from Jabesh-Gilead to be interred in the sepulchre of his fathers; (2 Samuel 21:12-14).

Nothing has been done for him, said the servants of Ahasuerus. This was a disagreeable truth which they could not conceal from the king. But the evil was not irreparable. Mordecai was still alive, and the king could yet testify his sense of the benefit received.

Verse 4. – *And the king said, Who is in the court? Now Haman had come into the outer court of the king's house to speak to the king to hang Mordecai on the gallows which he had prepared for him.*

'Woe to them that devise evil upon their bed,' or before they go to bed, *'and when the morning is light practise it.'* Haman rose up early in the morning to obtain the accomplishment of his malicious designs against Mordecai. It is much to be lamented that the children of the wicked one are often more active in the prosecution of their corrupt intentions, than the children of light in the accomplishment of their pious and charitable designs.

'Who is in the court?' said the king. He slept not for the whole night; and he heard, at the fittest time for God's purpose in keeping him awake, that Haman was in the court of the palace. When he was newly informed that Mordecai had never been rewarded for saving his life, he asked the question, *'Who is in the court?'*

Verse 5. – *And the king's servants said to him, Behold, Haman stands in the court. And the king said, Let him come in.*

When the king had formed the resolution that Mordecai should be immediately rewarded with the highest honors, he was glad that Haman had come so opportunely to give him his advice what honors were fittest to be conferred on him.

Verse 6. – *So Haman came in. And the king said to him, What shall be done to the man whom the king delights to honor? Now Haman thought in his heart, To whom would the king delight to do honor more than to myself?*

Long as Mordecai had been overlooked, the king discovers a warm gratitude for his good service when it is called to remembrance. This teaches us one happy means of exciting gratitude in our hearts to our benefactors. Let us call to remembrance their benefits, and we must be more brutish than oxen or asses if we feel not grateful impressions on our hearts. It was by this method that David awakened his soul to the praises of God for all his benefits.

You may likewise be of great use to your neighbors, by reminding them, when it appears necessary, of the benefits which they have received, either from their fellow-men, or from their Maker. You see in this part of the history of Ahasuerus, what happy effects a word read or spoken may have.

The king delighted to honor the man who had saved his life. What honor is due to our parents who have given us life? To those who have been instrumental in saving us from eternal wrath? Above all, to Him who gave himself for us, that we might be preserved from everlasting destruction? (1 Cor. 6:20; 2 Cor. 5:14,15).

Now Haman thought in his heart, To whom would the king delight to do honor more than to myself? – This proud conceit of Haman did not seem to be without ground. If the king had not wanted his sleep the foregoing night, it would have been well founded. How uncertain is the favor of men! and how much are those to be pitied, who mistake the rolling wave for a solid rock, on which they may build the foundation of their happiness!

Verses 7,8,9. – *And Haman answered the king, For the man whom the king delights to honor, let the royal clothing be brought, which the king usually wears, and the horse that the king rides upon, and the royal crown which is set upon his head. And let this clothing and horse be delivered to the hand of one of the king's most noble princes so that they may dress the man whom the king delights to honor, and bring him on horseback through the streets of the city, and proclaim before him, This is what shall be done to the man whom the king delights to honor.*

Haman thought with himself that he was certainly the man whom the king delighted to honor; but he did not say so. The vainest of the sons of men affect modesty, to obtain gratification to their vanity. If the king had asked Haman what honor he wished for himself, he would not have asked what he now supposed he was asking for himself, without incurring the danger into which Adonijah brought himself by asking the concubine of David to wife. The kings of the East were jealous of all that affected, or seemed to affect, any badge of royalty. Alexander the Great, when he was sailing upon the river Euphrates, and allowed the diadem to drop from his head into the waters, punished with death a seaman who brought it out of the river upon his head.

But it was not professedly for himself. It was for the man, unknown to him, whom the king desired to honor, that Haman asked the glory, not hitherto allowed to any subject, of wearing for once the royal apparel, and of riding through the city on the favorite horse of the king, adorned with a royal coronet, under the care of one of the king's most noble princes, who was on that day to be the servant of the man whom the king delighted to honor. We see in what Haman placed the chief happiness of man. He could not hope to obtain the admired dignity of sitting upon the royal throne: but the happiness next to that, in his estimation, was to be adorned for once with some of the ensigns of royalty; to be served by the greatest of the king's princes during the exhibition of his royal pomp; and to be declared the favorite of the king. What an empty, what a transient shadow of felicity was this! Surely the man who sought it from the king was a child in understanding; and yet such children are the greatest part of mankind. What is there more solid or satisfactory in any of the objects of human pursuit, while men are unilluminated from above? *'Vanity of vanities, vanity of vanities, all is vanity?'* But we can see and despise the folly of other men walking in a vain show, when we ourselves walk in a show equally vain. *'Surely every man is vanity!'*

Verse 10. – *Then the king said to Haman, Make haste! Take the clothing and the horse, as you have said, and do even so to Mordecai the Jew, who sits at the king's gate. Do not fail to do any of all the things you have spoken.*

This is a great infelicity which attends worldly pursuits, that there is no proportion between the pleasure of success and the pain of disappointment. How unsatisfactory to Haman would the wearing of royal ornaments for a small part of a day have been, and all the other honors which he expected to enjoy only for a few moments! We can scarcely suppose that the pleasure of this feast to his vanity would have lasted longer than a night, or a week. But how dreadful a stroke was given to him, by hearing that the man whom he mortally hated was the man whom the king delighted to honor; that he was to be invested with that royal pomp to which Haman himself looked as the perfection of felicity; and that he must become the servant of that man for whom he had erected a gallows fifty cubits high! What exquisite misery, if he had lived to endure it, must have been his portion, at the galling remembrance of his own disgrace, when the erection of the lofty gibbet published to the whole city the height of his hopes and the bitterness of his disappointment!

Do not fail said the king, *to do any of all the things you have spoken.* –

He counted no honors too great for his benefactor. He would compensate by his liberality the time which Mordecai had lived unrewarded and unhonored. If we have neglected to do good when we should have done it, let us use double diligence in doing it, if time is still left us to repair our omissions.

Verse 11. – *Then Haman took the clothing and the horse and dressed Mordecai, and brought him on horseback through the street of the city, and proclaimed before him, This is what shall be done to the man whom the king delights to honor!*

Do you complain that you must deny yourselves, and take up your cross in following Christ? But who is the man that is exempted from trouble, or the man that does not find it necessary to deny himself on many occasions? And is it not better to deny ourselves for Christ, than to deny ourselves for the sake of any earthly object? You see that Haman, great as he was in the court of Ahasuerus, must serve Mordecai as his lacquey, and perform to him those services which to Haman himself appeared the most glorious of all others, when he would have given thousands of gold and silver for a warrant to slay him. The greatest earthly princes must often do things displeasing or omit things pleasing to themselves, for temporary advantage, or even without the prospect of advantage. What could Haman gain from Mordecai, or from Ahasuerus, for doing what he could not do without the most extreme reluctance? But the least instance of self-denial for the sake of Christ shall be attended with a great reward, worthy of the bounty of the Giver.

Mordecai was too wise to value those childish honors which appeared so glorious to Haman. He was, undoubtedly, struck with amazement when Haman brought to him the royal robes, and the royal horse. But it was necessary for him to yield obedience to the king's pleasure; and, doubtless, he saw the gracious hand of God in what was done to him. Mordecai had more sagacity than the friends of Haman, who saw his fall before Mordecai the Jew presaged by this instance of his humiliation. Jacob saw the love of God in the face of his reconciled enemy. Mordecai saw the favor of God in the reluctant services performed by an enemy as full of malice as ever, and was cheered by the dawnings of that deliverance to his nation for which he had been praying and looking.

Verse 12. – *And Mordecai came again to the king's gate. But Haman hurried to his house mourning, and having his head covered.*

If you desire to be happy, be clothed with humility, and mortify pride. Haman in prosperity was miserable, and in adversity was doubly miserable, because he was the slave of pride. Mordecai preserved the even tenor of his soul in prosperity and in adversity. When he was led in royal state through the city, and publicly proclaimed the king's favorite, he was the same man as before; and returned without noise to the duties of his humble station. Haman's disappointment crushed his spirits. He hastened to his house, to pour out his sorrows to his friends, who could give him no comfort. He came back with his face covered, in token of that anguish which preyed upon his heart, and that shame which would not allow him to show his face. Yesterday he went out from the king's presence merry and joyful in heart. To-day he goes to his house pierced with incurable grief. For, since Adam was upon the earth, *'the triumphing of the wicked is short, and the joy of the hypocrite but for a moment;'* (Job 20:5).

Verse 13. – *And Haman told Zeresh his wife and all his friends everything that had happened to him:* –

He would have acted as wisely, if he had left his sorrows concealed in his own bosom; but this was impracticable. They were too violent to be concealed. He probably expected some mitigation to his griefs from the kindness of his friends. But miserable comforters were they all! Their words were the piercings of a sword.

Then his wise men and Zeresh his wife said to him, If Mordecai is of the seed of the Jews, before whom you have begun to fall, you shall not prevail against him but shall surely fall before him.

Who were these wise men? Either sages whom Haman patronised, and from whom he expected wise counsel when he required it; or diviners, who were believed to know more than men could know, without some communication with superior beings. Many of the heathens put much confidence in diviners, but we have learned better things from the word of God. By making it our counsellor at all times of perplexity, we shall find peace to our souls; (Isaiah 8:19,20; Psalm 119:24).

If Mordecai is of the seed of the Jews, before whom you have begun to fall, you shall not prevail against him but shall surely fall before him. – If Mordecai had been a native Persian, or a Babylonian, or an Egyptian, would they not have prognosticated equal success to him against Haman? No; it plainly appears that the dispensations of divine providence in favor of the Jews were so far known to them, as to assure them that Providence watched over their interests in a manner peculiar to their nation. Although most men are disposed to think that their own country is happy above others in the divine favor, and although the Persians at this time seemed to have good reason to flatter themselves with a special interest in the favor of Heaven, yet these wise Persians plainly confessed, that the Jews scattered through the nations were the special objects of the divine care. The wonders done in Babylon were known to all the world, and could not fail to impress all considerate persons with high sentiments concerning the God of Israel. Haman's wise men might have read the sacred books of the Jews, in which they would find that their God had wrought as great wonders for them in times past, as in the period of the Babylonian captivity. They learned instruction from the works of God. They saw that the same God who had preserved Daniel and his companions watched over the safety and fortune of Mordecai; and they concluded that Haman, his irreconcilable enemy, would fall under the weight of his vengeance.

But it is strange that these wise men, and even the wife of Haman, whatever they thought, expressed to him their mind so fully. If they did not choose to flatter him, might they not at least have concealed their dismal conjectures, especially as he was led by their counsels to that public disgrace in which he had involved himself, by building a gallows for the man who was appointed to be the king's favorite? for although it was built in the court of his own house, yet the news of its erection was soon to spread. It appears from the freedom they used with Haman, that they already considered him as a lost man, whom it was useless to flatter. They were his friends as long as his friendship could profit them; and now they seem to have cared little whether he accounted them his friends or his enemies. Their prophecy must have been as unpleasant as the howling of a dog, or even a sentence of death, to his ears. The rich have many friends; but when poverty is seen coming like an armed man, they vanish away like snow in the days of sunshine.

We may, however, learn useful instruction from a prophecy, dictated by reflection on the works of the Lord. Blind heathens have been forced to see that God takes care of his people; that he often interposes wonderfully for their deliverance; and that he leaves not his gracious works in their behalf unfinished. Why do not God's own people, in the day of their distress, call to remembrance his judgments for their consolation, and for the support of their faith? When he begins to deliver them, why do they indulge distrusting fears about the accomplishment of that work which he has taken into his own hand? Why are they not thankful for the day of small things, as the beginning of months of joy? After Jesus undertook to heal the daughter of Jairus, strong temptations met the mourning parent, when Jesus was on the road to complete his work, and fears began to overwhelm his soul. But what said Jesus? *'Fear not, only believe.'* He believed, and received his daughter back from death.

DISCOURSE XI.

HAMAN'S FALL AND DEATH.

CHAPTER 6:14 – CHAPTER 7:10.

Verse 14. – *"And while they were still talking with him, the king's officers came. And they hurried to bring Haman to the banquet which Esther had prepared.*

When Haman, on the former day, left the queen's banquet, he went forth joyful and glad of heart. One reason of his joy was that he was invited to a like banquet next day. *'Boast not yourself of to-morrow, for you know not what a day may bring forth.'* Are you invited to a banquet? You do not know whether you shall partake of it, or whether it will give you any pleasure to partake of it. Haman was in no haste to this day's banquet. He waited till he was sent for; and would have gladly gone to a house of mourning, rather than the house of feasting, for his mind was ill-fitted for the joys of a banquet. But he is not his own master. He must comply, as far as he can, with the will of the king. With a heart full of grief he goes to a feast where he must eat the bread of sorrow, and drink his own tears.

Chap. 7:1,2. – *So the king and Haman came to the banquet of Esther the queen. And the king said again to Esther on the second day of the banquet of wine, What is your petition, queen Esther, that it may be granted you? And what is your request? And it shall be performed, even to the half of the kingdom.*

Haman, honored with the king's society at the banquet of wine, might expect to be consoled for his late disappointment, by new expressions of the royal favor. But soon did his hope, if any remained, prove like the giving up of the ghost. He was brought to the banquet, not that he might enjoy the queen's smiles, but that he might hear an accusation against himself, which touched his life, and to which he could not answer.

The king persisted in his kind sentiments towards Esther. For the third time he promises, whatever her petition was, to grant it, even to the half of the kingdom. Who would not have been emboldened by a promise so often given? To have deferred the petition any longer would have but argued an ungrateful distrust of the king's sincerity. Let us remember how much greater encouragement we have to present our requests to God; and what distrust we discover of his faithfulness, if we do not come before his throne of grace with boldness. No less than six times, in the compass of one sentence, does our Lord Jesus assure us that our prayers shall be heard; (Matt. 7:7,8).

Verse 3. – *Then Esther the queen answered and said, If I have found favor in your sight, O king, and if it pleases the king, let my life be given me at my petition, and my people at my request:*

Esther, at last, ventured to bring forth her request. The nature of the case pressed her. The king's solicitations urged her. His kindness and his promises encouraged her. Unnecessary delays are dangerous, especially in matters of great importance.

The request was for her life, and the life of her people. The king was no less surprised at this petition, than Festus was at hearing the accusation of the Jews against Paul. It was, certainly, not for any such thing as the king supposed. It never came into his mind that his beloved queen could have any occasion to present a petition to him for her life. Although by his own authority, (but without his knowledge,) a sentence of death had been pronounced against her, it must have astonished him to hear that she and her people were doomed to destruction; and it must astonish the reader of this history, that the king, five years after his marriage with the queen, should have passed a sentence of death upon her whole nation, without knowing it. Into such absurdities are princes led, who are too indolent to look into their own affairs, and leave them to be managed without control by favorites, who have their own interests to serve, and their own passions to gratify.

Verse 4. – *For we are sold, my people and I, to be destroyed, to be killed, and to perish. But if we had been sold for men-slaves and women-slaves, I would have held my tongue, although the enemy could not make up for the king's damage.*

The good queen enforces her petition with resistless eloquence. *'I and my people are sold to be destroyed, to be killed, and to perish.'* These words are borrowed from the king's edict against the Jews. The king must have been greatly moved to hear that the queen was sold like a sheep to be slaughtered; and not the queen herself only, but all her friends, and, what was more, her whole nation. His heart must have been a thousand times harder than flint, if he had not been moved at this representation of the danger to which she and her people were exposed. If a humane prince will exert his power for the protection of the meanest of his subjects exposed to unmerited danger, what might not the great king of Persia be expected to do for the preservation of a beloved queen, and of all that were dear to her!

It is plain that she was not putting her husband to unnecessary trouble by her petition, which was extorted from her by the most pressing danger; and she informs him, that if the danger had been less dreadful, she would have been silent. If she and her people had been sold like bond-men and bond-women, then she would have left it to time to convince the king that his own interest required his interposition, or she would have left their deliverance to be effected by the gradual operation of divine providence in their behalf. But the case was very different as matters stood. The year was not to end before their utter destruction, unless something was presently done for their preservation; and it was not to be expected that God would show wonders to the dead, and make them to arise and praise him. The king could not bring them again from the dust of death, however he might regret the loss of so many faithful subjects.

But would it not have been the duty of Esther to supplicate for their relief, although they had been doomed only to slavery? Perhaps she might have seen it her duty to do it, if this had really been the case. But at present, her mind was so deeply possessed with the awfulness of their danger, that she thought if their misery had been any thing else than what it was, she could have borne it without troubling the king with her complaint. Thus, a man racked with the pains of a gravel, thinks, that if it had been only the gout, he could have borne it with patience; or, if he finds his life endangered by a sore disease, he will tell the physician that his anxiety is raised only by the dangerous symptoms, and that if these could be removed, he could easily endure the pains of his distemper.

It is to be remembered that what the queen desired from the king, however necessary and reasonable, was difficult to be granted, because the laws of the Medes and Persians could not be altered. It was therefore necessary to assure the king, that nothing but bitter necessity could have induced her to give him so much trouble. Modest petitioners are heard with favor, when impudent beggars are repulsed with scorn.

The king's interest was deeply concerned in this request on other accounts. The safety of a prince consists in the multitude and happiness of his people. If the Jews had been sold for slaves, the enemy could not have compensated the king's damage, although he had given twice ten thousand talents into the royal treasury. Far less could he have compensated the loss to be sustained by the king in the destruction of so many thousands of useful and laborious subjects, scattered throughout every part of his empire. Divine Providence has so closely connected the interests of princes and people, that the throne is established by righteousness and mercy, and subverted by unrighteousness.

Verse 5. – *Then the king Ahasuerus answered and said to Esther the queen, Who is he, and where is he who dares presume in his heart to do so?*

What! to compass the death of the queen; and, as if that were too small a wickedness, the destruction of all her people also! Was a man so wicked to be found in any of the hundred and twenty-seven provinces of the king's dominions? If there were such a daring criminal to be found, no death was too terrible for him.

What, then, will our Lord do when he rises up to revenge the wrongs done to himself in the persons of his brethren; of those who *'are espoused to him in righteousness, and in judgment, and in loving-kindness, and in mercies?'* Will he not account the wrongs done to them to have been done to himself? When he makes inquisition for blood, woe to them that are stained with bloody crimes against his people! The wrath of Ahasuerus against the enemies of the Jews was a fruit of God's wrath against them. He forgot not his promise to Abraham, '*I will bless him that blesses you, and I will curse him that curses you.*'

Who is he, and where is he who dares to do this thing? – What if Ahasuerus himself is the man? although it would have been unwise in the queen to tell him that he was. He was, certainly, though unconscious of it, a partner in this wickedness; and yet he was filled with horror at hearing that any person could dare to load himself with such guilt. Thus David was filled with anger against a man who was only the emblem of himself; (2 Sam. 12). Consider what abhorrence you have of the sins of other men, and consider how like your own sins are to theirs, and let your souls be humbled within you. Take care how you speak of the sins of other men, lest your tongues condemn yourselves. Your sins are probably much liker to theirs than you could imagine till you have well considered the matter. Perhaps they are a great deal worse, when every circumstance is considered.

Verse 6. – *And Esther said, The man who is our adversary and enemy is this wicked Haman. Then Haman was afraid before the king and the queen.*

Haman now finds for what reason he was invited by the queen to her banquet. It was to be accused to his face of the blackest of crimes. He had an opportunity of saying what could be said (is anything could be said) in his own vindication, or in mitigation of his offense. But if he had nothing to say, it was to be expected that the confusion of his face would be a witness against him.

This was actually the case: '*Then Haman was afraid before the king and the queen.*' He had too good reason to tremble for his life. The queen had brought a dreadful accusation against him, and his guilt was too apparent to be denied, or to be extenuated. And it was of a nature fitted to excite the king's fiercest indignation, and bitterest rage.

In what light did Haman's pride and greatness now appear to him? If he had possessed worlds, he would cheerfully have parted with them to have his former conduct buried in oblivion. In all our conduct let us have an eye to that future day which will assuredly come, when our behavior will appear to ourselves in its true light; and to that day which may come before we quit the world, when it will be followed with its just consequences. How many things that are done would be left undone, if, at the doing, men would realise in their own minds what will be realised one day by the divine providence!

There was a time when Haman thought that life was not life, unless all men bowed the knee to him. But how happy would he now have been if he could have obtained life upon any terms! What did all his honors formerly avail him, while he saw the hated Mordecai at the king's gate? But in his fear he would gladly have bowed the knee to Mordecai as the price of life.

Verse 7. – *And the king, arising from the banquet of wine in his wrath, went into the palace garden. And Haman stood up to beg for his life from Esther the queen, for he saw that evil was determined against him by the king.*

The king was agitated by his indignation to a degree beyond what we can well conceive. The angry passions rage in the breasts of men, in proportion to the sense they have of their own dignity, of the insults they apprehend to be offered to them, and of the obligations violated by the offender. Ahasuerus was so great a king, that he would think the smallest offense against himself almost unpardonable; but an attempt to destroy his beloved queen was the greatest of all crimes, next to an attempt upon his own life. How unpardonable did this crime appear in one whom he had loved, and trusted, and honored above all his subjects! No punishment which his power could inflict appeared to him equal to a crime so atrocious. And yet this was not the worst of the matter. Haman, by his artifice, had drawn his master into partnership of his own crimes. It is probable that Ahasuerus now saw that Haman's guilt was the decree obtained against the Jews, passed by the consent and authority of Ahasuerus himself. For how could Haman, without such authority, destroy a whole nation of the king's subjects? His wrath must have burnt like a furnace, when he considered how he had been betrayed into a decree so absurd, so wicked, so infamous, that might have proved so fatal to the wife of his bosom, and to all her kindred.

Ahasuerus could not keep his seat. He could not bear the sight of Haman. He ran to the garden, not to give his wrath time to cool, but to give it time to devise proper means for executing all the furiousness of its rage upon a man whom he had devoted to destruction. While Haman was already suffering for his wickedness by the terrors that tormented his heart, Ahasuerus himself suffered some part of what his rashness deserved, by the fiery indignation that raged in his bowels. How miserable is it to feel the torments which either of these passions inflict, when they obtain dominion over the soul!

Haman wished still to live, though in disgrace, and made supplication for his life to a woman whom he had offended beyond hopes of forgiveness. Although it was her duty to forgive him so as to wish well to his soul, it was not her duty to desire his pardon from the king, after he had involved himself so deeply in the guilt of blood. Or, if she had interceded for his life, it was not to be hoped that the king would spare the serpent that had almost stung the wife of his bosom to death. The case was hopeless; but drowning men will grasp at straws or shadows, when they can find no better supports.

The wicked now *'bows before the righteous;'* and Haman was not the first, nor will he be the last, of the enemies of God's people, that shall be made to *'bow before them, and to lick the dust of their feet;'* (Isa. 49:23; Rev. 3:9).

Verse 8. – *Then the king returned out of the palace garden into the place of the banquet of wine. And Haman had fallen upon the bed on which Esther was. The the king said, Will he also force the queen before me in the house? As the word went out of the king's mouth, they covered Haman's face.*

When men are enraged, neither their thoughts agree with facts, nor do their words agree with their thoughts. Haman could not well be thought a worse man than he was, and yet the king was disposed to put a worse construction upon his conduct than it deserved. It is not, however, to be supposed, that the king really thought he meant to force Esther before him in the house. Anger is a short madness; and the words of an angry man are like *'the speeches of one that is desperate, which are as wind.'* If we desire, therefore, to behave uniformly like wise men and like Christians, we must keep our mouths as with a bridle when our hearts are hot within us; and we must keep our hearts with all diligence, that our passions may not overpower our reason.

It is likewise necessary for us to beware of all irritating behavior, that we may not kindle up fierce passions in the breasts of other men. If they should think, or speak, or act unreasonably, when we have strongly tempted them to be angry, a share of the blame belongs to us; and if we condemn their fury, we should condemn ourselves as sharers of the guilt. Surely the king could not imagine in good earnest that Haman meant to force the queen in his presence; yet Haman, by snares laid for her life, gave the king too good reason to suspect him of everything wicked..

The king's fury drove him from the palace to the garden, and from the garden to the palace. It had the entire government of his thoughts, of his temper, and of his actions. A petition from any of the king's servants, or from Esther herself, at this time, in favor of Haman, would rather have increased than abated his fury. But, indeed, Haman had no friends in the king's house to take his part. Some of the king's servants covered his face, and others of them brought in new reports to his disadvantage. A proud man may be flattered, but he cannot be loved. When he falls from prosperity into adversity, he begins to know what sentiments are entertained concerning him.

While he spoke these words, they covered Haman's face; which the king could not now behold without detestation. The faces of the condemned used to be covered; and sentence of death had already been passed against this wicked man. What a miserable change did a single hour produce! How justly may the words of Bildad concerning the wicked be applied to this wretched man! – *'Yea, the light of the wicked shall be put out, and the spark of his fire shall not shine. The light shall be dark in his tabernacle, and his candle shall be put out with him. The steps of his strength shall be straitened, and his own counsel shall cast him down. For he is cast into a net by his own feet, and he walks upon a snare;'* (Job 18:5-8).

Verse 9. – *And Harbonah, one of the officers, said before the king; Also look! the gallow fifty cubits high which Haman made for Mordecai, who had spoken good for the king, stands in the house of Haman. Then the king said, Hang him on it!*

New charges are produced against Haman, when it was seen that the king was no longer his friend. Had Haman taken care to gain the love of his inferiors during the time of his greatness, he might have found some few, perhaps, that would have expressed their gratitude when he fell; and not many would have assisted in pushing him lower. But his misery was that he trusted in the multitude of his riches, and in the favor of the king. When the king was his enemy, all men were his enemies; and he had given abundant occasion to complete his destruction. His own hands had made the cords with which he was now girded and strangled.

Harbonah told the king of the gallows that Haman had erected for Mordecai, fifty cubits high. Here was an instance of his intolerable presumption, that he had built this gallows without the king's previous knowledge. But what was sure to inflame the king's revenge beyond measure was that the servant of the king, for whom the gallows was prepared, was the very man to whom the king owed his life when it was endangered by two wicked conspirators. It looked as if Haman had been in a confederacy with these men, and wished to revenge their death.

Then the king said, Hang him on it! – The king was impatient to have such a viper crushed, and removed out of his sight. He had been considering with himself, perhaps by what means he might chase him out of the world, so as best to express his own detestation of his conduct, and load him with ignominy. The words of Harbonah decided the business. What can be more ignominious for him than to be hanged on a gallows higher than most of the houses of the city; on a gallows constructed by himself for one of the king's friends; and on the very day on which Haman hoped to have enjoyed the pleasure of seeing Mordecai hanging on it till he died! – *'Hang him on it!'*

Verse 10. – *So they hanged Haman on the gallows that he had prepared for Mordecai. Then the king's wrath was pacified.*

There is no law more just, says an ancient author, than that the contrivers of destruction should perish by their own contrivances. Who pities Haman hanged on his own gallows? Who does not rather rejoice in the divine righteousness, displayed in that destruction which his own art brought upon him? In his dismal end, how fully verified are the words of David! *'He (the Lord) ordains his arrows against the persecutors. He has made a pit, and digged it; and he is fallen into the ditch which he has made: his mischief shall return upon his own head, and his violent dealing shall come down upon his own pate. I will praise the Lord according to his righteousness;'* (Psalm 7:13-17).

Let the workers of iniquity tremble, and turn to the Lord, and seek pardon through the blood of Jesus. Saul of Tarsus was a persecutor, who sought the utter destruction of the Israel of God; and yet he obtained mercy, and the grace of our Lord was abundant to him. *'But the Lord shall wound the head of the wicked, the hairy scalp of him that goes on still in his trespasses.'*

Let not the children of Zion despair, when their enemies are successful, and no hope seems to be left them. God knows how to find expedients in desperate circumstances, and to turn the blackest darkness into light. He knows how to bring upon the head of his enemies that destruction which they prepare for his own people, and to save them that love him from the greatest deaths.

The king's wrath was never pacified till Haman received the punishment which he so justly deserved. Then his mind enjoyed some ease when he heard that Haman was hanged on his own gallows. But he soon found that much yet remained for him to do, to put away the mischief of Haman the Agagite. *'When the wicked perish, there is shouting;'* but their wickedness may outlive them, and cause much distress and toil when they are gone to receive their reward.

DISCOURSE XII.

MORDECAI IS ADVANCED TO GREAT HONORS – LIBERTY IS PROCURED FOR THE JEWS TO DEFEND THEMSELVES AGAINST THE INTENDED MASSACRE.

CHAPTER 8:1-14.

Verses 1,2. – *On that day king Ahasuerus gave the house of Haman the Jews' enemy to Esther the queen. And Mordecai came before the king, for Esther had told what he was to her. And the king took off his ring, which he had taken from Haman, and gave it to Mordecai. And Esther set Mordecai over the house of Haman.*

Be not solicitous about treasuring up the riches of this world. What you can gain is to-day yours, to-morrow you know not whose it shall be. Should it fall into the hands of your children after you, you know not whether they will be wise men or fools; whether they will be losers or gainers by the possession of it. Nay, you know not whether it may not fall into the hands of your most abhorred enemies. This is often the fate of ill-gotten riches. '*The wealth of the sinner is laid up for the just.*' With what vexation would Haman have thought of that wealth in which he gloried, if he had foreseen that it was to be possessed by a Jewess! Would he not rather have chosen to live a beggar all his days, than leave his wealth to persons whom he so mortally hated?

The queen was enriched beyond her expectations and wishes. Yet the wealth bestowed upon her would enable her to perform important services to her beloved nation. The donation of it by the king, to whom it was forfeited, was a testimony of his affection, to which she still must have recourse, with new petitions for her people. Above all, this donation was a remarkable testimony of the kindness and justice of the divine providence, which put into her hands that immense wealth of the enemy of her nation, by which he would have bribed the king, if a bribe had been necessary to procure their destruction. The Lord had already not only wrought deliverance for her, but had given her an accession of riches out of the snare that had been laid for her kinsman; and she was thereby encouraged to hope that he would bring to a happy conclusion that great work that occupied her mind.

Her kinsman, too, was highly advanced, both on her account and his own. The king had formerly caused his favor for Mordecai to be proclaimed through the city of Shushan; but now he loaded him with real and substantial honors, which would put him into a proper condition for protecting his nation, exposed to danger for his sake.

It was now the fifth year since the adopted daughter of Mordecai was seated upon an imperial throne, and hitherto it was not known that he stood in any relation to the queen, or had showed to her the kindness of a father.

The king must, surely, at least have condemned his own thoughtlessness in inquiring so little after Esther's friends. He now discerned, that besides his unrequited obligations to Mordecai for saving his life, he owed to him likewise the graces and accomplishments of his queen, and almost her life; for he had been to her a second father, without whose kind care none knows what might have befallen her in her tender years.

It would be, likewise, a powerful recommendation of Mordecai, that he had hitherto lived quietly in a low station, without so much as mentioning his claims to preferment. It appeared plainly that he was more careful to deserve the king's favor than to enjoy it, and that greatness had no charms but the opportunities it might give him of doing good, or preventing evil. Those are fittest for high stations that are best satisfied with any station in which Providence is pleased to put them.

The king put Mordecai into Haman's place; and the queen, who now thought it highly expedient to inform the king of Mordecai's kindness and relation to her, did likewise make him her steward. To her dying day she forgot not the kindness showed to her in the days of her youth, and behaved as the best of daughters to the best of fathers.

Gratitude to benefactors is essential to a virtuous character. If you call a man ungrateful, you need say nothing more of him, you have already said everything that is bad; nor will the highest elevation excuse forgetfulness of benefits received in a lower condition. The blessed Jesus, exalted above men and angels, forgets none of the kindnesses shown to him in the persons of his brothers in a low condition upon earth; but what is done to the least of them is rewarded as if it had been done to Himself. We need not envy those women who ministered to him of their substance in the days of his humiliation the glorious rewards bestowed upon them in his state of exaltation. We still have it in our power to feed Him when he is hungry, to give Him drink when he is thirsty, to clothe Him when he is naked; and He will not be unrighteous to forget our works and labors of love to His name. Did Esther in her royal condition retain such a kind remembrance of the friends of her low estate, and shall we doubt of the infinitely superior virtues of him who is the fairest among the children of men; to the operation of whose Spirit we owe everything that is lovely in our temper and conduct?

Esther, on the throne, retained the kindness of her youth, not only to Mordecai, but to all her friends and all her people.

Verse 3. – *And Esther spoke yet again before the king, and fell down at his feet, and begged him with tears to put away the evil of Haman the Agagite, and his plot which he had plotted against the Jews.*

Esther now appeared to be in a very safe condition, and her friend Mordecai had little reason to be apprehensive for his life, when he was honored to be the king's favorite; but neither of them thought themselves safe or happy till their brothers and people were placed in a like condition. They would have rather chosen, if it had been the will of God, to perish, if their people could obtain deliverance and enlargement, than to live and see the misery threatened fall upon them. Esther, therefore, again ventures to trouble the king with her requests. She falls down before him. She weeps and makes supplication with floods of tears for her people. Happy were they in such an intercessor. Her beauty, her tears, the strong emotions of her heart apparent in her gestures, the amiable virtues which shone forth in her generous concern for her poor friends, were sufficient to have melted the most marble-hearted prince in the world. The humane Ahasuerus could stand out against such forcible and pleasing importunities. He was requested to do what might expose him to difficulties and dangers; for the fundamental laws of Persia deprived him of the power of abrogating his own laws. But what he could do he would doubtless perform, at such importunities of such a suppliant.

Although Esther had wept and made supplication to God for her people, she did not reckon that she had done what was incumbent on her, without weeping and supplicating the king likewise, at the risk not only of displeasing him, but of her head. When she had by her supplications made some progress in the important business, she wept and supplicated the king a second time, till she obtained all that could be obtained for her people. It is not enough to begin a good work, but we ought to hold on till it is completed, although great difficulties meet us in the face, which it may appear almost impossible to surmount. When we stop short before we have finished what we were called to perform, may we not be confounded by that question, '*You did run well, who did hinder you? Are you so foolish, having begun in the Spirit, to end in the flesh?*'

The queen solicits the king to undo the mischief of Haman. The king himself might, with too good reason, have been implicated with Haman. He was under obligations, from strict justice, to put away the mischief which could not be done without his consent. But the queen wisely overlooked this important consideration, and chose rather to address herself to the king's mercy than to his justice. '*Grievous words stir up anger; soft words turn away (or prevent) wrath.*' It was, indeed, highly proper that the king should be sensible of his own part in the wrong done to the Jews; but his own conscience would not fail to perform that office, and probably it operated the more powerfully in him, that the Jews themselves kept silence. We feel most powerfully the injuries that we have done, when those to whom they are done show little disposition to complain.

Verse 4. – *Then the king held out the golden scepter toward Esther:* –

She would now venture with greater boldness than before to go in before the king, for she was assured of his favor. When we know that we are beloved by superiors, we can go to them with boldness to ask any reasonable favor; yet so variable are the tempers of men, that we may be sometimes deceived in our hopes.

Esther was not, at this time, ashamed of her hope of the favor of Ahasuerus. God himself was her hope, and he inclined the king's heart to favor her.

Verses 4,5. – *So Esther arose and stood before the king, and said, If it please the king, and if I have found favor in his sight, and if the thing is right before the king, and if I am pleasing to his eyes, let it be written to bring back the letters (a sly plan by Haman the son of Hammedatha the Agagite), which he wrote to destroy the Jews who are in all the king's provinces.*

Observe with what humility and modesty, yet earnest importunity, she presents her request to the king. Esther was well furnished with those amiable qualities which must endear a wife to her husband, and obtain from him every reasonable request. Pride and petulance can obtain nothing without reluctance on the part of him that grants. Humility and submission are the weapons by which a wise woman will encounter opposition in her husband, and the means by which she will obtain what can be obtained by any methods fit to be used by a wife.

If Esther had any interest in the king's favor, the great use she desires to make of it is for the preservation of her people from the mischief devised by Haman. Patriotism and piety were shining ornaments of this princess. She desired not great things for herself. She was well satisfied with her own condition, if she could but see peace on Israel; for Jerusalem was near to her heart, and the welfare of the people of God was dearer to her than either grandeur or life.

Verse 6. – *For how can I bear to see the evil that shall come upon my people? Or how can I endure to see the slaughter of my kindred?*

Esther was now the queen of Persia, but still the people of Israel were her people and her kindred. Let a true fearer of God be placed ever so comfortably among the sons of men, still it will be his leading desire to *'see the good of God's chosen, to rejoice in their joy, and to glory with God's inheritance.'*

The king could not grant Esther everything that she requested. But he assures her that is great enemy of her people, and her security under the king's protection, would be of small avail to her, if her kindred must perish. Her life was bound up in their life. If her heart was broken and crushed by their ruin, what good could her life do her, or what pleasure could the king have any more in beholding her when she was drowned in perpetual sorrows?

There was a consideration that endeared the people of Israel to the queen still more than their relation to herself. They were the people of the Lord of hosts, the God of Israel. Esther did not think fit to mention this motive of her tender regard to her people when she was presenting her supplications to the king, because he could not have felt the force of it. Thus Nehemiah, in his supplication to the king for Jerusalem, does not speak of it as the center of the Jewish religion, as the city of the God of Israel, but as the place of his fathers' sepulchres. The king could easily understand the interest that his cup-bearer must take in the place of his fathers' sepulchres; but he knew nothing of that delight which good men take in *'the habitation of God's house, in the place where his honor dwells.'*

Verse 7. – *Then the king Ahasuerus said to Esther the queen and to Mordecai the Jew, Behold, I have given Esther the house of Haman, and have hanged him upon the gallows, because he laid his hand upon the Jews.*

The king could not grant Esther everything that she requested. But he assures her that it was not for want of good will, either to herself or to her people, that he did not in direct terms reverse the decree procured by Haman. His love to Esther appeared in the rich present of the confiscated estate of Haman. His good wishes to her people appeared in the ignominious death of their capital enemy. But kings cannot do everything. The most noble and potent prince in the world had not the power of rescinding his own decrees, however desirous he might be of undoing foolish things done by himself.

Verse 8. – *And you write for the Jews as it pleases you, in the king's name, and seal it with the king's ring. For the writing which is written in the king's name and sealed with the king's ring, no man may turn back.*

The king himself could not reverse it; and therefore we find that Darius the Mede labored in vain till the going down of the sun, to save Daniel from the lion's den, and passed a miserable sleepless night in the anguish of a fruitless repentance, for passing a mischievous law, which he could not abolish. The Persians thought their kings highly honored in that law by which their decrees were made inviolable. But this honor, like some others enjoyed by absolute princes, was a burden too heavy to be borne by mortals. It precluded them from the comforts of repentance, too often necessary for vain men, who though they would be wise, are born like the wild ass's colt.

The king, therefore, could not give Esther and Mordecai a warrant to pass an act rescissory of his own decrees against the Jews. But he allows them to frame a decree in his name, and to seal it with his ring, for counteracting its effects. As the first decree retained its force, the king could not legally punish those wicked enemies of the Jews who might take the advantage of it to gratify their malice. Their murders were already legalized by a decree that could not be altered. But a law for the protection of the Jews, which did not rescind the former, might possibly be devised by the wisdom of Mordecai; and to establish such a law, the king gave him his ring. He had been too ready on the former occasion to lend his authority; but now he commits it to a safe hand, and under necessary restrictions. He gave his ring to Haman, to seal a bloody decree; he now gives it to Mordecai, to seal a just and necessary decree for the preservation of many precious lives. The inviolability of the king's decrees, which gave him so much trouble by guarding the wicked laws procured by Haman, would guard the intended decree from violation.

Verses 9,10,11. – *Then the king's scribes were called at that time in the third month, that is, the month Sivan, on the twenty-third of it. And it was written according to all that Mordecai commanded to the Jews, and to the lieutenants and the governors and rulers of the provinces which are from India to Ethiopia, a hundred and twenty-seven provinces, unto every province according to the writing of it, and to every people in their language, and to the Jews according to their writing and according to their language. And he wrote in the name of king Ahasuerus and sealed it with the king's ring. And he sent letters by riders on horseback, and riders on mules, camels, and young dromedaries. In them the king granted the Jews which were in every city to gather themselves together, and to stand for their life, to destroy, to kill and to cause to perish, all the power of the people and province who desired to attack them, both little ones and women, and to take what they owned for a prize.*

Glad would Mordecai and Esther have been, could they have written to all the provinces letters in the king's name, recalling the permission given to the enemies of the Jews to destroy them. But this the laws of Persia would not permit. What, therefore, must be done to save the devoted nation? They are permitted by a new decree to defend themselves, and to destroy their enemies. This, it might be hoped, would have much the same effect as a decree repealing the bloody decree passed against the Jews. When it was known that the queen and the prime minister were Jews, and that the king favored their cause, it might have been presumed that few would be bold enough to attack them; which would be, by the new edict, to rush upon their own destruction, and to expose the lives of their wives and children, as well as their own. Some, indeed, might entertain such deep-rooted malice against the Jews, as to take advantage of the former edict; but the fault was their own, the risk was chiefly their own; nor could anything be done by Mordecai or Esther to prevent the mischief. It was to be attributed, not to them, but, in the first place, to the king's former rashness in gratifying the bloody enemy of the Jews; and, in the second place, to that fundamental, but absurd law of the empire, that the king's edicts, whether good or bad, could not be repealed. If men will presume to claim the prerogative of immutability in their counsels, let them take the consequences. Men are never more foolish than when they affect the perfection of wisdom.

We regret that permission was given in this edict to the Jews to destroy the wives and children of their enemies that might rise up against them. But the manners of ancient times are to have some allowance made for them. Jesus, the light of the world, had not yet humanized the nations by the light of his gospel. Besides, it was natural to think, that this permission to the Jews would be a means of preventing the effusion of blood; because many who will risk their own lives, will neither risk the lives of their wives, nor of their children, to gratify their passions. Retaliations in war sometimes involve the destruction of innocent persons, and yet are thought necessary to prevent greater mischief. But we are not bound to justify all that may be done by good men, or every circumstance of good actions. Mordecai and Esther might err, but their errors were not voluntary. It was their desire to prevent, and not to promote, the shedding of innocent blood.

The decree which they framed was sent to every nation of the empire in its own language. All wise lawgivers will address their subjects in a language they understand. God himself wrote the great things of his ancient law in the language of his chosen people; and the laws and doctrines of Christianity were communicated to the world in the language then most generally understood. It is better to speak five words in a known tongue, than ten thousand in an unknown language. Mordecai would have shown little regard to the life and comfort of his brothers, if he had not caused the decree to be translated into the languages of the different provinces. Those preachers of the gospel discover as little regard to the eternal life of their hearers, who do not use great plainness of speech, in showing unto them the way of salvation. Obscurity in our own language is not much less prejudicial than the use of an unknown tongue.

The decree was no sooner passed, and translated into the different languages, than copies of it were sent through every part of the empire, and the swiftest methods of conveyance were used. Mordecai and Esther had sufficient time to give seasonable intimations of the new decree to the Jews and to their enemies. Yet, considering the distance of some provinces, the possibility of untoward accidents, and the advantage of early information, they had no time to lose. Why should that be deferred till another day, which may be better and more safely done at present? How many have lost the seasons of good works, or the benefits expected from them, by deferring them! How many by delays have lost their precious souls! (Eccles. 9:10). But in the present case, the greatest possible expedition was likewise requisite, for the comfort of the trembling Jews. Let us not leave those persons under the power of despondency a single hour, whom we may cheer by happy tidings, or by other effectual methods of consolation. If happiness is preferred by ourselves to misery, we do not to others what we wish them to do to us, if we allow them to languish under heaviness of heart, when we may, by a good word, make them glad.

Verse 12. – *Upon one day in all the provinces of king Ahasuerus – upon the thirteenth day of the twelfth month, which is the month Adar.*

The day was fixed by Haman, but the disposing of the lot by which he fixed that day was evidently of the Lord. The lateness of the time gave sufficient opportunities for spreading the new edict, by which the day intended for the destruction of the Jews became a day of destruction to their enemies.

Verse 13. – *The copy of the writing for a commandment to be given in every province was announced to all people, even that the Jews should be ready against that day to avenge themselves on their enemies.*

It was published to all the people, that all the king's subjects might know the real wishes of the king, and might take their side accordingly, as they valued his favor. The knowledge of the decree might make many friends to that nation, and, doubtless, affrighted many of their enemies. *'Where the word of a king is, there is power; for all men seek the favor of the ruler.'*

It was published unto all people, chiefly as an alarm to the Jews, that they might prepare themselves to resist their enemies, if any enemies make their appearance. They were not so entirely to depend on the favor of their sovereign, as to be unprepared for the contest. He had bound up his own hands from assisting them, or revenging their wrongs. All that he could do for them was to give them the liberty of self-defence, and to afford them his countenance. They must stand up for their own lives, and for the lives of their little ones, if they were attacked. It is to be expected, that those who are not only forewarned of danger, but instructed in the proper means for guarding against it, and encouraged with the prospect of success in the use of them, will be ready for the day of decision. Do not they well deserve to perish, who are careless about their own safety? Who will bemoan those who may be safe in the day of evil, and despise the things that belong to their peace till they are hid from their eyes?

Verse 14. – *So the posts that rode upon mules and camels went out, being hurried and pressed on by the king's commandment. And the order was given at Shushan the palace.*

The posts were hurried by the king's commandment. – He was now made sensible of the great wrong he had done to the Jews, and made all possible haste to undo, as far as he could undo, what he had done. Are you sensible you have done wrong? Make haste, and delay not to repair the wrong, if it is in your power. How can you say that you repent of the evil that you have done, if you hold it fast? The light of nature teaches men that they ought, with the first opportunity, to put away the evil of their doings, and to redress the injuries done by their hands, or their tongues, or their pens. As soon as Jesus brought salvation to the house of Zaccheus, he said, *'Lord! if I have wronged any man by false accusation, I restore him fourfold.'* Is it your intention, in some future part of your life, to compensate the wrongs you have done in the former part of it? But are you sure that you shall see another week, or even another day? Boast not yourself of to-morrow, unless a prophet of as good credit as Isaiah has brought a message from God that some more years of life are allotted you.

And the order was given at Shushan the palace. – Little good was now expected by the people of God to come from Shushan the palace. From Shushan came the edict for their destruction. But God can make good to spring up to his people where it was least expected. In the very place where it was said, *'You are not my people,'* has it been said, *'You are the children of the living God.'* The valley of Achor is made by divine wisdom and grace a door of hope. The best of all things in the world came out of Galilee and Nazareth.

DISCOURSE XIII.

MORDECAI'S GREATNESS, WITH THE HAPPY CHANGE IN THE CONDITION OF THE JEWS.

CHAPTER 8:15 – CHAPTER 9:5.

Verse 15. – *And Mordecai went out from the presence of the king in royal clothing of blue and white, and with a great crown of gold, and with a garment of fine linen and purple. And the city of Shushan rejoiced and was glad.*

Mordecai, not long before this time, was clothed with sackcloth; and refused, at the request of the queen, to put it off. But now he is clothed with royal apparel, and his head is encircled with a crown of gold. What happy changes has God often made in the outward condition of his people! Let us never say in our prosperity, that *'we shall never be moved.'* Let us never say in the day of aversity, that *'our eyes shall never more see good;'* or, whatever our outward condition may be, let us not despair of obtaining those changes in our inward condition which the Redeemer, whom we are called to trust, has accomplished in innumerable instances. The Lord anointed him *'to comfort all that mourn, to give unto them the oil of joy for mourning, the garments of praise for the spirit of heaviness.'*

Mordecai was now adorned with the ensigns of that high station to which the king advanced him. Perhaps some may ask, whether Mordecai's happiness was increased by his elevation, or not? It certainly was. The greater part of men are fitted to enjoy more happiness in a middling, than in a high condition. But, when men are furnished with talents and opportunities for public usefulness, and when their pleasure lies more in doing good to others than in the enjoyment of ease and social delights, a station that enables them to gratify their wishes, and to exert their power for the public welfare, must afford them more exquisite and sublime pleasure than they would have enjoyed in domestic felicity, or in the endearments of friendship. Joseph was happier in the government of Egypt, which fitted him to be *'the shepherd and stone of Israel,'* than in the tents of his father Jacob; although he was his father's delight. David found much more trouble on a throne than ever befel him when he was following the ewes with young; but he was happier on the throne, because his elevation enabled him to do greater services for God and for Israel. Mordecai was raised on high by Divine Providence to be a saviour to Israel, and enjoyed the sublime pleasure of knowing that millions blessed God on his account.

Let us not, however, envy the great. Multitudes of them might have been far happier, if they had moved in a lower sphere. We are not all Davids or Mordecais. Agur was a very good man, and yet he prayed that God might give him neither poverty nor riches. Think not that you are better fitted than Agur to resist the temptations attendant on riches. Christ tells us, that *'it is as easy for a camel to pass through the eye of a needle, as for a rich man to enter into the kingdom of heaven.'* But nothing is impossible with God; and Mordecai, amid all his wealth and power, hastened towards the possession of that kingdom which cannot be moved.

The city of Shushan rejoiced and was glad for the fall of Haman, and the exaltation of Mordecai. *'When the righteous are in authority, the people rejoice; and when the wicked perish, there is shouting.'* Mordecai was an exile, and a worshipper of the God of Israel; yet the people of Shushan, who now knew his virtues, rejoiced that he was put into the place of Haman, who undoubtedly was an oppressor to other subjects of the king besides the Jews. The perplexity into which the city was thrown by the cruel decree against the Jews, prepared it for rejoicing in the exaltation of a man who employed his power for their protection. Bloody men are abhorred by their fellow-creatures, and virtue recommends itself to the admiration of those whose practice is not in all things conformable to its rules. A Herod venerated John Baptist.

Verses 16,17. – *The Jews had light and gladness and joy and honor. And in every province, and in every city where the king's commandment and his order came, the Jews had joy and gladness, a feast and a good day. And many of the people of the land became Jews, for the fear of the Jews fell upon them.*

Many expressions are used to signify the joy and exultation of the Jews on this occasion, and no expressions are sufficient to describe those transports of gladness which they must have felt when the king's commandment and decree came abroad. According to the days wherein they had sorrow, and wherein they had seen evil, they were made glad. Let us never sink under the weight of affliction, if the Lord is our God. Who had ever more reason than the Jews, in the interval between the two edicts, to say, *'The Lord has led us, and brought us into darkness, and not into light?'* The Babylonian captivity was a less hopeless calamity than the situation to which they were reduced by a general sentence of death. But the Lord *'brought them again out of darkness and the shadow of death, and broke their bands asunder.'* Now might they sing with pleasure these delightful words of David, *'You will save the afflicted people, but will bring down high looks; for you will light my candle. The Lord my God will enlighten my darkness.'*

'No affliction for the present is joyous, but grievous;' yet afflictions have often terminated in joys never felt by those who never had changes: men never feel the joys of health that were never sick; and those whose souls have been failing within them, through trouble, oppressions, and fear, know best the pleasure of ease and safety. It will be a great enhancement of the blessedness of heaven to redeemed saints, that they were once in a state of sin and sorrow. When we are in trouble, let us consider by what means joy may be brought out of it, that we may learn to rejoice in hope. Through the grace of God,

thorns may be made to bear grapes, and thistles figs, for he is *'wonderful in counsel, and excellent in working.'*

There is one thing that deserves observation in this joy of the Jews, that it was occasioned, not by a full security given them for their safety, but by that liberty which was given them to defend themselves from their enemies. They had still reason to dread an attack, but they had reason, too, to hope for victory. We would never taste joy in the things of this world, if we could not take pleasure but in prospects altogether unclouded. Who can say that he shall never more meet with dangers, or taste sorrows? We may be assured, on solid grounds, that all things shall work together for our good, and that heaven shall be our final portion; but what unpleasant things, in the present life, may appear to divine wisdom a proper preparation for our final happiness, we cannot tell. This we know, that when our prospects are in some degree pleasant, we ought to be thankful, and especially when the dark prospects are brightened, although the events in question cannot be certain. Some of the Jews might lose their lives, yet God had wonderfully interposed for their safety; and they had good reason to praise God for what was done, and to trust him for what was yet to be done.

They had *'a feast and a good day,'* wherever the king's decree came. *'A feast is made for laughter.'* Feasts, on proper occasions, are not unbecoming the people of God. Jesus himself did not refuse his presence to feasts. Doubtless, on this feast and good day the hearts of the Jews were enlarged, not only with joy, but with kind affections towards their brothers, *'partakers with them of the benefit,'* and with gratitude to the God of their salvation. While they congratulated one another, and praised the exertions of Mordecai and Esther, they did not forget to praise the Lord, who had turned the heart of the king of Persia to favor them; (Ezra 7:27,28); and who had turned a gracious ear to the voice of their prayers and their supplications. These are pure and lasting joys which terminate in God, the Father of lights, from whom every good and perfect gift comes.

The Jews had honor, as well as light and joy. The Babylonian captivity, and their dispersion among the nations, brought them into contempt: *'They were made a reproach unto their neighbors, and a by-word among the people.'* But God's signal interposition in their behalf filled beholders with wonder and respect. They appeared to be the favorites of the God of heaven. *'They said among the heathen, The Lord has done great things for them.'* God has promised to wipe away the reproach of his people, and get them fame and glory, when he rises up to plead their cause. Let us *'never fear the reproach of men, nor be afraid of their revilings.'* Our honor, as well as our life and property, is in the hand of God; and those who are precious in his sight will sooner or later be honorable in the eyes of men.

And many of the people of the land became Jews, for the fear of the Jews fell on them. – It is not impossible for those who are not sprung from Abraham to become Jews. *'They are not all Israel that are of Israel;'* and those may be *'Israelites indeed'* who are sprung from Japhet or from Canaan.

'Has a nation changed their gods, which are yet no gods?' says Jeremiah. Under the Old Testament dispensations, the nations were steady to their false religions. No nation changed their gods, which yet were no gods (if you except the Edomites, who were subdued by Hyrcanus, and adopted the Jewish religion; but those Edomites were only a part of the nation that had taken up their residence in the land of Judea). It was reserved for the glory of the New Testament dispensation, that nations under it should be born in one day to God; yet, in the days of old, many individuals became Jews after their return from the Babylonian captivity, especially at those seasons when God showed forth his glory in doing marvellous works for his people.

'The Lord is known by his judgments.' He was made known to many of the heathen throughout the Persian empire at this happy time, when the king Ahasuerus's heart was so unexpectedly turned to favor God's people. They saw that the God of heaven was the God of Israel, and that works were done by Him which no other god could do. The fear of the Jews fell upon them, for they saw that the greatest man, next to the king, in the

whole empire, was broken and crushed in his contest with them.

If the observation of single acts of the divine procedure had such happy effects in the conversion of the Gentiles, what effect ought the consideration of all God's works of wonder to have upon our hearts? The salvation of the Jews, in the days of Ahasuerus, is one of the manifold salvations which God wrought for his people in ancient days. But what are all the temporal salvations wrought for ancient Israel, to the great salvation wrought for Jews and Gentiles by our Lord Jesus Christ! and how wonderful are the salvations that have been wrought in different ages for the church! *'Among the gods there is none like unto you, O Lord! neither are there any works like your works. All nations whom you have made shall come and worship before you, O Lord! and shall glorify your name. For you are great, and do wonderful things; you are God alone!'*

Who could have believed that the contrivances of Haman for the destruction of the Jews would have terminated in the increase of their nation? The lovers of the name of the God of Israel would tremble at Haman's devices, lest the name of Israel should be put out, and the worship of the God of Israel should be extirpated from the earth. But the revolution of a few weeks convinced them that their God was the same God that he had ever been; and that wherein his enemies dealt proudly, he was still above them. Death and destruction are in the hand of the Lord, and he can make them instrumental for the life, and for bringing about the safety, of his people. *'Before him darkness becomes light, and sorrow is turned into joy. He takes the wise in their own craftiness, and carries the devices of the froward headlong. So the poor have hope, and iniquity stops her mouth.'*

Chap. 9. Verse 1. – *Now in the twelfth month, that is the month Adar, on the thirteenth day of the same, when the king's commandment and his order came to be done, in the day that the enemies of the Jews hoped to have power over them (though it was turned around, so that the Jews had rule over the ones who hated them).*

'The hope of the righteous is gladness, but the expectation of the wicked shall perish.' Of the truth of this maxim of wisdom, we have a remarkable instance in the events of the month Adar, when the decree of king Ahasuerus was put in execution. The enemies of the Jews had looked forward to that day with great pleasure. It was to be the day on which the name of Israel was to be abolished, and the worship of their God utterly extinguished. But, by the good providence of God, it was a day in which the bitter enemies of the Jews were destroyed, and their nation blessed with a testimony of the favor and power of their God, which made his name known through all the hundred twenty-seven provinces of the Persian empire. *'The God of their mercy prevented them;'* and at the time when their enemies had hoped to gain a complete victory, they were subdued and destroyed. Little do the enemies of Zion know the intention of the God of Zion, when he covers her with a cloud, and gives scope to their malice. Their conjectures appear to be built on solid grounds when they predict the downfall of Zion; but the wisest conjectures of men must give place to the most improbable predictions of the word of God, which assure us that the enemies of Zion shall be covered with confusion, and that God himself will establish her. The times have been, when many nations were gathered against her, that said, *'Let her be defiled, and let our eyes look upon Zion: – But they knew not the thoughts of the Lord, neither understood they his counsel; for He gathered them as sheaves into the floor, and made the horns of the daughter of Zion iron, and her hoofs brass, that she might arise and thresh, and beat in pieces many people, and consecrate their gain unto the Lord, and their substance unto the Lord of the whole earth.'* Wait patiently for God in the day of clouds and thick darkness. He often makes the day dark with night, when at the evening-time it shall be light.

Verse 2. – *The Jews gathered themselves together in their cities throughout all the provinces of the king Ahasuerus, in order to lay hand on any who sought their harm. And no man could withstand them, for the fear of them fell upon all people.*

'You shall not kill.' This commandment, in some cases, binds us to kill. It requires us to use all lawful endeavors to preserve our own life; and in preserving our own lives, we may be reduced to the unpleasant necessity of taking away the lives of other men. The Jews

were compelled, on the thirteenth day of the month Adar, to take arms into their hands, to destroy all that might rise up against them; and they acted wisely in uniting themselves in large bodies to resist the power of their enemies. Had they stood single in arms, they might all have been destroyed with ease. But their combination in the various cities of the king's dominions made them terrible and irresistible. Let us learn from their example to stand fast in one spirit, and with one mind striving together against the enemies of our souls, who endeavor to rob us of our faith, more precious than our lives.[1] The church is terrible, like an army with banners, when her rulers and members are closely united under the Captain of salvation, to oppose her enemies.

No man could now withstand the Jews, for the fear of them fell upon all people. They had the king, the queen, the prime minister upon their side; and what was still more, they had the providence of God upon their side. *'He caused judgment to be heard from heaven,'* as audibly as if an angel had proclaimed his favor to the Jews, and his indignation against their enemies. The wonderful works of Providence have often struck terror into the hardiest enemies of Zion; (Psalm 48:5,6).

Verse 3. – *And all the rulers of the provinces, and the lieutenants, and the governors and officers of the king helped the Jews, because the fear of Mordecai fell upon them.*

There were two decrees in equal force, which might have given them a fair pretense for taking the part of the Jews, or of their enemies, as they pleased; but it was plain that the king's favor was towards the Jews, and that if they expected any favor from him, it was necessary to secure the good-will of Mordecai. They chose that side in the contest which their own interest prescribed. What a pity is it that all princes do not favor the cause of religion! If they did, iniquity would be compelled to stop her mouth, and those men who do not value religion would treat it, at least, with respect.

Verse 4. – *For Mordecai was great in the king's house, and his fame went out throughout all the provinces. For this man Mordecai became greater and greater.*

He was famous for his virtue and wisdom, as well as for the honors to which the king had advanced him. He gained more and more respect the better he was known, and all the respect entertained for him by the king, or by his subjects, contributed to the success of the Jews in the day when their fate was to be decided. It was this that made Mordecai's fame and greatness a pleasure to himself, and the cause of thanksgiving from him unto God. He had been formerly as an humble shrub in the valley, and then his obscurity was so little disagreeable to him, that he never called to the king's mind the great services he had done for him in saving his life, nor would allow the queen to make any mention of his relation and kindness to her, although by the bare mention of these, the king would have been induced to place him in a much higher station. He was now like a tall cedar, with spreading branches, and a shadowing shroud; and he was highly pleased with this change in his condition, because it enabled him to afford shelter to all his people.

Verse 5. – *So the Jews struck all their enemies with the stroke of the sword, and slaughter, and destruction, and did what they would unto those who hated them.*

It may appear strange that the Jews now found any enemies bold enough to contend with them in battle. The king was their friend, God was their friend, what could those expect who sought their lives, but destruction to themselves? It is indeed wonderful, but not uncommon, for men to value the gratification of their malignant passions above their best interests, and above their safety. At the destruction of Jerusalem by the Romans, it is well known that the Jews themselves did more mischief to one another, than all the harm they suffered from the fury of their conquerors. The different parties, when they found respite from the Romans, destroyed one another within the walls, and destroyed their provisions, and thus brought upon themselves a famine, which destroyed them by thousands. But we need not look seventeen hundred years back to see the tyrannizing power of malice and hatred over the minds of men. Are there not many who subject themselves to bitter remorse, to ruinous fines, or to an ignominious death; are there not many more who subject themselves to the curse of God, merely to gratify their accursed spite against their fellow-men?

Many of the enemies of the Jews, doubtless, were overawed by the power of Mordecai, and either sat quiet in their dwellings, or joined with the Jews. Many chose rather to be quiet than to venture their lives in battle with enemies that were sure to be victorious. But there were others, not in small numbers, who chose to venture or rather to sell their lives, and the lives of all that were dear to them, rather than lose the opportunity given them by law, of attempting to destroy a race of men whom, though innocent, they hated with a deadly hatred. These men combined in the different cities to fight against the Jews. But their confederacy was against the God of heaven, who spoiled them of their courage, and gave them into the hands of the Jews, to do to them as they would. They were so far from gaining their malicious purposes at the expense of their lives, that victory, and glory, and triumph to their hated enemies, were the fruit of their cruel attempt. Vain it is to fight against God, or against those whom he loves and protects. If God is against us, who can be for us? If we harden ourselves against the Almighty, we cannot prosper. It were better for us to dash our heads against the craggy rock, than to rush upon the thick bosses of the buckler of the Almighty.

Why should men fight against God? And yet there are too many who fear not to carry the weapons of an unrighteous warfare against their Maker and their Judge. *'Whatever you have done, or not done, to one of the least of my brothers,'* says Christ, *'you have done, or not done, to me.'* Enmity against the people of God is enmity against God himself; and surely *'all that are incensed against Him shall be ashamed.'*

DISCOURSE XIV.

NUMBERS OF THE SLAIN – A SECOND BATTLE AT SHUSHAN.

CHAPTER 9:6-19.

Verses 6-10. – *And in Shushan the palace the Jews killed, and destroyed five hundred men. And Parshandatha, and Dalphon, and Aspatha, and Poratha, and Adalia, and Aridatha, and Parmashta, and Arisai, and Aridai, and Vajezatha, they killed the ten sons of Haman the son of Hammedatha, the enemy of the Jews. But they did not lay their hands on the spoil.*

Even in Shushan the royal city, under the eye of the king, there were more than five hundred men that combined, in defiance of the king's known sentiments, to attack the Jews. But they meddled to their own hurt. When we consider the audacity of that behavior to which their malice prompted them, we see that Mordecai had too much reason to tell Esther that she would not be safe in the king's palace if she did not intercede with the king. The men that could take the pretense of a law to attack the Jews to their certain destruction, might have been prompted by the same outrageous malice to attack Esther in the palace, when they could plead the king's authority for their enterprise.

These five hundred men in Shushan, who sold their lives in this desperate cause, were, doubtless, some of Haman's creatures, who had learned from him to hate the Jews with a bloody hatred. Haman's ten sons were at the head of them, and shared in their fate. They were, doubtless, trained up by their father in the hatred of that nation; and his miserable end, instead of opening their eyes, irritated their resentment, to their own destruction.

It was natural, some will say, for Haman's sons to account that people their enemies, by the means of whom their father suffered an ignominious death. It was natural, it must be confessed; but it does not follow that it was right. Children are to honor their parents while they live, and venerate their memory when they are dead, but not to follow their example in anything that is evil. The children of wicked parents ought to remember, that their duty to their Maker must have the precedency of all other duties; and that to rebel against God because their parents rebelled against him, is not more excusable, than for a man to be a thief, or a yraitor, or an adulterer, because his father was so before him. God commanded his people, when they were carried away captives for their transgressions, to confess their own iniquity, and the iniquity of their fathers. The holy son of the wicked Ahaz made a full confession of the sins committed by his father, and by the people under his influence, and deserved high praise for reversing all his wicked institutions; (2 Chron. 29). Jeroboam had only one son in his house who discovered a dislike of his father's conduct, and was the only member of the family who died in peace. *'Fill up the measure of your father.'* said Jesus to the Jews; warning them that their fathers' example would be so far from justifying their wicked conduct, that the vengeance of Heaven was brought the nearer to them that their sins were but a continuation of the sins of their progenitors.

Parents! pity your children, if you will not pity yourselves. You know what force the example and influence of parents has. If you profess bad principles, you of course train up your children in the profession of the same. If you openly practise wickedness, you teach your children to practise it likewise. Thus you pull down vengeance, not only upon yourselves, but upon your houses. You see that Haman was the enemy of the Jews, and of the God of the Jews; and the punishment of his wickedness fell heavy, not only on himself, but upon all his family, which was probably rooted out of the earth. His sons might have been allowed to live in obscurity, if they had been willing to live peaceably. But they had drunk deep of their father's spirit, and followed his example; and ten (probably all) of them perished on that fatal day on which their father, a few months before, had hoped to feast his eyes with the blood of those whom he chose to account his enemies.

But they did not lay their hands on the spoil. – It is not always good to seize all the money to which one has a legal right. There are many cases in which a regard to our own credit, and there are others in which a sense of duty, resulting from singular circumstances, should bind up our hands from receiving what we might otherwise take without injustice. The king's edict gave the Jews a right to take the spoil of their enemies; (Chap. 8:11). But for their own honor, and for the credit of their religion, they chose to leave the spoil of their enemies to be enjoyed by others. The tongue that slanders might have alleged that they had slain innocent persons with the guilty, to enrich themselves.

They had been accused as a wicked people, whom it was good for mankind to destroy from the face of the earth. Their noble disinterestedness was a refutation of this calumny. It was evident from their conduct that they were not lovers of money; and *'the love of money is the root of all evil.'* The apostle Paul showed disinterestedness of spirit in a higher degree, when he labored for years in places where, for the honor of that gospel which he preached, he would receive no recompense from his hearers, that it might not be accounted a fable cunningly devised for the profit of them who preach it; (Acts 18:3).

Verses 11,12. – *On that day the number of those who were killed in Shushan the palace was brought before the king. And the king said to Esther the queen, The Jews have killed and destroyed five hundred men in Shushan the palace, and the ten sons of Haman. What have they done in the rest of the king's provinces? Now what is your petition, that it may be granted you? Or what further request do you have? And it shall be done.*

The king had an account brought to him of the number of the slain in the imperial city. It was highly proper that he should cause this account to be brought before him. If husbandmen are diligent to know the state of their flocks, and look well to their herds, how much more ought kings to inform themselves of the affairs of their kingdom! Ahasuerus might learn wisdom from the account brought him of the slaughter of the enemies of the Jews. By his rashness he had occasioned the slaughter. If five hundred men were slain in Shushan, what numbers might be supposed to be slain throughout all the provinces? What bloodshed had been the fruit of one thoughtless act of government! It may be hoped that Ahasuerus learned wisdom for the time to come. Never in the succeeding years of his reign was he chargeable with such folly. At a great expense he learned a very needful lesson, To do nothing without consideration of the consequences.

The king brings to the queen his information concerning the slaughtered enemies of the Jews. *The Jews have killed and destroyed five hundred men,'* says he, *'in Shushan the palace,'* besides the ten sons of Haman, the most formidable and the most enraged of them. The king could not yet tell how many were slain through the large extent of his dominions, but he justly infers from the number of the slain in one city, that it must be very great in all the cities and provinces together. This piece of information the king hoped would be very grateful to Esther, as it would ease her mind of those griefs which had long oppressed it. She, indeed, had good and well-grounded hopes before this time, that the enemies of her people would fall in the contest; and now she enjoyed the satisfaction of knowing that her hopes were realized.

We must not rejoice in the destruction of our enemies, nor must our hearts be glad when they stumble. This is the doctrine of the prophets, as well as of the apostles; (Prov. 24:17). Yet God's people have good reason to rejoice at the fall of their irreconcileable enemies, when they see the mercy of God to themselves, and when they see the safety of the church in the destruction of those who hated them: *'When God shoots at the wicked with an arrow, and wounds them suddenly, the righteous shall be glad in the Lord, and shall trust in him, and all the upright in heart shall glory;'* (Psal. 64:7-10).

Now what is your petition, that it may be granted you? Or what further request do you have? And it shall be done. – It is reported of Mary Queen of Scotland, that her household servants were always glad when she was put into a passion; for, when she was restored to good humor, she made them more than a sufficient recompense for all past unkindnesses. Thus Ahasuerus, sensible of the wrongs he had done to his queen, endeavored to banish all remembrance of them, by heaping upon her unexpected kindnesses. All of us are liable to starts of bad humor, and may behave unkindly to those who are dearest to us, or we may, through want of due consideration, give them much pain without intending it. When we are made sensible of such conduct, let us repair it with advantage. While our friends live, if we have treated them with unkindness, there is opportunity to obliterate the wrong. They may die, and then it will be sealed up, and nothing will be left for us but unavailing regret.

Verse 13. – *Then Esther said, If it pleases the king, let it be granted to the Jews who are in Shushan to do to-morrow also according to this day's decree, and let Haman's ten sons be hanged upon the gallows.*

'Dearly beloved,' says the apostle, *'avenge not yourselves.' 'Love your enemies,'* says Christ, *'that you may be the children of your Father who is in heaven.'* Was Esther not a daughter of the Lord Almighty? or was the spirit of the Old Testament dispensation of religion different from that *'spirit of love, and of a sound mind,'* which is given unto us?

Esther was undoubtedly a saint of God, and the spirit of love dwelt in her. We have already seen that the writers of the Old Testament, as well as those of the New, forbid revenge; (Prov. 24:17). But self-defence is licensed and required under the New, as well as the Old Testament. Esther knew that there were still many deadly enemies of the Jews in Shushan, who might, if they were allowed to live, harass or destroy them. She desires that they might receive the just reward of their malice.

Lukewarmness, and even cruelty, have often assumed the dress of charity. The children of Israel, after the death of Joshua, were cruel to the rising generation, when they spared the wicked Canaanites. Saul brought wrath upon himself, when he spared Agag. Samuel performed an act of humanity, when he hewed to pieces before the Lord a tyrant who had made many women childless, for a warning to other despots. *'Cursed is he,'* says Jeremiah on a certain occasion, *'who does the work of the Lord deceitfully. Cursed is he who keeps back his sword from shedding blood.'* A curse came upon Meroz, for sparing the blood of the Canaanitish enemies of Israel. A worse curse might have come upon Esther, if she had neglected the opportunity graciously afforded her by God, for securing the peace of Israel by the destruction of Haman's creatures. They were a race of vipers. Their venom was not diminished. If they had not been crushed, they might have found an opportunity to sting the man who had brought destruction on their companions in wickedness.

Beware of making a bad use of this piece of history. Such circumstances as those in which Esther was placed, will probably never occur to any of you. The care of the lives of all the people of God came upon her, and the enemies of the Jews, by their late behavior, were seen to be hardened beyond all hopes of reformation. When the hand of the Lord was lifted up, they would not see it, but rushed upon him, even upon the thick bosses of his buckler. Your enemies may be reclaimed. Your duty, according to Solomon and Paul, is, if your enemies are hungry, to feed them: if they are thirsty, to give them drink. Thus you will heap coals of fire upon their heads, and the Lord will reward you. Remember how Jesus, when he was dying for your sins, prayed for his murderers. You know not what manner of spirit you are of, if you draw into an ordinary precedent extraordinary cases, from the histories of Elijah, or Moses, or Esther. Christ left you an example to follow his steps on every occasion.

Let Haman's ten sons be hanged upon the gallows; on that gallows which their father set up for Mordecai. Kings can take away our lives, that is all they can do against us; and yet, when we are dead, they may expose our bodies to infamy. Haman's ten sons could feel no more pain from the hand of men. But their ignominious exposure on the gallows erected by their father was an awful warning to other enemies of the Jews. It was a standing proclamation of the favor of God to that nation; of his indignation against their enemies; and of the righteousness of his judgments. Those who saw them, saw good reason for saying, *'Truly there is a reward for the righteous; truly there is a God that judges in the earth.'* The Lord causes his wonderful works to be remembered. He would not have us forget his awful, any more than his pleasant works, that he may be glorified by us as a great God and a Saviour.

Verse 14. – *And the king commanded it to be done so. And the order was given at Shushan, and they hanged Haman's ten sons.*

From the ready acquiescence of the king in Esther's request, we may reasonably conclude that he saw it to be just and proper. After what had newly happened, it was not likely that he would give a rash assent to a bloody decree. But *'a wise king will crush the wicked, and bring the wheel over them.'*

By the king's commandment, *'the ten sons of Haman were hanged upon the gallows.'* The king soon relented after he had passed a too severe decree against Vashti; but he did not repent, nor had he any reason to repent, of what he did against Haman. All the children of that insolent favorite were given up to infamy after death. We need not on this occasion reflect on the uncertainty of royal favor. Haman and his family might still have enjoyed the smiles of the king if they had deserved them. Their own wickedness destroyed and disgraced them; for *'they drew iniquity to themselves with cords of vanity, and sinned as it were with a cart-rope.'*

Verse 15. – *For the Jews who were in Shushan gathered themselves together on the fourteenth day also of the month Adar, and killed three hundred men at Shushan. But they did not lay their hands upon the spoils.*

They provided for things honest in the sight of all men. When they did not lay their hands on the spoils, it would easily be believed that they had killed no innocent persons. It was evidently not the desire of gain, but a just regard to their own safety, that induced them to kill so many of their enemies.

These enemies of the Jews that escaped on the thirteenth day of the month, would think that the bitterness of death was past. The law, as it then stood, exposed them to no further danger. But these enemies of God who escape shall not flee away. *'Mischief shall hunt the violent man till he is ruined.'* If he is not ruined to-day, he will be ruined to-morrow; if not to-morrow, on some following day known to the Lord, and probably on a day when he is not expecting it. The bitterness of death cannot be past while the sentence of the Almighty is standing in force against the wicked.

Verse 16. – *But the Jews who were in the king's provinces gathered themselves together and stood for their lives, and had rest from their enemies, and killed seventy-thousand of their foes. But they did not lay their hands on the spoils.*

How many were the enemies of the Jews, even after they were known to be favored by the king, when, in all appearance, avowed enmity against them was to end in speedy destruction! But many as they were, there were more with the people of God than against them, and their enemies were made to lick the dust. Let not those who have God on their side tremble at the multitude and strength of their enemies. *'Associate yourselves, O people! and you shall be broken in pieces; and give ear, all you of far countries; gird yourselves, and you shall be broken in pieces. Take counsel together, and it shall come to nothing; speak the word, and it shall not stand; for God is with us.'* Immanuel is our security from every danger.

The Jews, in none of the provinces of the king's dominions, laid their hands upon the spoils. They had been in great fear of death, and they thought it a great matter to have their lives saved, without making gain of their enemies. *'The life,'* says our Lord, *'is more than meat, and the body than raiment.'* When men are in extreme danger of their lives, or have newly escaped from it, money goes for little. Were we possessed with a due concern about deliverance from that sentence of death which has passed upon all men, or with a fervent gratitude for deliverance from so great a death, our attachment to the things of the present world would be greatly weakened. What will money avail us, if we must perish? If we are redeemed from destruction, we will be happy and thankful, whether we possess much or little, or nothing at all, of the good things that perish in the using.

Christians have often censured the whole body of the Jews, as men of a selfish and rapacious spirit. The charge has, probably, exceeded truth. But, as far as occasion has been given for it, it has been owing, in a great measure, to the oppressions exercised upon that unhappy nation, which have irritated their spirits, and weakened or destroyed their sense of justice towards those whom they considered as their enemies. Certain it is, that they were far from discovering a rapacious spirit in the days of Esther. Many who name the name of Christ might learn from them to set their minds on things above rather than on things of the earth. They chose to adorn their profession, by making it apparent that they sought not riches by means which they disapproved, although they would have appeared safe and honorable to any others but themselves.

Verse 17. – *And on the thirteenth day of the month Adar, and on the fourteenth day of the same, they rested and made it a day of feasting and gladness.*

On the thirteenth day they fought for their lives, and on the fourteenth they rested and rejoiced in their preservation and victory. The battle was probably sore in some places where their enemies were strong and many; but everywhere they gained the victory, and the joys of God's salvation were an abundant recompense for their toils and dangers. Let all God's people patiently endure the tribulations assigned to them, and courageously fight those battles which they are called to sustain. There is hope in their latter end, and the greater their fight of affliction, the sweeter is that rest which the Lord will give from their sorrows and fears. Jesus fought and conquered, and entered into his rest; and *'it is a faithful saying, that if we suffer with him, we shall also reign with him;'* and, before the time of reigning with him is come, we may hope that in this world days of rest and joy will often succeed nights of sore afflictions; (Isa. 4:3; Psalm 125:3; Isa. 57:15,15; Chap. 40:1,2).

Verse 18. – *But the Jews who were at Shushan gathered together on the thirteenth day of it and on the fourteenth of it. And on the fifteenth of the same, they rested and made it a day of feasting and gladness.*

The Jews of Shushan did not so soon obtain rest, as the Jews of the provinces. They were fighting on the fourteenth day of the month, when their brothers were resting and delighting themselves in the abundance of God's goodness. Yet they rested at last, and had as good a day on the fifteenth as their brothers had on the fourteenth. We must wait God's time for days of rest and gladness, and His time is always the best. It was good for the Jews at Shushan to be employed two days in encountering and destroying their enemies. Their rest was the more pleasant when it came, that they had made an utter end of those who plotted against their life.

The day of feasting and rest was sweetened by the preceding days of labor and fear. Pleasant is health after sickness. Safety is delightful after extreme danger; and gladness is double joy to those whose souls were depressed with sorrow. In days of prosperity it is good to look back to days of adversity, that we may feel the value of our present enjoyments, and that our hearts may be filled with the praises of him who has turned our darkness into light, and our mourning into dancing.

Verse 19. – *Therefore the Jews of the villages, who lived in the unwalled towns, made the fourteenth day of the month of Adar a day of gladness and feasting, and a good day, and a day of sending portions to one another.*

Their hearts overflowed with joy and gladness. They wished never to forget what God had done for them, and therefore they resolved annually to observe that day on which they obtained joy and gladness, as a day of joy, and of the exercise of mutual benevolence. We ought never to forget the happy changes which God has made in our condition. Often should we call back to our remembrance the mercies of former days. This will be our wisdom and our happiness. It will be a frequent renewal of former joys, and a means of preserving alive that gratitude which we owe to the God of our mercies.

DISCOURSE XV.

ORDINANCE OF MORDECAI AND ESTHER FOR OBSERVING THE DAYS OF PURIM.

CHAPTER 9:20-32.

Verses 20,21. – *And Mordecai wrote these things, and sent letters to all the Jews who were in all the provinces of the king Ahasuerus, near and far, to establish this among that they should keep the fourteenth day of the month Adar, and the fifteenth day of the same, yearly,* –

Some of those days of the year in which God appeared in the glory of his power to his people, by working signal deliverances for them, or by giving them signal testimonies of his favor, were appointed by him to be annually observed as days consecrated to his honor. Thus the Passover was a yearly commemoration of the redemption of Israel from Egypt, and the Pentecost of the giving of the law.

But it is not within the power of men to give holiness to a day. God alone, therefore, has authority to appoint stated days for religious services. He alone can bless such days as means of spiritual improvement. Without His presence and blessing, we meet together for the worse, and not for the better; and therefore we must be assured, when we expect his blessing, that we have his warrant for our meetings. That occasional fasts and thanksgivings, on proper calls of providence, may and ought to be appointed by public authority there is no reason to doubt; but stated fasts or thanksgivings can be warrantably appointed by no less authority than His, on whose shoulders the government of the churches is laid. We must observe all things whatsoever He has commanded us, and nothing else, as a religious ordinance, and, lo! he will be with us always.

But why, then, did Mordecai appoint the feast of Purim? Surely Mordecai could not take it upon him to appoint a religious festival without a divine warrant. He knew that neither Joshua nor David had appointed holy days to be annually observed by the nation, as commemorations of their glorious victories, or of the happy settlement of the people in consequence of their victories. He knew that Moses himself, the lawgiver of the nation, had appointed no solemn feasts by his own authority. He would not even authorise those who could not observe the passover on the ordinary days to observe it on another day, till he had received commandment about it from heaven.

We must conclude, therefore, either that Mordecai was authorised by the Holy Ghost to appoint this festival, or, which appears rather to be the truth, that the feast of Purim was not one of the holy festivals, but a civil festival appointed for joy and feasting, in commemoration of an event that ought never to be forgotten. Mordecai gave no orders concerning sacrifices to be offered on this day, or even concerning any act of religious worship. He, doubtless, hoped that thanksgiving and praise would be offered to God on every return of this joyful festival, but did not reckon himself authorised to publish a law for this purpose. His intention was to perpetuate the remembrance of a glorious deliverance, and he left it to the consciences and grateful feelings of the people to determine what acknowledgements should be made to God, according to the general rules of his word.

Mordecai wrote to the people far and near, to keep both the fourteenth and the fifteenth day of the month Adar as days of rejoicing. They were both of them days of rest, the former day in the provinces, the latter in Shushan; and he would have the people, in every part of the world, to remember, not only their own particular deliverance, or those which their fathers obtained, but deliverances granted to others of their people. Jews were bound, and Christians are surely not less bound, to consider themselves as members one of another, and to consider the mercies bestowed upon their brothers as mercies to themselves.

Verse 22. – *As the days in which the Jews rested from their enemies, and the month which was turned unto them from sorrow to joy, and from mourning into a good day – that they should make them days of feasting and joy, and of sending portions to one another, and gifts to the poor.*

All things work together for good to the people of God, by promoting their happiness, as well as their holiness. The remembrance of their toils sweetens the rest which succeeds them. The sleep of the laboring man is sweet, although he should sup sparingly before he goes to rest. The tears which the Christian must often shed are remembered with joy, when they are wiped away by returning prosperity. Mordecai wished the Jews to be ever mindful to their sorrows, that their joy may be full.

The days of Purim were intended to be days of feasting and gladness. In the season of their distress, they would scarcely be able to eat that bread which was necessary to the preservation of their life: when they thought of their deliverance, and of the mercy of God in their deliverance, they would eat their bread with gladness, and drink their wine with merry hearts.

These days were to be *days of sending portions to one another.* Their common danger, and their common deliverance, would endear them to one another, and open their hearts to mutual kindness. How much more ought our common salvation by Christ from our general misery to bind the hearts of Christians to one another. We were involved in guilt and ruin by sin, and the same sin was the source of misery to us all. We are all redeemed by the same precious blood; we are all saved by the same Almighty arm: Let our common joy in Christ's salvation overflow in mutual love. If we are penetrated with the love of Christ, will we not love all those who are the objects of the same exceeding riches of grace?

And of sending gifts to the poor, was to be another of the duties of this happy day. There might be many poor Jews, who were not able to afford an entertainment for this day of joy.

But Mordecai would have the poor to rejoice as well as the rich. Although we find our circumstances unprosperous, we must not on that account reckon that we have no right, or that we are not bound, to rejoice in public mercies. That the poor may not be tempted to repine when others rejoice, as if they were cut off from the public happiness, we should be ready to communicate to them a share of our blessings, especially when our hearts overflow with joy in God's goodness to ourselves. Why should the rich eat their morsel alone, while others are pining with hunger? If you desire the continuance of your own happiness from divine mercy, endeavor to diffuse it by wise liberality. Every expression of divine goodness to ourselves is a new obligation laid upon us to do good, to those especially who have most need of our bounty. Above all, the redemption by Christ binds us to be merciful; (2 Cor. 8:9).

Verse 23. – *And the Jews undertook to do as they had begun, and as Mordecai had written to them; –*

They cheerfully promised to comply with Mordecai's wishes, both from a regard to his authority, and from a lively sense of the mercy bestowed upon them. It is a happy thing when superiors require nothing from their inferiors but what themselves see to be just and reasonable.

Mordecai's letters could not but have a mighty influence upon a nation who were indebted to him for their lives. He could not be blamed for bringing them into the dangers which they had escaped, because it was his steadfast adherence to his duty which provoked Haman's wrath. But he deserved no less praise than Esther herself for their preservation. Gratitude will induce us to do many things for those who have been the instruments of preserving our lives. What shall we render to the Author or our lives, and to him who has redeemed our lives from destruction?

Verse 24. – *Because Haman the son of Hammedatha the Agagite, the enemy of all the Jews, had plotted against the Jews to destroy them, and had cast Pur, that is, the lot, to finish them and to destroy them?* –

The remembrance of Haman's fearful plot against all the Jews, powerfully instigated them to observe those days of joy that were appointed by Mordecai. When they considered how formidable the enemy had been, and how bent upon their destruction, they could not think of their deliverance without surprise, and joy, and thankfulness.

It would be useful to us for increasing our joy in the Lord, to think upon those enemies of the church that have often brought her into extreme dangers, that we may see the glory of that grace and power to which she is indebted for existence. If we think upon the Pharaohs, the Hamans, the Sennacheribs, the Antiochuses, the Dioclesians, the beast with seven heads and ten horns, that have opened their mouths like dragons to swallow up the people of God, will we not see good reason still to sing that song of ancient times? – *'Many a time have they afflicted me from my youth, may Israel now say; many a time have they afflicted me from my youth; yet they have not prevailed against me.'*

Haman was the cause of much terror to the Jews, but this terror ended in triumphs and joyful feasts. Unhappy are the enemies of the people of God. They labor for the profit of those whom they hate. Among those things that are made subservient to the advantage of the people of God, are to be ranked all the devices of their most malicious enemies, Satan himself, their greatest enemy, not excepted. Sennacherib was a tremendous enemy of Judah, and struck terror into the minds of the most valiant of the inhabitants of Jerusalem. But what was the event of his formidable invasion? Disgrace and ruin to himself, gladness and joyful feasts to the Jews; as Isaiah foretold, when he was marching along in all the pride of his heart at the head of his innumerable army, collected from his extended dominions: *'They had a song, as in the night when a holy solemnity is kept; and gladness of heart, as when one goes with a pipe to come into the mountain of the Lord, to the mighty One of Israel.'*

Verse 25. – *But when Esther came before the king, he commanded by letters that his wicked plot which he had plotted against the Jews should return upon his own head, and that he and his sons should be hanged on the gallows.*

In Mordecai's letters, he puts the Jews in mind, not only of Haman's plot against them, but of the means also by which it was disconcerted. Let us observe and call to mind the procedure of the providence of God in the works which he accomplished for his church, or for ourselves in particular. Every step of his goings of majesty deserves to be remarked and admired. They are all beautified with wisdom and grace.

Who could have expected that Esther, whom the King had not desired to see for thirty days, should obtain such favor in his eyes, as to turn his wrath against his favorite Haman, whose face he saw every day with smiles? Yet, when Esther came before the king, the mischief of Haman was turned upon himself, and he and his sons were hanged on the gallows. Let us do our duty, and leave the consequence to God. Without the protection of his providence, Esther would have fallen under the sentence of that cruel law which made the king inaccessible to his subjects. But her life was preserved by that God to whom she had poured out her soul in fasting. She did great things, and prevailed; and her name shall live to the latest posterity in the records of those heroes and heroines, who *'wrought righteousness, escapea the edge of the sword, out of weakness were made strong, and turned to flight the armies of the aliens.'*

'Wherever this gospel is preached,' said Jesus, *'there shall also this that this woman (who poured precious ointment on his head) has done be told for a memorial of her.'* Mordecai hoped that what Esther had done would be told in every succeeding generation to her honor; and for the encouragement of women as well as men, to do everything in their power to promote the interests of the church. Women are too ready to say, What can we do to serve the public interest? our mode of life confines us to our own families. But Esther is not the only woman that has gained just praises by her public spirit. Lemuel's mother taught her son to be a blessing to his people, and has left lessons behind her, by which women, to the end of the world, will be taught to excel in virtue. To Priscilla, as well as to Aquila, all the churches of the Gentiles gave thanks for what she did for Paul; and many of them had reason to thank her for what she did to Apollos likewise. Males and females are one in Christ Jesus. They are equally saved by his grace; they are equally obliged to promote his interest in the exercise of virtue, and the practice of duties suited to their respective situations; and women, as well as men, have sometimes found singular opportunities of service to their generation, which they could not safely neglect to improve.

Verse 26. – *Therefore they called these days Purim after the name of Pur.*

The very name of these days afforded a useful lesson to the people of God, and might have afforded a useful lesson to their enemies. It appeared from the event of the lots which gave name to this day, that although time and chance happen to all men, yet nothing is contingent to God. Chance is under his management, and those things which to us appear most accidental, are managed by his providence to accomplish his designs of mercy to them that love him, and of vengeance to his enemies. Why, then, should the friends of God give themselves any anxious trouble about the most uncertain events? The whole disposal of the lot is of Him. Haman's lots directed his measures to his own destruction, and the salvation of Judah.

Verses 26,27. – *Therefore for all the words of this letter, and of that which they had seen concerning this matter, and which had come to them, the Jews ordained, and took upon them and upon their seed, and upon all such as joined themselves unto them, so as it should not fail, that they would keep these two days according to their writing, and according to their time every year.*

The Jews, partly induced by Mordecai's letter, and partly by what they had seen and what had happened to them, agreed that the observation of Purim should be considered as an ordinance and a statute in Israel throughout every generation. They not only engaged for themselves, but for their seed, and all strangers who should join themselves to their nation, to observe this festival.

They did not take more upon themselves than there was a probability of accomplishing, when they engaged that it should not fail. When a joyful festival is appointed by the rulers, with the cheerful consent of the people, to be observed annually, it is not likely to fail among posterity, if the occasion of it was some signal revolution in favor of the nation, especially if the very existence of the nation depended upon it.

It may be justly questioned, whether a nation can bind their posterity to any thing further than the laws of religion, justice, and good order in society, bind them. But posterity would not too narrowly inquire how far the authority of their fathers extended, in a matter no less agreeable to themselves than to their progenitors. This, however, is certain, that when men command their children and their seed after them to keep the way of the Lord, future generations cannot turn aside from the good way of their ancestors, without greatly aggravated guilt; (Jer. 2:10-13).

The Jews expected that proselytes would observe the festival with no less joy than the posterity of Abraham. If we have joined ourselves to the church, we ought to consider ourselves as deeply interested in all the ancient as well as the later dealings of God with her. We partake of the root and fatness of the olive, and therefore ought to bless God for all the care he has taken of this tree of righteousness, which by his goodness has been so long preserved from destruction, and made to flourish in beauty, and abound in branches and fruit.

Verse 28. – *And that these days should be remembered and kept throughout every generation, every family, every province, and every city – and that these days of Purim should not fail from among the Jews, nor the memorial of them perish from their seed.*

Not only did the Jews resolve and promise to observe these days, but they did everything in their power to promote the observance of them in every province and city where any of their brothers dwelt, and to perpetuate the observance of them among their seed. Such was the pleasure they felt for their deliverance, and such their gratitude to God their deliverer, that they wished all their brothers, wherever they were scattered, to rejoice with them, and to magnify the Lord together. Their posterity, to the latest generation, could not fail, they thought, while these days were observed, to admire, to praise, to glorify the God of their fathers, their King of old, by whom manifold salvations had been wrought in the midst of the earth. They would, while this deliverance was recent, be disposed to think that none of the ancient salvations was more worthy of remembrance; and that as they had no authority to appoint any religious festival for the commemoration of it, they could not do less than concur in the appointment of a common festival, which would annually recall it to mind.

Verse 29. – *Then Esther the queen, the daughter of Abihail, and Mordecai the Jew, wrote with all authority to confirm this second letter of Purim.*

Far be it from us to suppose, that either Esther or Mordecai had their own glory in view, when they were at such pains to promote and perpetuate the observance of the feast of Purim. It would be unjust, as well as uncharitable, to ascribe such selfish intentions to persons who had laid down their necks for the honor of their God, and for the deliverance of their people.

That their design was good in writing the second letter of Purim with all authority, cannot be reasonably doubted. It may, indeed, admit of question, whether they did not expect more than prudence could justify them in expecting, from the perpetual observance of this feast. They probably thought, that while the memory of the wonders of the month of Adar continued, all posterity would abound in thanksgivings to God. The reverse has been the case. The feast of Purim has long since been turned into a drunken revel. The blinded Jews, it is said, lay it down as a maxim, That they ought to be drunken with wine in remembrance of Esther's banquet. How strange is it for human creatures to think that they are delivered to work abomination!

Esther and Mordecai '*wrote with all authority.*' They thought that they could not use their power for a better purpose, than to perpetuate the remembrance of that day when God delivered their souls from death, their eyes from tears, and their feet from falling. But in the exercise of their authority, they forgot not that kindness which was due to their brothers, the Israel of God.

Verse 30. – *And he sent the letters to all the Jews, to the hundred and twenty-seven provinces of the kingdom of Ahasuerus, with words of peace and truth,* –

When we are exalted above our brothers, we are too ready to forget both them and ourselves, as if the change of our condition had raised us to a higher rank of creatures. Mordecai and his adopted daughter were not negligent in the exercise of their authority for purposes that appeared to them good and salutary to the nation; but they still retained their humbleness of mind, and their kind affections to their kindred. They sent these letters to all the hundred and twenty-seven provinces, '*with words of truth and peace;*' with expressions of the warmest benevolence. Nor were these expressions, like many of our mutual compliments, merely dictated by a politeness which too often conceals a perfect indifference to our neighbor's welfare under good words and fair speeches. Their words were words of truth, as well as of peace, when they expressed their desires and prayers, that the Lord might bless his people with peace.

Let men maintain that authority which God has given them, that they may attain the ends for which it is given them; but let it be always tempered with charity and gentleness. Paul, in his epistles, asserts his authority as an apostle of Jesus Christ; but he writes with words of peace and truth, when he prays for grace and peace to the churches from God the Father, and from the Lord Jesus Christ.

Verse 31. – *In order to confirm these days of Purim in their set times, according as Mordecai the Jew and Esther the queen had ordered them, and as they had decreed for themselves and for their seed the matters of the fastings and of their cry. And the order of Esther confirmed these matters of Purim. And it was written in the book.*

At the motion of Mordecai, the Jews were unanimously determined to observe the festival, and to enjoin the observance of it to their posterity. The Jews were confirmed in their resolution by the second letter of Mordecai, in conjunction with Esther. And one consideration which would dispose them to observe the commemoration of this deliverance with joy and exultation, was, that they had fasted and cried for it under the pressure of danger. They could not eat their ordinary food. They cried out with exceeding loud and bitter cries. They fasted and cried unto the Lord, and he heard the voice of their supplications.

Spring is the pleasantest season of the year, because it follows the dreary desolations, and the piercing cold of winter. Those days of health are especially delightful which follow days of extreme sickness, when we had the sentence of death in ourselves. Remember the dismal thoughts that engrossed your minds, the terrifying apprehensions that embittered your troubles, and the exquisite felicity which you promised to yourselves, if it should please God, beyond your expectations, to send you relief. Thus will the troubles you have endured spread happiness in the retrospect over the remaining part of your life. You still must meet with trials; but you will be thankful that they are so light and easy to be borne, when they are compared with those which you have formerly endured.

Have you fasted and cried unto the Lord, and has He graciously inclined his ear to your complaints? With what joy and peace ought you to recollect the mercy which has preserved you from going down to the chambers of the grave, perhaps to the regions of destruction! David will teach you what improvement to make of your fasting and cries, when the Lord has been pleased to grant you the deliverance which you supplicated: '*I love the Lord, because he has heard my voice and supplications. Because he has inclined his ear unto me, therefore will I call upon him so long as I live. The sorrows of death compassed me, and the pains of hell got hold upon me; I found trouble and sorrow. Then called I upon the name of the Lord: O Lord, I beseech you, deliver my soul! Gracious is the Lord, and righteous; yea, our God is merciful. The Lord preserves the simple: I was brought low and he helped me: I will walk before the Lord in the land of the living;*' (Psalm 116:1–6, and 9: Psalm 18, 19; Isa. 38:11–20).

Verse 32. – *And the order of Esther confirmed these matters of Purim. And it was written in the book.*

The high and beloved name of Esther was sufficient to establish the decree of Purim. She had been the saviour of the Jews. At the risk of her life she had preserved theirs. What do we not owe to Him who, not merely by endangering his life, but by giving up himself to an accursed death, has delivered us from the wrath to come?

And it was written in the book of the Jewish institutions, or in the register of the Jewish transactions. Books are necessary for recording those things that are intended for the use of posterity. Were it not for books, we would all be children in understanding. Let us carefully improve those things that were written aforetimes for our learning, especially those things which divine wisdom has directed the holy men of God to record for our benefit.

The feast of Purim is still observed, though not in a manner agreeable to Esther's intention. The observance of this and other festivals of the Jews, from the most ancient times, is attended with this great advantage, that it affords a convincing argument of the truth of those facts which they were designed to commemorate, when we take this into the account, that these facts were recorded in books at the time when they were instituted which are still extant. The observance of the ancient Jewish feasts is a public declaration of the firm belief of the Jewish nation in the Old Testament Scriptures. This is one of the most powerful rational arguments of the truth of our holy religion. If the Old Testament Scriptures are true, the Messiah expected by the Jews is come long ago into the world; and none but Jesus of Nazareth can be that Messiah. Thus the most determined enemies of Jesus give a decided, though indirect testimony, that he is the Son of God, by attesting the truth and divine authority of those ancient Scriptures that testify of him.

DISCOURSE XVI.

GREATNESS OF AHASUERUS – CHARACTER AND GRANDEUR OF MORDECAI.

CHAPTER 10.

Verse 1. – *And the king Ahasuerus laid a tax upon the land and upon the isles of the sea.*

Too many subjects are disgusted with the governments under which they live, when new taxes are imposed. Here we find that the increase of taxes is no new thing, and that it may be necessary under the best and wisest governments. When the tribute here spoken of was laid upon the land, and upon the isles of the sea, Ahasuerus had his counsels directed, not by Haman, but by Mordecai. Ahasuerus might perhaps have saved his subjects their new burdens, if he had been more frugal in his expenses. The multitude of his concubines must have put him to a very great, and a worse than needless expense; (Chap. 2). He was liberal in his donations. His wars could not be carried on without great sums; and when his wars with the Greeks came to an end, he expended much money in political intrigues, to preserve himself from more wars. He therefore found it necessary to lay new burdens upon his subjects. But the protection which government affords makes the payment of necessary taxes an act of justice. *'Rulers are the ministers of God to us for good; and for this cause we must pay them tribute, because they are the servants of God, waiting continually upon this very thing.'* We are not excused from this duty by the supposition that government ought to be more economical than it is. Who of us does not sometimes spend money that might be spared? It is one of the laws of the Turkish empire, that no new tributes can be imposed on the people. The consequence is, that when their government must have money, it must be raised by oppression of individuals, who, in their turn, indemnify themselves by oppressing others. The Persians were much more wise, when they allowed a tribute to be laid upon them which came with equal weight upon all. *'He laid a tribute upon the land,'* upon the vast regions on the continent under the Persian empire, and upon the many *'isles of the sea'* which they possessed. A burden borne by all will be light, when it would be unsupportable to a few.

Subjects may, under unwise governors, have too much reason to complain of burdens laid upon them; (Prov. 28:16); yet complaints of this kind are often without ground. Rulers can best know what sums are requisite for the honorable support of government, and for the defence of the country. Although we think our burdens heavy, let us bear them conscientiously. We claim support to our just rights from government, and must not defraud it of its own rights; (Rom. 13:6,7).

Verse 2. – *And all the acts of his power and of his might, and the declaration of the greatness of Mordecai, with which the king made him great, are they not written in the book of the chronicles of the kings of Media and Persia?*

The Bible is incomparably the best of all books, and yet it is not the only book from which we may derive instruction. Luther wished all his books might be burned, rather than men should be kept by them from reading the Scriptures. But we may daily read the Scriptures, and find some time likewise for consulting other books. We find the apostle Paul quoting the books of poets and philosophers; (Acts 17:28; Titus 1:12; 1 Cor. 15:33). Here the inspired writer refers to the chronicles of Media and Persia for a further account of the power and greatness of Ahasuerus; and for a confirmation of what has been said of the greatness of Mordecai. We are often referred by the sacred writers to uninspired histories for larger accounts than they were directed to give us of the lives of persons eminent for their stations, and for their virtues and vices. Much useful instruction is to be drawn from credible histories. We learn from them many of the works that God has done on the earth, and the perfect conformity between his words and works. Many examples of goodness are set before us, which we ought to imitate; many instances of vicious conduct, which we ought to abhor.

The registers of the ancient kings of Persia do not now exist; but the reference made to them is a confirmation of the history of this book. The writer would not have sent his contemporaries to the public records for further information, if he had written anything which did not agree with them. Learned men have made a happy use of ancient writings of heathens, as well as of Christians, to establish the authority and truth of Scripture, in opposition to infidels.

Although the records of the Persian kings are lost, we have books left us which inform us of the greatness, and power, and long reign of Artaxeres, or Ahasuerus, the husband of Esther. Many worthy deeds were done by him to the church of God, as we are informed by Ezra and Nehemiah; and he was well rewarded by Divine Providence. The prayers of the people of God for his prosperity were heard.

Although we have no account of Mordecai in the Grecian histories of this long reign, we have no reason to doubt of what is said concerning him in this book. The Greeks had but a partial acquaintance with the affairs of the Persian court, and the most ancient Persian histories, written by Persians themselves, give some cause to suspect, that through ignorance or partiality the Greeks have frequently omitted or misrepresented the most important facts. Mordecai the Jew, and Ezra, and Nehemiah, had access to the knowledge of many facts concerning the government of Ahasuerus, that were unknown to strangers.

Verse 3. – *For Mordecai the Jew was next to king Ahasuerus and great among the Jews, and pleasing to the multitude of his brothers, seeking the wealth of his people and speaking peace to all his seed.*

Mordecai the Jew was next to king Ahasuerus. This was wonderful; a poor man of the dispersion of Israel was raised high in dignity, by the favor of Ahasuerus, above all the princes of Persia. The elevation of men from the lowest to the highest rank is not unusual in the east, even at present. But Mordecai professed a religion which seemed an unsurmountable obstruction to grandeur in a land of heathens; and he held it so firm that he would not conform to the fashions of the court in anything that did not consist with a good conscience. Haman hoped that all the men whose laws and customs were so different from the king's laws would soon be extirpated. He little expected that one of the most inflexible adherents to those laws and customs would supplant and succeed him in the king's favor. *'There be many that seek the ruler's favor'* with such eagerness, that they will bend their consciences into a ready compliance with his wishes, whatever they are: *'But every man's judgment comes from the Lord.'* He exalted Daniel and Mordecai in the courts of Babylon and Shushan; and these were men that would not have turned a hair-breadth out of the path of duty to please any prince on earth. Their unshaken firmness might, very probably, be one cause of their advancement. Inflexibility in what is right must be a respectable quality in the eyes, not only of the good, but of every man of sense.

Ahasuerus showered favors upon Esther, upon Mordecai, upon Ezra; and upon Nehemiah, and yet continued all his days to adhere to the religion of his fathers. Herod Antipas did many things gladly because of John Baptist, and yet he was not a good man. Love to the brothers is a scriptural mark of a saint; but men that are not saints may have a warm attachment to good men, on account of qualities that all the world hold in esteem. We love the brothers, when we love believers as the children of God, as our brothers in Christ, partakers of the same divine nature. But integrity, generosity, unshaken constancy in virtue, are qualities for which men that have not passed from death to life may esteem and love their neighbors, whether they are saints or not.

Mordecai was great among the Jews, and pleasing to the multitude of his brothers. – They venerated and loved him as the saviour of their nation, as their father and protector. Envy too often attends the exaltation of one's equals. Joseph's brothers would rather murder him, or sell him to strangers, than see him advanced above themselves. Ingratitude too often follows the greatest benefactions. The children of Israel requited evil to the house of Gideon for the deliverance wrought for them from the hands of the Midianites, at the risk of his life. But Mordecai met with returns of the sincerest gratitude from the multitude of his brothers. He still behaved to them as a brother, and they considered him both as their brother and their prince.

It was a great happiness to the good man that he was accepted of the multitude of his brothers; for '*a good name is better than precious ointment, and loving favor is rather to be chosen than silver and gold.*' This, however, is a happiness not always to be expected by good men; and therefore, as our Lord teaches us, we must learn to do good without the expectation of a return from those to whom we do it. Paul was still happier than Mordecai, when he found ungrateful returns for the noblest services, and yet could say in sincerity, '*I am ready to spend and be spent for you, although the more abundantly I love you, the less I am loved.*' If we do not perform our good works to be seen of men, we will be content with the honor that comes from God only. The favor and gratitude of men are highly useful, by enabling us to be still more useful to them; but then we have the testimony of our own hearts that our works are wrought in God, when the course of our goodness is not interrupted by bad returns from its objects; (Heb. 6:9,10; Gal. 6:12-16).

Seeking the wealth of his people. – Many, when they have attained the utmost summit of their wishes, become unhappy, because they have obtained what they sought. Desire fails, and their hearts become like a stone in them, because they have nothing more to desire. This is the effect of selfishness reigning in the heart. Give a good man ten times more wealth or honor than he ever desired to possess, he is not unhappy because his wishes are completely gratified, for he will still find new desires operating in his heart. Although he has nothing more to wish for on his own account, he finds opportunities to do much good to others, which he did not formerly enjoy. His desires are roused by the means of executing them. Mordecai was, doubtless, richer than he ever expected to be, when he was made the queen's treasurer, and the king's favorite. But there was a nation in which he was deeply interested, and which he had new opportunities given him to serve. These opportunities he did not neglect. While he faithfully served a prince to whom he was highly indebted, he sought, and by all wise and honest means promoted, the wealth and prosperity of his people. A rare talent was entrusted to him, and he did not hide it in a napkin. When we have nothing to do for ourselves, it will be our wisdom and happiness to do much for others. '*The liberal man devises liberal things, and by liberal things shall he stand.*'

The Jews were Mordecai's people. This was one though not the chief reason why he sought their wealth. Patriotism is certainly a virtue recommended to us by the best of saints. The apostle Paul was, perhaps, worse treated by his countrymen than ever any other man, and yet he would willingly have died for them a thousand deaths. He '*magnified his office as the apostle of the Gentiles, that if possible by any means, he might stir up to emulation his brothers according to the flesh.*'

Paul could not procure the love of his kinsman, like Mordecai; although he certainly sought the welfare of his people with an affection no less ardent. The reason of the difference may be that Mordecai sought their outward prosperity, and Paul their spiritual advantage. We are not to suppose that Mordecai was careless about their spiritual interests. That expression which we translate '*the wealth,*' might have been rendered '*the good*' of his people. He sought their happiness of every kind. But his station gave him opportunities chiefly to promote their external prosperity. Paul labored for their spiritual advantage; and we know what difference men put between services done to their bodies and services done to their souls. If the preachers of the gospel, who call men to come and share in the unsearchable riches of Christ, should call them to come and receive thousands of gold and silver, not one of them would hear the invitation without a thankful compliance; and yet they will not come unto Christ, that they might have life. Alas! how little regard is paid to the words of the Wisdom of God: *'Receive my instruction, and not silver; and knowledge rather than choice gold. For wisdom is better than rubies; and all the things that may be desired are not to be compared with it;'* (Prov. 8:10,11).

And speaking peace to all his seed. – The generous soul of this good man was filled with kindness to the rising race, and projected the happiness of succeeding generations. *'He spoke peace to all his seed'* (or rather, their seed). He was courteous in his deportment to the young, and behaved so as to discover a warm regard for the welfare and happiness of the race that should be born. Thus Peter, in the view of laying aside his earthly tabernacle, took care that Christians should have necessary truths in remembrance, when they could not enjoy the opportunity of hearing them from his mouth.

The expression seems to imply that Mordecai procured the peace of the seed of Israel by the words of his mouth. *'Death and life are in the power of the tongue.'* Mordecai, by his credit with the king, gave him a favorable opinion of the Jews, and extinguished all suspicion that might be entertained by that prince to the prejudice of a nation whose laws were different from the laws of other people; and, by his influence with the Jews, promoted that spirit of loyalty and good behavior on which their welfare greatly depended.

Few have it in their power to be such benefactors as Mordecai: all have it in their power to do much hurt; and who has it not in his power to do some good? We are not required to do what we have it not in our power to do, or what is not competent to our station. But all of us are bound to live under the influence of those tempers which were eminently displayed in those great saints whose examples are recorded in the Bible. They obtained their good report through faith, which animated them in all their undertakings. If we live by the faith of Christ, we will be active according to the ability that God gives us, and the calls of his providence, in promoting his glory, and the best interests of men.

Fervent charity operated in Mordecai; and if our faith is genuine, it will work by love. Love is not a dead, but a vigorous affection. If the spirit of love and faith dwell in us, we will be trees of righteousness, whose leaves will not wither, and whose fruit will be produced in its proper season; for *'the fruit of the righteous is the fruit of a tree of life.'*

If we cannot reasonably hope to do much for posterity, we certainly may do something to promote the welfare of our own generation. If our goodness extend not far, it may reach to parents, servants, wives, and neighbors. Our dutiful behavior towards them, our example, our prayers, may greatly promote their present comfort, and their eternal welfare.

And why may not the most inconsiderable Christian hope to be of some use to posterity? Train up your children in the fear of God, and they will be a blessing to the next age. They will probably follow your good example, and thus you will be useful, by their means, to generations yet unborn. If you have no children, you may be useful to young persons around you: *'A word spoken in season, how good is it!'*

GOD'S PROVIDENCE UNFOLDED IN ESTHER

by

ALEXANDER CARSON

PROVIDENCE UNFOLDED, etc.

The great design of this portion of the Holy Scriptures is to display the wisdom, providence, and power of God, in the preservation of his people, and in the destruction of their enemies. We learn from it that the most casual events which take place in the affairs of the world are connected with his plans respecting his people, and that the most trifling things are appointed and directed by him to effect his purposes. It decides a question that philosophy has canvassed for ages, and never will fathom; recording a number of events, the result of man's free will, yet evidently appointed of God, and directed by his providence. From this book the believer may learn to place unbounded confidence in the care of his God in the utmost danger; and to look to the Lord of omnipotence for deliverance, when there is no apparent means of escape. It demonstrates a particular providence in the minutest things, and affords the most solid answer to all the objections of philosophy to this consoling truth. The wisdom of this world, with all its acuteness, is not able to perceive how God can interfere on any particular occasion, without deranging the order of his general plans. Philosophers account for the prosperity of the wicked, and the afflictions of the righteous, from the operation of general laws. A villain grows rich by industry, and oppresses the virtuous poor; a righteous man loses his all by a storm at sea, or is himself overwhelmed in the ruins of an earthquake. In all this the philosopher's god cannot interfere, for he is tied down by the order of a general providence. He is fettered by his own previously established laws, as effectually as the gods of the heathen were when they swore by the river Styx. He must quietly look on amid all the occasional mischief resulting from his plans, which, though upon the whole the best possible, yet have many unavoidable defects. Storms and earthquakes result from the operation of general laws established at first by the Author of nature; and the Almighty, it is supposed, without unsuitably counteracting the order appointed by himself, can neither prevent them nor deliver them from their dreadful consequences. Famine and war, with all the evils that destroy or afflict men, are accounted for on principles that exclude a particular providence. The arrogance of the oppressor cannot be restrained, nor the sufferings of the virtuous prevented, without an unbecoming deviation from the order of nature. Philosophy cannot see how her god could dispose every particular event without a miracle on every occasion of interference. On this supposition, she thinks that he must be continually suspending and counteracting the general laws which he at first established for the government of the world.

How different from this philosophic god is the Lord God of the Bible! Jehovah has indeed established general laws in the government of the world yet in such a manner that he is the immediate Author of every particular event. His power has been sometimes displayed in suspending these laws, but is usually employed in directing them to fulfil his particular purposes. The sun and the rain minister to the nourishment and comfort equally of the righteous and the wicked, not from the necessity of general laws, but from the immediate providence of Him who, in the government of the world, wills this result. Accordingly, the shining of the sun and the falling of the rain on the fields of the wicked are represented in Scripture, not as the unavoidable effect of general laws, but as the design of supreme goodness. A fowling-piece well aimed will strike a particular object; but divine truth has assured us that a sparrow cannot fall to the ground without the permission of the Ruler of the world. This book teaches us that God exerts his particular providence in an inconceivably wise and skillful manner, even by the operation of his general laws, and by the exercise of the free determinations of men. The very laws that in the opinion of the philosopher stand in the way of a particular providence are here exhibited as the agents that he deputes to effect his purposes. The most astonishing interferences that ever were recorded are here effected solely through the operation of general laws, and the actions of voluntary agents. The people of God are delivered out of the most imminent danger, and their enemies most marvelously overturned, without a single miracle. The glory of the Divine wisdom, and power, and providence shines here the more illustriously, because God effects his work without suspending the laws of nature, or constraining the determination of the agents employed in the execution of his work. He saves them, and destroys their enemies without going out of the usual path of his providence. Had the earth opened and swallowed the enemies of the Jews, the power of Jehovah would have been displayed; but when he saved them by a train of events according to the general laws of nature, each of which separately viewed seems fortuitous, yet when seen in combination must necessarily have been designed to bring about the one great end, the existence of a particular providence is proved, and the nature of it is delightfully illustrated. It is not merely taught in doctrine, but it is exhibited in example. In the history of the deliverance of the Jews through the exaltation of Esther, we have the whole history of the world in miniature. The book of Esther is the History of Providence. In the inspired account which we have here of an interesting portion of Jewish story, we have an alphabet, through the judicious use of which we may read all the events of every day, of every age and nation. This is a divine key which will open all the mysteries of providence. It is God's commentary on all that he has done and on all that man has done, since the finishing of the works of creation. All is natural and seemingly fortuitous; yet if the whole had been a work of mere fiction for amusement, the events could not have been better adapted to the end. There is all the simplicity of nature, yet all the surprise and interest of romance. The grand object is evolved like the plot of a regular drama; every event recorded contributes its influence in producing the effect. There is nothing wanting; there is nothing superfluous. Had the most trifling incident refused its aid, the whole plan would have been deranged – the most fatal results would have succeeded. From the first to the last, all parts are connected and influenced like the machinery of a watch. By a thousand wheels the main-spring guides the index. We have first a train of events to raise up deliverance to the Jews, even before they were brought into danger; next, we have a train of events to bring them to the brink of ruin; then follow the surprising means of their preservation, and the destruction of their enemies. To one or other of these objects every circumstance recorded in the history contributes, and the whole forms one of the grandest displays of the wisdom, power, and providence of God, that is to be met with in the Scriptures, and is well calculated to represent that noble plan by which the kingdom of Satan is overturned, and God's people are delivered from the power of their great enemy, through the very means intended for their utter extirpation.

In reviewing the train of events that provided the means of deliverance for the Jewish nation, before they were brought into danger, the first thing that presents itself is the great feast of Ahasuerus. At first sight nothing could have been more unconnected with the intended object. It is quite a fortuitous and ordinary matter. A royal revel would appear calculated to defeat the designs of Jehovah, rather than fulfil them. But the wisdom and omnipotence of Jehovah can use ordinary events to effect his purpose, and can fulfil his will by a worldly assembly, or even by a synagogue of Satan, as well as by a church of Christ. He reigns as absolutely over his enemies as among his friends. He works through Satan and his emissaries, as well as through the ministry of the angels of his presence; and employs the councils of sinners, as well as the loyal and loving exertions of saints. The occasion of originating this deliverance to the people of God was a feast to exhibit the glory of a worldly kingdom, and not a religious assembly. God employs his agents in work suitable to their character. Had the wisdom of men formed the plan of deliverance, the monarch would have been made a proselyte to the religion of the Jews, and the work would have been effected by him as a servant of the God of Israel. But God does everything by him while he continues, as far as we are informed, altogether uninfluenced by the law of the Lord of heaven. Had David sat on the throne of Persia, his zeal for the preservation of Israel and destruction of their enemies, could not have flamed with greater ardor than that of Ahasuerus.

What was the particular occasion of this feast we are not informed, and therefore it can be no way useful for our edification. Commentators are usually very obliging with their conjectures on such an emergency, and edify us with many a shrewd guess. But it is the duty of a Christian to learn everything that the Scriptures record; and it is equally his duty to remain in the most obstinate ignorance of everything that they do not reveal. Whether this was a birthday, or a feast for commemorating the accession to the throne, whether it was an annual festival, or an occasional revel, I know not – I care not. What I know is that God had evidently determined it as a link of the wonderful concatenation of ordinary events employed by him to effect his glorious purpose of delivering his people. Though the free appointment of man, it was also the appointment of God. It was necessary to give birth to the events that follow.

The whimsical, tyrannical, and indecent thought that struck the mind of the monarch in his wine, though originating with himself, was according to the appointment of a wise Providence. Why did such a thought come into his mind? It was evidently contrary to the custom of Persia, for Vashti to make such an appearance, as the females of this occasion feasted apart. It was extremely indecorous for the female majesty of the empire to be exposed to the formal survey of such an assembly, heated with wine. The queen's disobedience of the orders of an absolute monarch, accustomed to universal obedience, shows how much the thing required was contrary to the general sentiments of decorum. Had such a thing been usual, it would not have been so offensive to the queen. It may be said it was a drunken frolic. But was the king never drunk before? Is this the only time that he acted under the influence of wine? Why did the thought strike him now rather than at any other time of his drinking? Why is it that this is the only instance of the kind on record? God's intention undoubtedly was that a thing might be enjoined on the queen with which she would not comply, that her disgrace might make way for the exaltation of the deliverer of his people. Yet though in one point of view it was the appointment of God, in another it was the result of the actions of free and voluntary agents. God's purpose is brought about by those whose only view is to fulfil their own purposes. How inscrutable are the mysteries of Providence! how unsearchable are his counsels in the government of the world! Men are his enemies – they hate him, and disobey him; yet in all their plans and actions they fulfil his will. The regularity of the heavenly bodies in their courses is wonderful; but they are not voluntary agents; they are constantly urged on by the hand of their Creator. But men think, and resolve, and act for themselves; yet they fulfil the plans of Jehovah as much as the sun, moon, and stars. His very enemies in opposing him are made the instruments of serving him. How consoling to the believer is this view of Providence! When he looks around him he sees everywhere men trampling on the laws of God, and openly putting dishonor on him. Is God disappointed in the end that he proposed by his works? is he really overcome and thwarted by the prince of darkness? No! Jehovah is executing his purposes even through the wickedness of men and devils: and all things that have taken place from the creation must minister to his glory. Though Satan has usurped the throne of God in the world for so many thousand years, yet in all this God has been executing his own plans; and he now rules on earth as absolutely and as unreservedly as he does in heaven. This is a depth which we cannot fathom; but it is a truth necessary for the honor of the character of God; and one of which the Scriptures leave no room for doubt. The sin and misery that are on the earth – the endless perdition of wicked men and devils – are subjects of melancholy consideration to the man of God; but let him be consoled with the thought that Jehova'. works all things according to the counsel of his own will, and that the darkest spots on the book of God may appear in the brightness of meridian light in the world of glory. *"The Lord has made all things for himself; yea, even the wicked for the day of evil,"* (Prov. 16:4). The Apostle Paul declares that he was a *"sweet savor unto God,"* as well *"in those that perish,"* as *'in those that are saved."* A fool may ask, How can these things be so? and the wisest man on earth cannot answer him. But is it not enough that God has said it? Shall little children receive the word of their parents with the utmost confidence of conviction, when they testify the most incredible things, and shall we hesitate to receive the word of the God of truth?

The queen's refusal is another providential circumstance which we are here called to observe and to admire. Notwithstanding the singularity, the indelicacy, and the unreasonableness of the command, it is remarkable that the queen should venture to disobey a despot heated with wine. She could scarcely expect to escape with impunity. Even Esther herself, with all her surpassing beauty, was exceedingly reluctant to venture uncalled into his presence. She was not willing to risk her life on his caprice, whether he would hold out the golden sceptre, or allow her to perish in her rashness. What, then, must have been the danger of Vashti? What must have been the intrepidity of the daring woman that refused to obey him? Her conduct was singularly bold and imprudent. Her resolution was no doubt suggested by her pride, or by her sense of decorum; but a regard to self-interest is usually stronger than these principles, especially in courts. Why, then, did her delicacy at this time prevail over her prudence? Not one woman in a thousand would have acted in this manner, in the same circumstances. Why then did a woman of such spirit fill the situation of queen at this critical moment? Why was not her beauty accompanied with an abject spirit of servility, as is usually the case among the slaves of eastern despots? The reason evidently is God had provided this high-spirited woman for the occasion which he meant to serve by her. He had determined her character and conduct as the means of executing his purposes; and by the ordinary course of events, his providence had given a consort to the monarch who was fitted for the part which he designed that she should act. As a voluntary agent she ignorantly fulfilled the will of Him whom she knew not, when she was influenced solely by a regard to her own feelings.

The advice of the king's counsellors on this occasion is also remarkable. The sycophants around despots are generally distinguished for caution. Even in their revels they are seldom off their guard. Now it was at the utmost hazard that they gave this advice. They must succeed, or fall. Though pure love could not influence the breast of a licentious eastern monarch, yet it is evident that Ahasuerus admired the beauty of his queen. The favorite mistress of despots is known to prevail against the most subtle and most powerful ministers. We see how readily this very monarch gave up to Esther the man whom he had most singularly honored and raised above all the princes of the empire. If the counsellors of the king should fail in displacing Vashti from the affections of their master, they were evidently planning their own ruin. Had the king refused to listen to their counsel, and the queen been restored again to power, their overthrow was certain. Why, then, did not the supple statesmen take the wisest course, and make their court to the queen by interceding for her pardon? After all the provocation of the king by the queen's disobedience, it was still possible that a man who admired her beauty, and had provoked her transgression, might not instantly put it out of his power to forgive her. She might have been disgraced in such a way as not to prevent her restoration, or repentance. Such a bold step in the ministers of a despot is certainly remarkable. But whatever might influence them, God had determined their counsel as the means of fulfilling his own.

That the king should subject her to a temporary degradation or disgrace, even though his own improper command was the occasion of her transgression, is very natural; but that, for the cold-hearted purpose of setting an example to the wives of the empire, he could consent to give up forever one whom he so much admired, discovers more stoicism than is generally to be found in absolute monarchs. Their treatment of their wives is usually more influenced by passion than by a view to the public good. In the heat of his fury it would have been less strange that he should have given orders for her death, than that he should divorce her for an example to the wives of his subjects. Yet, to the frigid morality of his wise men does this eastern sensualist sacrifice his beautiful queen. By a harsh decree she is divorced forever. But this great feast – this capricious command – this imprudent disobedience – this rash advice – this unfeeling consent – this sacrifice of affection to policy – this harsh decree, are all necessary in the plans of Providence. Vashti must be removed, that Esther may be exalted to her place.

Let us next contemplate, for a moment, the elevation of a poor fatherless Jewess to the rank of queen of the Persian empire, and admire the wonderful providence of God in her destination. Is there any man so blind as not to perceive that it was entirely providential that one of the small number of captive Jews should be found more beautiful than all the virgins of a hundred and twenty-seven provinces? Can any one question that God gave her exquisite loveliness for the very occasion? Known unto God are all his ways from the beginning; and in the formation of Hadassah he had an eye to the plan which he intended to execute through her. Had not God provided a Jewess of beauty surpassing all the virgins of the Persian dominions, the previous events would have been useless. Esther was found the most lovely of women, that through her beauty she might deliver the people of God.

In this circumstance we have a key to the Divine procedure in adjusting the various events in providence to the fulfilling of his plans and declaration with respect to the kingdom of his Son. All the persons who are called to take a part in the advancement or defence of the cause of God are gifted by him with the necessary qualifications. Many of these qualifications are given in their birth or education, though they may not for a length of time be called to use them. Sometimes they may even for years employ them in opposition to God. Such was the case with Paul, and doubtless some points of the character of this eminent apostle were bestowed on him in his very constitution, with a view to the service of Christ. He had many things by immediate gift; but he had some things by mental temperament and education. Any one who reads the History of the Reformation with an eye to this characteristic in Divine Providence, will see it surprisingly illustrated in innumerable instances. The character and circumstances of Luther alone will afford a multitude of such providential provisions. By a single gift was Esther fitted to be the deliverer of Israel: by a multitude of talents and acquirements, in the most wonderful complexity, was Luther fitted for the work to which he was called by God. Indeed, the history of the Reformation bears a very striking resemblance to this deliverance of the Jews. Without a single miracle, God wrought a deliverance as surprising as the preservation of Israel, and many of those employed to effect it were as ignorant of God as the king of Persia. He used the passions and the interests of worldly men in bringing about his purposes, as well as the love and zeal of his own people. The preservation of the cause and people of God at that period was as much the work of Divine Providence as the deliverance of the Jews from the destruction to which they were destined by the wicked Haman.

All the learning, ability, and acquirements – the riches, birth, rank, and influence, through which at any time the cause of God has been served, have been conferred by God, in his providential government, to fulfil the purposes of his grace. Not only does he gift his own people for this end, but many who belong not to any of the tribes of Israel have been made hewers of wood and drawers of water for the service of the temple. Many able defences of the Scriptures – many satisfactory vindications of their doctrines, and illustrations of their contents, have been afforded by Providence through the instrumentality of men as ignorant of the true grace of God as they who deny their authenticity. The very ravens are made to feed the people of God, rather than that they should want.

In God's conferring on Esther this exquisite beauty, that he might raise her to royal rank, and to influence over the throne itself, we may see that the same thing may, in one point of view, be the Divine appointment, and in another may be the sinful action of men. This is a doctrine clearly taught in the Scriptures. It is here exemplified in the government of

Providence. It is a truth, however, that the wisdom of this world cannot fathom, and therefore cannot receive. That God should in any sense appoint, or intend to bring about, what he has in his word forbidden, is indeed one of the deep things of God. It is the abhorrence of the wise, while many even of those who have professed to have become fools that they may be wise, in effect deny it by their explanations. But this is a doctrine that the sagacity of men will never penetrate; it is a depth that human intellect will never be able to fathom. Who can by searching find out God? Can nothing be true of him and his ways but what is to be comprehended by such worms as men? Is it not enough to command our belief, that God has said it? Is he not virtually an atheist who requires more? A Christian who rests the reception of the Divine testimony on his ability to comprehend the thing testified is more inconsistent than a deist. One who recommends any truth of Scripture on such grounds insults God. The voice of Providence combines with that of Scripture in testifying to the truth of the doctrine to which I have referred. God evidently provided the beautiful Hadassah for the bed of Ahasuerus. But does the Holy One approve of this connexion? Are the seraglios of sensualists according to his word? Does the divine law sanction the divorce of Vashti for such an offence? What can be more abominable in the eyes of God than this manner of choosing a queen? What could be more hurtful to the interests of men, or more repugnant to their feelings? How unreasonable that a brutal sensualist should possess all the beauty of his vast empire? How many of the fairest females were thus lost to society, and consigned to perpetual misery in the palace of the sensual despot? Can anything be more palpably contrary to the end of marriage, not only as it is declared in the word of God, but even as it has been understood by heathens? Yet God performed his purpose through this great wickedness of men. He has no share in human guilt, while the transgressors of his law are made to fulfil his purposes. Such wisdom is too wonderful for us; it is high; we cannot reach it. But it is God's wisdom; let us receive it with submission.

We may here see also the way in which God regulates the events in his providence for fulfilling his plans, by adapting them to the instruments which he intends to employ in their execution. It was beauty that he gave to Esther, because beauty only could be the means of her elevation. All other accomplishments would have utterly failed. Had God given Esther greater riches than any subject of the hundred and twenty-seven provinces, she would not have been a single step nearer the throne. Had she been the daughter of the most powerful man in Persia, or a person of the highest birth, God, in his providence, could have made her a convert, or a friend to the religion of the Jews; but this would not have forwarded her progress to the throne. Had she possessed all the wisdom of Solomon, or all the accomplishments of her sex, with the exception of beauty, she might as well have been an idiot or a rustic. Personal beauty only could raise her, and personal beauty the God of providence gave her, that she might be raised. This affords a key to God's plans in his providence, by which he governs a world that is at enmity with him. In this way he makes them obey his will who know him not, who hate him, and, what is still more strange, even while they fulfil his will, transgress his laws. How unsearchable are the counsels of Jehovah! His way is in the sea, and his path in the great waters, and his footsteps are not known.

The providence of God appears conspicuous even in the ignorance of Mordecai and Hadassah. A marriage with a heathen was forbidden to the Jews. Now, had Mordecai and his kinswoman known their duty, her exaltation could never have taken place. But it seems very surprising that a man like Mordecai should be ignorant of this law of his God, or that he should know it, and join in the breach of it. Commentators are very willing to excuse him in this business. Mr. Scott says – "It does not seem to have been left to the choice either of Mordecai or of Esther;" And Dr. Gill is willing to believe that the fair Jewess went by constraint. But, were this true, is it a justification of a breach of the law of God? Why did Mordecai so uselessly hazard his own life and expose his whole nation to destruction, by obstinately refusing to honor Haman, and yield so readily to this vile prostitution of Esther? If danger will warrant us to violate the law of God, we will never want a pretext. But there is no evidence that there was any reluctance in this business. There is no account of a search, nor of concealment on the part of Esther. So far from hiding Hadassah when the king's commandment was heard, it appears that Mordecai was uncommonly solicitous to promote her exaltation. Mr. Scott, indeed, attempts to plead his vindication in this, by alleging, that as he could not prevent her from becoming one of the concubines of Ahasuerus, he might thus endeavor to have her made queen. But even this reasoning is not good. Had she been violated by the despot, she would not be justified in afterwards becoming his wife. Mordecai's zeal, then, to have her made queen is, in every point of view, unjustifiable. It was contrary to the law of God, yet it was in another point of view, God's own appointment. Instead of eagerly seeking a union with the king, Hadassah should have chosen the scaffold in preference. Her crime was much heightened by submitting to become his concubine before she became his wife. How many chances were against her that she might never have been called a second time into his presence?

Mr. Scott alleges, that "in her peculiar circumstances, the ritual of not giving their daughters to those of another nation might not be thought obligatory." But can any circumstances justify the violation of a law of God? Very likely, indeed, Mordecai might have some way to excuse himself. The command, as contained in the law of Moses, could not be unknown to him. But, like many good men now, he might have some way of excusing himself from obedience. But whatever this might be, he must have deceived himself. Neither times nor circumstances can relieve from the obligation of obeying God's law. Could there be stronger circumstances to disannul the restriction as to marriage than those which existed in the return from the Babylonian captivity? Wives had been married, and therefore ruined if the marriage is broken; children are born of these marriages, and, if the marriage will not stand, they must not only be bastardized but even deprived of a father's roof, and education by him in the knowledge of the God of Israel. Yet all this was a matter of no consideration. Both wives and children must be disowned and driven away forever. Let us read the Book of Ezra, and learn how sinful such marriages were accounted by all that feared God.

It is this wretched shift of times and circumstances that has subverted the whole order of Christ's house, and changed every ordinance of his kingdom. The laws of the kingdom are read in the book of God; but, by some peculiarity in their situation, good men plead their excuse from observance, or, by forced explanations, conform the canons of Scripture to their own conduct. It requires but little ingenuity to devise a plausible pretext for not doing that to which we are averse, or for doing that we like.

Mordecai and Esther, then, were guilty in this affair. But this unaccountable ignorance of their duty prepared them to execute the part that God had allotted them in this wonderful display of his providence. Who can read this story without being convinced that this marriage was God's plan for delivering the Jews from the approaching danger? Can anything be clearer than that it was contrary to the law of God? In some point of view, then, God appoints what the sin of men effects. He ordains actions which are entirely free, and in which men have all the guilt. This is as clear as the authority of Scripture can make it. Ask me to explain it, and I confess myself a child. I would as soon attempt to fathom space, or calculate the moments of eternity. I believe it, I confess it before the world, I urge the reception of it on Christians, because God has testified it in his word. Let God be true, and all men liars.

From this we see that the very ignorance of duty in the people of God may sometimes be providential, and serve his purposes. I have no doubt that there are still in Babylon many Mordecais and Esthers, whose ignorance in their unlawful situation is turned to the glory of God and the good of his people. But the good effected by them in such a situation does not lessen their sin in violating the law of God. It is the hand of the Almighty that brings good out of evil, and makes the ignorance of his friends, as well as the wrath of his enemies, to praise him. He will pardon them, but they will suffer loss, both in this world and the next. Even in this world, the most gainful violation of God's laws is a loss to a Christian, and obedience, at the cost of the most expensive sacrifices is a gain. What says the Lord Jesus to this question? – *"Then Peter began to say unto him, Lo, we have left all, and have followed you. And Jesus answered and said, Verily I say unto you, there is no man that has left house, or brothers, or sisters, or father, or mother, or children, or lands, for my sake and the Gospel's but he shall receive an hundred-fold more in this time, houses, and brothers, and sisters, and mothers, and children, and lands, with persecutions; and in the world to come eternal life."* The hundred-fold in this life cannot be of the things of this world, for then obedience would be a merely mercenary speculation. God does not bribe us to do our duty. It appears to me that it must be in the increase of light and enjoyment of God. The value of discovering God's mind in the Scriptures, and of beholding the glory of his character and ways, is incalculably great; and no one who has experienced it would exchange it for kingdoms. He is a blessed man who is the least in the kingdom of God; but there are many Christians who would not exchange with their brothers of the lowest attainments their views of divine things, as they have been taught by the Word and Spirit of their God, for all the glory of this world. The man who knows most of God is the first man on earth.

There is no reason, then, to envy the condition of believers, who, from ignorance, can enjoy lucrative situations, even if there were no future loss. The peace of God, which will always be enjoyed in proportion to knowledge and obedience, is beyond all the treasures of the world. This view of things is highly useful, for sometimes Christians may not only be tempted to envy the prosperity of the wicked, but even the condition of their brothers, whose ignorance allows them to possess more of the popularity, honors, and gains of the present world. Peter himself, when informed of the manner of his death, appears to have felt more from jealousy lest the beloved disciple might not be called to like suffering, than he did for the thing itself. *"Lord,"* said he, *"and what shall this man suffer?"* It behoves us all to attend to the answer. *"Jesus said unto him, If I will that he tarry till I come, what is that to you: follow me."*

There is an obvious advantage in knowing and doing the will of God. Paul says, *"If any man's work shall abide, which he has built on the foundation laid by him, he shall receive a reward. If any man's work shall be burned, he shall suffer loss, but he himself shall be saved; yet so as by fire."* He who got the greater number of talents, and made the best use of them, was made ruler over the greater number of cities. And what talent can be compared with the knowledge of the will of God?

Some people are willing to believe that whatever is lost by obedience to the will of God, will in some way be made up to them, even in this world, though it is their duty to obey without this consideration. But this view is false, fanatical, and hurtful. Though in every situation, we have a right to look to God, for this world as well as for the next, yet we know not to what sort of trials it may seem good to God to expose us. There is no safety in anything but in counting all things but loss for the excellency of the knowledge of Christ Jesus our Lord, and to be ready for him to suffer the loss of all things.

Sometimes the servants of Christ excuse themselves from complete conformity to his institutions, and vindicate the observance of the commandments of men in the things of God, by alleging the field of usefulness that accomodation in these things lays open to them. If they can point to any good done by them, they suppose that it is God's approbation of their situation. But in this they deceive themselves. Their conduct, as a transgression of the law of God, remains sinful, though his sovereignty turns their ignorance to his glory and the good of his people. Obedience is better than sacrifice, and to hearken than the fat of rams. It is a foul calumny on God to suppose that it is necessary to disobey him, in order to do good. This takes it for granted that his laws defeat their own end. When in the wisdom of God, he makes the ignorance of his people to serve his purpose, this no more excuses their ignorance and their conduct that results from it, than the good effects of the death of Christ will justify the crime of Judas Iscariot. God will, no doubt, forgive the ignorance of his people, but he will never hold it innocent. He will never approve it. Through the instrumentality of his people who understand not the nature of his kingdom, God provides that multitudes hear the gospel, who are to those in a scriptural situation altogether inaccessible. Yet this does not warrant the situation. Some of the people of God are in mystical Babylon, and, no doubt, will in some way serve God's purposes in that vile situation, yet the voice of God does not cease to sound in their ears, "*Come out of her, my people, that you are not partakers of her sins, and that you do not receive of her plagues.*" A Christian who knows his duty would not break the least of the commandments of Jesus, to enable him to turn the revenues of all the kings of the earth to the service of the cause of Christ. I might be asked, if all men would embrace my views of the nature of a church of Christ and his ordinances, and act on them with rigor, what would be the consequence? Millions who now constantly hear the gospel would be entirely shut up from it, and the hundreds of thousands of pounds that are raised annually for the spreading of the gospel would fail. If none are to be embodied in the church except such as appear to be born again by the Spirit through the belief of the truth, how would the gospel be supported? How would it be spread over the world? And so asks the child, If the moon is not nailed to the sky, will it not fall? This is a preposterous fear. Leave God's province to himself; fill your own well. Follow Jesus, though it should leave the whole world to be involved in darkness. But there is no fear of such a result. Though God now makes use of the ignorance of his people to support and advance his cause; if they all knew their duty, he would give still more signal success. The silver and the gold are his. When it served him, Jesus said to a rich man, "*Zaccheus, come down; for to-day I must abide at your house.*" All the wealth of the world is at his absolute disposal, and the moment he needs it, he will call for it. Let not the servants of God do evil that good may come. Let them not disobey him, that they may put themselves in a condition to serve him. I would not set at nothing the least of Christ's little ones. I will acknowledge all who know him, as far as I can know them, notwithstanding all the ignorance they may labor under. But I will not, out of complaisance, cease to declare what I learn from the word of God; I cannot cease to call on Christians to follow Jesus. Their ignorance is sin. The good which they do through ignorance is no justification of it. Esther saved the Jews, but by being in a situation to do so, Esther transgressed the law of her God.

The providence of God is seen in every step of the progress of Esther to her destined elevation. As in the case of Joseph, when sold into Egypt, God provided friends for her in all who had the means of seeing her. He filled every heart with good-will towards her at first sight. The king's chamberlain was pleased with her from the first moment of her arrival, and accelerated her progress by every means in his power. "*So when the king's commandment and his order was heard, and when many young women had been gathered together unto Shushan the palace, into the hand of Hegai, Esther was also brought into the king's house, into the hand of Hegai, keeper of the women. And the young woman pleased him, and she received kindness from him. And he quickly gave her the ointments for herself, with such things as were set aside for her, and seven young women who were fit to be given her, out of the king's house. And he moved her and her maids to the best place in the house of the women.*" When her turn came to approach the king, "*she asked nothing but what was chosen by Hegai the king's officer, the keeper of the women. And Esther had favor in the sight of all who looked upon her.*" Surpassing as her beauty was, this universal favor cannot be ascribed to it. In courts, envy and intrigue often prevail over every claim. Had not God disposed the hearts of those who beheld her, some far inferior beauty might have been the general favorite.

Notwithstanding her incomparable beauty, it was possible that the king's affections might have been anticipated by some of those who had previous access, or, from caprice or peculiarity of taste, he might have preferred another. But the providence of God had ordered this also, and no one pleased the king before the approach of the lovely Hadassah; and she obtained an instant preference. "*So Esther was taken to king Ahasuerus into his royal house in the tenth month, which is the month Tebeth, in the seventh year of his reign. And the king loved Esther above all the women, and she received grace and favor in his sight more than all the virgins. So much so that he set the royal crown upon her head, and made her queen instead of Vashti."*

The conspiracy of two of the king's chamberlains is another event in which we may see the hand of God, for effecting the elevation of Mordecai, preserving him from the wrath of Haman, and investing him with authority for the defence of his people, as well as the destruction of their enemies. A plot for the assassination of the sovereign is indeed nc unprecedented thing in the courts of absolute monarchs. It is granted that the onl impulse on the mind of the conspirators, exciting them to the murder of their master, wa their resentment on account of whatever injury or provocation they had received. Thei motives were not, in the remotest degree, to fulfil the counsel of God; nor are the sanctioned by him. They are therefore themselves solely responsible for their wicke intentions. But that this conspiracy was ordered of God, cannot surely be a matter o doubt with any who connect this fact with the others recorded in this history, and wh believe the narrative to be the word of God. It is here as evidently brought in t contribute towards the general issue as any incident in a drama. Take it away, and th whole chain is broken. Let us then admire the wonderful ways of Providence, in bringin about events through the freedom and the sins of human action. Why did these office receive provocation at this particular time? Why did they attend more to the gratificatio of their revenge than to their safety? Is a conspiracy to slay the sovereign the usual resu of every great injury done by him to individuals? Why was not the conspiracy bett conducted? why was it made known and frustrated? above all, why was Mordecai th man by whom it was discovered? why was he the man to whom it was known? Take awa this link of the chain, and all the other links are useless. Whatever, then, was the means bringing it to the knowledge of Mordecai, it was God that made it known to him, as muc as if he had revealed it in a supernatural manner. Indeed, as Dr. Gill observes, "the latt Targum says, it was showed unto him by the Holy Ghost;" for the wisdom of man cann see how the providence of God can arrange human actions to fulfil his purpose witho any miracle. How many chances were there, humanly speaking, that no conspiracy shou have existed at this time, or that it should not have been found out; or, if discovered, th Mordecai should not have been the discoverer? Was not the event evidently intended lay a foundation for the future safety, elevation, and power of Mordecai? How e couraging is this document! The Lord's people are frequently in danger. Their enemies l snares for them, which no human wisdom can enable them to escape. How consoling is for them to reflect on this wonderful narrative! Here is a fact that ought to encoura them in their most trying difficulties. The Lord laid a plan, and prepared means for t deliverance of his people in the Persian empire, even before their enemies had prepare the plot for their destruction! When therefore we are encompassed on every side, let look to the hand of the Lord to execute the plan which he may have prepared for o deliverance. When Hagar cried unto the Lord, he showed her a well, which is as wonderf in Providence, if the fountain had been there from the creation, as if it had been opene by miracle.

Having considered God's wise and gracious provision for the safety of his people durin the approaching storm, we shall now attend to the events by which it was raised. We ma discover the hand of God in this, no less than the former. The providence of God brin his people into danger, not because he is unable to ward off even the appearance of it, bu that he may glorify himself in their deliverance, and exercise their graces. Were they neve in danger, they would be deprived of some of the greatest opportunities of praising th wisdom, kindness, and watchfulness of his providential care; his enemies would want a occasion of manifesting their enmity to them and him; and their faith would be withou its necessary trials. But though, in one point of view, God wills the persecution of hi people, the sin of the persecutor is all his own. He is ignorant of God's purpose, and hi enmity to them arises from his enmity to him. Though he fulfils the appointment of God yet he wickedly gratifies his own evil dispositions. It is a curious fact, but not a singula one, that God raised up Haman to bring his people into danger, as well as Esther to deliver them. In this, as in other things, the Divine wisdom is distinguished from the human in a striking manner. No man would nurture the wretch whom he should know to be the future enemy of himself and his offspring. But God exalted Haman in the court of the great king, above all the princes of the empire, for the very purpose of giving him an opportunity of manifesting his enmity against his people, and of attempting the destruction of the whole nation. He puts his enemies in the most favorable situation to oppose him, that he may show with what ease he can discomfit the utmost efforts of their malevolence; nay, he makes the very wrath of man to praise him, and the plans of his enemies to destroy his cause are made to effect its establishment.

The motives of Ahasuerus in the promotion of Haman were, no doubt, such as usually influence absolute sovereigns in conferring their favors, and in choosing the objects of their particular bounty. In the caprice of affection, they set no bounds to their liberality, and the most unworthy men in the empire are often their favorites. It is not strange, then, that it should have been so on the present occasion. But the direction of Providence is clear even amid apparent casualties. It was God raised Haman, as well as he had for a like occasion raised Pharaoh. The individual, the character, the crisis of his exaltation, the height of his elevation, are linked together by Providence for a good purpose. In such a light is this combination of circumstances exhibited in the inspired text. It is brought forward as one of the grand incidents which contribute their influence to bring about the result. *"After these things king Ahasuerus promoted Haman, the son of Hammedatha the Agagite, and advanced him, and set his seat above all the princes who were with him."* Why was Haman the favorite at this time? Why was he raised to such a pitch of glory?

The next event that presents itself to our consideration, as contributing to bring the Jews into danger at this time, is the refusal of Mordecai to honor Haman, according to the king's commandment. Notwithstanding all that the commentators have said to justify Mordecai, I cannot but think that this part of his conduct arose from ignorance of his duty, and that he might lawfully have done the thing which he refused to do. Were it certain that Haman was an Amalekite, the fact would not vindicate a Jew in refusing him honor in the court of Persia. The command to extirpate the Amalekites was given to Israel only as a nation, and as living in their own land. *"Therefore it shall be, when the Lord your God has given you rest from all your enemies round about, in the land which the Lord your God gives you for an inheritance to possess it, that you shall blot out the remembrance of Amalek from under heaven; you shall not forget it."* (Deut. 25:19). What had Mordecai to do with this command in his present situation? But if Haman was really an Amalekite, and if this was the ground on which Mordecai refused to honor him, whether it was valid or invalid, the providence of God is visible in the matter. Why was the favorite an Amalekite? Why was one of that nation, at such a time, preferred to all the subjects of a hundred and twenty-seven provinces? On this supposition, had he been a Persian, Mordecai would have honored him without scruple, and so no storm would have arisen against the Jews.

It is alleged in favor of Mordecai, that an idolatrous reverence might have been required. Dr. Gill makes wonderful sketches to justify or excuse his conduct. As divine honors were given to the kings of Persia, he thinks that they might also have been exacted for their favorites; but of this he gives no proof. *It might be* will prove nothing; and nothing to justify such a supposition is in evidence from the passage. On the contrary, the thing which he is said to have refused, is what he might lawfully have given. The king's command enjoined all his servants to *"bow down and reverence Haman."* What should prevent any man to comply with this injunction of supreme civil power? But Dr. Gill's ingenuity finds even in this an argument on his side. The face that *"the king had so commanded concerning him.* shows, he thinks, "that it was more than civil honor and respect, for that in course would have been given him as the king's favorite." But this would not have been in all cases a matter of course, and that it was enjoined, there is the evidence of this record. The king requires nothing but to bow and reverence. Even had Haman pretended to be a god, of which there is not the slightest evidence, this would not excuse any one from bowing to him according to the king's commandment. Caius made himself a god, but should this have hindered his Christian subjects to bow down to him and reverence him? Even if there was a danger that it might be mistaken by some for religious worship, let the principle on which it is performed be declared, but let not what is lawfully due be withheld.

Dr. Gill argues, that it must more than civil respect that was required, because that the Jews did not refuse to give in the most humble and prostrate manner. This is just like saying that no Christian could refuse to uncover to the king, because Christians in general do this without scruple; yet William Penn would not uncover to King Charles. Besides, if Mordecai's conduct was influenced by a consideration of the nation of Haman, or anything in his individual character, this argument has no bearing. I cannot say why he refused: what I say is that he might have lawfully yielded all that was required.

That nothing more than civil honor was required for Haman by the king's command, is clear from the 9th verse of the fifth chapter – *"Then Haman went forth that day joyful and with a glad heart. But when Haman saw Mordecai in the king's gate, that he did not stand up nor move for him, he was full of fury against Mordecai."* Here his offence was that he did not stand up, nor even moved himself to Haman. Can any sober mind interpret this of religious worship? was there any idolatry in rising out of respect to the second man in the Persian empire? Whatever ceremonial might have been in approaching great men in that country, on this occasion there is no ceremonial, for there was no approach. The great man is passing, and Mordecai will not stand up, nor even move to notice him. Dr. Gill himself admits that this was civil respect; but, then, Mordecai, it seems, refuses even this, lest it should be interpreted as religious worship. Was ever greater violence used in special pleading? So then not even the smallest respect ought to be given to heathen rulers who claim divine honors. But this, it seems, was only part of his reason. Mordecai was influenced, he says, partly by knowing that Haman had planned the destruction of the Jews. And would this justify him in refusing to obey the king's commandment? Another thing that weighed with Mordecai, he alleges, was that he confided in Esther's influence to save the Jews, and therefore treated Haman with marked contempt. But may rulers be disobeyed when this can be done with impunity? Ought the man to be treated with contempt who is commanded by an absolute monarch to be honored above all his subjects? Is this the way in which Christians are to recommend the doctrine of Christ to the world?

But where is the necessity of arbitrarily supposing that this reverence must have had something idolatrous in it, when nothing but what is lawful is required in the words of the command? Was Mordecai perfect in knowledge, and infallible in conduct, that such a violent stretch must be made to justify him?

It is argued by Mr. Scott that Mordecai was accepted of God in what he did, and therefore that his conduct must have been justifiable. But God's acknowledging him, and interfering to deliver him, are no proof that he approved of this part of his conduct. If God would not deliver his people from the consequences of their ignorance, they would soon be destroyed. Is there any passage in this history which, either by implication or expressly, commends Mordecai for not bowing to Haman? I admit that his motives may have been good. If he intended to honor God, his motives would be approved, though his conduct might be the effect of ignorance. We see from Rom. 14 that God accepts his people even in their ignorance, when they are influenced by a regard to his authority. But this does not change error into truth, nor sin into duty. I think it is manifest that Mordecai acted on principle, for even when he saw the frightful consequences of his conduct, he persisted in it with the utmost steadfastness. The text also seems to insinuate that he considered his being a Jew as a reason for refusing honor to Haman. But whether this had an eye to the nation or character of Haman, or in what way he supposed his being a Jew could justify this conduct, is not said, and cannot be known.

It has also been properly replied, that the homage required does not seem to differ from that paid to Joseph by his brothers and by the Egyptians, or from those forms of civil reverence which the greatest saints of whom the Old Testament gives an account, observed without scruple before their superiors. Ezra and Nehemiah, and even Mordecai himself, must have rendered the same homage to the king of Persia. It is answered, that in these cases, with respect to the Persian monarch, the forms of approach may have been dispensed with, in the approach of the Jews. But this is gratuitous, and exceedingly unlikely. It is not in evidence, and cannot be accepted as proof. But what will utterly destroy this forced supposition is that Esther, in her first approach to the king, must have complied with the ceremonial; and she could not have been excused by her nation, for it was not known that she was a Jewess. And in all this she followed the counsel of Mordecai. What is still more, even after the nation of Esther was known, she not only did without scruple what Mordecai refused to Haman, but she prostrated herself before the king. *"And Esther spoke yet again before the king, and fell down at his feet, and begged him with tears to put away the evil of Haman the Agagite, and his plot which he had plotted against the Jews."* (Chap. 8:3). Here she submits to the humblest prostrations to the king. Mordecai refuses to stand up, or even to move, in honor of Haman; Esther prostrates herself at the feet of Ahasuerus. It is utterly vain by special pleading to hope to save Mordecai in this matter.

This point is of no great importance in itself, but the forced interpretations and violent suppositions that are used in order to justify Mordecai is a specimen, in the disciples of Christ themselves, of the effects of human wisdom, to conform the word of God to itself, instead of implicitly bowing to its dictates. Had the learned and good men who have recourse to this criticism, in order to justify a man of God, met such an instance of outraging the inspired text, in the writings of the opposers of the doctrines of grace, they would have justly exclaimed with wonder, indignation, and horror. But they can consecrate the same licentious principle to make the text speak agreeably to their own wisdom. I have often observed that, in vindicating their own errors, the disciples of Christ avail themselves of the most licentious of the principles of criticism, which are the usual resource of the wildest heretics. On the contrary, the man of God ought to accustom himself in all things to conform himself to the word of God, to make his own wisdom bow to the Scriptures, and to receive implicitly whatever they teach.

Here, then, we see that even the ignorance of God's people is employed to fulfil his purposes. Mordecai's ignorance was sinful; but had he been better instructed in his duty, he could not have been employed on this occasion. Many a piece of service God has, in every age, allotted to some of his people, for which they are fitted by their ignorance. That he should bestow gifts on his people, to enable them to fill the station allotted to them, is not a matter of surprise to any; but that the very ignorance of his people should fit them for certain situations for which he has designed them could hardly be anticipated.

From this fact we may also perceive, that our ignorance of duty may frequently bring danger and persecution upon ourselves and the whole body of Christians with which we are connected. Haman's resolution to destroy the whole Jewish nation was occasioned by Mordecai's refusal to honor him. It is true, indeed, commentators are willing to believe that Haman's including the whole Jewish nation with Mordecai was influenced by the conviction that they were all of the same sentiment on this subject. This, however, is not only not in evidence, but it is direct contrary to the reason assigned by the Holy Spirit in the narrative. *"And when Haman saw that Mordecai did not bow nor worship him, then Haman was full of wrath. And he scorned to lay hands only on Mordecai, for they had revealed to him the people of Mordecai. Therefore Haman sought to destroy all the Jews, who were throughout the whole kingdom of Ahasuerus, the people of Mordecai."*

Mordecai is then fully chargeable with all the natural effects of his ignorance, even though a merciful Providence prevented the execution of the threatened vengeance. When an ill-formed Christian manifests refractory, unsubmitting spirit towards his superiors, it brings odium and persecution on all connected with him. That God should give the government of the world to his enemies, and demand submission to the wicked, is not what the wisdom of this world could expect. If Christians will listen to the counsel of their own hearts, rather than to the dictates of the Divine word, they will think it very unreasonable that the children of the Great King, the heirs of God, should tamely yield to the evil men in power, and honor their persecutors. But such is the law of that kingdom which is not of this world. That spirit that refuses honor to worthless men in power is not the spirit of the gospel. That proud and insolent piety that refuses the customary tokens of respect even to majesty, was not practised by the patriarchs, nor was it inculcated by the apostles. If it finds shelter in the conduct of Mordecai, it ought to be known that it is sanctioned only by Mordecai's sin.

The next providential circumstance we shall review is Esther's concealing of her kindred. Had it been known to Haman that Esther was a Jewess, and the near kinswoman of Mordecai, he certainly would not have attempted any violent measures against either Mordecai or the Jews. Notwithstanding his mortification on account of the insult, he would have found it prudent to smother his resentment, or to gratify it in a more indirect way. He could not have expected to prevail, as long as Esther retained any share in the affections of the king. Mordecai's intention in enjoining Esther to conceal her descent, was, no doubt, lest her being a captive Jewess might prevent her advancement to the situation of queen. The odium of her religion, as well as the captivity of her nation, would appear to him to stand in the way of her elevation. God's intention by that concealment was to preclude a circumstance that would have prevented the danger of his people. He designed to bring them to the very brink of ruin, that he might manifest his power in their deliverance. It was ignorance and carnal policy in Mordecai; yet in another view, it was ordained by God for a wise purpose.

From this fact we may see that worldly policy in religion naturally leads to disappointment and trouble. When by their wisdom, Christians seek preferment, or endeavor to escape the cross, by concealing any part of the truth, they are generally preparing a scourge for their own back. Esther, by the advice of Mordecai, concealed her religion, for the purpose of obtaining a situation that would enable her to protect the cause and people of God; but by that concealment the ruin of her whole nation would have been effected, had not a merciful God interposed to ward off the intended blow. Every means contrary to the word of God promises affliction to the people of God. Believers who conceal the truth to obtain any worldly advantage may congratulate their policy when they succeed; but let them look about, for danger and sorrow are pursuing them. They have made a pit in which they will sink, if a merciful God prevent not the natural tendency of their conduct. From the bold and independent spirit of Mordecai, we may reasonably infer that his desire of the advancement of his kinswoman was more influenced by zeal for the good of his nation than by any views of private advancement. The advantage of her exaltation to the cause of the captive Jews would blind him to its sin. How often do Christians, reasoning on the same principle, overlook the laws of God! Jesus Christ, by his apostles, separated his disciples from the world for observance of the ordinances of his kingdom; but human wisdom has violated this order, and sought protection and power to the cause of God, through a marriage with the world. In the writings of the apostles we everywhere meet with the distinction between Christ's people, who are called "*Christians,*" "*believers,*" "*saints;*" and the rest of mankind, who are called "*the world,*" those who are without, etc. But by the marriage of Esther with Ahasuerus there is now no world: there are none without; for every man in Christendom either belongs to what is called the church, or may belong to it if he chooses. That this marriage has produced some good effects, I am not the person to deny. It may often have been a shield to the people of God. But with all the advantages that it has ever had, the bans are forbidden, for the marriage is contrary to the word of God. None ought to have a place in the church of Christ but such as appear to be his disciples. When the Lord shall stand upon the wall that was made by a plumb-line, with a plumb-line in his hand, the high places of Israel shall be desolate, and the sanctuaries of Israel shall be laid waste, (Amos 7:7). The greatest possible good to the cause of God cannot justify the smallest deviation from his commands. Let the ark of God itself fall, rather than attempt to uphold it with a human hand.

Let us adore the mercy of our God, who steps forward in the time of our danger, to rescue us from the consequences of our own policy. He might justly have given up Mordecai and Esther, to reap the reward of their sin. But as their conduct was the effect of ignorance, he saves them from ruin, and promotes them to honor. Their devotedness to the cause of God is unquestionable. He forgets not the glory of his own name, and though his people are ignorant and sinful, he looks to the perfection of the righteousness of the Substitute, his own dearly beloved Son.

Not only was the great elevation of Haman providential; the commandment of the king for all to reverence him in a marked manner was also directed by the Divine counsel. The favor of the king would indeed naturally have procured respect for the object of it; but the royal command made the neglect a breach of the laws of the king, and exposed it to the notice of the other servants, who made it known to Haman. *"Why do you transgress the king's commandment?"* is a question which shows that the offence was considered not a breach of courtesy merely, but the violation of the royal authority. Without this commandment, Mordecai might have escaped. That Haman was immediately informed of the people to whom Mordecai belonged was also providential, for he had not previously known this. Had not this been discovered, the body of the Jewish nation would have escaped the danger to which Mordecai was exposed. But a wise Providence took care that this fact should not lie hid, that his name might be glorified in the salvation of his people, and in the destruction of their enemies. Why was Esther's descent unknown, though she was advanced to be consort to majesty, while Mordecai's was notified as soon as his offence? Yet the other servants themselves had not previously known this. It was on this very occasion that he himself discovered his kindred; *"for he had told them that he was a Jew."* Here we see, that as the caution of Mordecai in advising Esther to conceal her nation was the means of bringing it into the utmost danger of total extinction, his voluntary discovery of his descent was now to have the same effect. The utmost exertions of human wisdom may often be employed to bring about what they are intended to prevent.

But what above all calls for our wonder is that a monarch, who ought to consider himself the father of all his people, shall, for no purpose but the gratification of a wicked favorite, give up a whole nation to perdition. If no sentiments of duty or of pity had any weight with him, why did not his interest as a sovereign forbid his compliance with the cruel request? Yet, in defiance of every principle of humanity, justice, and policy – without even the pretence of any misconduct – he gave the lives of the whole Jewish nation, *"both young and old, little children and women,"* a present to his unprincipled favorite. The unsubstantial reasons alleged are not weighed, but received implicitly, without examination. After all, there is nothing in the history to show that Ahasuerus was a cruel or tyrannical man. His conduct in this instance is an easy, unsuspecting compliance, in a matter that required the utmost deliberation and caution. Let us attend a moment to the argument employed by the crafty favorite to overreach his master, and destroy the people of God. *"And Haman said unto king Ahasuerus, There is a certain people scattered abroad and dispersed among the people, in all the provinces of your kingdom. And their laws are different from all people, neither do they keep the king's laws. Therefore it is not for the king's gain to allow them to live. If it pleases the king, let it be written that they may be destroyed. And I will pay ten thousand talents of silver to the hand of those who have charge of the business, to bring it into the king's treasuries."*

What was the head and front of the offence of this people? Their laws were different from those of all other nations. They would not observe the religious institutions that were ordained by man. The civil law of the countries of their captivity it was their duty to obey. Their God commanded them to *"seek the peace of the city whither he had caused them to be carried away captive, and to pray unto the Lord for it,"* (Jer. 29:7). But to neglect the ordinances of their God, or to observe the religious rites appointed by man, they had no license. Why were the Jews to be blamed for the singularity of their institutions, for their scrupulous separation from other nations, and for their firmness in refusing compliance with the rites of all other religions? If their laws were singular, were they not the laws of God? Why do kings and rulers pretend to interfere between God and his people? Why do wretched mortals assume an authority to set aside what God enjoins? Let Christians in every country render to Cesar the things that are Cesar's but to God the things that are God's. If rulers must usurp the throne of God, let them attempt to alter the rising of the sun, or regulate the changes of the moon; but let them not dare to meddle with the laws of the kingdom of Christ.

The allegations of Haman against the Jews are still substantially the ground of accusation against those who fully follow the churches planted by the apostles, and refuse compliance with all the institutions of man in the things of God. They are held up as a singular kind of people, who, by the peculiarity of their religious observances, and their uncompliant spirit with respect to every deviation from the ordinances of God, manifest disaffection to the government of the country. In their religious observances, they are accused as being *"diverse from all people."* Fear of this accusation, more, perhaps, than any other cause, keeps the people of God from discovering the ordinances of Christ, and induces them to accommodate, as far as possible, to some of the great sects in the countries where they live. Israel grew weary of the government of God, and desired a king, that they might be like other nations. How long will the children of God neglect the laws of his kingdom! when will they return to the order and ordinances of his house!

How grateful ought Christians to be who live in a land of liberty! What a blessing it is to have the exercise of their religion secured to them by the laws of the state! If any of them are so ill-informed as not to be impressed with the value of this privilege, let them think of the Jews in the time of Esther – let them think of the state of Christians in this country in ages past - and in some other countries at the present moment. What a wretched thing it is to live in a country whose rulers assume the authority of God, and dictate in the things of religion! What a revolting idea to live in a country where an incensed favorite may receive a present of the lives of a whole nation! How degraded is the state of man in a country where an insolent coutier offers the sovereign a price for the lives of a whole people!

Yet the Christian has nothing to fear in any country. If he is called to suffer, it will be for God's glory and his own unspeakable advantage. If God has no purpose to serve by the sufferings of his people, he can, even under the most despotic governments, procure them rest. Jesus rules in the midst of his enemies, and is master of the resolves of despots. He restrains their wrath, or makes it praise him. If he chooses, he can give his people power even with the most capricious tyrants. They are as safe in the provinces of the empire of Ahasuerus, as in the dominions of Great Britain. The history of the book of Esther demonstrates that there is no danger from which the Lord cannot rescue his people, even through the medium of the ordinary course of events. Without a single miracle, he brings them from the very brink of ruin, and precipitates their enemies into the abyss. We see them, as a nation, formally given over to destruction by an irrevocable decree; yet they escape without the suffering of an individual. *"And the king took his ring from his hand, and gave it unto Haman, the son of Hammedatha the Agagite, the Jews' enemy. And the king said to Haman, The silver is given to you, the people also, to do with them as seems good to you."* Even the power of the king himself could not revoke this grant. Letters were sent to all the provinces of the empire, to secure the entire extirpation of the hated race. The enmity of the nations to the Jews is stimulated by their avarice. They are permitted *"to take the spoil of them for a prey."* Can human wisdom descry any possible means of escape for the captives of Israel in the midst of their enemies? Yet God is their deliverer!

Haman now thought his victory secure. The royal decree is obtained, and messengers are sent out with it to all the king's lieutenants in the provinces, in the languages of all the nations subject to Persia. *"And the king and Haman sat down to drink, but the city of*

Shushan was perplexed." Little did that unthinking monarch reflect on the misery to which his rash indulgence of a favorite had consigned so many of his innocent subjects. Could absolute monarchs get a view of the mischief caused by the oppression of their wicked favorites, they would often shrink from it with horror. Many a bloody decree originates not so much in the cruelty of their nature, as in the seducing flatteries of their courtiers. They watch the pliant hour, and in the moment of good-humor, they obtain the fatal grant. From that moment they keep the matter at a distance from his ear, and divert his attention by the gratifications of intemperance and debauchery. How insensible is the mind of men in certain situations! "*There is no flesh in man's obdurate heart, it does not feel for man.*" Despots and their sycophants sit down to their drunken banquets, after giving decrees that involve whole nations in misery!

As God can protect his people under the greatest despotism, so the utmost civil liberty is no safety to them without the immediate protection of his Almighty arm. I fear that Christians at present in this country have too great a confidence in political institutions, and in the enlightened views of the public on the rights of conscience. We hear more boasting of the march of mind than of the government of God. It is thought impossible, into whatever hands power may fall, that rulers in this country should ever attempt to effect uniformity in religion, or apply force in the affairs of religion. Such an opinion is as unfounded in the philosophy of human nature, as it is destitute of the authority of history and of the word of God. There are not wanting some symptoms of the rise of Haman, and if he does not at length obtain a present of the lives of his enemies, it will be owing, not to the light of our politicians, but to the overruling providence of God, in opposition to that light. At all events, let Christians confide in the power and watchfulness of their God, not in the schemes of fanatical politicians. Even at the present moment, I am confident that there are many places in the empire where there is not entire liberty of conscience. There may be the liberty of the statute book, when there is danger from the mob; and where there is not perfect safety for the Christian in exercising, and in publishing, and spreading his religion, there is not practical liberty of conscience. To have liberty of conscience, we must not only be freed from all force constraining us to profess a religion which we do not assume; we must also be safe in the most active and public efforts to spread our own.

Let us now attend to the providence of God effecting the deliverance of his people from this awful danger, and precipitating their enemies into the pit which they had prepared for others.

The disposal of the lots cast before Haman, to ascertain the most lucky day for striking the intended blow, attracts our attention as the first providential circumstance for the salvation of the Jews. Even before Haman had obtained the royal consent for destroying them, he had used divination to discover the most fortunate time for executing his purpose. Shall the oracle of Satan be compelled to speak for God? Shall the god of this world lose all his sagacity when he comes to fix the destruction of the people of the Lord? Why did he choose the last month in the whole year, when the execution of his plan would have been promoted by immediate despatch? "*The lot is cast into the lap, but the disposal of it is of the Lord.*" He works his own will by the counsels of devils, as well as through the agency of the angels of his presence. "*In the twelfth month, that is the month Nisan, in the twelfth year of king Ahasuerus, they cast Pur, that is, the lot, before Haman, from day to day, and from month to month, to the twelfth month, that is, the month Adar.*" From the direction of this oracle, the day of execution was fixed on the thirteenth day of the twelfth month, that is, more than eleven months after the decree. Whether the laws of nature, or the agency of infernal spirits, guided this answer, it was evidently ordained by God for the salvation of his people. Had the day of execution been immediate, there was nothing to prevent Haman's wicked purpose from taking effect. But his very superstition is made to co-operate in God's plan for the preservation of Israel. When the devil himself is consulted, he gives the most foolish advice to his friends, when God has any purpose to fulfil by it. He that was a murderer of the saints from the beginning is here made an instrument to effect their preservation.

We have here a key to the providence of God with respect to the heathen oracles. Though they uttered the responses of demons, they were made the means of fulfilling the purposes of God. Satan by them ruled the world, but God in them overruled Satan himself. While the devil was the God of this world, and held men captive at his pleasure, Jehovah ruled the earth as absolutely as he did the angels of heaven. While men in general were serving the prince of darkness, the Lord effected his own sovereign purposes through their agency. Human wisdom may exclaim, How is this! Let it fathom the depths of the Divine wisdom before it repeats the question. If God is God, the rebellion of devils and of men must be in some way for his glory.

By a like expedient, Jehovah provided that Jonah should be cast into the sea. He raised a tremendous storm against the ship in which the refractory prophet was sailing. But what providence is in a storm? The philosopher sees in this nothing but what he calls nature, and the laws of nature. *"But the Lord sent out a great wind into the sea."* Although storms, and earthquakes, and pestilence, and thunder, and war, and famine, may all be brought about by natural causes, they are all the work of the Almighty. But when the storm is raised, how is it to manifest Jonah? It is through the impression of the heathen mariners that it was sent as a judgment. Why were they struck with this impression now? Did they look on all storms in this light? or did they judge from the peculiarly tremendous nature of this tempest? In whatever manner the impression came, it was to fulfil the purpose of God. But even with this impression, how is the guilty person to be detected? How are these heathens to find out the will of the God of Israel? It is through the means of their own superstition. It is by casting lots; and though God always disposes the lot, there is no reason to believe that he will always in this way manifest a guilty person. Were this the case, rulers would have no difficulty in detecting guilt, and discriminating between the guilty and the innocent. But the heathen mariners acted on their own superstitious opinion, which was nothing better than the origin of dueling; and in this instance God spake through their oracle: *"So they cast lots, and the lot fell upon Jonah."* Here, then, we see the way of Providence. The Ruler of the world effects his purposes by every agent, and makes use of the opinions and motives, of the resolutions and actions, of all men. Nay, he overrules their very crimes to fulfil his plans. In these sentiments of the heathen mariners, however erroneous they are in some respects, yet it is pleasing to see the strong conviction of an overruling Providence. This is strikingly obvious, both in their opinion of the cause of the storm and in their expedient of the lots. As Aelian has observed, "Atheism is the refinement of speculation, and not the dictate of human nature. No one of the barbarians," says he, "ever fell into atheism, or started a doubt as to the existence of gods. They have no such discussions as, Are there gods? and if there are gods, do they take care of us? Neither Indian, nor Celt, nor Egyptians, ever conceived such a notion of Epicurus and the atheistic Grecian sages." Now, this observation of the heathen historian is of great importance. In whatever way the impression has been received, it is general that Divine Providence rules in all the affairs of men. This view of nature is only stifled by some of the greatest fools in human shape, who style themselves philosophers.

But let us return to the history of Mordecai. How wonderful is the providence of God in restraining Haman from taking immediate vengeance, on receiving a fresh insult, as he returned in triumph from Esther's banquet! *"Then Haman went forth that day joyful and with a glad heart: but when Haman saw Mordecai in the king's gate, that he did not stand up, nor bowed for him, he was full of indignation against Mordecai. Nevertheless Haman held himself in!"* Haman held himself in! There is something more wonderful in this than even in a miracle. In my view, Almighty power would not have been so illustriously displayed, had God interfered to save Mordecai, by causing the earth to open and swallow his adversary, as by ruling his impetuous passions without interfering with the freedom of his determinations. Haman has a royal irrevocable decree for the destruction of the whole Jewish nation; he is elated beyond measure by being the only person invited to the queen's banquet with the king; he is again insulted by the man whom he so much abhorred; his mind is full of wrath; yet he holds himself in from immediate violence! Where did he learn his self-command? Look at the mouths of the hungry lions with Daniel before them; look again at the enraged Haman, and Mordecai untouched in his presence. God, who stopped the mouths of lions, and preserved his children in the furnace, manifested here a more wonderful power in directing the free will of a bloody persecutor, armed with the authority of the Persian empire. It was Haman's own action – *"he held himself in!"* yet it was the working of the providence of God. Not so wonderful would it be to see a ship standing motionless in the midst of the tumult of the waves, or the raging billows rolling to the shore without touching the rocks, as to see Haman holding himself in on this occasion. Let the children of God read, and believe, and rejoice. When their enemies are maddened with rage, their God can make them restrain themselves, even without changing their heart. By his inscrutably providence, they willingly resolve to refrain from injury, or to delay vengeance, even while they feel no pity.

We may recognize the hand of Providence in overcoming the fears of Esther when solicited to approach the king in behalf of the Jews. By going uncalled into the inner court, she would subject herself to death by law. Judging from the manners of our own country, we may think that her risk was small. But in estimating her danger, we ought to take into account the caprice of despots in countries where polygamy prevails. This moment they devote to destruction the object on which they doted the moment before Besides, Esther had reason to apprehend an alienation of affection, or at least a coldness, as she had not been called into his presence for thirty days previously. Here, indeed, is another providential circumstance that ought to excite our wonder. Whatever was the reason why the king had so long neglected her, the thing was undoubtedly a part of the Divine plan, that Esther's danger might be increased, her faith put to the severer trial, and his own power more fully manifested in obtaining for her a gracious reception. Let the children of God look at this and take a lesson. When he calls them to arduous duties, instead of smoothing the way and removing the appearance of difficulty or danger, he often, by his providence, throws obstacles in their way. A wife, in following Christ, instead of delighting her husband, may give him the greatest offence. Children may make their very parents their enemies by their obedience to their heavenly Father. Instead of inducing his disciples to discover his laws and ordinances, by the prospects of greater acceptance with the world, he promises them nothing but ridicule and hatred. Instead of flattering every instance of obedience with additional honors and rewards from men, the discovery of the laws and institutions of Christ's kingdom may be followed by the loss of all things. God will not bribe his people to serve him. He will not secure their allegiance hiding them from danger. They must give their life, if he calls for it, or give up the hope of the heavenly inheritance. They must count the cost, and be willing to incur it; they must take up the cross and follow him. They are not to fear him who has power to kill the body, but rather him who can punish both soul and body in hell for ever. Jesus must be obeyed in the prospect of every danger. He that loves his life, shall lose life eternal. Yet, in general, it may be observed, that when Christians are made willing to face every danger for Christ's sake, the greatest real dangers that they may have dreaded are turned away from them. When God has tried them sufficiently, he removes the trial. Esther's apparent danger was heightened by her long neglect. Yet, after all, her God procured her acceptance with the king.

It is absurd in any at this time to underrate the trial of Esther. She must herself, doubtless, have been a better judge of the extent of her danger than we can now possibly be; and she estimated it so highly, that at first she altogether refused to comply with the request even of Mordecai, to whom she had in all other things paid the deference due to a father. *"All the king's servants and the people of the king's provinces know that whoever, whether man or woman, shall come to the king into the inner court, who is not called, there is one law of his to put him to death, except such to whom the king shall hold out the golden sceptre so that he may live. But I have not been called to come in unto the king these thirty days."* Her life, then, was actually forfeited by the act; and to spare her was the pardon of a criminal condemned to die. Besides, she must, in this approach to the king, appear in a new character, as a captive, as a Jewess, as one of these already given up to death in the grant of Haman. In such circumstances, she might well be apprehensive that by her death he might make way for a successor. What trust is to be put in the affections of a capricious despot? What confidence is to be placed in the unfeeling man who could give up the beautiful Vashti? Might not some reasons of state operate to the destruction of Esther?

Her apprehensions of the magnitude of her danger appear evidently in the preparations with which she thought it necessary to approach him. All the Jews in Shushan fasted three days, night and day, before she ventured on the dangerous service. It is also evident, in the words in which she expressed her determination, that having counted the cost, she was prepared to give her life as a sacrifice for her friends. *"If I perish, I perish."* She consented not to undertake this mission till she overcame the fear of death.

What a blessing is marriage according to the institution of God! Was she truly a wife who could not trust her life with her husband? Better to be the wife of a Christian peasant, than the queen of a Persian despot. In the midst of all her regal honors, what happiness could Esther enjoy in her situation? Yet with what preposterous artifice did she and her guardian court the dangerous height! The prospect of wretchedness will not deter the fallen human mind from seeking the glories of this world, even at the expense of the soul. Man is a strange compound of meanness and of pride.

Let us take a glance at the arguments by which Mordecai prevailed on the queen to undertake to intercede for the Jews. They are such as were calculated to produce the desired effect, and were, no doubt, suggested by a gracious Providence. The faith, manifested by Mordecai in the Divine protection, approaches to that of Abraham himself. If, then, faith if the gift of God, there is no doubt that Providence directed the resolution of Esther. *"Then Mordecai commanded to answer Esther, Do not think within yourself that you shall escape in the king's house more than all the Jews. For if you are completely silent at this time, then relief and deliverance shall arise to the Jews from another place, but you and your father's house shall be destroyed. And who knows whether you have come to the kingdom for such a time as this?"* Notwithstanding the greatness of the danger, Mordecai appears confident that his God would raise up deliverance from some quarter. He rightly interprets the intention of Providence in raising her to royalty for this very occasion. Here we have a beautiful example of the view of Providence entertained at that time by the people of God. Mordecai knew well the events that led to the exaltation of Esther. He knew that she was raised in the ordinary course of human affairs. He knew that her exaltation was owing to the divorce of Vashti, and to her own surpassing beauty. An atheist would have no difficulty in accounting for it. Yet Mordecai believed also that God raised her, and justly concluded from the present danger, that his purpose in raising her was for the very purpose of interceding for the Jews. At all events, he concluded, that as she had it in her power to make an effort for their preservation with probable hopes of success, should she refuse to make trial of her influence, she might expect that God would signally punish her, and save his people in some other way.

Let all Christians learn from this, not to be backward in using their influence to protect the people of God, and serve the interests of his kingdom. If they hide their face, God will provide other instruments, and they shall not be without chastisement. If from apprehensions of danger they decline any service that the providence of God lays before them, the very thing that is dreaded may come upon them, and others may be honored to do the work in safety. *"You therefore,"* says God to Jeremiah, *"gird up your loins, and arise and speak to them all that I command you: be not dismayed at their faces lest I confound you before them. For behold I have made you this day a defenced city, and an iron pillar, and brazen walls, against the whole land; against the kings of Judah, against the princes thereof, against the priests thereof, and against the people of the land. And they shall fight against you, but they shall not prevail against you, for I am with you, says The Lord to deliver you."* (Jer. 1:7-19).

By the gospel the elect of God are to be saved from a greater destruction than that which threatened the Jews in the time of Esther. The gospel is to be spread over the world by the means of the disciples of Christ. Let them therefore brave danger, and shame, and loss, in publishing the glad tidings of salvation. Why have eighteen centuries passed since the giving of the command to preach the gospel to all nations, while many have not yet heard of the name of Jesus? The Lord's time indeed may not be come, but this does not excuse the indolence of his servants. The commandment is come, which is the only thing with which we are concerned: The Lord, will, no doubt, raise up instruments to effect his purpose in the proper time, but this will not make up the loss, or excuse the neglect of his slumbering servants.

By the institutions of Christ, his children are to be nourished and advanced in the knowledge of him. But the nature of his kingdom is yet little understood; and every one of his ordinances having been changed in Babylon, still remained incrusted with superstition and human inventions. The children of God, then, are deprived of much of that wholesome nourishment which the pure ordinances of God are calculated to yield. Let allegiance to Jesus and the love of his people influence his disciples, who know his will, to zeal in making it known to others. Let no mistaken complaisance with respect to the corruptions of divine institutions, prevent them from denouncing everything contrary to the word of God. Let not the emolument of office, the reproach of the world, or deference to the prejudice of God's people, induce them to practise what is not taught in Scripture, or to decline adopting everything enjoined by the authority of Christ. Has he not himself said – *"And why do you call me Lord, Lord, and do not do the things that I say? You are my disciples if you do whatever I command you."*

Let not Christians, who know the law and ordinances of Jesus, fear to exert themselves in their defence. The corruptions of the ordinances of Christ are sanctioned by so many prejudices, and strengthened by so many interests, that Christians in general are irritated when they are called to inquire. The wise virgins have laid themselves down to slumber, and they are peevish with those who attempt to awake them. If they do arise for a moment, it is usually to plead for a little more sleep, and to remonstrate against the violence and cruelty of the untimely intruders. He who will revive all the ordinances of Christ, and denounce everything human in religion, must be prepared for a kind of martydom even from Christians. This is much more painful than the enmity of the world; but even this he is not to fear. If believers, from the apprehension of becoming unpopular even with the churches of Christ, hide their knowledge, or decline to employ their talents according to their opportunities, let them learn from the lesson of Mordecai to Esther, that God can do his work without them; and that in some way they may expect the Divine displeasure. There cannot be a doubt that a Christian consults his good, upon the whole, by boldly and unreservedly doing the will of God. The more he shows himself dead to censure and to praise, the more he disregards gain and loss, when they stand in the way of duty – the more he will have reason to rejoice in the end. Let his ambition always be fired with the hope of ruling over ten cities. Esther, to save the people of God, flung herself at the feet of the despot, at the hazard of her life; but, instead of being put to death, Esther met with a most gracious reception. A day will come at last when obedience to the most disagreeable of Christ's commandments will appear great gain.

We may also perceive here the good effect of wholesome admonition on a stumbling servant of God. The fear of man had prevailed over the love of her brothers, in the mind of Esther. But faithful admonition kept her from falling. How forcible are right words! From the suggestion of Mordecai, it appears, that though the royal decree consigned the whole Jewish race to death, yet that she counted on safety in the palace, as the wife of the king. But Mordecai undeceives her on this, and took away her flattering hopes. By declining to do duty, she put herself from under the Divine protection, and engaged the displeasure of Providence to seek her out for destruction. Notwithstanding all her confidence in her situation, he denounces death to her and her father's house, if she declined the dangerous service. It is always under some false confidence that the children of God decline to obey him. To expose them, is, by the Divine blessing, the means of recovering the stumbling individual. Let not the servants of God perceive one another going astray. or halting on the Christian race, without endeavoring to recover them. By the words of Mordecai, through the Divine blessing, Esther was brought from a state of abject timidity, to the confidence and boldness of a martyr. *"If I perish, I perish!"* Such ought to be the resolution of all God's servants. They should count the cost, and be willing to part with property, fame, popularity, friends, relatives, life, for the sake of the Lord Jesus. *"If any man come to me,"* says Christ, *"and hate not his father and mother, and wife and children, and brothers and sisters, yea, and his own life also, he cannot be my disciples. And whosoever does not bear his cross, and come after me, cannot be my disciple"* (Luke 14:26,27). An apostle says, *"As Christ laid down his life for us, we ought also to lay down our lives for the brothers."*

An incidental remark or an allusive application of the words in which Esther expressed her devotedness, may not be useless. People in a certain state of mind are represented as saying – *"If I perish, I will perish at the feet of Jesus!"* Surely there can be no similarity between the situation of a person approaching a despot, contrary to law, at the hazard of life, and that of one approaching the merciful Redeemer, by the command of God, with the assurance of pardon. There is no possibility of perishing at the feet of Jesus. Men perish through unbelief, in refusing to come to him. *"You will not come to me that you may have life."* Whosoever comes to Jesus shall not be cast out.

From the conduct of Mordecai on this occasion, we may see that confidence in God does not preclude the use of means. Mordecai had immediate recourse to the influence of Esther, though, it is evident, he ultimately relied on the power and providence of God. It is obvious, from his observations, that he expected preservation from God through the use of means, even had Esther declined the intercession. *"If you are completely silent at this time, then relief and deliverance shall arise to the Jews from another place."* Let us learn from this, that as God has promised to protect us and provide for us, it is through the means of his appointment, vigilance, prudence, and industry, that we are to look for these blessings.

We shall now view the providence of God in the reception of Esther. Life and death are on the countenance of the despot, and according to the will of God he frowns or smiles. Had God designed her death, she would have found the king in another temper. But is not the king's heart in the hand of the Lord? Does he not turn it as he pleases? Esther is received most graciously and accosted in the most affectionate manner. The coldness that had overlooked her for thirty days gives place to the utmost warmth of affection, and instead of the denunciation of death that she at first feared, she now hears the expressions of the most extravagant bounty. *"Now on the third day Esther put on her royal clothing, and stood in the inner court of the king's house, across from the king's house. And the king sat upon his royal throne in the royal house, across from the gate of the house. And when the king saw Esther the queen standing in the court, she received favor in his sight. And the king held out to Esther the golden sceptre that was in his hand. So Esther drew near, and touched the top of the sceptre. Then the king said to her, What do you desire, queen Esther? And what is your wish? It shall be given to you even to half of the kingdom." "And when the king saw Esther the queen standing in the court, she received favor in his sight."* This favor was the spontaneous affection of the king's own heart; but in another point of view, it was God who gave her that favor. Who is so blind as not to see the hand of God in this? Who is so stupid as not to ascribe the glory to the Almighty in this matter? Who does not here recognise Joseph's God? *"But the Lord was with Joseph, and showed him mercy, and gave him favor in the sight of the keeper of the prison."* Who does not see the Lord that always interfered for Israel, and will always interfere for the deliverance of the true Israel of God? Who gave favor to the Israelites in the sight of the Egyptians on their leaving of Egypt? *"and I will give the people favor,"* says God, *"in the sight of the Egyptians; and it shall come to pass, that when you go you shall not be empty."*

Christian, see here the security of God's people in doing duty; see the encouragement to confidence in his protection. From this learn the importance of humbling yourself before your God in the hour of trial. See the duty of fasting and prayer in the time of trouble and of danger; see the resource of God's people in the time of their calamity. If we need the protection of men, let us first ask it from God. If we prevail with him, the power of the most mighty and of the most wicked must minister to our relief. Esther and her friends first cried unto the Lord, and humbled themselves before him, and then she went to the king. *"Then Esther told them to return to Mordecai this answer – Go, gather together all the Jews who are present in Shushan, and fast for me, and neither eat nor drink three days, night and day. My maidens and I will also fast in the same way. And so I will go in unto the king, which is not according to the law. And if I perish, I perish."* How often do Christians look first to the means of deliverance! how often do they try every resource, before they go to God with a simple and confident reliance on him! how is their unbelief rebuked here! What encouragement does this hold out to confidence in God in the utmost danger! Only let us believe, and all things are possible.

Esther's delay in preferring her request is another providential circumstance. It is strange that she did not hastily take the advantage of the good-humor of the monarch, before she gave him time for reflection and bad counsel. She might not find him again so complaisant. Her impatience also to be delivered from a state of suspense must have favored an immediate application. Yet without any assigned reason, she declined an explanation, not only at that time, but also at the first banquet. Whatever may have been Esther's design, the design of providence is obvious. Had she at that time declared her request, Haman would not have had an opportunity of performing his part in the drama. This man of glory and of guilt must be allowed another scene on the stage of time, to exhibit his character in all its bearings, and to show the disappointment and misery of the enemies of God. His vanity is not yet at the highest pitch; he must be brought to the pinnacle of vain-glory. When he arrives on the summit of earthly magnificence next to majesty itself, he must grasp at the shadow of royal splendor. But in the grasp he must begin to totter to his fall. The crown he had devised to wear for a day, he must fix on the head of his greatest enemy. He must be made to minister to the man of God, whom he thought to destroy. Then shall he fall, never more to rise at all: he must prepare a gallows for Mordecai, but he must himself be hanged thereon.

Thus it shall be with the proud and prosperous wicked. Though they may not, like Haman, meet a retribution in this world, their honor will be succeeded with everlasting shame and misery. From the pinnacle of earthly glory they shall be hurled into the depths of hell. This prosperity is not to be envied by the poorest Christian. *"Fret not yourself because of evil-doers, neither be envious against the workers of iniquity, for they shall soon be cut down like the grass, and wither as the green grass"* (Psal. 37:1,2).

How vain is earthly glory! How irrational are the struggles of statesmen and courtiers for the giddy height of power! This moment their counsels may direct the destinies of nations; the next they may be hurled into the abyss of eternal misery. This day they may sit at the helm of empire; tomorrow they may appear before the dread tribunal of God. Now they are at the head of nobles and princes, and attract the notice of admiring millions; in an instant their souls may be required of them, and they may be covered with shame and everlasting contempt. Look at Haman Was ever statesman or courtier more highly honored and advanced? He is drunk with worldly glory, but his soul is still thirsty. To what purpose is he mounting yon dangerous height? It is that he may tumble into the abyss below. While his happiness appears to the beholder to be complete, his own bad passions make him miserable. Infamy and ruin hover over him while he ascends, and he falls a monument of the vanity of earthly glory. What a sudden and dreadful reverse! what a lesson to all the children of pride! what an example to statesman and courtiers!

We may here see also, that even in this world the most successful ambition is always disappointed in the hope of happiness from the enjoyment of its object. The scholar, the man of science, the senator, the warrior, having gained the utmost eminence to which their throbbing hearts aspired, are not only unsatisfied with glory, but are perhaps more miserable than the lowest of the class to which they belong. There is still something that makes disappointment prey on their souls. In all his glory Haman confessed himself miserable, on account of the disrespect of an insolent Jew. *"And Haman told them of the glory of his riches, and the multitude of his children, and all the things in which the king had promoted him, and how he had advanced him above the princes and servants of the king. Moreover Haman said, Yes, Esther the queen let no man but me come in with the king unto the banquet that she had prepared. And also tomorrow I am invited to her banquet, with the king. Yet all this avails me nothing as long as I see Mordecai the Jew sitting at the king's gate."*

All men are in the pursuit of happiness, and all, by nature, seek it in the things of this world; but in them it never can be found. Even the acquisition of the things in which they suppose happiness to consist will disappoint them in the enjoyment. Man, at enmity with God, cannot be happy. The curse denounced against sin has entwined itself with all human enjoyments. It is seen not only in the thorns and briars, but also in the most voluptuous enjoyments of that royal luxury that crops the sweetest buds of a terrestrial paradise. It lodges not only in the cottages of the poor, but seats itself on the thrones of princes. Solomon has found that all earthly enjoyments are but vanity of vanities. Sinner, return to God through Jesus Christ. There is no real happiness either in this world or the next, but in the favor of Him from whom you fly. You children of pride, see in Haman the disappointment of your hopes! How unsatisfactory are your present enjoyments! how soon must you exchange your earthly splendor for the abodes of endless and unmixed misery! The basest of your menials, if he knows the Saviour of sinners, is a happier man than you. Seek happiness, then, where it is to be found – in the knowledge of God. *"Behold the Lamb of God, that takes away the sin of the world!"* Until you are delivered from your sins, the curse of God rests on you, and Divine wrath must pursue you both in this world and the next. Lay them on the head of the Lamb of God, and be free from guilt, pollution and misery. *"The blood of Jesus Christ cleanses from all sin."* Mordecai, with the threatening of death against himself and his whole nation before his eyes, was evidently a happier man, from confidence in the Divine protection, than Haman in the midst of the unbounded profusion of royal power. The children of God are, indeed, frequently sorrowful, but, paradoxical as the assertion may appear, if they enjoy their privileges they are always rejoicing. *"Though now, for a season, if needs be, they are in heaviness, through manifold trials, yet even now they rejoice with a joy unspeakable and full of glory."* They endure as seeing him who is invisible. Moses chose rather to suffer affliction with the people of God, than to enjoy the pleasures of sin for a season, esteeming the reproach of Christ greater riches than the honor of Egypt: for he had respect to the recompense of reward. Even in the midst of all the afflictions to which he may be called for Christ's sake, the Christian has peace and joy. He is given strength for his day – faith in proportion to his trials. *"Beloved,"* says the apostle Peter, *"think it not strange concerning the fiery trial which is to try you, as though some strange thing happened to you; but rejoice, inasmuch as you are partakers of Christ's sufferings, that, when his glory shall be revealed, you may be glad also with exceeding joy. If you are reproached for the name of Christ, you are happy; for the Spirit of glory and of God rests upon you."*

In this history of providential interposition, there is nothing more wonderful than the process that led to the exaltation of Mordecai. We already noticed the circumstance that put him in the way of royal notice. He had discovered a conspiracy against the life of the king. But why was he not rewarded immediately on the discovery? why was he so long neglected or forgotten by the king? The smallest services to majesty usually meet an immediate and a magnificient retribution. Why was the greatest service that could be rendered to man overlooked till it was entirely forgotten? Is the saving of the life of a sovereign of so little estimation? Are absolute monarchs wont to disregard the saviours of their lives? Shall such profusion of royal bounty be showered on the head of Haman, while Mordecai remains unrewarded? What can account for this strange conduct? One thing can account for it, and nothing but this can be alleged as a sufficient cause. The thing was overruled by Providence, for the fulfilment of the Divine purposes. God not only works his will through the actions of all men, but their very abstaining from action is employed by him for the same purpose. Had Mordecai been suitably rewarded at the time of his service, there would have been no opportunity for the wickedness of Haman, and the danger of Mordecai, to be so wonderfully manifested. Had Mordecai been already advanced, Haman would not have sought his ruin. But by the delay, Haman is insulted; Mordecai is brought to the brink of ruin, from the wrath of the haughty favorite. Who is so blind as not to see the hand of God in this?

But if the reward of Mordecai at the time of his service would have been unsuitable to God's design in manifesting the wickedness of Haman, and his own power in the defence of his people, to have delayed it for a single day longer would have been ruin to the unbending Jew. His immediate death is planned by his enemies, and the next day would have seen him hanged on a gallows fifty cubits high. Haman was to ask the life of his enemy from the king; and to ask it was to obtain it. *"Then Zeresh his wife and all his friends said to him, Let a gallows fifty cubits high be made, and tomorrow speak to the king that Mordecai may be hanged on it. Then go in merrily with the king to the banquet. And the thing pleased Haman, and he caused the gallows to be made."* Mordecai, what miracle shall deliver you now? Shall God speak from heaven, or destroy your enemies with his thunder? shall the earth open, and swallow them up that seek you life? shall the angels of the Lord carry you away, and hide you from your pursuers? No! your God will save you by his providence, in a way suitable to the rest of his conduct manifested in this book. Death hovers over your head, but he shall not strike you; the wings of Providence shall overshadow you, and turn aside the dart; you shall have both life and glory without a miracle. But if you were neglected at the time of so eminent service, what probability is there that you shall now be thought of? What friend of yours shall your God send to the king, to remind him that he owes you his life? who shall put him in mind of his obligation at this critical moment? Another day, and you are a dead man! But your God is not asleep, nor unmindful of you in the time of danger. What is it that he cannot make the minister of his mercy to his servants? A remarkable interposition of his Providence shall bring you into notice this very night. Though you have no friend to speak for you, your God shall cause the thoughts of the king to roam in the paths where he shall find your claims displayed. Even in the unseasonable hour of night, the memorial of your good deed shall come before him. The king lies down, but he cannot sleep, nor shall he sleep till he hears of Mordecai. *"On that night the king could not sleep, and he commanded to bring the book of records of the chronicles. And they were read before the king. And it was found written that Mordecai had told of Bigthana and Teresh, two of the king's officers, the keepers of the door who tried to lay a hand on king Ahasuerus. And the king said, What honor and dignity has been done to Mordecai for this? Then the king's servants who served him said, Nothing has been done for him."* Astonishing! *"On that night!"* O, gentle sleep, why did you forsake the king's couch on that critical night? There is indeed nothing strange to find you leaving the bed of state, and fluttering with your downy wings over the sooty cribs in the cottages of hardy industry. But why did your caprice choose to leave the couch of Majesty in the critical moment? Did you not act as the minister of Heaven? Sleep, it was God drove you on that night from the bed of Ahasuerus.

Let us here learn to trace the hand of God in the most trivial events. There is nothing fortuitous – nothing without God. Who would think of ascribing to God so seemingly unimportant a matter? Yet this link is essential in the chain of the wonderful providences by which the Ruler of the world executed his plan on this memorable occasion. Take this away, and the whole chain is useless. Another night would have seen Mordecai on the gallows, or in the grave. This fact teaches us, that there is nothing really casual as to God, even in a restless night of a human creature. How wonderful is the providence of Jehovah! how minute, how amazingly diversified, are its operations! The eye of the Lord beholds, and his wisdom directs, all the events with respect to all the creatures in the universe. This would be too much trouble, and too mean an employment for the God of the philosophers. But the God of the Scripture not only created all things at first, and established laws by which he governs them, but he continually works in his Providence. It is in him we live, and move, and have our being. It is by his immediate power that creation is sustained in existence, that every function of animal life is performed, and that every motion in the universe is effected. The blindness and enmity of the mind of man wish to put him at a distance, and to consider him no farther the governor of the world, than as the Author of the general laws of nature, according to which all events take place. But the Bible brings God before us in all things that occur. Of the innumerable insects that inhabit a blade of grass, there is not one whose vital functions are not carried on by the power of God. To him the lion roars for his prey, and he feeds the ravens. He ever works without weariness. Epicurus removed his gods to a distance from the earth, that they might feast without disturbance from the tumults of men. He gave them a luxurious ease, far above the clouds, and did not interrupt their festivities with the government of the world. And infidel philosophy, in modern times, does nearly the same, under the name of Christianity, by ascribing to God only what it calls a general providence. This is not the God of the Bible. The Christian may recognize his God as shining in the sun, breathing in the air, and living in all life. His immediate power is as necessary to sustain all things in existence, and to effect every change in their state, as it was to create them at first. His Providence is as necessary for the care of a microscopic insect, as for regulating the motions of a solar system.

Why, then, O monarch of the east, did your sleep forsake you on that memorable night? When it fled, why did you not pursue it, and with your instruments of music force it back to your royal chamber? Call your minstrels, and woo it with softest sounds of sweetest melody; lure it to your couch with the voice of song. Come forth, you harmonious choirs; raise your most enchanting airs, and lull your monarch in repose. Tell me, you wise men of the world, why nothing could amuse the king at this time but the chronicles of his kingdom? Is this the usual requiem of an eastern monarch? Is a dry register of facts a likely expedient to hush the restless thoughts, and induce the gentler influence of sleep? Tell me, Ahasuerus, why that thought passed across your mind at this time? Where shall I find its origin? Out of a million of millions of thoughts, this appears the least likely to strike you at such a time. You are silent, O monarch! on this you know no more than the bed on which you do lie. It came, but from where it came you know as little as you do of the birth-place of the wind. And why did you yield to it when it came? What made your free will prefer to indulge this thought? Was not the thought your own? Was not compliance with its suggestions your own action? Of this it is impossible for you to doubt. How then can this your thought be ascribed to God? In what mysterious sense can this action be the appointment of God? All is light, yet all is mystery. The facts are as certain and as obvious as the mind of man can wish; yet to adjust their boundaries is as impossible as to draw a line between the colors of the rainbow. The most obvious truths may be incomprehensible to man. This thought, and the action which was its result, are the king's; yet they are the instruments through which the Almighty Ruler of the world performs his purpose. Take these away, and you destroy the whole chain of Providence exhibited in the Book of Esther. But even when the book of the chronicles comes, are there not a thousand chances that the suitable part may not turn up? What directed the reader to the proper place? In so extensive a subject as the annals of the Persian empire, what probability is there that the reader will happen on the few lines that record the service of Mordecai? He might have read till morning without touching this subject. What finger guided him to this story? Is it not more likely that the curiosity of the king would prompt him to hear some of the transactions of former reigns? This was the hour for the deliverance and exaltation of Mordecai, and it was the finger of God that pointed to the record of his service. Every step we advance in this wonderful history, we see a display of an overruling Providence. The Book of Esther is a book of wonders without a miracle.

The king hears the record of the conspiracy, and inquires about the reward of his services. He takes it for granted that he must have received a suitable recompense in honor and dignity; but finds that he is yet unrewarded. Strange! very strange! inexplicably strange! But God's design is clear. The Divine plan required that Mordecai's exaltation should be delayed till now. But it shall be delayed no longer. God's providence requires that this very moment Mordecai shall be raised; for Haman is at the door to demand his life. Keep Mordecai's services another hour unknown to the king and the servant of God is given into the hand of his enemy. How injudiciously are royal favors often conferred! The man who deserved of the king more than any subject in his empire is neglected, while that worthless minion, Haman, rose almost to royal honors!

In the preservation of the life of the king, we may learn the duty of the servants of God to their civil rulers. Mordecai was in the land of the captivity of his people, yet, instead of forwarding a scheme for the murder of the sovereign, he saved him by a discovery of his danger. Christians ought to stand at the utmost distance from every scheme that tends to overturn or embarrass civil government. Their duty and their safety in every country demand submission to the ruling powers.

There is something worthy of admiration in the conduct of Mordecai during the time of his being neglected after his important service. We find no unbecoming intrusion on the notice of majesty, no cringing at the knees of Haman and the minions of a court, to forward his claims to preferment. Yet, when honors came, they are received without any affectation of stoical indifference; he appears in the splendor of royalty, and becomes greater and greater in the Persian empire. Unlike an Aristides or a Diogenes, he spurns not the favor of the king, nor returns a rude reply to the kindness of majesty. A Christian ought never to show himself lower than an heir of heaven; but to affect a disregard to all worldly comfort is the affectation of philosophic pride.

While in Mordecai we find something to blame, we may find in him much more to praise. God accepted him as his servant, though he was ignorant of some points of duty. In him we find the strongest faith in the Divine protection, and the most heroic devotedness to the cause of God and his people. Should not this be a lesson to us all? And while we faithfully bear our testimony against errors of every kind, let us be willing to acknowledge the servants of God in all the various denominations where they are to be found. We have all our own errors; and though this ought not to induce us to look on error as innocent, it ought to keep us from despising the weakest of the people of God. Is it not a most surprising thing that any Christian can find a difficulty in recognising those whom God has recognised and sealed with his Holy Spirit?

At the critical moment of the king's inquiries about Mordecai, Haman had come into the outward court, to solicit for his immediate execution. Mark the Lord of providence in every step. Had not the king been kept from sleep – had not the book of records been called for his amusement – had not the account of the conspiracy turned up to the reader – Mordecai would now have been given into the hand of his enemy.

Mark the providence of God, also, in having Haman at hand, that by his mouth the honors of Mordecai might be awarded, and that by his instrumentality they might be conferred. Why did the king think of referring the reward of Mordecai to another? Why did he not himself determine the dignities to be conferred on his preserver? Or, if he refers to another, why does he not immediately leave the matter to those now about him? why does he ask, Who is in the court? why was Haman there at this moment? why was he the only one that waited so early on the king? why did Ahasuerus put the question in such a manner as to conceal the object of the royal favor? why does the king, instead of plainly naming Mordecai, use the periphrasis, *"The man whom the king delights to honor?"* why does this form of the question allow Haman to suppose that he was himself the happy man for whom the honors were intended? At this time the king knew nothing of the designs of Haman, and had no design to insnare him. Every circumstance here is wonderfully providential. From this we see that God can make the greatest enemies of his people the means of advancing their interests. Whom then ought the Christian to fear, but God?

Behold the retributive justice of God in the death of Haman! One of the chamberlains, who probably had seen it when he went to call him to the feast, mentioned the gallows that Haman had prepared in his house to hang Mordecai. *"The king said, Hang him on it."*

But we are not yet done with the wonders of Providence in this affair. Even with all the good intentions of the king, how can the Jews be preserved? The first decree could not be revoked; how then could a handful of Jews, scattered over all the provinces of the empire, stand up against their enemies in all nations? Although they had the royal license to defend themselves and destroy their adversaries, how could one small nation, so widely dispersed, escape destruction, when impunity invited the assault, and instigated malice? Their escape is secured by the awe inspired into the nations by the elevation of Mordecai. The God who so often filled the hearts of the most numerous armies with the dread of his people, few in number, now filled the nations of the Persian empire with the fear of them. *"The Jews gathered themselves together in their cities throughout all the provinces of the king Ahasuerus, in order to lay hand on any who sought their harm. And no man could withstand them, for the fear of them fell upon all people. And the rulers of the provinces, and the lieutenants and the governors and officers of the king helped the Jews, because the fear of Mordecai fell upon them. For Mordecai was great in the king's house, and his fame went out throughout all the provinces. For this man Mordecai became greater and greater. So the Jews struck all their enemies with the stroke of the sword, and slaughter, and destruction, and did what they would unto those who hated them."* Fear not the malice of your enemies, children of the most High. Your God can deliver you out of their hands. Lift up your heads, Christians, for your redemption draws nigh. You shall yet *"have light, and gladness, and joy, and honor."*

But in the book of Esther we are not only to attend to the wonderful interpositions of Providence manifested in the facts of the history. From the manner of revelation, in innumerable other instances, we are warranted to consider this history as prophetical and typical. In the deliverance of the Jews on this occasion, we may see God's method of preserving his church in the time of the fourth beast; and the final triumph of the saints of the Most High. When the Reformation opened the gates of Babylon, many Christians have remained there, or in some of its provinces. They are thus exposed to loss and danger; but they shall not be destroyed. Their enemies plot their ruin, but the mischief will ultimately fall on their own heads. In Haman we see a striking type of the man of sin; he seeks to destroy the whole Israel of God; but his effort will only bring on his own ruin. All must honor this wicked Haman. He indeed seeks divine honors, and there is a temptation here to stretch the type to the antitype, and find Haman guilty of claiming divine worship. But this is not in evidence, and there is no necessity that there should in all things be a perfect correspondence between the type and the antitype. This likeness is seen sufficiently in the honors that his imagination suggested for the man whom the king delights to honor, when he supposed that he was himself the person. It is astonishing that he presumed to award royal honors to any subject of the empire. Was not this likely to awaken the jeolousy of a despot? Yet such was the arrogance of this man of sin that Haman Haman answered the king, *"For the man whom the king delight to honor, let the royal clothing be brought, which the king usually wears, and the horse that the king rides upon, and the royal crown which is set upon his head. And let this clothing and horse be delivered to the hand of one of the king's most noble princes so that he may dress the man whom the king delights to honor, and bring him on horseback through the streets of the city, and proclaim before him. This is what shall be done to the man whom the king delights to honor."* Can there be a more correct figure of the blasphemous pretensions of the man of sin, who has usurped the honors of God? These honors, however, were without scruple awarded to Mordecai by the king. *"then said the king to Haman, Make haste, and take the clothing and the horse, as you have said, and do even so to Mordecai the Jew, who sits at the king's gate. Do not fail to do any of all the things you have spoken."* And if Mordecai is a type of the Son of God, how justly were these honors awarded! The Father delights to have him honored even as himself.

In the unchangeable laws of the Medes and Persians, we may see one of the features of the kingdom of the man of sin, whose infallible decree cannot be altered. Yet notwithstanding the irreversible decree that determines the destruction of all heretics, the providence of God has made other provisions for their safety. The decree never dies, but it may slumber. Other laws may be made by the state to counteract it.

In the fall of Haman, let us anticipate the overthrow of all the opposers of the kingdom of Christ. All the schemes devised for overturning Christianity will not only prove abortive, but will finally bring down vengeance on the heads of their authors.

We may here see how God can bring down the man of sin by the ordinary course of providence, without employing a single miracle. He can make his very enemies the instruments of effecting his designs. By them he usually cuts off those whom he devotes to temporal destruction; and by them also he can deliver his own people. When Haman was cut off *"many of the people of the land became Jews; for the fear of the Jews fell upon them."* How well does this correspond with the increase of the true kingdom of Christ by genuine converts, when destruction shall have fallen on mystical Babylon! No king but the Messiah can reign in the midst of his enemies, and perform his will by those who design to oppose it.

This history, that has been thought by some unworthy of a place among the inspired writings, discovers, when attentively considered, the most surprising series of events brought about without a miracle, that ever was exhibited to the consideration of the human mind. Among the most admired works of genius, of all ages and countries, we will not find that the invention of man has been able to form a story, and connect a series of surprising events, like this true history. Homer, and Virgil, and Milton, and all the writers of epic poetry, have been obliged to use supernatural agency upon all critical occasions. To interest their readers, they must depart from the ordinary course of nature, and employ means that never really existed. Gods and demons, and muses, are so necessary to the poet, that they still have their impression on the phraseology of poetry. If you prevent him from invoking the inspirations of his muse, from conversing familiarly with Apollo and the nine, from mounting to the top of Parnassus, and from drinking of the Pierian spring, you deprive him of the chief resources of his art. To have recourse to his machinery is universally granted to be his privilege, as often as there is a *"dignus vindice nodus."* But the book of Esther presents us with the most interesting and surprising narrative; it gives us a series of wonders in producing danger and deliverance, yet the means employed are so much in the ordinary course of nature, that a careless reader scarcely perceives the hand of the Lord. Every event appears the natural and obvious result of the situation in which it is produced, but to create and combine these situations is as truly a work of Divine wisdom and power, as to create the world, or to fix the laws of nature. It is thus God rules the world; he is continually working, yet blind men perceive him not. Nature or chance is worshipped instead of Him whose power is necessary to the life, motion, and existence of every being.

This book, then, whose inspiration has lately been called into question, by ignorance, speaking from the chair of learning, commends its claims to me, in the most convincing manner, by its own internal evidence. No human pen could have produced it. The characteristic feature which I have pointed out proves it to be a child of God. Had man been its author, it would have been crowded with miracles. I challenge the world to produce anything resembling it, in this point, from the writings of uninspired men.

There is another feature in this history that proves it to be of heavenly birth. There is no instance in which it gratifies mere curiosity. While it informs us of facts, it informs us no farther than they contribute to the design of the Holy Spirit, and are important for instruction. In this feature it shows its resemblance to the teaching of our Lord, and to the writings of the apostles. So far from gratifying idle curiosity, our Lord declined compliance with respect to some points in which human wisdom would think it important to be informed. His communications manifest a striking reserve; and even when pressed, he could not be induced to reply to any curious questions. In the writings of the evangelists and the apostles, how often do we wish that they had been a little more communicative? And, assuredly, had they spoken from their own wisdom, they would have made a larger Bible.

Now, with this in his view, let any one read the Book of Esther. In how many points do we wish more information! Facts are stated simply where we would wish to see them standing in connection with their origin. To see this argument illustrated in a striking light, let any one cast his eye over Gill's commentary on this book, that he may see, from the Talmuds and Rabbinical writings, the additional information that human wisdom seeks in vain in the book of God. There is not one point interesting to curiosity but what is supplied by their traditions or their conjectures. Had the book of Esther been written by the wisdom of men, it would have manifested its origin by gratifying curiosity in a similar way. Let us illustrate this remark by a reference to a few particulars in this history. The first I shall mention is the account of Mordecai's conduct in reference to the marriage of Esther. How human wisdom endeavors to justify or excuse him in this business may be seen by looking into almost any of the commentaries. But this history relates the fact, without any observation either in justification or condemnation of him. We are left to acquit or blame him, according to the light of the Scriptures.

With respect to the conspiracy against the life of the king, who is it that would not wish a little more information? What uninspired writer would not have given us at least a sketch of the cause of the discontent of the conspirators, and of the means by which it was discovered to Mordecai? What a human author would have done on this subject, we may see from what human wisdom has actually supplied. Dr. Gill tells us that the Jewish writers say that the two conspirators were Tarsians, and spoke in the Tarsian language, supposing that Mordecai did not understand it, but that he, being skilled in languages, understood what they were saying. According to Josephus, it was discovered to Mordecai by Barnabazus, a servant of one of the chamberlains. The latter Targum says, that it was revealed unto him by the Holy Ghost, but the Spirit of God, speaking by the writer of the book of Esther, deigns not to inform us how Mordecai came to know the matter. He only declares that the thing was known to Mordecai.

The account of the rise of Haman affords us another specimen of this Divine wisdom. In giving an account of the rise of a favorite, every historian informs us of the ground of his acceptance with his sovereign; but not one word on this head here. We are merely told, *"After these things did Ahasuerus promote Haman, the son of Hammedatha the Agagite, and advanced him, and set his seat above all the princes that were with him."*

Whether the conduct of Mordecai, in refusing to reverence Haman, was blameable or justifiable, and the grounds on which he acted are things that no human author would have overlooked. But whether he was right or wrong, or what was the principle on which he refused obedience, in this instance, to the royal mandate, this book says nothing. It merely states the fact – *"But Mordecai did not bow, nor did him reverence."* In order to justify him, the Targum and Aben Ezra say that Haman had a statue erected for himself, and had images painted on his clothes. Dr. Gill, who does not rely on this, strains hard to make out a good case for his client from the passage itself, and from conjecture. He thinks Haman claimed divine honors, because they were given to the Persian kings, and might have been given to their favorites. But there 'might have been' is a very bad foundation for an argument, though it is sufficient to remove a difficulty in a case that is attested by other credible testimony. This disposition to acquit the hero in an interesting narrative, in every part of his conduct, whatever may be its success in this instance, proves clearly that if the writer had not been guided by Divine wisdom, he would have given us a few remarks in justification of Mordecai.

The last instance to which I shall allude is the account of the affair that brought

Mordecai into royal notice. We are not told what diverted the monarch from sleeping, nor what induced him to call for the book of the chronicles of his kingdom, nor what led to the reading of one passage more than another. Human wisdom would have gratified us on all these points, but the Spirit of God says no more than, *"On that night the king could not sleep, and he commanded to bring the book of records of the chronicles. And they were read before the king. And it was found that Mordecai had told Bigthana and Teresh, two of the king's officers, the keepers of the door who tried to lay a hand on the king Ahasuerus."*

But though I perceive internal evidence in this book, confirming its authenticity and inspiration, I do not submit to the dogma on which some modern critics seem to act, that the authority of the canon is not sufficient to entitle a book to be admitted to the rank of inspiration, and that it is necessary for each book to be separately tried on the independent evidence from its own contents. Modern critics, in acting on this principle, resemble the lawyers, who excite litigation in order to obtain clients. They have an opportunity of displaying the treasures of their learning, and the reach of their ingenuity, in defending the claims of the Scripture without the authority of the canon. In judging of this internal evidence, they lay down first principles that are not entitled to that rank, and overlook first principles that demand universal respect. A first principle of the latter description in that testimony is a sound source of evidence, and that the books of Scripture are to be received on the authority of the canon. In ascertaining whether the book of Esther, among other books, is inspired, we have to inquire, Was it in the collection called Scripture in the day of our Lord? If it was, its inspiration is past dispute. Jesus Christ recognised the Jewish Scripture as the word of God. The apostle Paul represents it as one of the chief privileges of the Jews, that they are the depositaries to whom were intrusted the oracles of God, and neither the apostles nor their Master charge them with unfaithfulness in their trust. Now, the book of Esther, as Dr. Gill observes, has been generally received as canonical both by Jews and Christians. "It stands," he says, "in Origen's catalogue of the books of the Old Testament; nor is it any material objection, that it appears not in the catalogue of Melito, since in that list is comprehended under Ezra, not Nehemiah only, but Esther also, which Jerome mentions along with it."

As in rejecting the inspiration of this book, some modern theologians disclaim a first principle entitled to the most confident reception, so they admit some first principles that are mere figments of the imagination. Why is the book of Esther denied as a book of Scripture? Because it has not the name of God in its whole compass. Here it is taken as a first principle, that no book can be inspired, that does not contain the name of God. But where have they got this axiom? It is not self-evident, nor asserted by any portion of Scripture, and is therefore entitled to no respect. Whether a book may be inspired, though the name of God is not mentioned in it, depends not on any self-evident first principles, but on matter of fact. And matter of fact determines,in this instance, that a book may be inspired, although it does not express the name of God.

This objection, though it affects an appearance of wisdom, manifests a very inadequate conception of the nature of the word of God. It considers every book in the collection as an independent whole, standing unconnected with the other books. But the Bible is like the human body; all the books together form one whole, and there is no reason that one book should serve the place of another more than that the hand or the foot should perform the duty of the eye or of the ear. It is enough if the whole will of God is learned from the book as a whole. If it is contended that every book of Scripture must contain the name of God, a like demand may be made with respect to every chapter, or any small division. The prophecy of Obadiah contains but one chapter; must it prove its divine origin by containing a whole body of divinity? Let the Christian form his views of the characteristics of Scripture from itself, and not from the arbitrary conceits of his own mind.

But if God is not expressly named in this book, he is most evidently referred to by the people of God.

This book, then, that exhibits the providence of God, is composed in a manner suited to its subject. God is everywhere seen in it, though he is not named. Just so God is every moment manifesting himself in the works of his providence, though he works unseen to all but the eye of faith. He supports and moves the heavenly bodies, while his name is not expressly written on the sun, moon, or stars, and though no herald voice proclaims him in the execution of his office. The Christian also has many ways of acknowledging God, without expressly naming him. The sun, from the time he rises till he sets in silence, preaches the God that made and upholds him: the book of Esther, from the beginning to the end, proclaims the providence of God, though it does not expressly name him.

But not only is the objection invalid, but every one of the same class is utterly unworthy of respect. A book may disprove its divine origin by what it contains, but in no case by what it does not contain. What is to be expressed in any divine communication is not for man presumptuously to determine by his own wisdom, but lies entirely with a sovereign God. We may as well say that God would not make the sun or moon, without writing his name on it, as that he could not inspire a book that did not mention his name. Vain man will be wise, though he is born as the wild ass's colt. Even in the things of God he must, by his own maxims of wisdom, pronounce on the authenticity of the inspiration of the All-wise!

Another objection alleged to the inspiration of this book is that it is not quoted in the New Testament. Now, who made this a first principle? What authority establishes the dogma that a book of the Old Testament cannot be inspired unless it is quoted in the New? Is it a self-evident truth? By no means. Does the New Testament teach this doctrine? No such thing. Where then has it obtained its authority? In the presumption of man. To be quoted in the New Testament is indeed proof of the inspiration of a book of the Old, and may therefore be used very properly as a confirmation; but not to be quoted is no proof of a want of inspiration. The inspiration of the Old Testament is independent even of the existence of the New. Many books of the Old Testament, indeed, are quoted in the New; but this does not discredit such as are not quoted. To make quotations by the New Testament essential to the recognition of the inspiration of the books of the Old Testament, is as unreasonable as to demand the quotation of every chapter and of every verse. It is perfectly sufficient that there is nothing in the book of Esther that contradicts the New Testament. As far as they teach on the same things, they perfectly agree. To the inspiration of the book of Esther there is not one objection that deserves a minute's consideration; and it bears in every page the impression of the finger of God.

The opinion that the settling of the canon is a matter of criticism, and lies fairly open to discussion, is a wicked and pernicious error. It is the suggestion of Satan to upset the authority of the whole Scriptures. It is impossible to deny the inspiration of one book of Scripture on principles that will not overturn any other. If the book of Esther is to be rejected because it does not express the name of God, then any person is equally at liberty to reject any other book, because it wants something that his wisdom thinks an inspired book ought to contain. That an inspired book must express the name of God, is a principle as arbitrary, and as far from self-evidence, as any other conceit that the human mind may entertain. If, then, its authority is acknowledged, equal indulgence must be granted to every other demand of human wisdom. If the book of Esther is to be rejected, because it is not quoted in the New Testament, then there is not a book in the New Testament that must not be rejected, because there is no inspired authority quoting them; and, by consequence, every book of the Old must also be rejected, because the recognition of it in the New will in that case be of no authority. If the books of the New Testament can on sufficient grounds be received as inspired, although the canon is not settled by the quotations of inspired authority, then may the books of the Old Testament likewise. To reject one book, then, must admit principles that will overturn the inspiration of all. The settling of the canon is not a matter of criticism, but of testimony;

peripharasis, and the strongest confidence in him is manifested by Mordecai. The faith of that illustrious servant of God is among the most distinguished examples of faith that the Scriptures afford. *"Then Mordecai commanded to answer Esther, Do not think within yourself that you shall escape in the king's house more than all the Jews. For if you are completely silent at this time, then relief and deliverance shall arise to the Jews from another place, but you and your father's house shall be destroyed. And who knows whether you have come to the kingdom for such a time as this?"* Is not this a reference to God, and confidence in him as the God of Abraham, Isaac, and Jacob? *"From another place."* Can there be any doubt as to the place from which he expected deliverance? Is not this an obvious reference to God? Does not this reasoning to persuade Esther, express the fullest confidence that the Jews would be eventually delivered, though the danger was so great and so inevitable, that no human eye could discern the means of preservation, should not Esther undertake the intercession? As Abraham counted him faithful who had promised, and believed that though Isaac should die on the altar, he should by him be the father of the Messiah, so Mordecai believed that when every apparent means of safety failed, God would on this occasion be the deliverer of Israel. Is it not from the retributive justice of God that he threatens destruction to Esther and her father's house, should she decline the intercession through unbelief? The very Providence that is illustrated in this book is exhibited in the faith of Mordecai. He looked for deliverance through means, and if all apparent means should fail, still he believed that Providence would raise up means.

How clearly and strongly is this view of Providence expressed in the question to Esther – *"And who knows whether you have come to the kingdom for such a time as this?"* He justly concluded, from the occurrence of such a danger, that the reason why Providence had raised her to the rank of queen, was to be the deliverer of her people. Mordecai's view of Providence is that which is inculcated in all the wonderful events of this singular narrative. It is the view of Providence which I wish to press on all my brothers in Christ. If times of trouble are before us, what better preparation for it, than the study of the book of Esther? If the great Antichrist, under any form, is yet to meditate the destruction of the whole Israel of God – if there is any just apprehension from the prophecies of Scripture, that great calamities are still before the Church of Christ, ought not every Christian to be nourishing his faith with this wonderful display of Providence, as the deliverer of those who put their trust in him? Surely there can be no harm in watchfulness and apprehension, when the enemies of the cross are so rapidly increasing, and when indecision and lukewarmness so fearfully characterise the great body of the people of God. All the other symptoms of danger are not so dreadfully alarming as that spurious liberality that begins to look with complaisance on the enemies of Christ; an affection of that love of man that manifests disaffection to some parts of the character of God.

Esther also manifests confidence in God, and a resolution to die for his people, if that should be the result of her application in their favor. She approaches the king, not confiding in her charms, nor hoping to escape destruction from the love or pity of a husband, but in the way of Divine appointment, in the time of danger, by much fasting and prayer. This is an exhibition of a true servant of God. The power of Jehovah, and the love of his people, are strongly manifested in the conduct of these two illustrious Israelites. If God is not mentioned by name, he is seen in all their conduct.

In the exhibition of the conduct of Esther on this occasion, we have a strong internal evidence of inspiration. Had human wisdom formed a heroine, it would have been likely to represent her from the first moment as intrepid and ready to encounter the greatest dangers with more than masculine bravery. But Esther is not presented to us in this light by this history. She comes before us in the usual character of her sex, and of the ordinary attainment in the Divine life. She at first declines the hazardous undertaking for fear of losing her life. Her timdity is overcome by such arguments as ought to influence a believer in the God of Abraham; and she finally displays resignation and confidence, though not althogether unmixed with fear. Such is the usual conduct, such is the usual confidence, of and however mortifying it may be to the pride of the learned, they must receive it on the same gounds with the illiterate. The man of literature may indeed go a step or two beyond the unlearned. He may examine the books in which the testimony is contained, and with his own eyes he may read the catalogues of Origen and Melito, with any other accessible evidence. But even here he must rest on testimony. He has not seen the original manuscripts; and though he possessed the very autographs of the apostles, he must depend on testimony that they are really such. The canon of Scripture, then, the critic is not to ascertain by the rules of his art, but he must take it on the authority of testimony, and commence with it as a first principle.

It may appear surprising to some that the Christian public has not been more shocked with the late attempts to shake the authority of the canon, and to displace so great a portion of the word of God from its high rank. But the reason is obvious, from the quarter from which these attempts have proceeded. Had the reasons that some have alleged for rejecting the book of Esther, the two books of Chronicles, and the Song of Solomon, been urged by professed infidels, or noted heretics, they would have been rejected with horror. But when they had been ushered into the world from the pens of reputedly orthodox divines, and, for anything I know to the contrary, men of real godliness, the sinfulness of the attempt, and the danger of the principle on which the opinion is founded, have been concealed from general notice. The very grounds of rejection have a show not only of wisdom, but of concern for the honor of God and his word. Satan appears as an angel of light when he teaches that the book of Esther should be rejected, because it does not express the name of God, and because it is not quoted by the New Testament. What zeal does this manifest for the honor of God! what a high regard for the authority of the New Testament! Baxter says that the Jews were in the habit of casting the book of Esther to the ground before reading it, to express their sense of its deficiency in wanting the name of God; and the thought is quite in the style of Jewish piety, and of the human wisdom of Christians. It is just such a thought as Satan will be likely to suggest to mistaken piety. But Satan conceals from them that by their zeal for the honor of God they rob themselves of all the advantages of that book. They do not see that they give up to him all the treasures of the knowledge of Providence that are contained in that precious record. He gives them a bauble, as the Europeans have done to barbarians, and he takes from them the most valuable diamonds. Satan suggests that the book of Esther cannot be a book of Scripture, because it is not quoted in the New Testament. Who would think that the infernal spirit of darkness has such a respect for the writing of the apostles? Arch deceiver! your respect is affected for the purpose of overturning the writings for which you do profess this respect. Though the dupes who are deceived by you perceive it not, your keen eye discerns that this principle will overturn the Bible. When you deceive the profane and the ungodly, you will employ a Carlisle or a Taylor; but when the children of God are to be robbed of a part of his word, you do prefer an evangelical divine as the deceiver.

It is on this very principle that the grand deceiver has overturned the foundation of all knowledge, through the affected wisdom of the philosopher. Perceiving that false first principles lead to every error, Des Cartes resolved to take nothing for granted but the existence of his thoughts. He did not admit even his own existence as a first principle. This must be proved from his thinking. Here he imagined he had a foundation for all knowledge. But in rejecting his own existence as a first principle, and other first principles equally entitled to respect, he laid the grounds of universal scepticism, on which Mr. Hume afterwards built with such success. If nothing is self-evident but the existence of individual thought, no man has any evidence of the existence of anything but of himself. Some of his followers never advanced farther than this. The Egoists believed in their own individual existence, but, with matchless fortitude, each of them refused to believe that there is any being in creation but himself.

Now, this is just the spirit of the modern efforts to rest the authority of the books of Scripture, not on the canon ascertained by testimony, but on their internal evidence. For the authority of a book of Scripture they seek a surer foundation than testimony, however unexceptionably ascertained. They reject the solid foundation on which God himself has rested the authority of the canon, and have adopted a foundation that sinks from under the whole building. Like Des Cartes, they may themselves adopt many truths, notwithstanding their foundation will not bear them; but others, like the Egoists, may reject almost any part of the Divine word. This wisdom, then, is both impious and foolish. In pretending to add strength to the bulwarks of God, it takes away their foundation. To reject a sound first principle is equally injurious to truth as to admit a false one. Either of them lays a foundation for error.

The book of Esther abounds with valuable instructions. To rob the Christian of the edification and comfort which it affords, is to do him the most serious injury. When critics find themselves at a loss for a field in which to exercise their ingenuity, let them indulge their vanity on the writings of the ancient Greeks and Romans. Here let them gambol with the most frantic movements, and approach as nearly as they choose to the opposite boundaries of credulity and scepticism; but let them cease from the word of God. Let them not dare to put their unhallowed hands on the ark of Jehovah. Let the children of the Most High possess his word in its utmost extent; let them possess it without addition. The curse of God pursues both him that adds and him that diminishes.

One most conspicuous advantage afforded to the Christian by this book is, that it gives him a commentary to all the events recorded in history, with respect to the rise and fall of empires, the prosperity and adversity of nations, the progress and persecution of the Church of Christ, and the exaltation and degradation of individuals. In reading history, people in general look no farther than to the motives, designs, and tendencies of human action. Some are contented even with the knowledge of facts, without attempting to discover their course or to trace the connection of events. But in the book of Esther the Christian may learn to refer every occurrence in the world to the counsels of God, and to behold him ruling with absolute sway, amid all the confusion of human agency, over all the purposes and actions of men and devils. In the afflictions of virtue, in the oppression of the righteous, in the prosperity of the wicked, in the insolence of power, in the persecution of truth, the philosopher finds it difficult to defend his god, and cannot defend him without making him different from the God of the Scriptures. He excuses his supineness by bringing him forward to reward virtue in another state, by the unavoidable necessity imposed on omnipotency through the establishment of general laws, from which it is impossible to deviate. But the book of Esther teaches the Christian, that the rise, and progress, and triumph of the man of sin, as well as his decline and fall, are according to the purpose of the Almighty – the All-Wise – the eternal. His glory is secured by the exertions of his enemies, as well as by those of his friends. He raises up Haman and Pharaoh, as well as Esther and Moses. Such a God is too wonderful for the discovery or the approbation of human wisdom. This is too dazzling a light in which to view the Divine character, for any who are not taught of God, and who are not accustomed to submit in the most absolute manner to the decisions of his word. It is only the eagle can gaze on the sun. Many of those who, in some measure, are taught of God, are too weak-sighted to look on him in this blaze of light. They prefer to view him through the dark glasses of some human system of theology. My fellow Christians! I entreat you, as you value the authority of God, as you regard your own edification, study the book of Esther, and see your God ruling even over sin. Behold him in all the ways of conquerors – in all the intrigues of courts – in all the changes of empires – in all the caprices of monarchs – in all the persecutions of truth – as well as in all the progress of the Gospel.

The book of Esther teaches us to see the hand of God, not only in the great events of the world, but in all the transactions of men. It calls on us to see him in every occurrence of every day in our lives; and to trust in him for provision, protection, health, comfort, peace, and all the blessings of life. Innumerable dangers are around us every moment; it is only the arm of God can ward them off from us. The most trifling accident might destroy us, as well as an earthquake; it is the watchfulness of Providence must guarantee our safety. How then is this book calculated to nourish our gratitude, increase our dependence on God, and invigorate our confidence! As we need the Almighty protection in all things, even when we see no danger, so even when the most terrible disasters threaten, he can defend. From how many evils has he delivered us in the course of our lives! How many wonders of Providence may we recount in our own escapes! Christians, study the book of Esther, and view God on your right hand, and on your left, all the day long. See his watchful eye upon you, and his guardian hand around you, both night and day. *"He will not allow your foot to be moved; he that keeps you will not slumber. Behold he that keeps Israel shall neither slumber nor sleep. The Lord is your keeper; the Lord is your shade upon your right hand. The sun shall not smite you by day, nor the moon by night. The Lord shall preserve you from all evil: he shall preserve your soul. The Lord shall preserve your going out and your coming in from this time forth, and even for evermore."*

In Esther's success we find encouragement to undertake the most dangerous service to which duty calls us. We are indeed to count the cost, and be willing to serve the cause of God at the expense even of life. But in this example, let us see that God is able to preserve us in doing his will, even when danger is most appalling. There may be safety in the midst of danger, when we go forward in the path of duty; but death itself is preferable to disobedience. *"If I perish, I perish,"* is the spirit in which the people of God ought to encounter the most appalling dangers in doing his will. In this spirit we can die in triumph, or live with joy and a good conscience

If times of trouble are before us – if God is about to call his people to suffer for his sake, let us in the book of Esther alleviate our sorrow with the consideration that God rules in the storm. He can disperse the darkest clouds; he can preserve us in the midst of the thunderbolts; so he can give us peace and joy in the most violent death. Is it not consolation that persecution is by his appointment, and that in the end it will turn out for his glory as well as our good?

Even persecution may be commissioned to benefit the Church of God. It may effect what prosperity has kept far away. It may bring Christians into one body, as they have the one Lord. Their common sufferings will tend to unite them, and the afflictions of the house of God will tend to its purification. The millions who are Christians only in name, and who now by their union with the people of God, defile the temple, and cramp the exertions of believers, may then take their proper place. The interests, the prejudices, and the habits of Christians combine to keep them in ignorance of the nature of Christ's kingdom, and of the laws and institutions with which he has furnished them. When worldly temptations cease to deceive, Christians may become more tractable, and what they did not learn in the time of their peace, they may soon learn in a time of danger. A man may learn at the stake what he could not see in the pulpit.

The consideration that the whole course of affairs on earth is directed by the overruling hand of Providence, as it is kept so conspicuously before our eyes in this book, may be highly useful to Christians in regulating their zeal in the cause of God. The mountains that lie in the way of the Gospel appear so impassable, that any means that promises to facilitate the passage is sometimes eagerly employed, without reference to the authority of divine appointments. The end is made to sanctify the means; evil is done that good may come; means are employed that God has not ordained – that God has forbidden. And means are supposed warrantable, if it appears that the thing cannot otherwise be effected. It is to this baleful principle that the union of the church with the world owes its origin. The nations of the earth, in all their sins, are made a sort of Christians by name, and the enjoyment of the ordinances appointed only for the people of God. In all the worshipping assemblies in Christendom, separate the disciples, and what a poor figure will they make in the eyes of the world! How would they support the Gospel! To act on this principle would, in the opinion of many, be to banish Christianity from the earth. However reluctant some may be to desecrate the ordinances of Christ, they think they must do it, or suffer Satan to triumph over Christ. They complain of the decay of religion – they pray for better times – they strive to breathe life into the dry bones – they warn sinners of their danger; but still they give them the ordinances of Christ, for they cannot work without them. Numbers are necessary for the existence of a sect; and Christ's ordinances must be misapplied in order to promote his system.

Now I entreat Christians who act on this principle to consider what an affront it casts on the Head of the church. Who is it that governs the world? Has Jesus given up to the devil the power he received from his Father after his resurrection? Does he not still hold all power in heaven and on earth? does not the book of Esther show that his providence extends to all events? May they not learn here, that their Lord directs the actions even of his enemies to fulfil his will? Look here, and behold a few scattered Jews defending themselves, and destroying their enemies in all the provinces of the Persian empire. In the cause of God, then, let them employ no means but such as are sanctioned by the appointment of Jesus. Let the ark of God itself fall, rather than put a hand to it contrary to Divine authority.

It is from the same principle that such an eagerness is always discovered to enlist the authority of kings and rulers in the cause of Christ, although they themselves may give all the weight of their example to the kingdom of Satan. Christians in general seem to think that there is no hope of protection for Christianity from civil rulers, unless they are nominally embodied in the ranks. For the sanction of power they barter the ordinances of Christ. In the book of Esther let them learn that their Lord is the King of kings and Lord of lords – that he rules in the midst of his enemies – and that he can make the most tyrannical princes the protectors of his people, when he pleases. Ahasuerus, who had by an irreversible decree doomed to destruction the whole Jewish people, was, without any conversion to God, without any proselytism to Judaism, made the most zealous friend that ever appeared in favor of the house of Abraham. He not only with the utmost zeal co-operated for their deliverance from the intended destruction, but gave up to them, to the immense injury of his kingdom, all their enemies in his dominions. He gave them unlimited authority to kill their enemies and spoil their substance. The kings of the earth are the ministers of God; as such they ought to be honored; but give them not the throne of the Lord Jesus Christ. If they are not Christians by being born again through faith in the great propitiation made on the cross, and walk in newness of life, let them not be called Christians – give them not the ordinances of the house of God.

In the book of Esther the conductors of the various religious societies ought to take a lesson. I am afraid there are few of them that do not need it. The craft, the management, the bartering of the Christian name with Neologians and heretics for co-operation, money, and countenance, that some of them have employed, would induce one to think that they consider the Lord Jesus Christ to be dethroned, and that his friends must work without him till the restoration. I rejoice in all the good done by any of them. I wish I could convince them that they will do the more good the more closely they abide by the means afforded by the Head of the Church. Jesus rules on the earth as well as in heaven, and those who honor him he will honor to do his will. What have the Samaritans to do in building the temple of God? Has Jesus lost command over the treasures of the earth, that we must have recourse to the bounty of Satan? He will give us his contribution, no doubt; but he will have a niche in the edifice, in which his statue must be worshipped. It would be more pleasant for me to be bandying compliments with the religious world, than to incur their displeasure by acting as their censor. But wholesome admonition is better than praise. Though the generality may despise it, some Christians may receive benefit. They may be led to see that in the propagation of the gospel the Lord Jesus has no need of the countenance or co-operation of his enemies. The book of Esther will teach them that he can effect his purposes, even through those ignorant of him, without embodying them among his disciples.

In the Book of Esther the Christian may see the union of two things apparently irreconcilable – the free agency of man, and the over-ruling appointment of God.

Philosophers have exhausted their ingenuity in endeavoring to fathom this abyss; but their line has proved too short. Some have erred with respect to both sides of the question. They have held that actions are not free, and that they are necessary in such a sense as to render man inexcusable in guilt. On this foundation some ground the duty of charity. If a man sins under a necessity of this king, there is no propriety in blaming him for his conduct. In the book of Esther we may see that man's actions are his own, yet that they are, in another point of view, the appointment of God. We see here that man is accountable and blameable when he sins; yet we see that these very sinful actions are the appointment of God to effect his own purposes.

The philosophers who contend for the freedom of human actions, generally deny the eternal decrees of God; because their wisdom cannot reconcile these two things with one another. And must not the penetration of philosophers fathom the deep things of God? Proud worms! can nothing be true of God, but what your minds can penetrate?

In reading the writings of philosophers on this subject, nothing can be more evident, than that one party has proved that men act freely, and that the other proves as clearly that the foreknowledge of God implies the certainty of all actions as they are foreknown. In so far each is right on his own side, but wrong as to the other. They will fight as long as the devil has use for the discussion, for, on their own principle, the dispute never can be settled. The human mind is not able to fathom the subject; they are struggling to grasp infinity; they are both right, and both wrong; truth lies between them; each of them has a hold of its skirt, but neither of them entirely possesses it; it cannot be seized, except it is believed without being comprehended. This removes it altogether out of the road of the philosopher, for he cannot receive anything for which he cannot account. While the philosophers dispute, and, under the specious name of lovers of wisdom, prove themselves fools, let the Christian, from the book of Esther, behold the freedom of human actions in union with divine appointment. Let him not affect to strut in the buskins of the schools, and pretend to explain what on this subject he receives on the authority of God. Let him receive it, because the word of God exhibits it; not because his wisdom can fathom the depth of the Divine counsels. The most illiterate man of God, who receives with meekness what the Scriptures lay before him, is, with respect to the deepest subjects of philosophy, a greater philosopher than any of the mere sons of science. They may seize truth by the garment and tear away a shred, but the Christian, believing the Divine testimony, possesses the substance. I am sorry to be obliged to remark that Christians too generally affect the philosopher on this subject. They have separated what God has joined together, because they could not comprehend the union; and, from prepossession in favor of one part of truth, have been led to give up or explain away the other. Some, out of zeal for the doctrine of the freedom of the human will, have, in opposition to the clearest testimony of Scripture, denied the decrees of God; while others, from a false zeal for the honor of the Divine counsels, have denied the freedom of human action. Both of them, inconsistently with their character as Christians, act on the same principle of unbelief with the philosopher. They deny what they cannot comprehend. Like infidels, they assume it as a first principle, that nothing is to be received as truth that is not comprehensible to the mind of man.

When will Christians cease from their own wisdom? when will they in all things submit to the testimony of God? when will they practically admit, that God may know, and therefore call upon them to believe, what they cannot comprehend? Will man never cease to make himself equal with God? will the Christian never learn that he is nothing? Disciple of Jesus, go to the book of Esther, and acquaint yourself with the deepest point of philosophy. There see the solution of the question that has occupied the wise from the very cradle of philosophy, but which philosophy has never solved – which it is not capable of solving, on any other principle than submission to the testimony of God. Degrade not your Master, my fellow Christians, by modelling his doctrines according to the profane speculations of the schools. If any man will be really wise, let him become a fool in the estimation of the world, that he may be wise in the estimation of his God.

Let us read the book of Esther, and in the view of the overruling government of God, let us console ourselves in contemplating the melancholy prospect of this world, in which the counsels of nations in every age are conducted by the enemies of God. We hear much of Christian nations and Christian rulers; but where is the nation in which the counsels of the ungodly do not prevail? where is the government that is conducted strictly on Christian principles? Statesmen, it is true, seek to manage Christianity like every other state engine, and therefore affect to support it. But where is the assembly of legislators, in which it is visible that the Lord God is feared as he ought to be feared? This is a gloomy subject for the contemplation of the man of God. But let him turn his eyes to the book of Esther, and behold the Lord God omnipotent reigning, and working his will by the very instruments employed by Satan to defeat his purposes. God rules even in the counsels of the ungodly. God will glorify himself even by the very empire of Satan.

It is a heart-rending thing to reflect on the sin and misery that prevail in this world. Let us relieve ourselves, in some measure, by this consideration, that God has done all things according to the counsel of his own will. Is the Almighty disappointed in his work of creation? has Satan prevailed over him because of his strength? or will any real dishonor attach to God by the rebellion of men and angels? Impossible; away with the accursed thought! These clouds before my eyes are dark and lowering – I cannot penetrate that gloom – I see nothing but confusion and wretchedness. The very glory of this world is vanity; its highest enjoyments are unsatisfying. But though I cannot see through this dreadful darkness, I will look beyond it by the eye of faith. God reigns; all things therefore must issue in the glory of his name, and the happiness of his people.

FOOTNOTES

RUTH – CHAPTER 5

[1]This discourse was delivered in a time of scarcity.

CHAPTER 8

[1]An ephah contained three pecks and three pints. – Calmet

ESTHER – CHAPTER 1

[1]Sir William Temple.

[2]Dr. Lawson lived at a time long before the modern Temperance Reformation originated. In his day, a moderate indulgence in the use of intoxicating beverages on festive, and indeed we may say on ordinary, occasions, was considered fitting and proper; and conducive to health, as well as esential to hospitality, even by Christians and ministers of the Gospel. And they practised according to their light. Yet it is instructive to note, that the essential principle of the modern Temperance reformation is recognised and enforced in this passage by our author. The only difference is, that that principle is now extended by us in practice. Our author here inculcates the obligation of 'refusing to drunkards the means of gratifying their intemperate appetites'; we now go farther, in accordance with our increased light and knowledge, and insist on the duty of ourselves abstaining from, and withholding from others, the means of forming intemperate appetites. We know (what our fathers did not know,) that intoxicating drinks are 'deadly poison' in their own nature and effects to all who indulge in their use; and woe will be unto us if we do not obey the superior light we enjoy. – Ed.

CHAPTER 4

[1]The recent foul assassination of his Excellency Abraham Lincoln, President of the United States of America, who was so universally respected and beloved for his integrity and and amiable qualities of a man, and for his eminently patriotic administration as the Chief Magistrate of the great American Republic during the late deplorable rebellion, adds fresh point and emphasis to our author's observations, in regard to the peculiar dangers that beset supreme rulers and princes. Christians should, from these considerations, be impressed with the duty and obligation which specially rest on them as Christian citizens, to offer up prayers to God for the preservation of the life of their chief Magistrate. The Scripture prayer – 'God save the King!' or, God save the President! should as earnestly and constantly go up to heaven from millions of Christian hearts, as the prayer – 'Give us this day our daily bread!' – Ed.

CHAPTER 9

[1]Referring to the House of Steward. – Ed.

CHAPTER 8

[1]These weighty sentences fully vindicate the defensive leagues and covenants entered into by the Reformed Christians of the churches of the Reformation – such as the Huguenots of France, the Lutherans of Germany, and the Covenanters of Scotland, not to mention the primitive evangelical churches of the valleys of the Alps – by which they solemnly bound themselves to defend, even by resort to arms if necessary, their civil and religious rights and liberties, more precious to them than their lives, against the intolerable oppressions of Popery and the tyranny of their rulers. They equally condemn the principle of the 'Society of Friends' and our modern 'Peace Society' and others, who maintain that even defensive warfare for a just cause is unchristian and wrong; and who would even forbid to the individual the resort to self-defence for the security of his life and property. Away with such weak and contemptible principles as these! They are equally opposed to the dictates of nature, or the Word of God. – Ed.

www.ingramcontent.com/pod-product-compliance
Ingram Content Group UK Ltd.
Pitfield, Milton Keynes, MK11 3LW, UK
UKHW021522300726
14060UKWH00015B/732

9 781589 600591